**Banish Dirt from Your Castle
Forever with 2,047
Queen-Tested Tips**

The Queen of Clean's

COMPLETE
CLEANING GUIDE

LINDA COBB

#1 *New York Times* Best-Selling Author

RODALE

We hope this advice provides the answers to many of your household needs. However, total success cannot be guaranteed in every case. Care and caution should be exercised when using remedies, products, and methods presented in this book. All cleaning treatments should be tested in an inconspicuous place prior to application. This is highly recommended and strongly encouraged. Please read and follow with care all information contained on product labels. Linda Cobb, The Win Holden Company, and Rodale Inc. hereby disclaim any liability and damages from the use and/or misuse of any product, formula, or application presented in this book.

Mention of specific companies, organizations, or authorities in this book does not imply endorsement by the publisher, nor does mention of specific companies, organizations, or authorities imply that they endorse the book.

Internet addresses and telephone numbers given in this book were accurate at the time it went to press.

Originally published as *Talking Dirty with the Queen of Clean®*, *Talking Dirty Laundry with the Queen of Clean®*, and *A Queen for All Seasons* by POCKET BOOKS

Printed in the United States of America
Rodale Inc. makes every effort to use acid-free ∞ , recycled paper ♲ .

Cover and text design by Tara A. Long

Library of Congress Cataloging-in-Publication Data

Cobb, Linda.
    The queen of clean's complete cleaning guide : banish dirt from your castle forever with 2,047 queen-tested tips / Linda Cobb.
        p.   cm.
    Includes index.
    ISBN 1–57954–660–9 hardcover
    1. House cleaning.   2. Housekeeping.   I. Title.
TX324 .C64   2002
648'.5—dc21   2002010033

        10   9   hardcover

RODALE

WE **INSPIRE** AND **ENABLE** PEOPLE TO IMPROVE
THEIR LIVES AND THE WORLD AROUND THEM

To my Mom, the Queen Mother.

*Without her love, guidance and the fact that she made me clean my
room and learn to do laundry, none of this would be possible.
She's 90 years old, and I learn something from her every day.
Thanks Mom, I love you!*

*My Dad. You will always be a candle burning brightly
in my heart.*

ACKNOWLEDGMENTS

There are many people to thank for their help and friendship through the years. Some I will thank by name, but all of you know who you are and I bow to you in thanks.

My husband John, kids David and Janette, Victoria, Pat and Laura, Nancy, and Nanette and David. Thanks for putting up with the craziness.

Win and Carolyn Holden, without you none of this would be possible.

Everyone at Good Morning Arizona—KTVK Television. Nobody does it better!

Beth McDonald and Bill Austin, KESZ Radio. You are number one in the ratings and in my heart.

Duane Dooling, a friend for all seasons.

The Palace Pussycats, Zack and Zoey Elizabeth. Without them I wouldn't be an expert in pet stains and odor.

Our neighbors, who help us all they can and put up with TV satellite trucks parked in the driveway at 1:00 AM and never complain.

Brenda Copeland, your advice and friendship mean so much.

Ellen Phillips and Karen Bolesta, who did a fantastic job editing this book, and Tara Long, Jennifer Bright, Kathy Dvorsky, and Karen Neely for their talent and energy.

The people of Arizona. You made me Queen, and I love you.

CONTENTS

Part 4: Seasonal Palace-Cleaning Program

Part 5: Everything You Need to Be a Queen

MEET THE QUEEN

INTRODUCING HER ROYAL HIGHNESS OF HOUSEKEEPING! Linda Cobb, the Queen of Clean®, is no stranger to the cleaning business. She is the former owner of one of the largest cleaning companies in Michigan. Not only is she an authority on carpet cleaning, upholstery cleaning, and wall and window washing, but she also has faced all types of cleaning challenges. In fact, her firm specialized in some of the most difficult cleaning tasks in the industry: disaster restoration and fire, smoke, and water damage.

As the Queen of Clean®, Linda is a featured guest on more than 70 local and national talk radio and television shows across the country. She recently made her debut on Oprah Winfrey's TV show *Oprah*. In addition, Linda is a regular guest on KTVK-TV's top-rated morning show *Good Morning Arizona* in Phoenix, as well as Home & Garden Television's *Smart Solutions*.

Linda is also a top-notch speaker, wowing audiences across the country with her knowledge and unusual cleaning methods, such as using Tang in the toilet and Massengill on the dog! Her natural cleaning methods are easy and even fun, something that never fails to astound her audiences. There's a standing challenge to audiences to stump the Queen, but so far nobody has been able to do it.

As a complement to her myriad appearances, Linda publishes the bi-monthly *Queen of Clean®—The Newsletter*, which goes into thousands of homes across the United States and Canada. On the air, in print, and on the Web, Linda does it all, but the crown jewels of her achievements are her three *New York Times* best-selling books, *Talking Dirty with the*

Queen of Clean®, Talking Dirty Laundry with the Queen of Clean®, and *A Queen for All Seasons.* In *The Queen of Clean's® Complete Cleaning Guide,* Linda brings together her vast knowledge of cleaning and house-keeping—plus a generous helping of her wonderful sense of humor and tips for really enjoying life and living.

Linda lives in Phoenix with her husband. Visit her on the Web at www.queenofclean.com.

So sit down, put your feet up, take a sip from your coffee or cola (no spilling, now!), and let the Queen give you the keys to her kingdom. It's a nice, clean place to be.

1
Castle-Cleaning Essentials

The Queen's Annual Cleaning Checklist

I've been at this cleaning business a long time, and still I'm surprised by the number of people who get hung up on what to clean and when. Seems that for some people, *cleaning* is a dirty word. They want to know how often to clean this, when to put away that—as if there's going to be a big test at the end of the cleaning semester. But life's not like that. Sometimes you win. Sometimes you lose. Sometimes your house is clean. Sometimes . . . well, let's just leave it at that, shall we?

I don't believe in keeping to someone else's schedule and someone else's rules. I believe in making my schedule work for me, and I have only one rule: If it's not dirty, don't clean it. We're all busy, and we all have better things to do than clean house. No one but the Marines wears white gloves these days, so we don't have to be concerned with the white glove test. That said, few of us are happy living in a home that's dirty or unkempt. It's hard to relax when the dust bunnies are having a rodeo in the corner of your living room.

Sit back and think for a moment. What does clean mean for you? How organized do you want to be? Are you the type of person who's just dying to rearrange the magazines at the dentist's office, the one your coworker runs to when she spills cola on her keyboard? Or are you the type whose idea of cleaning is to hide the dirty dishes in the oven and whose laundry schedule is determined by "Can I get away with this for another day?"

Chances are, you won't have to think too much about this. You already know who you are. You know what makes you comfortable and how you like to live. I suspect that despite our natural tendencies, most of us flit between one group and the other. There are times when we feel that things are ordered and under control, just as there are times when chaos rules. I'm not trying to get you to change teams, to convert you, or to give you a cleaning citation. I want you to find your comfort level, to do the things that will get you there and help you stay there.

And that's where this book comes in. I've started off with a list of things to think about, from everyday household tasks that you'd never overlook (like washing dishes) to those uncommon tasks and easy oversights, such as flipping your mattress and cleaning the gutters. I'd like to encourage you to find out what's right for you. Some people, for example, may like to change their sheets every week. Others may find that every 2 weeks is often enough for them. A schedule only works if it's flexible and realistic. Start with that in mind, and you can't go wrong.

It's about Time

So here it is: the Queen's annual cleaning checklist. Read it over, and see if it works for you. If not, whip out a pen and start making changes. Or better yet, make a few copies and make your changes on *them,* so you'll be able to read the final version.

Daily Duties

Personally, there are only two things that I do *every* day: kiss the King and feed the cat. I make the bed most days (it's so much nicer to come home to), and I do try to see that the dishes are done, but sometimes I'm just so busy or distracted that even the simplest tasks fall by the wayside. We're all very busy. We all have too much to do. That's why I've kept this list of daily chores short. Carry out these few tasks on most days, and you'll find your life running smoother than you could imagine. Miss a day and . . . well, the dishes will still be there tomorrow.

❑ Make beds.

❑ Put dirty clothes in the hamper.

❑ Hang up clean clothes.

❑ Clean up spills.

❑ Wash dishes.

❑ Wipe counters and stove top.

Twice Weekly

I've kept this list gloriously short—only one item! You can actually get away with vacuuming carpets just once a week (6 days is the average gestation period for dust bunnies), but vacuuming twice weekly will prevent the dirt from getting ground into the fibers, and will therefore prolong the life of the carpet.

❑ Vacuum carpets.

Weekly

Weekends were made for more than housework, so try spreading these tasks out through the week if you can.

❑ Sweep hardwood floors.

❑ Dust hard furniture.

❑ Dust knickknacks.

- ❏ Do the laundry.
- ❏ Change sheets.
- ❏ Clean sinks.
- ❏ Clean showers and tubs.
- ❏ Clean toilets.
- ❏ Clean bathroom mirrors.
- ❏ Empty trash cans, put out garbage. (Clean the trash can if odors remain.)
- ❏ Sweep porch, patio, and doormats.

Biweekly

- ❏ Vacuum stairs.
- ❏ Dust TVs, VCRs, stereos, and so forth.

Monthly

- ❏ Replace the bag in your vacuum.
- ❏ Vacuum upholstery.
- ❏ Clean makeup brushes and sponges.
- ❏ Clean hairbrushes and combs.
- ❏ Vacuum drapes.
- ❏ Clean mirrors.
- ❏ Vacuum or dust blinds and shutters.
- ❏ Dust ceiling fans.
- ❏ Dust woodwork.
- ❏ Wash kitchen and bathroom area rugs.
- ❏ Vacuum carpet edges.
- ❏ Check hard floors and rewax heavy traffic areas if needed.

- ❑ Clean out the refrigerator.
- ❑ Spot-clean the kitchen cabinet fronts.
- ❑ Clean the fronts of stove, refrigerator, dishwasher, and so forth.
- ❑ Check the furnace filter: Change or clean if needed.
- ❑ Hose off entry mats.
- ❑ Sweep out the garage.

Quarterly

- ❑ Sweep or wash walkways and driveways.
- ❑ Change or clean the furnace filter.
- ❑ Wipe off lightbulbs as you dust (be sure they are cool).
- ❑ Wash or thoroughly clean any knickknacks that require more than dusting.
- ❑ Flip the cushions on chairs and sofas for even wear.
- ❑ Clean humidifiers and dehumidifiers.

Twice a Year

- ❑ It's got to be done: Clean the oven.
- ❑ Clean the stove hood and/or exhaust fan.
- ❑ Discard foods in the freezer that are past their freshness. Clean freezer.
- ❑ Flip the mattresses on beds.
- ❑ Wash any plastic, vinyl, or leather furniture.
- ❑ Clean scatter rugs.
- ❑ Dust books on shelves, making sure to dust the shelves under the books.
- ❑ Vacuum the heat registers and cold-air returns.
- ❑ Vacuum under furniture.

- ❑ Check silverware, and clean if necessary.
- ❑ Replace that little box of baking soda in the refrigerator.
- ❑ Dust all the things you haven't been able to reach all year long.
- ❑ Clean bedspreads and slipcovers.
- ❑ Clean closets as you change seasonal clothes.

Annually

- ❑ Wash blankets and comforters.
- ❑ Dust down walls.
- ❑ Wash walls. (I actually think every 2 years is often enough for this.)
- ❑ Strip any waxed floors and rewax.
- ❑ Wash all windows and screens.
- ❑ Wash or dry-clean drapery.
- ❑ Move and clean under and behind large items.
- ❑ Wash blinds.
- ❑ Clean carpet and upholstery.
- ❑ Clean any areas you have avoided all year long.
- ❑ Have the air conditioner checked and cleaned.
- ❑ Have the furnace checked and cleaned.
- ❑ Sort through the medicine cabinet, clean it, organize it, and discard old medicine.
- ❑ Clean out kitchen cupboards, wash, and reorganize.
- ❑ Replace the batteries in smoke detectors and other safety devices.
- ❑ Check the batteries in flashlights.
- ❑ Clean rain gutters.
- ❑ Wash all exterior windows.
- ❑ If you have a chimney, clean it.

So there you have it. Your annual cleaning checklist. (Now, that wasn't so bad, was it?) But that's just the beginning of what this book is about—establishing a routine that works for you. The other part? How to clean everything—and I mean *everything!*—so you'll have the tools and know-how you need when you're ready to use them.

And of course, there's fun stuff, too. I've even included some recommendations from my four-legged cowriter, Zack, the Palace Pussycat. Zack helped me with my last two books (mainly by sitting on the manuscripts), and this time he wanted to contribute further, so look for his suggestions in "The Cat's Meow" and "A Word from Zack." His segments provide advice from the feline point of view, and, of course, he reminds us that behind every successful woman there's usually a rather talented cat. As you can see, this is not your typical cleaning book. But then again, I'm not your typical Queen!

Five Palace Essentials You Should Never Be Without

There are five cleaning products you should never be without, and most of them are things you already have in your home. You can purchase generous-size containers of all of them for a total of $10, and they will last for months. They can be used alone, together, or in conjunction with other common household products such as salt or dishwashing liquid to help you handle most of the cleaning problems in your home. They are especially good for people with allergies and for those of us who want to cut back on the amount of chemicals in our homes.

Now we'll take them in order and talk about their many uses. As you'll see, cleaning your castle is only the beginning! I've included tips for safe, natural pest and plant disease control, royal beauty secrets, and a few holiday hints. Even Zack, the Palace Pussycat, has a few things to say for himself!

IMPERIAL SHOPPING LIST

Here's your shopping list. If you don't have all these products at home, the Queen hereby decrees: Go buy them!

White vinegar

Baking soda

Lemon juice

Club soda

Spot Shot Instant Carpet Stain Remover

White Vinegar

Use white vinegar to remove heavy soap scum and mineral deposits from showers, tubs, and sinks. Warm the vinegar and put it in a spray bottle. Spray on showers, tubs, and sinks, and let soak for 10 to 15 minutes. Then use a nylon scrubbing sponge to remove scum. Respray if necessary. To remove mineral deposits from around drains, close the drain and pour in enough white vinegar to cover the drain area. Let soak overnight, scrub with a nylon scrubbing sponge, drain the vinegar, and rinse.

To remove scum and mineral buildup from showerheads and to keep them free-flowing, put undiluted white vinegar in a plastic sandwich bag. Tie the bag around the showerhead and leave it on overnight. Scrub the head and poke any loosened mineral deposits with a toothpick, rinse, and enjoy your next shower.

To remove soap scum and mildew from plastic shower curtains and liners, fill the washing machine with warm water, 1 cup of white vinegar, and your regular laundry detergent. Add the curtains, along with several old, light-colored towels. Run through a complete cycle, then re-hang the curtain immediately.

Add 2 to 3 tablespoons of white vinegar to hot water along with your regular dishwashing liquid to cut grease on dishes and crystal.

Add ¼ cup of white vinegar to the washing machine during the final rinse to soften clothes and remove lint from dark clothes.

Use vinegar to clean the glass shelves of your medicine cabinet.

Apply undiluted white vinegar to the skin with a cotton ball to deter bugs: They'll hate the way you taste, but the odor disappears immediately from your skin.

A WORD FROM ZACK, THE PALACE PUSSYCAT: Neutralize pet urine odor with diluted white vinegar (25 percent vinegar to 75 percent water) sprayed on carpets. Always test in an inconspicuous spot before treating a large area.

Clean stainless steel sinks with a paste of baking soda and vinegar. Don't let the foaming scare you—it works great!

Make a window cleaner in a spray bottle with ¼ cup of white vinegar added to 1 quart of water.

Make an air freshener in a spray bottle with 1 teaspoon of baking soda, 1 tablespoon of white vinegar, and 2 cups of water. After the foaming stops, put on the lid. Shake before using.

Clean vinyl floors with ½ cup of white vinegar to 1 gallon of warm water.

Keep drains free-flowing with ½ cup of baking soda and ½ cup of white vinegar poured down the drain. Cover the drain for 15 minutes (it will foam). Then flush with cold water. Do this once a month.

Clean mirrors with a solution of half vinegar and half water. Wet a sponge, soft cloth, or paper towel with the solution, wash the mirror, and then buff dry.

ROYAL DECREE: *Never* spray water onto a mirror! Moisture that gets into the edges and behind mirrors ruins the silvering on the mirror, resulting in dark spots.

Spray vinegar on the underarms of clothes and let soak for 15 to 30 minutes to deodorize and minimize underarm stains.

Make an excellent toilet cleaner with borax and vinegar. Pour 1 cup of vinegar over the stained area of the toilet, then sprinkle 1 cup of borax over the vinegar. Soak for 2 hours, and then brush and flush.

Kill weeds with a natural toddy of 1 ounce of white vinegar, 1 ounce of inexpensive gin, and 8 ounces of water. Pour this on the weeds and say "goodbye."

Remove road-salt stains from boots by wiping them with a mixture of 1 part water and 1 part white vinegar.

Keep Easter eggs from cracking by adding 1 tablespoon of white vinegar to the boiling water. (Vinegar will seal any cracks and help the eggs congeal.) To dye your eggs, put out several glasses of hot water (plastic will stain, so use glass). Add 1 tablespoon of vinegar to each cup. The acid in the vinegar will help the dye adhere to the eggshells.

Keep flies away from your picnic by wiping the table with some undiluted white vinegar.

ROYAL BEAUTY SECRET: Your nail polish will last longer if you apply a little white vinegar to each nail. Just coat each nail using a cotton swab prior to applying your nail polish. The acid in the vinegar encourages the polish to stick to the nail, so you get better coverage and longer-lasting wear.

Baking Soda

Baking soda is a great deodorizer, cleaner, and mild abrasive. Use it as you would a soft-scrubbing product or cleanser in tubs and sinks.

Keep food disposals fresh and free-flowing by putting the stopper in the disposal and adding 3 inches of warm water and a handful of baking soda. Remove the stopper, turn on the disposal, and let the water run out.

(continued on page 16)

QUEENLY PRODUCT RECOMMENDATIONS

Sometimes you'd just rather buy a conventional cleaner or stain remover instead of making your own. But how can you choose among the thousands of products out there? Unless you know exactly what you want, strolling through the cleaning aisles of your favorite grocery store can be intimidating. There are so many products that seem to do the same thing, and they all claim to be the best. They can't all be the best, but how do you know which to trust?

I give my Seal of Approval to products that stand alone in their categories. Of all the products that do what these do, the ones that have my Seal of Approval are the best. The Palace Picks on page 17 are products that are similar, but are far and away better than anything else on the market.

So there . . . your shopping has just become a little bit easier.

The Queen's Seal of Approval

The Queen of Clean's® Seal of Approval is awarded to a product that exemplifies the very best in its category. I have tested *every single one* of these products. I don't rely on press kits that say that "Product X" is the greatest thing since sliced bread. I've put this stuff through the ringer. Believe me, I try a lot of products, but these are the ones that work, work well, and work consistently. Truly fit for a Queen! (Look on page 30 in the next chapter for more great laundry products.)

Soapworks

Soapworks is the manufacturer of wonderful, nontoxic user- and earth-friendly laundry and personal-care products. Originally designed for allergy and asthma sufferers, Soapworks products are very effective. In addition, they are economical, so everyone can use them. Call (800) 699-9917 or visit them online at www.soapworks.com for more information on their line of healthy, effective products.

- Fresh Breeze Concentrated Laundry Cleaner (powder or liquid)
- Brilliant Bleach (made with peroxide, spectacular for whites and colors)
- Rain Fresh Dishwashing Machine Powder
- Sun Shine Concentrated Dishwashing Soap
- Gentle Shower Body Wash and Shampoo
- Natural Touch Bar Soap
- At Home All-Purpose Cleaner

Odorzout

This is a fabulous, dry, 100 percent natural deodorizer. It's nontoxic, so you can use it anyplace you have a smell or stink. It is especially effective on pet urine odors, and because it's used dry, it's simple to apply. If you have anything in your home that has a smell, there is no better product made than Odorzout! For more information, call (800) 88-STINK or visit their Web page at www.88stink.com.

Clean-X Clean Shield

Formerly Invisible Shield, this is a truly wonderful product. It turns all of those hard-to-clean surfaces (tubs, showers, shower doors, sinks, counters, stovetops, windows—any surface that is not wood or painted) into nonstick surfaces that can be cleaned with water and a soft cloth. No more soap scum or hard-water deposits! It never builds up on surfaces, so it won't make them slippery. Also, it's nontoxic, so you can use it on dishes and food surfaces, too. Call (800) 528-3149 to find a supplier near you.

Euronet USA

Euronet USA is the U.S. distributor of the ACT Natural microfiber cloths and mops. They contain patented ACTEX fibers that clean and disinfect without chemicals. They have been scientifically proven to remove germs and bacteria and even come with a great warranty. They are easy to use, since no cleaning chemicals are involved great for people with allergies, and can be cleaned and sanitized in the washer. This is a big plus with the mop. Use these products in the kitchen and bathroom; to spot-clean carpet; on windows, mirrors, and hard furniture; in the car; and even to spot-clean clothes while you're wearing them—virtually anywhere you clean! Call (888) 638-3552, or visit them at www.euronetusa.com. Remember, in microfiber cloths, you get what you pay for. Don't be fooled by cheap imitations. Euronet USA offers a 100 percent satisfaction guarantee and 2-year performance guarantee with these products.

Dial

Dial Corporation makes a few of my very favorite products. Some of them have been around since the 1800s, such as 20 Mule Team Borax and Fels-Naptha Heavy Duty Laundry Bar Soap. Zout Laundry Stain Remover is one of the newer products. Dial also makes my favorite laundry detergent—Purex. It works great on whites and colors, has a wonderful pricepoint, and is gentle on clothes. Dial products are available in most grocery stores.

Remove perspiration stains and odor from clothing by applying a paste of baking soda and water and letting it soak for 30 minutes prior to laundering.

Mix 1 gallon of warm water and ¼ cup of baking soda. Soak freshly washed socks in this for 30 minutes. Do not rinse out the solution, spin out in the washer, dry, and you will have odor-eating socks.

Clean smudges on wallpaper with baking soda and water.

Baking soda on a soft, wet cloth is great for cleaning your car's chrome, headlights, and enamel.

Remove crayon from hard surfaces with baking soda on a damp rag.

Use on any hard surface as a mild abrasive to remove stains.

Use baking soda as a bug killer for aphids. Use 1½ teaspoons of baking soda per pint of water and apply every 7 days.

To clean grout (any color), mix 3 cups of baking soda with 1 cup of warm water. Scrub grout with a brush and rinse.

When you replace that little box of baking soda in your fridge with a fresh one twice a year, don't let the old one go to waste. Pour the old box down the drain, and chase it with ½ cup of white vinegar. You'll create a little volcano to naturally clean and freshen the drain.

Use baking soda on a damp cloth to polish silver.

To remove burned food in a casserole dish, fill the dish with hot water, add 1 tablespoon of baking soda, and allow to soak.

To get grass stains off fabric shoes like Keds, clean them with baking soda. Dip a wet toothbrush into some baking soda and brush vigorously. Rinse well and dry out of the sun.

Remove dirt and mildew from a child's wading pool by flushing with warm water and baking soda.

Put some baking soda in your car's ashtray. It may not discourage smokers, but it will help neutralize the odor.

Clean screen stain and mineral deposits off windows by dipping a soft, wet cloth in baking soda and rubbing gently. Follow by washing windows as usual.

No need to use chemicals or expensive products to clean lawn furniture. Just rinse with warm water and baking soda. Sprinkle dry baking soda directly on stubborn marks—this natural abrasive will take them right off!

A WORD FROM ZACK, THE PALACE PUSSYCAT: To clean up pet vomit, sprinkle on a heavy coating of baking soda. Let it absorb moisture and dry, then scoop or vacuum up. The baking soda will neutralize acids and help prevent stains. Follow with Spot Shot Instant Carpet Stain Remover.

Remove dark heel marks from hard floors with a damp cloth and baking soda.

Remove streaks and greasy films from car windshields with a thin paste of baking soda and water. Rinse well.

Here's a great natural way to control black spots on roses: Add 1 tablespoon each of baking soda and vegetable oil to 1 gallon of water. Then add 1 drop of liquid detergent and shake well. Spray directly on the foliage, and spray every 5 to 7 days during humid weather. Make sure you wet both sides of the leaves.

A WORD FROM ZACK, THE PALACE PUSSYCAT: Put baking soda in the bottom of cat litter boxes to help eliminate odor. Put in a thin layer of baking soda and then add the litter as usual. This works with clay or clumping varieties.

Lemon Juice

QUEENLY COMMENT: Lemon juice is nature's bleach and disinfectant.

Apply lemon juice to clothes, undiluted, to remove fruit-based stains. Let soak for 30 minutes and then launder.

Remove rust from clothes by applying undiluted lemon juice and laying the garment in the sun. It disappears like magic.

Bleach spots off Formica counters by using straight lemon juice or mixing it into a paste with baking soda.

Clean brass and copper with lemon juice and salt. Sprinkle salt on half of a lemon and rub the metal with it, then rinse thoroughly. If you don't have fresh lemons, you can also mix bottled lemon juice and salt.

Make a cleaner in a spray bottle with 2 cups of water, 2 tablespoons of lemon juice, ½ teaspoon of liquid dish soap, 1 tablespoon of baking soda, and 1 teaspoon of borax. Shake before using to clean any hard surface.

Remove tarnish from silver with a paste of lemon juice and baking soda. Apply the mixture with a soft toothbrush, then allow to dry. Remove with a clean, dry toothbrush and polish with a clean, soft cloth.

Apply lemon juice to chrome and buff to a shine.

As a bleach alternative, use ¼ cup of lemon juice and ¼ cup of white vinegar mixed in 1 gallon of warm water, and soak clothes for 15 minutes prior to washing.

Lemon juice is great for removing stains from your hands. Bottled or fresh-squeezed, just massage the lemon juice into your hands before washing them with good old soap and water.

If food has left any stains on your good china, make a paste of lemon juice and cream of tartar and rub gently. Rinse the piece well when you're done.

Bleach a wooden breadboard by applying lemon juice and letting it sit overnight. Wash and rinse in the morning.

ROYAL BEAUTY SECRET: Make your own hand cream by mixing 2 parts glycerin to 1 part lemon juice. Massage a little into your hands after washing and at bedtime. This absorbent cream works well and smells lovely!

Club Soda

QUEENLY COMMENT: Club soda is the best emergency spot-remover there is.

Keep club soda on hand to clean up spills on carpets and clothing. Remember to react as soon as possible to a spill. If you act fast, a spot shouldn't become a stain. Club soda will remove red wine, coffee, tea, soda (yes, even red soda!), Kool-Aid, and any other spills you can think of. Lift any solids carefully off carpet or clothes and then pour on the club soda, blotting with an old rag until all the color from the spill is removed. Don't be afraid to really wet the carpet, it won't hurt it: Carpet goes through countless dippings in water as it is made. Blot carpet easily by folding a rag and standing on it, turning the rag as it absorbs moisture and color from the spill. The carbonation in the club soda brings the offending spill to the surface so that you can blot it up, and the salts in the soda will help prevent staining.

If you spill on your clothes in a restaurant, ask for a little club soda or seltzer and use your napkin to blot the stain until it is removed. At home you can pour the club soda directly onto the spot, flushing it out.

I have found that club soda will even work on many old stains. Always keep several bottles on hand.

Spot Shot Instant Carpet Stain Remover

Every home needs a good all-purpose carpet stain remover. Skip the kinds that foam, dry, and require vacuuming up: They leave residue in the carpet that attracts dirt. Spot Shot Instant Carpet Stain Remover has never failed me in years of cleaning. It effectively removes water- and oil-based stains. Use it on pet stains, lipstick, makeup, hair dye, food spills, mystery spots—even old spots. Follow the label directions, and you will be amazed at how well it works. It's inexpensive and available at grocery stores, Target, Wal-Mart, and hardware stores. Make sure you have a can on hand for emergencies. It works great with the club soda method discussed above.

Spot Shot Instant Carpet Stain Remover even removes grass stains. Just follow the directions on the can. For stubborn stains, apply rubbing alcohol; wait 10 minutes, blot, then treat with Spot Shot.

The Last Word on Laundry

When I think of laundry, I picture miles of aisles . . . not in my own palace, but in the grocery. All those detergents, bleaches, starches, fabric softeners—even mysterious bottles of things like bluing. How do you know which ones to choose? And, even more to the point, what do you do with them all when you get them home? Never fear, the Queen is here. I'll tell you which products are the best, when you don't need the fancy stuff (and when you do), how to make your own, and how to use them effectively. Plus I'll give you the real dirt on home dry-cleaning kits, the scoop on spots and stains, and more . . . Read on!

Laundry Detergents and Queenly Alternatives

I don't think there is a greater laundry challenge than walking down the soap and detergent aisle and deciding which products to buy. We are constantly bombarded with ads about how well this one cleans, how good that one smells . . . this one contains bleach, that one contains optic brighteners, and that one over there . . . well, it contains every cleaning agent known to man—and woman. Arrrggh! But what really matters in a laundry detergent? When is more just too much?

I have a rule that I follow with laundry detergent, and it's this: Less is more. When I want a laundry detergent or soap, I want that and only that. Period. I want to be the one who determines when I need bleach, softener, or other additives, so I opt for the simplest product, the one that basically does only one thing: removes and suspends soil from my clothes and leaves them clean and fresh. Now by *fresh,* I don't mean having a smelly odor after the wash. I like to leave the house without advertising what detergent I use by the way I smell! I like the labels that read "Free." I don't want odor or artificial color, just the cleaning product. It is healthier for your body *and* your clothes.

(♛) **QUEENLY COMMENT:** If I want to have a fragrance, *I* will choose it! I don't want to smell like a combination of laundry products all mixed together.

Basic laundry detergent. This is where it all starts. Choose your laundry product (bearing in mind my lecture above), and measure it into the machine. Remember to adjust the amount of detergent used to the size of your load. (You may need to adjust the amount if you have hard water. More about that on page 38.) More is not better where laundry soap is concerned. It's just harder to rinse out. Detergent residue makes fabric sticky, and that makes it attract soil faster.

Which laundry detergent do I use? I've tested them all, and believe me, that was a challenge. Sometimes the detergent that gets out the most spills and spots is not the one that is best for your clothes—or your family. Some laundry detergents are particularly hard on colored fabrics, fading them and giving dark colors a whitish cast.

After more testing than you can imagine, I have picked one detergent that I believe can be all things to all people: Purex. It is gentle on clothes and gentle on you, and available in enough varieties so that you can decide whether you want additives, fragrance, and so forth.

Purex is gentle on colors, tough on whites, and, with the addition of 20 Mule Team Borax, can remove the very worst messes. For general laundry, just follow the directions on the box or bottle. I myself am a liquid soap kind of Queen, because I like to measure out my detergent in the cap, and then do a little prespotting with it before I toss the clothes and the balance of the detergent in the machine.

Laundry additives. If you have a particularly soiled load of clothes and feel that your detergent needs a kick, try a safe additive like 20 Mule Team Borax. This will help detergent work better, without bleach. It removes soils and stains, brightens clothes, and freshens laundry without an artificial smell. It's been around since 1891, so it's definitely passed the test of time! Use about ½ cup per wash load when you need extra cleaning power for things such as work clothes, towels, rugs, and so forth.

Need something for diapers? Try 20 Mule Team Borax. It's completely safe for baby clothes and hand washables. It's also a great deodorizer and has more uses in cleaning than I can name.

Allergy-free products. Many people, particularly children, have allergies and asthma problems that seem to be directly related to the cleaning and laundry products we use in our homes. If your family appears to be allergic to underwear (no, I'm not kidding), it may be your detergent. I've been researching allergy-free, nontoxic cleaning products for a long time, and I'm happy to tell you that I have found environmentally friendly products that work to avoid these reactions. I've tested these products. They work safely on laundry for the whole family, babies to adults.

The following products are made by a company called Soapworks. They were created by a woman in direct response to her son's severe, life-threatening asthma.

Try the Fresh Breeze Laundry Powder or the Fresh Breeze Liquid. They are made from natural ingredients such as coconut and palm kernel soap. Fresh Breeze can be used to safely spot-treat clothes and presoak, too, and has a light, fresh scent of natural ginger. Cost for the powder soap works out to about 5 cents per load, compared to about 18 cents a load for a reasonably-priced detergent.

Soapworks also makes Sun Shine Liquid Soap for dishes and washing delicates—and again, it is all natural—and Soapworks Brilliant Bleach, which is a hydrogen peroxide-based bleach.

There is something for everyone in the laundry aisle, but a word of caution: Not all clothes require those heavy-duty products. They can be hard on fabrics and on the environment. Grandma didn't need those additives, and her clothes lasted a long time.

Be a Spot Hotshot!

I love natural products, and I love things that I can make for pennies that work better than the products I could buy at the store. Here are some of my favorite laundry spot removers. Use them just as you would over-the-counter products, but take note: Many of them are designed to take care of specific spots and stains.

Start with a clean spray or squeeze bottle, and always remember to label any product you make. It's important to know what the bottle contains and what it was intended for. I like to include the recipe on the label, too—that way, I can easily mix up additional product. Cover the label with clear packaging tape or a piece of clear adhesive sheet to protect the label from moisture.

These spotters are all intended for washable fabrics. If in doubt, test on an inconspicuous area, such as a seam.

General All-Purpose Laundry Spotter
Combine the following ingredients to make a generic spotter that works on a wide variety of stains:

  1 part rubbing alcohol
  2 parts water

If you use a large spray bottle, you can add 1 bottle of alcohol and 2 of the alcohol bottles filled with water. Spray this on spots and spills, wait a few minutes, and then launder as usual.

Beverage, Fruit, and Grass Remover
Combine equal portions of:

  White vinegar
  Liquid dishwashing soap
  Water

Shake well, and work the solution into the spot. Let stand a few minutes and then launder as usual.

Nonoily Stain Remover
Combine equal portions of the following ingredients:

  Ammonia
  Liquid dishwashing soap
  Water

Shake well, and work the solution into the spot. Let stand a few minutes and flush with water. This solution works well on stains such as milk, blood, perspiration, and urine. *Do not use on washable wool, silk, spandex, acrylic, or acetate.*

Oily Stain Remover
Combine the following ingredients:

  1 tablespoon glycerin
  1 tablespoon liquid dishwashing soap
  8 tablespoons water

Work the solution into grease and oil stains. Let sit a few minutes, flush with water, and then launder as usual.

ROYAL DECREE: All of these spotters are for washable fabrics only, and none of them are for silk, wool, spandex, acrylic, or acetate. When in doubt, test first!

Bringing Out the Big Guns

It's time to talk about the big guns of laundry spotters. We all need them from time to time. But what's best? What really works? Read on. I've tried them all, so you won't have to!

ROYAL DECREE: I am counting on you to test a small, inconspicuous area on the fabric for colorfastness *before* you use any of these spotters. Don't let laundry spotters dry. Launder soon after spotting to prevent the spot from becoming a stain. Don't let me down!

Energine Cleaning Fluid. This is a terrific can't-be-without spotter for dry-clean-only clothes. Blot it on until the stain is gone and then blow-dry to avoid a ring.

Fels-Naptha Heavy Duty Laundry Bar Soap. This is that old-fashioned brown bar soap that your grandmother used. It has been around for 100 years—literally!—and it's a great spotter for numerous spots and stains. Wet the bar and simply rub the stain, working it in well. Let it sit a few minutes. This spotter still works even if allowed to dry on the fabric. Great for ring-around-the-collar and perspiration stains.

Ink Away. Ink and marker can be a challenge to remove, but this product, made by the makers of Goo Gone, really proves its worth. Follow package directions carefully and be sure to read the list of things *not* to use it on before you start.

Spot Shot Instant Carpet Stain Remover. This one wins the prize for the most unusual laundry spotter, but it's *still* one of the Queen's favorite products. Yes, that's right, it's not just for carpet. It's also a great laundry prewash spotter—and boy, does it work! It is safe for all colorfast washables and works in all wash temperatures. Spray the stained area thoroughly, saturating the stain. If the stain is difficult or stubborn, work it between your thumbs. Allow Spot Shot to sit at least 60 seconds, then launder as usual. Do *not* allow it to dry on the fabric, and do not use it on silks, fabrics labeled "dry clean only," or noncolorfast fabrics. This

SPOTS & SPLATTERS
Unclogging Spray Cans

Dear Queen:
What is your method for unclogging spray cans?

The Queen Responds:
I've had success with a few methods. Sometimes running the nozzle under a forceful stream of hot water will do the trick. Other times soaking it in a little rubbing alcohol works well. If neither technique does the trick, try carefully inserting a sewing needle into the clogged end. Gently rock the needle back and forth, then rinse the nozzle again with hot water. Remember to always use care when working with aerosol cans.

product works on oily stains, ink, pet stains, cola, shoe polish, lipstick, blood, and others. It's a must-have in the laundry room.

Wine Away Red Wine Stain Remover. Don't let the name fool you—this product is much more than a red wine stain remover. It works great on Kool-Aid, grape juice, red soda, cranberry juice, orange soda, coffee, and tea, as well as red wine. I even took red food coloring out of a shirt with it once. Wine Away is made from fruit and vegetable extracts and is totally nontoxic—I love that!

Zout Stain Remover. This is a super-concentrated stain remover that works great on ink, blood, grease, fruit juice, grass, and hundreds of other stains. A little goes a long way with this. Simply saturate the stain, work it in, wait 5 to 10 minutes, and then launder as usual.

Stain Removers from Your Cupboard

You may not know this, but some of the very best spot and stain removers are things you use every single day! Not only do these stain removers work great—they're right at your fingertips!

Alcohol. Rubbing alcohol is great for grass stains and so much more.

Ammonia. This is *the* perspiration stain fighter.

Automatic dishwasher detergent. Keep this on hand as a bleach substitute and whitener/brightener even if you *don't* have a dishwasher. Liquid, powder, and tablet forms all work well. If you choose the tablet, make sure it has dissolved in the water before you add clothes. Pour the mixture directly on the stains, or soak stains in the detergent.

Baking soda. Baking soda removes odors.

Club soda. This is my favorite "Oh my gosh, how did I do *that?!*" spotter. Use it on any fabric or surface that can be treated with water. A slight dabbing on dry-clean-only fabrics is also permissible—just be sure to test first! Use club soda on any spill (ask the waiter for some if you're dining out). Just dab it on then blot it off. Club soda keeps spills from becoming stains and brings the offending spill to the surface so that it can be easily removed. I always make sure to have a bottle on hand.

Cream of tartar. I bet you have this in the kitchen cupboard! Mix cream of tartar with lemon juice, and you have a wonderful bleach for white clothes with food or other stains. It's effective on rust stains, too.

Denture-cleaning tablets. The cure-all for white table linens with food stains and white cotton with stains? Denture-cleaning tablets! Dissolve one tablet per ½ cup of water. Pour directly on the stain or spot.

Dishwashing liquid. Use dishwashing liquid undiluted on tough stains.

Glycerin. You can remove tar, tree sap (think "Christmas tree"), juice stains, mustard, ketchup, and barbecue sauce with glycerin.

GOJO Crème Waterless Hand Cleaner. This product is totally awesome for removing grease and oil, including shoe polish.

Hydrogen peroxide. Three percent hydrogen peroxide is super for removing blood stains, especially if they are fairly fresh. It also is a wonderful bleaching agent for stubborn stains on white clothes. Combine ½ cup of hydrogen peroxide and 1 teaspoon of ammonia for an unbeatable stain removal combination. Just make sure to use 3 percent and *not* the kind you use to bleach your hair.

Lemon juice. This is nature's bleach and disinfectant. If you have spots on white clothes, apply some lemon juice and lay them in the sun.

Apply a little more lemon juice prior to laundering, then launder as usual. This is really effective on baby-formula stains.

Meat tenderizer. A combo of meat tenderizer (unseasoned, please, or you'll have a whole new stain!) and cold water is just the answer to protein-based stains such as blood, milk, and so forth.

Salt. Sprinkling salt on spilled red wine will keep the wine from staining until you can launder it. Mixed with lemon juice, salt will remove mildew stains.

Shampoo. Any brand will do. Cheap is fine. I save the small bottles from hotel/motel stays and keep them in the laundry room. Great for treating ring-around-the-collar, mud, and cosmetic stains.

Shaving cream. Shaving cream is one of the best spot and stain removers available. That's because it's really whipped soap! If you have a spill on your clothes (or even your carpet), moisten the spot, work in some shaving cream, and then flush it with cool water. If the offending spot is on something you're wearing, work the shaving cream in and then use a clean cloth to blot the shaving cream and the spot away. Finish off with a quick touch of the blow-dryer to prevent a ring, and you're on your way. The best thing about shaving cream is that even if it doesn't work, it won't set the stain, so the spot can still be removed later. Keeping a small sample can in my suitcase while traveling has saved me more than once!

WD-40 lubricant. If you don't have any, pick up a can the next time you're at the hardware store. Why? Because we've all had those nasty grease stains and oil stains on clothes: Salad dressing misses the salad and gets the blouse, or grease splatters when you are cooking—or crayon, lipstick, or Chap Stick gets on your clothes! WD-40 is your answer. Spray some on, wait 10 minutes, then work in undiluted liquid dishwashing soap and launder as usual. Works well on everything *except* silk.

White vinegar. Use white vinegar undiluted as a great spotter for suede. It's also a wonderful fabric softener. Just put ¼ cup in the final rinse.

It's worthwhile to keep these things on hand. As you can see, most are inexpensive *and* have other uses. They'll make you the laundry Queen (or King!) in your home.

QUEENLY PRODUCT RECOMMENDATIONS

I promised you some more of my favorite product recommendations back in chapter 2. And here they are—the best of the best for clean, fresh laundry.

The Queen's Seal of Approval

To qualify for the Queen of Clean's® Seal of Approval, a product has to simply be the best in its category. These are. I use them all.

Borateem

Borateem Color Safe Bleach helps keep clothes looking new longer by powering out soil and stains. It also helps safely preserve colors. Look for Borateem in the laundry section of your local grocery.

Fels-Naptha Heavy Duty Laundry Bar Soap

Fels-Naptha Laundry Soap is a wonderful laundry spotter and cleaner. Great for ring-around-the-collar and perspiration stains. You can find Fels-Naptha in the laundry or bar soap section of your local grocery.

Purex

Purex laundry detergent is formulated for powerful everyday cleaning at a great value price. Purex keeps your whites white and your colors brilliant. Plus, Purex leaves your clothes smelling great! Purex is available in liquid, powder, and tablets. For more information, visit www.Purex.com.

20 Mule Team Borax

Put a kick in your laundry detergent! 20 Mule Team Borax helps remove soils and stains, brighten clothes, and freshen your laundry. This product can also be used throughout your house for cleaning and deodorizing.

Zout

Zout laundry stain remover is a super-concentrated stain fighter that helps remove tough stains, even old set-in ones. With Zout, stains are quickly and safely eliminated from all colorfast washable fabrics. For more information on Zout and stain-fighting tips, visit www.Zout.com.

I mentioned the following two in chapter 2, but they're for laundry, too, so I'm going to tell you about them again. That's my Queenly prerogative!

Odorzout

This is a fabulous, dry, 100 percent natural deodorizer. It's nontoxic, so you can use it anyplace you have a smell or stink. It is especially effective on pet urine odors (just ask Zack!), and because it's used dry, it's simple to apply. If you have anything in your home that has a smell or a stink, there is no better product made than Odorzout. For more information, call (800) 88-STINK or visit their Web page at www.88stink.com.

Soapworks

Soapworks is the manufacturer of wonderful, nontoxic, user- and earth-friendly laundry and personal-care products. The two Soapworks products for laundry are Fresh Breeze Concentrated Laundry Cleaner Powder or Liquid and Brilliant Bleach (made with peroxide, spectacular for both whites and colors). Originally designed for people with allergies and asthma, Soapworks products are very effective. In addition, they are economical, so everyone can use them. Call (800) 699-9917 or visit them online at www.soapworks.com for more information on their line of healthy, effective products.

Bleach 101: Whiter Whites, Brighter Brights

Are you one of those people who thinks that directions are what you read to find out what you did wrong? Then pay attention. I'm going to give you my do's and don'ts of bleach basics.

Do's

Here's the Royal Road to clean, bright clothes.

- Read the directions on the container of bleach. Don't just browse or speed-read, either, there's lots of useful information on labels.

- Check the labels on the fabric you wish to bleach. If the label says "no bleach," it says it for a reason.

- Test the bleach if you are unsure. To do this with chlorine bleach, mix 1 tablespoon of chlorine bleach with ¼ cup of cold water. Find a hidden area on the piece of clothing and place a drop of the solution on it. Leave this for a minute or two and then blot to determine if there is any color change. If there isn't a color change, it's safe to use on that garment. If there is a color change, forget using chlorine bleach.

- To test all-fabric bleaches, mix 1 teaspoon of the bleach with 1 cup of hot water. Again, place a drop on an inconspicuous area on the garment. Wait at least 15 minutes, blot, and check for any change in the color.

- Of course, if any color change takes place, don't use that type of bleach on that type of fabric.

- Always be sure to rinse bleach out of fabric thoroughly. If you don't, you run the risk of getting bleach on your other clothes when you launder them.

Don'ts

To avoid disaster when bleaching, resist the temptation to do any of the following four Unqueenly acts.

- Absolutely never allow undiluted chlorine bleach to come in contact with fabrics.
- Never use any kind of bleach directly on fabric without testing it first.
- Never use more bleach than called for. It can damage fabrics, and it's wasteful, too!
- *Never, ever* use chlorine bleach and ammonia in the same wash! It can generate deadly fumes.

Now let's talk about the bleaches one by one.

Chlorine Bleach

The strongest, fastest-acting bleach available, chlorine bleach is very effective on cottons, linens, and some synthetics when used properly. Used improperly, it can weaken cloth fibers, causing them to disintegrate. It can even cause holes. Always follow container directions with care, and never use chlorine bleach on silk, wool, spandex, acetate, fibers treated to be flame-resistant, or dry-clean-only fabrics.

Most of us have had a bad experience with chlorine bleach, so use care. Never pour it on hand washables, and never pour it onto clothes that are in the washing machine. Pour it in the bleach dispenser, if your washing machine is so equipped, or into the washer while it is filling with water and *before* you add the clothes. For hand washables, dilute it prior to adding the clothes, and be sure to adjust the amount accordingly for the amount of water being used.

👑 **QUEENLY COMMENT:** Name brands and store brands of chlorine bleach work the same, so purchase the product of your choice, or the one with the best price.

All-Fabric Bleach or Oxygen Bleach

This is a much milder form of bleach. It works well on delicate fabrics or those requiring gentle care. It is slower-acting than chlorine bleach, and it is less effective in restoring whiteness to fabrics. It may be effective, though, through regular use. This bleach can be used on all fabrics, even silks, as long as the care tag does not say "no bleach." Add this bleach when you add your detergent, and do not pour it directly on the clothes. More is *not* better, so measure, don't just pour.

A New Generation of Bleach

Soapworks has come up with a new generation of bleach that is effective, user-friendly, and safe for use by people with allergies and asthma. It is hypoallergenic, nontoxic, biodegradable, 100 percent natural, safe for septic tanks, and contains no chemicals, dyes, or fragrances.

This product is called Brilliant, and it is just that! Created with hydrogen peroxide—which is the safest whitener and brightener for fabrics—this natural bleach can be used effectively on both whites and colored fabrics. Clothes can be soaked safely for 24 hours or more without harm to either fabric or color.

Brilliant is also a softener, so no additional softening agent is required. Add ¼ cup to the washer as it fills with water. As with any bleach product, test in an inconspicuous area when in doubt.

Bluing

Bluing is a whitening and brightening agent that has been around for a long, long time. Available in liquid form, bluing contains blue pigment, which actually counteracts the yellowing that occurs in some fabrics. Always dilute this with water as directed on the bottle, and never pour it directly on clothes or spill it on other fibers or surfaces. Look for it in the laundry aisle at the grocery store. This product will even remove the yellow from gray hair!

Making Your Own Bleaching Agents

Yes, you *can* create your own effective bleaching formulas with things you already have at home.

Lemon juice. Nature's bleach and disinfectant, lemon juice can be used to whiten clothes. Take 1 gallon of the hottest water possible for the fabric you're bleaching and add ½ cup of bottled lemon juice or the slices of one or two lemons. Soak the clothes for 30 minutes or even overnight. This works especially well on white socks and underwear and is safe for polyester fabrics. Don't use lemon juice on silks, though.

Automatic dishwasher detergent. Fill a bucket with the hottest possible water for the fabric you are working with, and add 2 tablespoons of any brand of automatic dishwasher detergent. Soak white clothes for 30 minutes or even overnight. Then dump them into the washer and launder.

To use this bleaching technique in the washer, fill the machine with water and add ¼ cup to ½ cup of automatic dishwasher detergent. Agitate for several minutes and then add clothes. Soak as directed above and then add detergent and launder as usual.

Hydrogen peroxide. This can be used to bleach delicate items such as wool or wool blends. Soak them overnight in a solution of 1 part 3 percent hydrogen peroxide to 8 parts cold water. Launder according to care directions.

Fabric Softeners—The Soft Sell

Fabric softeners are used to make fabrics soft and fluffy and to minimize static cling. They can also reduce wrinkling and make ironing easier.

If your detergent already contains softener (read the label), you may not need additional softener unless you are getting a lot of static cling in your clothes.

Here are the two types.

Liquid softeners. These should be added to the final rinse cycle by the automatic dispenser (if your washing machine has one), or by hand if not. Carefully follow the directions on the label, and make sure to measure: Too much is not better, nor is too little.

QUEENLY COMMENT: If you are using an automatic dispenser, add the softener, then follow with an equal amount of water to help disperse the softener. This will help to eliminate softener spots on clothes.

Fabric softener sheets. These paper-thin sheets soften clothes, and they also work with the heat of the dryer to reduce static electricity in the load, which means that your dress won't cling to your panty hose and your trousers won't stick to your socks! I find store brands work just as well as higher-priced varieties, so go ahead and make your choice by fragrance or price. Whatever suits you.

By the way, if static cling is a problem (and it happens to the best of us, especially when you're at an important event), try smoothing your skirt with a damp pair of hands. A little bit of hand cream on top of your panty hose works well, too.

ROYAL DECREE: Dryer softener sheets can cause buildup on towels, which can make them feel slippery and reduce their absorbency. Use the softener only once every two or three washings to avoid this and keep towels fluffy and soft.

Making Your Own Fabric Softener Sheets

Believe it or not, you can make your own fabric softener sheets. Simply take an old washcloth, mist it with a mixture of 1 part of your favorite liquid fabric softener and 2 parts water, then toss it in the dryer with the clothes. Remist for each new load of clothes, and occasionally launder it when washing towels to remove any softener buildup and soften the towels at the same time.

I keep a mixture in a small spray bottle on the shelf in my laundry room along with a few old washcloths. I find that ⅓ cup of liquid fabric softener and ⅔ cup of warm water make a good quantity. Shake prior to spraying on the cloth.

ROYAL DECREE: Always label the bottle of any mixture you make yourself to keep it from being misused accidentally.

RETIRED SOFTENER SHEETS

Once you have used that little fabric softener sheet, you can use it to clean off the lint filter in your dryer before you toss it. Here are some other ingenious uses for those retired sheets.

- If you have a casserole or pan with burned-on food, fill it with hot water, toss in a softener sheet, and let it sit for several hours (overnight is fine). The burned-on food will slide right out.
- Run a needle and thread through a sheet to prevent static from tangling the thread.
- Wipe the television screen, venetian blinds, or any other surface that attracts dust with a used sheet to reduce the static electricity that acts as a dust magnet.
- Place a sheet in a coat pocket to avoid the shock you get when getting in and out of the car in winter.
- Place a used sheet in luggage, drawers, closets, trash cans, under car seats, and in your laundry bag or hamper to provide a fresh scent.
- Tuck a used sheet into shoes before placing them in your luggage. The shoes will smell fresh, and you can use the fabric softener sheet to buff them and remove dust after wearing.
- Use a fabric softener sheet to polish chrome to a brilliant shine after cleaning.
- Use a sheet to wrap Christmas ornaments or other fragile things before boxing them for storage. The dryer sheet will protect them, and you can wipe Christmas ornaments prior to hanging on the tree to reduce static electricity and repel dust.
- Wipe car dashboards with a used sheet to shine and repel dust.

Retired fabric softener sheets have plenty of use left, so don't waste them. And don't use new softener sheets for any of these purposes! Pick up a used, or, as I like to call them, "retired" sheet instead! I put my used fabric softener sheets in an empty tissue box that I keep in the laundry room. This way they are always handy.

Fabric Softener Spots on Clothes

No matter how hard you try, at some point you will probably pull out a load of clothes and find either blue spots from liquid fabric softener or "grease"-type spots from dryer softener sheets on your clothes. Here's what to do.

Liquid softener spots. If spotting occurs, wet the item and rub with undiluted dishwashing liquid, then rewash. Wetting and rubbing with shampoo seems to work, too. Do *not* rub with laundry detergent. It won't remove the spot—in fact, it may set it in.

Fabric softener sheet spots. If spotting occurs, rub the area with a wet bar of soap, such as Dove, and then relaunder.

To avoid spots from fabric softener sheets, place the sheet on top of the clothes in the dryer rather than mixing it in, and start the dryer immediately. Do not use a sheet when you are using the air fluff cycle without heat.

ROYAL DECREE: Do *not* use dryer sheets on children's sleepwear or other garments labeled as flame-resistant, as they may reduce flame resistance. These sheets are *not* nontoxic, so keep them out of reach of children and pets to avoid accidental ingestion. And many dryer sheets contain perfumes that can irritate baby's skin.

The Hard Truth about Water Softeners

If you live in an area that has hard water, you will be well-acquainted with the graying or yellowing effect that hard water minerals can have on your clothes. You may also have noticed that, rather than suds in your washing machine, you have gray-looking water and, sometimes, scum on the water surface.

Still not sure if you have hard water? You can check with your local water-supply office—they will tell you the degree of hardness in your water. If you have well water, you might want to call a water-treatment company. They'll be able to test your supply. Of course, you can also look out for these telltale signs.

- Fabrics look dull and gray.

- Fabrics feel stiff instead of soft.

- Soaps and detergents don't lather well.

- White or green residue appears around drains and faucets, and on glassware; you may also find hardened deposits on spigots.

If your water is not *too* hard (less than 10.6 grains of hardness per gallon), you can help alleviate the problems associated with hard water by adjusting the amount of detergent you use. Start by using half the amount of detergent called for. You can also give your detergent a "kick" by using Arm and Hammer Washing Soda or 20 Mule Team Borax along with your detergent, following package directions. These products are found in the laundry additive section at the grocery store or at discount stores. If you find that your clothes still do not have the degree of cleanliness and softness that you desire, you may need to try a liquid softener that you can add to your laundry along with your detergent, or go to a mechanical means of softening.

Making Your Own Water Softener

Combine the following in a labeled 1-gallon container. Plastic gallon milk jugs that have been washed well work great.

½ pound Arm and Hammer Washing Soda
¼ pound 20 Mule Team Borax
1 gallon warm water

To use: Add 1 cup of the solution to each load of wash water along with your normal laundry detergent.

If you still find that your wash is dingy and you are not getting any lather from your bar soap in the shower, then you may need to turn to a mechanical softener, which is attached to the house water system.

Starch and Sizing

Starches and sizing restore body to fabrics that have become limp through washing or dry cleaning. They also form a protective barrier to repel dirt. Fabrics such as cotton or linen respond particularly well to these products.

Starch. Starch comes in spray, liquid, and powder forms. Liquid and powder starches should be combined with water—the directions on the package will tell you what proportions to use. Mix to a thick paste if you want your clothes to have a crisp, starched appearance. A thinner consistency will give you a lighter look. You can also add starch to the final machine rinse if you like. Just be sure to follow the directions carefully. Spray starches provide a light effect. Use powder or liquid if you prefer a heavier starch.

(crown) **QUEENLY COMMENT:** The easiest form of starch is spray starch, which you apply while ironing. Just spritz it on the clothes and iron. It's that easy!

Sizing. A lighter cousin to starch, sizing is applied in the manufacturing process to provide protection and body to fabric. General wear, moisture, perspiration, and washing or dry cleaning will eventually break down the sizing, though, so you may want to reapply it. Buy it in a spray can and spritz it on garments as you iron.

(crown) **ROYAL DECREE:** Don't use too much of these spray products! And don't use your iron on a high heat—the starch or sizing will flake off if you do.

Cry Me a River—The Color Ran!

Ever turned your white underwear pink? Then you know what I'm talking about when I say that some dark colors bleed during initial washing. Not all colors are what we call "colorfast," so you must be careful to prevent the dye of one garment from running on to another. No point in ruining the royal robes!

Is It Colorfast?

How do you know if an item is colorfast? Test it! Try this simple color-fast test before you launder new fabrics. You'll save yourself a lot of time and heartache if you do.

- Place a drop of water on an inside seam or another inconspicuous spot. Blot with a white cotton ball or towel.

- If the cotton ball remains clean, it is safe to wash with other clothes. If it picks up some color from the fabric, then you must wash the garment separately.

Be careful not to drip-dry fabrics that are not colorfast. The color can streak. Instead, roll these clothes in a towel to absorb excess moisture, then hang to dry, away from other fabrics.

Uh-Oh . . .

What happens if a pair of new black socks was somehow washed with your favorite white blouse? Fugitive color happens, that's what! Don't despair. Some products can help you do away with color runs.

Synthrapol. This is a wonderful product used by quilters to eliminate color runs in quilts. Used in a basin or in the washing machine, it will remove fugitive color without damage to the original color or fabric. In simple terms, if you washed a white T-shirt with a red T-shirt and the white T-shirt turned pink, Synthrapol will remove the pink and return the shirt to its original white.

Synthrapol works best on cottons, but I've had success with polyester and blends, too. Try it in an inconspicuous spot first, unless the item is a total loss and you feel you've got nothing to lose. This is a fairly strong chemical, so be sure to follow the directions carefully.

Carbona Color Run Remover. One box of Carbona will restore a whole washload of clothes dyed from mixed-wash bleeding. You *must* test the fabric to be sure that it's colorfast: Otherwise the garment's original color will be removed along with the fugitive color! Follow the directions carefully and use great care. This, too, is a strong chemical. It may be harmful to synthetic materials, denim, or bright, fluorescent, and khaki colors. Zippers, buttons, and so forth may become discolored, so you might want to remove what you can prior to treatment.

Retayne. A color fixative for cottons, Retayne is an interesting product that you should use *before* washing a garment that is likely to bleed. Just think of this as an ounce of prevention.

For best results, treat the garment with Retayne prior to laundering for the first time. Not only will this prevent bleeding, it will also help to keep colors brighter longer. Again, as with everything, try in an inconspicuous area first and read the directions carefully.

QUEENLY COMMENT: All three of these products contain chemicals that can be harmful to children and pets, so please make sure you take adequate storage precautions.

How to Rescue Things That Reek

Odor can be a big laundry problem. There are a number of perfumed products that claim to remove odor and leave fabric fresh-smelling. It's been my experience, however, that most of these products just mask smells. I don't know about you, but I'd rather not have lilac-scented perspiration!

Putting white vinegar in the final rinse will remove some odors. But for difficult odors, such as smoke, urine, pet smells, garlic, gasoline, and so forth, you need a much stronger product. I highly recommend Odorzout, a 100 percent natural product with no odor of its own. Use it dry or wet. It doesn't cover up odors—it actually absorbs them! And it's safe for people with asthma or allergies, too!

To use Odorzout dry, sprinkle it directly on clothes that have an offensive odor, and allow them to sit for several hours. Intense odors, such as gasoline, can be treated for several days with no harm to the fabric. Just make sure you allow air to circulate—the product won't work in an enclosed space.

To use wet, simply fill the washing machine and add 1 to 2 teaspoons of Odorzout. Agitate for a minute and then add the clothes and your detergent. Launder as usual.

Odorzout is great when sprinkled on pet bedding several hours before laundering. You can also use it to control odor in hampers and diaper pails. It is safe and nontoxic for use around kids and pets, which is a big plus.

Try the Odorzout Pouch as well. You can put the pouches in empty shoes to eliminate smells, and in cupboards and drawers to keep odors at bay. I love the convenience.

Another good general odor remover for laundry is 20 Mule Team Borax. Add this to any odorous load of laundry. Just follow the directions on the box. This product is safe for all washables.

(👑) **QUEENLY COMMENT:** Remember, if it stinks, it's best to treat it immediately, before the odor can be passed on to other items.

The Dirt on Home Dry-Cleaning Kits

You've seen them—those home dry-cleaning kits available in all the stores. What are they good for? Well, if you expect to open the dry-cleaning bag and find clean, sharply pressed clothes straight from the dryer, you'll be disappointed. If, however, you want to extend the time between professional dry cleanings, these kits may be for you.

I have found home dry-cleaning kits to be effective on items such as sweaters, cut velvet, velvet, dry-clean-only blouses, and those garments that are delicate and hard to hand-wash and lay flat to dry. They are also great for freshening small blankets, bedspreads, comforters, and draperies. But do not force a large bedspread or blanket into the bag. It will be filled with wrinkles when you remove it.

Home dry-cleaning kits do work on suits, although you'll give up the sharply pressed finish. (You may even find occasional spotting on the suit's lining.)

All of these kits come with treated cloths and reusable dryer-safe bags. Some come with separate spotting solution and spotting blotters. They all work approximately the same way.

First, you spot the garment, either with the same sheet that you toss in the bag during the cleaning process, or with a separate spotting liquid. Spotting the garment well is important because, as we all know by now, heat can set stains. Take your time with the spotting procedure and look over the garment well.

Look for the kits at grocery, drug, and discount stores. Follow the directions carefully for the kit you have selected. Do not overcrowd the dryer bag, or your clothes will be very wrinkled and require a lot of work with the iron—and that defeats the purpose.

SPECIAL HINTS FROM THE PALACE

Follow these Queenly tips to get the most from your dry-cleaning kit.

- Remove the clothes from the dryer bag immediately, and hang or fold them—whichever is appropriate. Some pressing may be required, depending on the type of fabric.
- Do not use any bag other than the one which is provided in the kit, and do not use any additional cleaning chemicals.
- If you don't like the odor of perfume fresheners, check out each kit individually and try several. Some have more perfume than others.
- Last but not least, follow the directions closely.

Are these kits worth the money? Ultimately, that's up to you to decide. If you have a lot of things you want to freshen between cleanings, and if that crisp, pressed look is not vital to you, then yes, give them a try. If, however, your wardrobe consists mostly of business suits and crisply creased trousers, you will probably be disappointed. Will these kits replace your regular trips to the dry cleaner? I don't think so. But I don't think they were intended to.

Health and Budget Basics

Health matters to me—yours, mine, the planet's. It's a queenly concern! That's why I always try to use cleaning products that are safe and environmentally friendly as well as super-effective. Of course, I want a clean, fresh house—but not at the expense of the good health of the King, the Queen Mum, my own majestic self, or Zack, the Palace Pussycat! I also don't want disease-enhancing mold, mildew, and other evil, germy things growing in my house. And I'm sure you don't either! So read on for some truly regal ways to rid your palace of yucky mold, get the gunk out of your ducts, turn down the allergy meter, and help cut down those bills and save your budget—and the environment!

Stop the Science Experiment: Mold and Mildew

Left unchecked, dampness in a home or basement can rot wood, peel paint, and promote rust and mildew.

Find the Source

Here is a simple test to determine if dampness is caused by seepage or excessive humidity.

Cut several 12-inch squares of aluminum foil. Tape them in various spots on the floor and walls; seal the edges tightly. If moisture collects between the foil and the surface after several days, waterproof the interior walls. If moisture forms on the foil's surface, take the following steps.

- Close windows on humid days.

- Install a window exhaust fan.

- Vent your clothes dryer to the outside.

- Use a dehumidifier, especially during summer months.

If you need to waterproof your interior walls, treat the walls with epoxy-based waterproofing paint or masonry sealer. (To clean walls in preparation for paint, look for special mildew cleaners in home centers.)

QUEENLY PRODUCT RECOMMENDATIONS

One thing I have found is that most people associate clean with what they smell. We want everything to smell clean. And mold and mildew definitely don't smell clean! For all of us who've ever been in a mildew-infested gym shower room, that smell is unforgettable. Ecch! If you're looking for a foolproof product that you can purchase to use in eliminating all odors with success, I highly recommend Odorzout.

This is a 100 percent natural product that stops many odors almost on contact, including mold and mildew. It is made of blended natural zeolite minerals, contains no perfumes, and is 100 percent safe for use around children or pets. (**A word from Zack, the Palace Pussycat:** You can even use it in the cat's litter box!)

In my testing, I have found no odor that it didn't work on. Call (800) 88STINK for more information or ordering, or visit the Web site: www.88stink.com.

Make Your Own Treatment

You can make your own mildew treatment by mixing 1 quart of chlorine bleach and 1 tablespoon of powdered nonammoniated laundry detergent with 3 quarts of warm water. Scrub the mildew-stained surface with the solution and allow it to work until the discoloration vanishes, then rinse thoroughly and allow to dry.

ROYAL DECREE: Be sure to wear goggles, rubber gloves, and protective clothing when using this mildew treatment. Never allow it to come in contact with carpet or fabrics, and clean the shoes you wear before walking on carpets. Use this solution outdoors or in a well-ventilated area.

Cleaning Your Air Ducts

You've had smoke damage in your home . . . you have allergies . . . you just purchased an older home. Here's some healthy advice for cleaner air and a fresher smell.

Picture yourself in this situation: Your home has had smoke damage. All the cleaning and repainting is done, and now you are ready to turn on the furnace. You go to the thermostat and turn it up. You hear the furnace spring to life. The central blower is activated . . . and, suddenly, you run screaming from the house. What's wrong? All the odor that collected in the duct system during the smoke damage has just been blown full force from the duct system and into the house! It smells like the house is on fire again. As if the smell isn't enough, you now see black sooty residue blowing out in a dark cloud and settling all over the newly cleaned walls, carpet, and furniture. How could this happen? Nobody thought to clean the duct system prior to cleaning the house and turning on the furnace.

But duct cleaning and deodorizing is not just for houses that have had fire or smoke damage. It is very beneficial in older homes where dust and allergy-causing bacteria have accumulated in the ductwork and are blown through the home each time the furnace runs. Duct cleaning can be very beneficial for people who have allergy problems, too.

How *Do* You Clean Those Ducts?

Duct cleaning involves removing register covers and vacuuming out all the ductwork that leads to the furnace. After some elaborate preparatory vacuuming and cleaning procedures, which include cleaning all the register covers, a duct sealer is introduced into the system in the form of a fine mist. This sealer is a plasticlike resin. The chemical itself actually neutralizes odor and seals the loose soot, dust, and dirt that remain after vacuuming onto the interior walls of the system. During this process, all odor is eliminated, and minor residues remaining in unseen or unreachable areas are permanently sealed onto the interior surface of the ducts.

This process gives you a dirt-, dust-, and pollen-free environment. If allergies run in your family, you will immediately notice the difference. This is particularly good in older homes that, naturally, have the original duct systems in place.

ROYAL DECREE: When you have your ducts cleaned, I recommend that you have your furnace cleaned at the same time. Many furnace companies clean ductwork, too, as do many disaster-restoration or cleaning companies.

Allergy Sufferers: Don't Despair!

The experts say that allergies are reactions to harmless substances that don't bother most people. Huh! If that's the case, why do so many people suffer from them? Seasonal allergies are caused by factors such as tree, grass, and other types of pollen. Year-round allergies are reactions to things like dust particles, animal dander, mold, and dust mites. Whatever their cause, allergies can make us sneeze, sniff, cough, and generally feel miserable. But you don't have to take it lying down!

Can You Do Without It?

Many detergents contain petroleum distillates—a major irritant for people with allergies. If freshly laundered clothes make you sneeze or itch, consider changing detergents. Be selective. Look for products marked "dye- and perfume-free," and check the label for colors or perfumes—you'll want to steer clear of them. I like Purex, a gentle detergent that does a great job on laundry. People with severe allergies or asthma may benefit from environmentally friendly products, such as those manufactured by Soapworks. If you or anyone in your family experiences allergies, you owe it to yourself to shop around.

ROYAL DECREE: If you have allergies, use pump dispensers rather than aerosol sprays, which can fill the air with minute particles of irritants.

Here are other Imperial ways to avoid getting struck down by "spring fever."

- Dryer fabric softener sheets can exacerbate allergies, so it's best to do without them.

- If you must use hair spray, apply it outside the house so that the fumes won't linger.

- Look through your cleaning supplies and eliminate the ones with a strong scent, the ones that are loaded with chemicals, and the ones you've had for a long time. Products can undergo changes after time, and irritants can increase.

- Don't mix chemicals.

- Look for natural cleaning products such as baking soda, lemon juice, club soda, and white vinegar.

- Furniture polish can attract dust and dust mites. It's best not to use it—simple dusting will suffice.

- Change the bag in your vacuum cleaner frequently. If you have a vacuum with a collection canister rather than a bag, empty it each time you vacuum.

- Stuffed animals are huge dust collectors, so if your children have allergies, it's best to limit their exposure. Any cloth or fuzzy toy can be a potential allergy problem. If your child is having difficulties with allergies, remove toys one by one to determine those that can be tolerated—and those that can't.

QUEENLY COMMENT: Stuffed fabric toys that can't be washed can still be cleaned. Just place in a plastic bag with some baking soda and salt, and shake vigorously a few times a day for several days. This should remove dust, dirt, and odors.

Allergies Underfoot

If you have severe allergies, you've probably already been told that you should consider hard floors such as wood, laminate, or ceramic (tile). These floors can be washed frequently and will do a lot to keep allergy symptoms at bay. For many folks, though, the carpeting needs to stay put, so here are a few tips I've learned over the years.

If you have severe allergies but are unable to remove carpets, apply benzyl benzoate dry foam or 3 percent tannic acid, then vacuum using a cleaner with an effective filter system. Tannic acid breaks down mite allergens, and benzyl benzoate dry foam actually kills mites and helps remove them and their waste products from carpet.

Avoid placing houseplants directly on carpets and rugs. Moisture in the plant can cause condensation, and that in turn can cause mildew—a powerful irritant to people with allergies.

Vacuuming can stir up dust mites and their droppings, so don't vacuum too frequently. Once a week is fine (isn't that grand?).

Queenly Declarations for People with Allergies

No need to sneeze and wheeze out there in allergy-land. Put these three suggestions to work for you.

- Vacuum hard floors prior to mopping so that you don't stir up dust.

- Wash all hard floors with a quality cleaner created with allergy sufferers in mind. Try At Home All-Purpose Cleaner from Soapworks. (See "More Queenly Product Recommendations.")

- Damp-mop hard floors with a good-quality mop that can be washed in the washing machine. Try the ACT Natural microfiber mop (see page 79 for more on mops).

Sofa, So Good

I don't know about you, but my sofa is my favorite throne. The King and I spend a lot of time sitting there. If you do, too, use these Queenly tips to keep allergy-causing monsters at bay.

- Stay away from fuzzy or flocked fabrics that are difficult to clean. Buy only upholstered pieces that can be cleaned with water.

- Vacuum upholstered pieces weekly.

- Stay clear of furniture with ruffles or fringes. They're notorious dust catchers—and are extremely difficult to clean.

- When shopping for upholstered furniture, look for pieces without loose pillows. Buy tailored pieces in tightly woven fabrics.

SPOTS & SPLATTERS

Allergic to . . . What?!

Dear Queen:

My asthmatic daughter's allergist informed me that molds grow almost everywhere—bedding, carpet, even snow! So I assume that mold can also grow in my houseplant soil. Is there any way to kill the mold without damaging the plants?

The Queen Responds:

Don't throw those houseplants away! Just don't water them too much. Check the soil between waterings to make sure it's not too wet, which would encourage mold. Here are more suggestions for reducing mold in your home and keeping your family more comfortable.

- Fix all sources of leaks. Remember, mold thrives in damp conditions.

- If possible, install air-conditioning in your home. This dries the air out, making it more difficult for mold to survive.

- Keep firewood outside.

- If you have a basement, keep it as dry as possible.

- Clean the shower floor frequently to ensure that mold doesn't accumulate.

- Clean the bottom of your refrigerator and underneath it.

- Ask your allergist about placing an air purifier in your home that emits negative ions and ozone. Some studies have shown these to be effective in destroying mold.

FILTERS: NOT JUST FOR COFFEEMAKERS

Dirty filters can aggravate allergies and asthma. And since you don't see them, they're easy to forget. So when you're cleaning house, don't forget your filters!

- If there's a filter, clean it! This means vacuums, fans, air purifiers, and so forth.
- Change the furnace filter at least once a month, or invest in one that can be washed. Make sure to wash it frequently.
- If your allergies are severe, consider wearing a filtration mask while vacuuming and dusting.

And So to Bed

We spend so much time under the royal canopy—which is to say, *sleeping*—that allergy aggravators have hours to creep up on us. Here's how to give them the royal boot.

- Sealing your bedroom door with weather stripping will give you more control over your sleeping environment.
- Keep pets out of your bedroom.
- Something as innocent as wallpaper can cause mildew, so keep walls—especially bedroom walls—free of papers and fabrics.
- Use an air purifier in your bedroom.
- Vacuum your mattress frequently. Invest in a good mattress cover—one that forms a protective cover but still allows the mattress to breathe.
- Wash all bedding in 130°F water at least every 10 days. That includes blankets, pillows, comforters, and mattress pads.
- If you can't wash pillows and comforters as frequently as you'd like, try placing them in the dryer on the air fluff cycle. That will help.

- Keep bedspreads, dust ruffles, decorator pillows, and so forth, dust-free. Better yet, get rid of that dust ruffle.
- Stay away from down and feather pillows. They can aggravate allergies, even if you're *not* allergic to them. Use foam pillows encased in hypoallergenic covers that can be zipped shut.

Fighting Allergies All around the House

Here are a few more tricks for keeping allergies out of your royal residence.

- Wash windows and screens frequently.
- Keep the house closed up as much as possible, especially on windy days.
- Plant flowers and trees that produce as little pollen as possible. Indoors, choose houseplants such as ivy, African violets, and leafy plants such as philodendrons, piggyback plants, creeping pileas, and prayer plants.
- Install an air cleaner on the furnace or invest in a stand-alone air purifier.
- Don't keep fresh flowers indoors, no matter how beautiful.
- Keep your fireplace clean, and make sure the damper is closed.
- Use natural lamb's-wool dusters. The lanolin in the wool traps the dust and keeps it from spreading.
- If you don't like to use lamb's-wool dusters, use a clean, damp cloth.
- Insects love stagnant water, so don't allow water to stand in fountains and plant bases.
- Remove dried flower arrangements. These dust catchers are very hard to keep clean.
- Invest in a dehumidifier and maintain it well. Empty it weekly and clean it, too. Wash it with a solution of 1 quart of warm water and

2 teaspoons of chlorine bleach. Make sure you wipe down the coils, and pay special attention to the container that catches the water.

- Make sure your curtains are made of synthetic fiber. Natural fibers contain more lint and may aggravate allergies.

- Dust mites survive in dampness, so do everything in your power to keep the air dry—except moving to my house in Arizona!

- Keep cooking pots covered to eliminate steam.

- Use an exhaust fan over the stove when you cook.

- Don't hang clothes in the house to dry.

THE CAT'S MEOW

Remember me, Zack, the Palace Pussycat? Well, I have a few things to say about allergies myself! Here's how you can have pets *without* aggravating your allergies.

- Brush your pet outside and often. Try to wash him weekly—if he'll let you!

- People with allergies should avoid cleaning litter boxes. (There! I bet you never thought there was anything *good* about having allergies, did you?) If that's not possible, use a filtration mask and dispose of waste outside—never in a trash can.

- If your pet hates a bath, wipe his coat with a damp ACT Natural microfiber cloth. This will remove loose hair, dander, and dry saliva, all of which contribute to allergy problems.

- Don't take your dog for a run in the woods, through fields, or in tall grass, where he can pick up allergy-causing mold spores, dried grass, leaves, and pollen. Hmpf . . . dogs!

—Zack

Tips for Conserving Energy and Water

Here's one case where what's good for the Queen is good for the castle. Why heat up your energy bills to new heights, or waste water and drown in high water bills, when you can cut back and enjoy it at the same time? For example, cuddling is an energy-efficient way to keep warm. Want to save water? Bathe with a friend! Of course, there are more serious ways to save on your energy bill. Here are my favorites.

ROYAL DECREE: I hereby decree that all money saved on energy and water bills should be spent by the King of *your* castle on shiny baubles and other delightful treasures for his Queen!

- Why heat an empty house? Lower the thermostat when your family is out during the day. Try 65°F or so and bring the heat back up in the evening. If you lower the temperature when everybody is toasty warm in bed, you'll cut your bill even further. A double setback thermostat can adjust the temperature according to your needs. It's well worth the money.

- Moist air retains heat, so invest in a humidifier (or adapt your existing heating system), and you could lower your thermostat by another 3 to 4 degrees. That can save you up to 12 percent on your heating bill.

- A gas-fired heating system should be professionally cleaned and serviced at least once a year to keep it working at maximum efficiency. Oil-fired systems should be cleaned and serviced twice a year. Those of you who have had the misfortune of a furnace backup *know* I'm giving you good advice. Cleaner is better.

- Shut the dishwasher off at the dry cycle and allow dishes to air-dry with the door partially open.

- Just cooked a nice roast dinner? Leave the door open a crack (once you've turned off the oven, that is), and let the heat warm the room as the oven cools. But don't do this if you have young children. (**Zack, the Palace Pussycat, adds:** Or curious dogs and cats!) Nothing is worth a potential burn.

- Keep radiators, registers, and ducts clean. Vacuum with the duster brush attachment. For hard-to-reach spots, use a telescoping duster. Make sure radiators, registers, and ducts are clear of debris and free from obstructions, such as furniture and drapes.

- Replace furnace filters frequently. A clean filter will distribute heat more efficiently. Check filters monthly—say, the first of every month. Vacuum to remove dust, and replace filters when vacuuming alone won't get the filter clean. Disposable filters should be replaced at least every 3 months.

- Heat can escape through air conditioners, so store yours if you can. If that's not possible, do your best to winterize the unit. Cover the outside of the air conditioner with cardboard cut to size, and then wrap it in a heavy-duty plastic. Drop cloths and plastic tablecloths are ideal. (Of course, plastic air conditioner covers are also available at home centers and hardware stores.) Secure the covering with a bungee cord, making sure to avoid corner flaps that might tear in the wind.

- Conserve energy in winter *and* summer by adjusting the rotation on your ceiling fan. A counterclockwise rotation will push the hot air from the ceiling down into the room—perfect for winter. A clockwise rotation will pull up warm summer air and replace it with a nice, cool flow.

- Conserve water by taking showers instead of baths. The average bath uses 25 gallons of water, whereas the average shower uses just 10 gallons.

- Don't leave water running while you brush your teeth. Turn it off until you're ready to rinse.

- That "small load" setting may save water, but the washing machine still goes through the same number of rotations. Avoid washing small loads if you can.

- Whenever possible, use cold or warm water for washing clothes. Always use cold water to rinse.

- Clean the lint filter on your clothes dryer each time you dry a load. Clothes will dry faster and more efficiently.

- That little black dress may be a hot number, but there's no reason to keep it warm. Keep closet doors closed to avoid having to heat areas where you don't actually need heat.

2
Polish Your Palace
Floor to Ceiling

The Queen's Royal Carpet Treatment

Carpet is one of the most expensive investments you will make in your palace. But never fear! If you're armed with proper knowledge about choosing a good-quality carpet that fits your imperial lifestyle and my handy cleaning and stain-removal guidelines, your carpet will give you many years of enjoyment and quality wear.

Know Your Carpet

Most residential carpet is made from one of four fibers: nylon, polyester, olefin, or wool (or a combination of these fibers). All of these fibers can make great carpet, although nylon is one of the most cost effective and durable.

Cleaning Your Carpet

Many people ask me how to go about hiring a firm to clean carpeting. Listed below are some general guidelines to follow. Always call more than one company to compare pricing. Ask each company the same set of questions, and remember that word-of-mouth is one of your best allies. Ask your neighbors, your friends, and the people you work with which companies they have used and how satisfied they were.

Questions to Ask a Carpet-Cleaning Company

What is the cost per square foot or room? Find out if there is a square footage limitation per room and if your room sizes fit within the limitation. Remember to ask about hallways, walk-in closets, and bathrooms, too. They may count as a whole room when companies offer room pricing. If the cost is figured by square foot, measure the length and width of your rooms and multiply length by width to achieve the square footage. Add the total square footage of all of your rooms and multiply by the cost per square foot. This should give you an accurate price.

Which method of cleaning is used? Steam cleaning or extraction is the preferable way to clean. Ask if the company uses a "truck-mounted unit." A portable cleaner will not generate the same powerful extraction process that a truck unit will.

Do they clean with hot or cold water? Cold water will not remove stubborn, greasy soil. A truck-mounted cleaning system should hook up to your cold water, usually at an outside tap, and heat the water as it flows through the truck.

Is the company insured? If they damage your furniture while moving it or bang into a wall, you want to be sure they can cover the cost of the repair.

How long have they been in the carpet-cleaning business? Be sure to ask about the company's experience and past clients. You want to be sure you are hiring trained professionals who do this for a living.

Before Carpets Are Cleaned

Follow these tips to make it easier for the carpet cleaners to do their job.

- Pick up all small items from carpets.

- Remove all items that are in and on furniture that will be moved.

- Whenever possible, remove dining chairs and other small, light pieces of furniture.

- Pick up all small area rugs.

- Remove things from the floor of the closet if the closet carpeting will be cleaned, too.

- Remove anything from under beds if the beds will be moved.

- Open windows, if weather permits.

- If the house is not left open, turn on the air conditioner or heat, whichever is appropriate.

- If possible, set fans so they blow across the carpet.

- Wash the soles of the shoes or slippers that you will be wearing on the damp carpet; otherwise, dirt from the soles will be transferred to the carpet.

- Do not move your furniture back until the carpet is completely dry; ask the carpet cleaner for her best estimate on drying times.

After Carpets Are Cleaned

Once your palace carpet has been returned to its pristine (well, almost pristine) state, here's what you'll need to do.

- *Beware* of slippery surfaces when you step from damp carpet to linoleum and other hard floors.

- Do not put towels or sheets or newspapers on the carpet.

- If you have had the carpet treated with carpet protector, you will need to allow extra drying time.

- Vacuum the carpet thoroughly after it is dry with a clean vacuum.

The Queen's Gallant Guide to Removing Spots

The number one rule of spot removal on carpet is to always keep several bottles of club soda on hand to use on spills on any kind of carpet. If you spill, follow my splendid spot-cleaning steps—they're terrific for most general spills and definitely will not cause any further damage.

How to Spot-Clean Spills

1. Blot up as much moisture as you can—laying old light-colored towels over the spill and standing on them is a great way to start.

2. Scrape up any solids.

3. Pour club soda on the spill. Don't be afraid to really pour it on. The carbonation in the soda will "bubble up" the spill so that you can blot it up. Again, cover the spot with clean, light-colored towels or rags and stand on them. This will really help to absorb the spill. Continue to pour and absorb until all color from the stain has been blotted up and the towel is coming up clean.

4. Follow up with a good carpet stain remover. I prefer Spot Shot Instant Carpet Stain Remover.

5. When you spot-clean carpet, never rub the stain, because it will only spread the stain further and it will cause abrasion to the carpet fibers.

Out, Out Special Spots

You never know what might soil the carpet in your fabulous foyer, princely parlor, or decadent drawing room—but never fear. The Queen has come the rescue with her tried-and-true techniques! I'll accept the challenge that any stain can offer.

Beer

You wouldn't cry over spilled milk, so why shed a tear over beer? First thing to do for a beer spill on the carpet is to blot up all the liquid you can, then flush the area with club soda and blot, blot, blot again. Now turn to a great carpet stain remover like Spot Shot Instant Carpet Stain Remover, and follow the directions carefully. Try to avoid carpet cleaners that contain stain repellents. If the beer doesn't come out during the first try, the repellent could lock in the stain, and you could be left with a permanent mark.

Candle Wax

Put ice in a plastic bag and lay over the wax, allowing it to freeze. Chip off all the wax that you can. Next, lay brown paper over the wax (a grocery bag works great; use the area without the writing) and press with a medium-hot iron. Move the paper as it absorbs so that you don't redeposit the wax on the carpet. Have patience and continue as long as any wax shows up on the bag. Next, apply a good carpet stain remover.

Chalk

Vacuum the chalky stain well, using the attachment hose to concentrate the suction over the chalk and chalk dust. If the chalk isn't removed by the vacuum, use a good carpet-spotting product.

Champagne

Champagne spills should be sponged immediately with club soda. The salt in the soda will help to prevent permanent stains, and the carbonation will draw the spill from the fibers. Two remedies for the price of one! After that, you can treat champagne spots with Spot Shot Instant Carpet Stain Remover. Just make sure to blot well with club soda first.

Chocolate

Chocolate stains on carpets should be treated immediately with your favorite carpet cleaner. Try Spot Shot Instant Carpet Stain Remover. For really stubborn stains, saturate the area with ½ cup of hydrogen peroxide mixed with 1 teaspoon of ammonia. Allow to sit for 20 minutes, and then blot. You may need to repeat this process. Once the stain is gone, flush the area with club soda and blot by standing on old, heavy towels. This should remove the moisture. Allow the area to dry fully before walking on it.

Cigarette Ash
Ash on carpet should be vacuumed using only the hose—no beater bar, which could grind the ash into the carpet.

Coffee
The best defense is a good offense when you spill coffee. First, act as quickly as possible. Hot coffee is the equivalent of brown dye. Blot up as much of the spill as you can and immediately apply club soda. If you don't have club soda (shame on you!), use plain cold water. Really pour it on and blot, blot, blot. Follow with a good-quality carpet stain remover. If a stain remains, you can attempt to remove it by pouring on hydrogen peroxide, waiting 15 minutes, and then blotting. If it is lightening the stain, continue applying hydrogen peroxide, waiting, and blotting. As a final step, rinse with cold water or club soda.

ROYAL DECREE: Shaving cream makes a great instant spot remover! If you have a spill and have no carpet stain remover available, grab the shaving cream. It is particularly effective on makeup, lipstick, coffee, and tea. Work it into the spot well and rinse with either cold water or club soda.

Glue
Try saturating glue with undiluted white vinegar. Working with an upward motion, work it out of the fibers and spot with Energine Cleaning Fluid. For rubber cement, use the same method as for gum. If the stain is from a water-based glue such as Elmer's School Glue, fold a paper towel and saturate it with warm water until it's almost dripping. Place this over the glue spot and leave on for 45 minutes to 1 hour to allow the glue to soften. Rub the glue spot with a wet rag in a circular motion to remove all the glue you can. Repeat this procedure until glue is removed. Follow with a good carpet stain remover.

Grass Stains

Grass stains on carpets should be removed with a good-quality carpet cleaner such as Spot Shot Instant Carpet Stain Remover. Just follow the directions on the can. For stubborn stains, apply rubbing alcohol; wait 10 minutes, blot, and then treat with the carpet cleaner.

Guacamole

Guacamole is my favorite, but what a cleaning disaster it is! Think about it: It's oily *and* green. Clean up guacamole spills on carpets and upholstery by scraping with a dull, straight edge, such as a credit card. (The one you used to pay for the party should do nicely.) Remove as much *gunk* as possible, and then flush with club soda and blot, blot, blot! Let the club soda sit for 10 minutes, and then flush with cool, clear water. Once the surface is dry, apply a good carpet and upholstery cleaner, according to the directions on the container. If you still have a green reminder, mix up a solution of ½ cup of hydrogen peroxide and 1 teaspoon of ammonia, spray it on liberally, let it sit for 15 minutes, and

SPOTS & SPLATTERS
Cleaning Mystery Carpet Stains

Dear Queen:
I know you have a "when-all-else-fails" solution for mystery carpet stains. The solution definitely contained ammonia and hydrogen peroxide. I tried it on a spot, and it worked when nothing else had. Now I have another spot and can't find the formula recipe. Can you help?

The Queen Responds:
Here's the formula: ½ cup of hydrogen peroxide mixed with 1 teaspoon ammonia. Heavily spray or pour the solution on the stain. Allow it to sit for 15 to 30 minutes, then blot the spot with a damp cloth. You might need to repeat this several times.

then blot. Continue until the stain is removed, flush with club soda, and blot until you have removed all the moisture possible.

Gum

Freeze with ice in a bag and chip off all that you can. Work a little petroleum jelly into the remaining residue and roll the gum into it. Scrape up and follow with a good spotter or Energine Cleaning Fluid.

Indentations

While they're not stains, indentations in carpet caused by furniture can still be eyesores. To remove indentations, lay ice cubes in the indentations, being sure to cover all of the indented area. Leave the ice cubes to melt overnight, and then fluff the carpet nap with the tines of a fork the next day.

Ink

Spray on hair spray or blot with rubbing alcohol. For heavy spots, try denatured alcohol. Blot well and follow with a spotter.

Markers and Felt-Tip Pens

To remove marker and felt-tip pen stains, dampen a few sponges with rubbing alcohol. Use a blotting motion to absorb the marks, changing the sponge as needed. Apply a good carpet stain remover, such as Spot Shot Instant Carpet Stain Remover, as directed on the can.

Mud

Cover wet mud with salt or baking soda and let it dry thoroughly before touching it. Once it is dry, vacuum it using the attachment hose to concentrate the suction on the mud. Use a good carpet stain remover, following the directions, to complete the process. For red dirt or mud, use a rust remover such as Whink or Rust Magic to remove any color residue. Make sure that you test the rust remover in a small area first.

Nail Polish

Blot up as much polish as possible with a tissue or anything handy. Then test the effect of nonoily nail polish remover on an inconspicuous part of the carpet. If there are no ill effects to the carpet pile, apply the nail polish remover with an eyedropper or a nonsilver spoon, blotting immediately after each application. Always use nonoily polish remover. If regular nail polish remover does not work, buy straight acetone at a beauty supply house, pretest again, and apply as directed above. Once you have removed as much of the stain as possible, follow with Spot Shot Instant Carpet Stain Remover. If color staining remains, apply hydrogen peroxide to bleach or lighten the stain.

Oil
Oil stains on carpets should be covered quickly with baking soda. Allow the baking soda to absorb the oil—this may take several hours. Vacuum up the baking soda, using the attachment hose to concentrate the suction on the spot. Vacuum very well with the hose before vacuuming with a beater bar to remove all of the baking soda. Finish off with your favorite carpet cleaner.

Red Soda and Kool-Aid
Grab the club soda fast and follow the steps in "How to Spot-Clean Spills" on page 66. If the stain is old, still try the club soda to help lighten the stain. Use a carpet stain remover, such as Spot Shot Instant Carpet Stain Remover. If the spot is still present, saturate with hydrogen peroxide or undiluted lemon juice. Wait 15 minutes and blot. Continue to apply and check your progress just to be sure you aren't lightening the carpet.

Red Wine
Grab the white wine and pour it on, or saturate the spot with salt and follow with the club soda and carpet stain remover.

Salsa
Salsa the sauce (not the dance!) tastes so good but stains so badly. For salsa spills, blot with club soda as soon as possible, then treat with Wine Away Red Wine Stain Remover or Red Erase. Both are fabulous at removing red stains from carpets (and from upholstery and clothes, too).

SPOTS & SPLATTERS

Cleaning Old Carpet Stains

Dear Queen:

We cleaned the living room carpet with a Hoover Deep Carpet Cleaner. After we finished, I noticed that it cleaned so well that there are very old stains showing up; these stains were never noticeable until we did the deep cleaning. I've tried just about everything I can think of to remove the stains. We are assuming the stains came from the former owner's pets. Can you help get our carpets looking clean again?

The Queen Responds:

Try mixing a solution of ½ cup of 3 percent hydrogen peroxide with 1 teaspoon of ammonia. Apply the solution with a rag, wait 30 minutes, and then blot. If the stains are lightening, continue with the hydrogen peroxide solution. If the stains don't respond to this treatment, you may need to contact a professional cleaner. Get recommendations from neighbors and friends, and always be sure to check prices.

Silly Putty and Similar Products

Scrape off as much of the clay as you can with the dull edge of a knife. Spray the area with WD-40 lubricant, let it stand for 10 to 15 minutes, and then scrape again. Respray the area if necessary, then wipe up the stain with an old rag. Once you succeed in removing the clay residue, apply rubbing alcohol to the stain and blot, blot, blot. Reapply as necessary.

Smoke Odors

While smoke odors aren't technically stains, the stale smell can be offensive to a nobleman's nose! Sprinkle natural Odorzout over the carpet and let it sit overnight. Vacuum in the morning.

Soot

Sprinkle with salt, wait at least 2 hours, and then vacuum, using the attachment hose to concentrate the suction. Spot-clean with a good spotter or Energine Cleaning Fluid.

Tar and Mustard

Work glycerin (available at drugstores in the hand cream section) into the spot. Let it sit for 30 to 60 minutes. Working carefully with paper towels, use a lifting motion to remove the spot. This may require multiple treatments. Follow with a good spotter, such as Spot Shot.

Watercolor Paints

Apply rubbing alcohol with a sponge, then lightly blot the stained area. Keep turning the sponge as you work and blot until no more of the stain is absorbed. You should be able to remove the rest of the stain with a damp sponge and a soft-scrubbing product. Rinse the carpet well.

Carpet is one of your most expensive investments (even if you're living like a King or Queen), so treat it with the care it deserves. It will last much longer and will look better if you clean it with a gentle touch.

SPOTS & SPLATTERS
Removing Mildew Stains from Carpets

Dear Queen:
Can you tell me how to get mildew stains off my variegated light-colored carpet?

The Queen Responds:
Treat those spots with heated white vinegar and then steam-clean the area, using Spot Shot Instant Carpet Stain Remover as your cleaning agent. Doing this won't leave soap in the carpet, and that's what's causing the stains to reappear after cleaning.

Floor Cleaning: Now Step on It

When the Royal Court holds session, you'll want everything in tip-top shape, especially the floors! You wouldn't want your palace slippers to get soiled, would you? Once you know a few basics, you can clean your floors quickly and easily just like the pros.

Ceramic Tile Floors

Sealing the grout in a ceramic tile floor is a must. Purchase a sealer from the store where you bought your tile or from a home center.

Ceramic tile is not porous—you can clean it effectively with warm water. Many cleaners leave a residue on the tile surface that looks like a smeary coating. A good neutral cleaner for tile is 1 gallon of warm water, 2 tablespoons of ammonia, and 1 tablespoon of borax. Never use vinegar. It is acidic and will eventually etch the grout.

SPOTS & SPLATTERS
Removing Tape Residue from Tile

Dear Queen:

How can I remove carpet tape residue from ceramic tile? I have exhausted all ideas, including paint thinner, Goo Gone, steel wool, and scraping. I would like to put down new rugs in the foyer, but I can't get this tape off the floor. Can you help?

The Queen Responds:

That's a sticky problem, all right! There are several things you can try; one of them (or a combination of all three) will be sure to remove the glue. First, heat some white vinegar and put it in a spray bottle. Spray the area heavily with heated vinegar and let it soak for about an hour. Use a dull straight edge (a credit card works great) to remove the glue residue. If the glue doesn't respond to that treatment, use heated baby oil in a spray bottle; let it soak, then scrape. Glue still there? Pick up some Un-Du (available at hardware stores and home centers), and follow the package directions carefully.

ROYAL DECREE: *Never* use a sponge mop on ceramic tile. It works like a squeegee, depositing the dirty water into the grout tracks.

To clean tile floors, sweep or vacuum the floor prior to washing. Use a rag or chamois-type mop, and rinse the mop as you work, frequently changing the water as it becomes soiled. If you have gloss-finish tile, it may be necessary to dry the tile. Use a clean terry rag under your foot to do it the easy way.

Wood Floors

The beauty of wood floors can't be beat, whether they're random-width planks in an old house or highly polished hardwood in new construction. Keeping these floors looking great isn't at all hard.

Removing Dirt and Debris

Use a dry dust mop to remove dust, or vacuum the floor, being sure not to use a vacuum with a beater bar—this can mar the floor.

Grit can scratch wood floors, so they should be swept before washing. Use long, directed strokes when sweeping, moving from the

SPOTS & SPLATTERS
Cleaning Garage Floors

Dear Queen:
I'm trying to find ways to clean our painted garage floor. When it's clean, it looks great, but it gets dirty quickly. Do you have any cleaning solutions?

The Queen Responds:
Throw a handful of trisodium phosphate (available at hardware stores and home centers) into a bucket of hot water, then wash down the floor using a chamois mop. Rinse the floor with hot water. Power washers are also great for painted garage floors. Look for one when it's on sale.

Janitorial supply companies and home centers also sell sweeping compound. This allows you to sweep the floor to remove dust and oily dirt, and keeps the dust from flying around. Sprinkle the sweeping compound on the floor, and then sweep up the dirt and sweeping compound with a push broom; pick up and throw out the dirt and compound when you are finished.

corners to the center of the room. Sweep all the grit—crumbs, cat litter, and any unidentifiable stuff—into a dustpan.

Somebody break a glass? It's bound to happen. Pick up the large shards first, and then use a cut potato to pick up the slivers. (Yes, a potato.) Just cut the potato in half and press down on the glass with the damp side. Vacuum the remaining small pieces, using the attachment hose to concentrate the suction, then vacuum thoroughly. Never use a vacuum with a beater bar to vacuum glass until you've picked up all you can with the potato and the attachment hose. The beater bar will only flip the glass around, making it even harder to clean up the debris.

If cigarette ash gets on hard floors, simply clean it up with a broom and dustpan.

Cleaning the Queen's Way

Now you're ready to wash with your favorite gentle floor cleaner. Don't have a favorite wood-floor cleaner? Try tea! The tannic acid gives the floor a wonderful shine. Brew 1 quart of boiling water with one or two tea bags. You can have a cup of tea if you'd like, but let the rest cool to room temperature before using it.

- Wring out a soft cloth in the tea. Make sure the cloth is damp, not wet. Overwetting the floor could warp it or damage the finish.

- Start at the edges of the floor. While on your hands and knees, wipe the floor with the soft cloth, starting at the edges of the floor and moving your hand across it in a small circular motion. In case you're not clear on this: *Yes, I am suggesting that you get down on your hands and knees.* Sorry, but anything else is just a shortcut, and if you want to clean your floors thoroughly, this is the only way to go.

- Keep the cloth well-rinsed and continue until the entire floor is done. This will clean the floor and cover many imperfections.

- Buff with a soft cloth if desired.

To fill scratches, use a crayon or combine several to match the floor. Wax crayons for wood are available at the hardware store. Work the crayon into the scratch, then heat the repair with a blow-dryer and buff with a rag. This will work the repair into the floor so well that you'll never know it's there.

Bruce Floor Care Products makes a floor cleaner that is a cleaner and wax in one. It comes in two colors, light and dark. If your floors are very badly scratched or damaged, you might consider trying this product before you spend the money to refinish the floors. Follow the directions on the can carefully, and allow plenty of time to do the job, working in one small area at a time.

Vinyl Floors

For cleaning vinyl floors (including no-wax floors, sheet vinyl, and linoleum), sweep or vacuum the floor well. Mix 1 gallon of warm water

THE MIRACLE OF MICROFIBER . . . OR IS IT?

Microfiber cloths and mops clean without chemicals—just water and the cloth or mop. Do these products work? Well . . . yes and no. The old adage "You get what you pay for" certainly holds true in the microfiber business. If you are purchasing these cloths dirt cheap, you are wasting your money. If they do not contain thousands of fibers, they won't clean as they should.

Here's the dirty lowdown on the very best microfiber mop I've used: Euronet USA makes the ACT Natural microfiber mop. A dry mop/wet mop with a telescoping handle, this miracle beautifully cleans vinyl, ceramic, marble, wood—any hard flooring—with nothing but water and thousands of little scrubbing fingers that pick up the dirt without scratching. Just wring out the mop in water, stick it to the Velcro pad, and off you go! It's doesn't leave a film, and the microfiber is machine washable. Check out www.euronetusa.com or call (888) 638-3552.

and 2 tablespoons of 20 Mule Team Borax. Wring out your rag well in the solution and wash the floor, keeping the rag clean. No rinsing is necessary. Using borax preserves the shine on floors, even those that have been waxed.

The Finale—Waxing!

When you wax a floor, it is wise to buy the wax from a janitorial store, which sells commercial products that hold up well to wear and traffic. On a clean floor, apply two thin coats of wax, allowing ample drying time between coats. It is imperative that the floor be clean, otherwise you will wax in the dirt. The next time you wax, wax only the traffic area where the wax is worn off, feathering it into the other areas to blend. This eliminates wax buildup around the edges of the room.

If you do have wax buildup, purchase a wax-stripping product from your local janitorial supply store. It is more efficient than ammonia and also very reasonably priced.

Off the (Castle) Walls

Unless you live in the round turret of a castle, you'll find that every room has four walls (more or less!), and sooner or later, those walls will need your undivided attention. Let the Queen of Clean® come to the rescue! I've washed more walls than I can count, and I've learned how to do it quickly and efficiently. (After all, a Queen has many more important things to attend to.) All my secrets are right here!

Wash Them like the Pros

Wall washing can actually be easy if you have the right equipment and do it the right way (and it can be a whole lot of fun if you don't have to work around gilded doorways and velvet tapestries). My tips for removing spots and marks and choosing the best tools for the task will have you finishing up the job in a jiffy.

HAVE ALL THE RIGHT STUFF

Three cheers for the loyal subjects who have assembled the proper tools for the job of wall washing! Get things together before you start and have the furniture moved away from the walls so that the washing process will flow smoothly. Do it like a professional. This list tells you what you should have.

- Two buckets
- Natural sponge (not one of those awful nylon ones), available at janitorial supply stores, home centers, and hardware stores
- Baking soda and a soft rag
- Art gum eraser
- Drop cloths
- Ladder
- Ingredients for the cleaning solution of your choice
- Two strips of washcloth or terry rags and two rubber bands

Removing Marks

The first thing you want to do is erase any marks on the wall. Use an art gum eraser that you keep on hand for this purpose and erase just the mark. This works on many types of marks. If you still have some stubborn spots, use a little baking soda on the corner of a white rag and rub gently, doing just the mark. Nongel toothpaste also is a good spot remover; use it on a cloth over the tip of your finger.

Crayon Marks

If you have kids, you have probably had crayon on the wall. To remove crayon easily, spray with WD-40 lubricant and wipe crayon away with a paper towel. Follow up with a soft cloth and a solution of hot water and a little dishwashing liquid, washing in a circular motion.

Ink and Marker Marks

To remove ink or marker, use hair spray (the cheaper the better) or rubbing alcohol. For really tough spots, denatured alcohol from the hardware store works great. Always apply these cleaners carefully, trying to do just the spot.

A Drop Cloth Saves Time

Use a drop cloth on the floor around the area you'll be washing; it will save you time and mess in the long run. A fabric drop cloth is preferable to plastic because it absorbs drips and isn't slippery when wet.

Anti-Drip Armbands

Before you start to wash your walls, wrap a strip of washcloth or Turkish toweling (made out of cotton terrycloth) around your wrist several times and secure it with rubber bands. This will keep drips from running up your arms when you are working with your arms above your head.

Where to Start Washing

You have the wall free of marks, your drop cloths are in place, your wrists are wrapped for drips, and you have your washing solution ready. Now wet your natural sponge. Begin washing at the bottom of the wall and work up, doing the ceiling last. Drips of water are much easier to wipe off a clean wall and won't leave marks as they do on a soiled wall.

GREAT WALL-WASHING SOLUTIONS

Try either of these wall-washing solutions.

- 1 gallon of warm water, ½ cup of ammonia, ¼ cup of white vinegar, and ¼ cup of washing soda (available in your grocer's detergent aisle)
- 1 gallon of warm water, 1 cup of ammonia, and 1 teaspoon of mild dishwashing liquid

For really professional results, wash walls with either of these solutions, then rinse walls with clear water. If you choose not to rinse, then be sure to change the cleaning solution frequently as it becomes soiled.

ROYAL DECREE: Don't skimp and use a nylon sponge or a rag; it will drag as you wash and take you twice as long. A natural sponge has thousands of "scrubbing fingers" and will get the job done fast, easy, and right.

Don't Stop in the Middle!

Once you start on a wall, don't stop in the middle. Complete one full wall or the full ceiling before you take a break. If you stop in the middle of a wall or ceiling, you will have "tide marks" where you stop and start again.

Keeping Walls Clean

You can make your own brushing tool to use between washing, to dust down the walls. Tie a clean dust cloth loosely around a broom head and

SPOTS & SPLATTERS

Removing Water Stains from Acoustic Tile

Dear Queen:
How can I remove brown water stains from white ceiling acoustic tile without having to paint?

The Queen Responds:
Mix ¼ cup of chlorine bleach with 1 quart of warm water and dab it onto the area with a white rag (an old washcloth works well). Use great care with the bleach because bleach will remove color from carpet and upholstery; you may want to cover up everything. Also, make sure to ventilate the area when using the bleach. You may need to repeat this process several times, but it usually works quite well. If you have to paint the area, be sure to stain-kill the area with KILZ (available at hardware stores and home centers), or the stain will bleed through again.

use it to dust the ceiling thoroughly from time to time and to dust down the walls. Give the broom a shake now and then as you are working to remove dust.

A Word about Wood Paneling
Clean wood paneling following the suggestions in chapter 6 on cleaning wood floors.

The Wallpaper Chase

No need to study long and hard to learn how to care for wallpaper. A simple washing will do the trick in most instances, and if you have any spots, I know just the solution. Read on!

Cleaning Wallpaper
Wash vinyl and washable wallpapers with one of the mild wall-washing solutions in "Great Wall-Washing Solutions" on page 83.

To clean grass cloth, burlap, or cloth wallcovering, vacuum it with the soft duster brush on the vacuum. Do this regularly to maintain the appearance.

Removing Spots on Wallpaper
Out, out, stubborn spot! Try these trusted ways to remove unsightly spots from your wallcoverings.

Grease Spots
Make a paste of cornstarch and water and apply to the grease spot. Allow it to dry, then brush or vacuum it off.

Apply a double fold of brown paper (a grocery bag works well, but don't use the part with the writing on it) and press over the grease spot with a warm iron. This may require several efforts. This method also works well on candle wax. Follow up with a little hair spray or alcohol.

SPOTS & SPLATTERS

Removing Wallpaper Borders

Dear Queen:
Do you know an easy way to remove wallpaper borders?

The Queen Responds:
Make a solution of 2 parts warm water and 1 part liquid fabric softener. Score the border and then spray on the solution. Start peeling up the border, reapplying the solution as needed.

Crayon Marks
Rub lightly with a dry soap-filled steel-wool pad. Do this very gently. You can also try rubbing with baking soda on a damp cloth. On vinyl paper, try using a little silver polish.

Smudges, Marks, and Mystery Stains
Erase with an art gum eraser. To remove marks from nonwashable paper, rub a scrunched-up piece of white bread over the marks. Rub very gently. You may need to repeat this a few times before you make progress.

Paint by Numbers

One of the questions men ask me most frequently is how to get through the job of painting quickly and easily. I've assembled this list of terrific time-savers and easy energy-savers to make all your painting jobs go much more smoothly.

Top Tips for Easier and Quicker Palace Painting

If you gather the proper tools in one place and take care of them after you've finished the job, you've won half the painting battle. All that's left to do is follow my nifty painting shortcuts and tips, and you'll finish painting in no time at all.

Short-Term Storage
If you need to store a paintbrush or roller in the middle of a project or between coats of paint, place it in a tightly sealed plastic bag and place it in the freezer. The brush or roller will not dry out for a day or two, and no cleanup is needed until you have completed the project.

Protecting Hardware
When painting woodwork, cover doorknobs, locks, and other hardware with a generous coating of petroleum jelly. If the paint splashes where it shouldn't, it can easily be wiped up.

Splatter Removal
For easy removal of paint splatters on windowpanes, use a round typewriter eraser with a brush on the end. It's safer than a razor and easy, too!

Painting Screws
To make painting hardware screws easier, stick them in a piece of foam packing material. The screw heads will all be facing up, ready to be sprayed or painted in one coat.

Cleaning Hands
Use vegetable oil to clean oil-based paints off hands. The oil is safer than paint thinner, has no fumes, and is mild to the skin. After using the oil, wash well with soap.

Preventing White Paint from Yellowing
To stop white paint from yellowing with age, put several drops of black paint in for every quart of white paint. Mix very well.

Keeping Cans Clean
Cover the rim of the paint can with masking tape if you are going to pour paint from the can. When you are done, remove the tape to clean the top.

Drip Realignment

If you are painting from the can, punch two or three nail holes in the small groove in the top rim of your paint can. As you wipe the paint from your brush on the rim, the paint will drip back into the can instead of collecting in the groove and spilling over and down the sides of the can.

Cleaning Brushes in a Second

To make a paintbrush easier to clean, wrap masking tape around the metal ferrule and about ½ inch over the bristles. Rather than drying on the bristles, paint will collect on the masking tape. To clean, remove the tape and clean the paint that remains on the brush.

Garbage Garment

Wear a garbage bag as a coverall when painting overhead. Cut holes for head and arms. You can cover your head with an old shower cap, too. No more paint splatters on clothes and hair!

Easier-Opening Cans

When sealing the lid on a paint can, wipe a thin layer of petroleum jelly around the rim. This will allow the can to open easily the next time.

Record-Keeping

Before you store leftover paint, list on the can the rooms you have painted with it. Touch-ups are easier if you don't have to try to figure out which can of paint you used for what.

Paint-Catching Wristband

If you paint like I do and have runs of paint going down your arms every time you paint over your head, wrap an old washcloth around your wrist, secure it with a rubber band, then remove it and throw it away when you are done painting.

Drying Brushes Completely

If you soak your brush between painting sessions, be sure to drain out all of the liquid, or you will have a dripping mess when you start painting again. One good way to do this is to stand the brush straight up in an empty can for a few minutes to let the fluid drip out. Or suspend it from a stick laid across the top of an empty can that is taller than the brush. To be absolutely sure that the brush is dry, take an old rag, wrap it around the brush, and squeeze the bristles from the top downward over the can.

Working Your Way Down
Start painting at the top of the wall and work your way down. That way, if paint drips down, it can be smoothed out as you go.

The Care and Hanging of Pictures and Paintings

Pictures and paintings are part of the personal touches that make a house a home (or a castle!). Here are some ideas for hanging and cleaning pictures and oil and acrylic paintings.

Finding the Stud the Easy Way

When you are ready to hang a picture, especially a heavy one, it is a good idea to find a stud to hang it from. Take an electric razor and run it across the wall. You will notice a distinct difference in the sound of the razor going over a hollow wall and the sound when it hits a stud. Use this whenever you need to find the stud to hang anything around the house.

Keeping Cockeyed Pictures Straight

Wind some adhesive tape around the center of the picture wire. The wire will be less likely to slip on the hanger.

Place masking tape on the back four corners of your picture and press against the wall. Wrap masking tape, sticky side out, around the middle of a round toothpick, and then slide out the toothpick from the loop. Place the tape loop near the bottom on the backside of the frame. Make a few more tape loops and place them as needed on the back of the frame.

Preventing Experimentation Holes

Cut a paper pattern of each picture or mirror that you plan to hang and pin to the wall. After you've found the correct positions for the hangers, perforate the paper with a sharp pencil to mark the wall.

When you want to avoid nail holes in the walls, hang pictures with a sewing machine needle. They hold up to 30 pounds and leave almost no marks on the wall.

Staining Unfinished Picture Frames

Stain them beautifully with ordinary liquid shoe polish. Apply one coat and let dry. Follow with another coat, and then wax with a good paste wax. Brown shoe polish gives the wood a walnut glow and oxblood emulates a mahogany or cherry color. Tan polish will look like a light maple. This hides scratches, too.

Cleaning Glass-Covered Pictures

Never spray any cleaner directly on the glass; it may seep under and onto the picture. Spray a paper towel with window cleaner, wipe, and polish with a dry towel.

Polish glass with a used fabric softener sheet to shine and deter dust.

Cleaning Oil and Acrylic Paintings

Give them an occasional dusting with a clean, lint-free cloth or a soft brush. Spot-clean if necessary with a barely damp rag or piece of white bread. If the painting is worth a lot of money or has sentimental value, take it to a professional. Even a soft dust cloth can snag and cause a chip.

Gilt Picture Frames

Remove stains from gilt picture frames by rubbing gently with a cloth moistened in milk.

Photo Emergency

If you have a picture that is stuck to the glass, immerse the glass and the photo in a pan of room-temperature water and keep testing until the photo pulls free. Don't try to rush it! Let the photo air-dry. Since most photo prints get a water bath during processing, there shouldn't be any damage, though this is not a 100 percent guarantee.

The Throne and Beyond

Over the years, I have found that there is one room that generates question after question, and that room is the bathroom.

Once when I was eating in a wonderful little Chinese restaurant, the proprietor, an elderly Chinese gentleman, followed me into the ladies' room to see if I thought his bathroom was clean. He was using the methods that I had recommended on television and was making his own cleanser from my recipe. Let me tell you, his bathroom was spotless!

It made me think that of all the rooms in your house, the bathroom is probably the room that most guests always see and have the most private time to observe. I have tried virtually every cleaning product on the market and developed many of my own concoctions for beating the bathroom blues.

These are the best and easiest cleaning tips I can offer.

Toilet Tips

If you have indoor plumbing, then you have to clean the toilet once in a while, whether you like it or not. These tips make cleaning the throne a breeze.

Tang Tune-Up

To keep your toilet clean and your dog happy, put several tablespoons of Tang Breakfast Drink in the toilet before you leave for work or at bedtime. Let it soak, use your toilet brush to swish around under the rim, and flush.

Removing Hard-Water Rings

Shut off the water at the toilet tank and flush. Spray undiluted white vinegar around the inside of the toilet, and then sprinkle borax onto the vinegar. Let the vinegar and borax soak about 30 minutes and then scrub the hard-water rings with a piece of fine drywall sandpaper (it looks like window screen and is available at hardware stores and home centers). If you have an old hard-water ring, you may need to repeat this several times.

Plop-Plop-Fizz-Fizz Cleaning

Drop a couple of denture-cleaning tablets into the toilet and let them sit overnight. Brush under the rim with your bowl brush and flush.

Sparkling Showers and Brilliant Bathtubs

It's always a pleasure to be the first one to take a shower or bath after the bathroom has been cleaned. Doesn't everything just sparkle? With my fast cleaning tips, you can have sparkle every day!

Cleaning Fiberglass Showers and Tubs

Heat white vinegar until it is hot (but not boiling) and pour it into a spray bottle. Heavily spray it on the shower and tub. Wait 10 to 15 minutes. Moisten a scrubbing-type sponge with more of the vinegar and scrub down the shower, using additional heated vinegar as necessary. Rinse well and dry.

Cleaning Porcelain Tubs

To clean and polish a porcelain tub and remove stains, make a paste of powdered alum (available in drugstores) and water. Rub well, as if using cleanser. For stains, make a paste of powdered alum and lemon juice; apply it and let it dry. Remoisten the stain with more lemon juice and rub well. Rinse thoroughly.

(👑) **QUEENLY COMMENT:** Borax and water is also a great cleaner for porcelain. Make a paste and rub well, then rinse.

Keeping Plastic Showers Clean

To make shower upkeep simple, apply a coat of car wax. Do not use this on the floor of the tub or shower. After showering, use a squeegee to wipe down the shower door and walls—your shower will stay clean, and you'll have fewer problems with mildew.

Removing Hard-Water Marks

Many plastic-type tubs have a dimpled slip-proof bottom that defies cleaning. I have found that using a good gel cleaner or a mild cleanser, such as the homemade types in "Making Your Own Cleanser" on page 94, and a piece of fine drywall sandpaper (it looks like window screen) works the best. Cut the sandpaper into a workable size, apply the cleaner, and rub it over the hard-water marks. Use this only on dimples in plastic and fiberglass tub and shower bottoms.

Stubborn Spot Remover for Showers

For stubborn shower spots and scum buildup, use a dry, soap-filled steel wool pad on a dry shower. Do not allow water to become involved in this process, as it will cause the steel wool pad to scratch. Follow up with the vinegar process described in "Cleaning Fiberglass Showers and Tubs" on page 92.

Removing Bathtub Decals

Lay a sheet of aluminum foil over the decals and heat with a blow-dryer on high. Work up the edge of the decal with a dull straightedge (credit cards work great) and keep applying the heat as you pull. If the decal is stubborn, lay down new foil, heat well, and peel again. To remove the residue, try petroleum jelly, denatured alcohol, or nail polish remover. Test these products in a small area first before applying them to the tub surface.

Cleaning Shower Door Tracks

Plug the drain holes in the door track with a little bit of paper towel made into a ball. Pour in undiluted white vinegar. Let this soak for 30 minutes, unplug the holes, and rinse the track with a spray bottle of water. Run a rag along the track; this will flush the accumulated buildup out of the track.

MAKING YOUR OWN CLEANSER

For a great nonabrasive scouring powder for disinfecting, combine:

   4 parts baking soda

   1 part borax

Store the powder in a shaker container.

For a nontoxic, grease-cutting scouring powder, combine:

   4 parts baking soda

   1 part washing soda

Store the powder in a shaker container.

Keeping Tile and Grout Clean

You can keep ahead of grout cleaning if you use a dry typewriter eraser on dry grout to remove mildew and stains as they appear. For bigger problems, make a paste of baking soda and chlorine bleach and apply it to the grout. Let it dry and then rinse the tile and grout thoroughly.

ROYAL DECREE: Apply the baking soda and chlorine bleach paste in a well-ventilated area, using care near carpet or fabric. Just the fumes of chlorine bleach can remove color from towels left hanging in the tub area.

Cleaning Bathroom Accessories

It's not just the shower or tub that need your attention. Soap scum, mineral deposits, and residue from beauty products can build up on shower curtains, faucets, and walls. Find all the cleaning advice that you'll need right here.

Plastic Shower Curtains

To clean soap scum and mildew off plastic shower curtains, put the shower curtain in the washing machine with 1 cup of white vinegar, ¼ to ½ cup of your favorite liquid laundry detergent, and several old, light-colored towels. Fill the washer with warm water and run through a complete wash and rinse cycle. Remove from the washer and hang on the shower rod immediately.

Showerheads

To clean mineral deposits from the showerhead, fill a plastic sandwich bag with undiluted white vinegar. Tie this around the showerhead and leave it there overnight. In the morning, remove the bag (save the vinegar to clean your drain; see my Queenly Comment). Scrub the head with a brush, and it's ready to use.

QUEENLY COMMENT: Put ½ cup of baking soda down the bathroom drain and follow with the vinegar from the showerhead cleaning. This makes a great drain opener. Wait 30 minutes, and then flush the drain with water.

Chrome Faucets

Use white vinegar on a cloth or sponge to remove water spots and soap scum. Dry and buff with a soft cloth. Rubbing alcohol is also a great spot remover. Apply, then dry and buff.

To shine chrome or any metal fixture in a hurry, use a used dryer fabric softener sheet on a dry fixture.

Removing Hair Spray Residue

You can use the following formula to remove hair spray residue from any hard surface—vanities, tile, floors, and walls. Mix a solution of 1 part liquid fabric softener and 2 parts water in a spray bottle. Spray on the surface to be cleaned, and wipe. Not only does it remove hair spray, but it also acts as a dust repellent and shines vanities beautifully!

9

The Palace's Grand Appliances and Gadgets

Keeping appliances and electronic equipment clean and in good working condition will surely make them last longer. Follow my quick tips for wiping, washing, and dusting, and you'll have plenty of time to practice ballroom dancing with your King.

Kitchen Patrol

You probably have more appliances, gadgets, gizmos, and surfaces to clean in the kitchen than you do in the rest of your castle rooms combined. (Not to mention all the miscellaneous stuff the King, Crown Princes and Princesses, and the like seem to drop onto any available counter space.) I don't think there is a room in the house that gets messy faster than the kitchen. So get on kitchen duty and clean up!

Keeping the Sparkle on White Appliances

Many of us have white appliances in the kitchen. In order to keep them from yellowing, I use a simple formula to clean the exterior.

Combine:

8 cups water
½ cup chlorine bleach
½ cup baking soda
2 tablespoons borax

Wash white appliances thoroughly (using care around carpet or fabric), rinse well, and dry.

Cleaning Appliance Exteriors

Rubbing alcohol makes a great cleaner for the exterior of all types of appliances; use care around flames though. Be sure not to grab your everyday dishcloth to wipe down appliances; it will transfer grease and smear the finish.

If you need a wonderful polish for the exterior of appliances, try club soda. The club soda doesn't have to be fresh or have fizz. It works great even if it has lost its carbonation.

Cutting Boards

Remove odors from cutting boards and breadboards by wetting them and then rubbing them with a little dry mustard. Let the mustard sit for a few minutes and then rinse. To disinfect cutting boards, especially wood ones, mix 1 quart of water and 3 teaspoons of liquid chlorine bleach in a spray bottle. Spray it on, let it sit at least 5 minutes, and then rinse the boards with hot water.

Automatic Coffeemakers

Depending on how often you use your coffeepot and how hard your water is, you may need to clean your coffeemaker once a month to once every 3 months.

SPOTS & SPLATTERS

A Peppery Problem

Dear Queen:
I inherited some very nice, old wooden pepper mills. How can I get them clean? I thought of using salt, but that may dull the blades. Can you help?

The Queen Responds:
Put some plain, dry rice in them, filling each mill about halfway. Shake the mills once a day for a few weeks (do a little cha-cha-cha). Empty the rice and fill the mill with a small amount of fresh pepper; grind it through the mill. Dump it out, add fresh pepper, and you're ready to begin using them.

Fill the water reservoir with undiluted white vinegar. Place a filter in the coffee basket and turn on the pot. Allow about half of the vinegar to run through and then shut off the pot. Let it sit for about 30 minutes, then turn the coffeemaker on and allow the balance of the vinegar to run through. Clean out the pot well, fill the reservoir with fresh cold water, and allow it to run through. Run the fresh water through twice—there are lots of coffee flavors on the market these days, but I don't think vinegar-flavored coffee should be one of them!

To clean the glass pot: Use lemon and salt and rub with a sponge, or use baking soda and lemon juice or water and rub with a sponge. Rinse well.

To clean the basket and other parts: For white plastic units, soak any removable parts in hot water with dishwashing liquid and about ¼ cup of chlorine bleach. Soak about 30 minutes and rinse well. This helps remove stains and oils. For dark-colored coffeemakers, use dishwashing liquid and about ¼ cup of white vinegar in the same manner as for the white parts above.

Chrome Burner Rings and Guards

Remove the burner rings from the stove. Lay a single sheet of paper toweling on each pan and moisten with ammonia. Place them in a plastic bag and close the bag. Leave for several hours or overnight. Open the bag (pointed away from your face because of fumes) and remove the parts. Wash, rinse well, and dry.

Dishwashers

To remove that milky film from glassware and clean the inside of your dishwasher, fill the dishwasher with your glassware (no metal, please). Do not use dishwasher detergent. Put a bowl in the bottom of the dishwasher and pour in 1 cup of household bleach. Run through the wash cycle, but do not dry. Fill the bowl again with 1 cup of white vinegar, and let the dishwasher go through the entire cycle. The film will be removed from your dishes, and the dishwasher will be clean—all in one easy step.

To eliminate dishwasher odor: Sprinkle borax in the bottom of the dishwasher and leave it overnight. Using a damp sponge, use the borax to wipe down the inside of the dishwasher, door, and gaskets. Rinse the

SPOTS & SPLATTERS
Up with Silverware

Dear Queen:
What is the correct way to load silverware in the dishwasher—handles up or handles down?

The Queen Responds:
Handles down is the best way because the eating surface of the utensil is exposed to more water. If you have narrow handles that fall through your silverware basket, then you'll have to put the silverware in handles up.

THE PAIN OF PALACE DRAINS

This is the best nontoxic drain opener you will ever use: Pour 1 cup of salt (table salt, rock salt, or any kind of salt) and 1 cup of baking soda down the drain. Follow with a kettle of boiling water. If the problem is congealed grease, it will be gone immediately. For the very best results, don't use the drain for several hours. If you need a stronger product, use 2 tablespoons of washing soda (available where laundry products are sold) dissolved in 1 quart of hot water, and pour it slowly down the drain. Flush with hot water after 10 minutes.

Once a month, pour a handful of baking soda into the drain and add ½ cup of white vinegar. A small volcano will erupt. Cover the drain for several minutes and then flush with cold water after 30 minutes.

If you have a garbage disposal, you can keep it clean and free-flowing by filling the sink with 3 inches of warm water and mixing in 1 cup of baking soda. Drain it with the disposal running.

Need to use a plunger on that clogged drain? There really is a special way to use a plunger to make it work more effectively. Close the overflow to the sink (if your sink has an overflow, it's usually a series of holes or a single hole in the front of the sink) by plugging it with an old rag. If you don't do this, the water will go down one hole and come back up through the overflow. Fill the sink with 4 to 5 inches of water. Put the cup of the plunger over the drain and press down hard. Then pull the handle up, push down again, and repeat 10 to 12 times. Adding a little petroleum jelly around the rim of the plunger gives even better suction.

inside of the dishwasher with water, then just get right to work on the next load of dishes.

To remove dishwasher rust: Fill both detergent cups with Tang Breakfast Drink and run through the normal cycle. If rust is bad, several treatments may be required. When doing this, don't put dishes or detergent in the dishwasher.

To keep your dishes spot-free: Combine 1 cup of borax and ½ cup of baking soda in a container with a lid. To use this terrific spot stopper, add 1 teaspoon of the mixture to the dishwasher along with your regular dishwasher detergent.

Microwave Magic

To clean your microwave quickly and simply, wet a dishcloth and place it in the center of your microwave. Turn on high and allow the cloth to "cook" for 30 to 40 seconds. The steam that this creates will help loosen any hardened spills. Once the cloth has cooled a bit, use it to wipe the inside clean.

ROYAL DECREE: Don't use the microwaved cloth immediately after removing it from the oven; you could suffer steam burns.

To give your microwave a clean, fresh smell, place a bowl of water in it and add three or four slices of fresh lemon or 2 tablespoons of lemon juice. Cook on high for 30 to 60 seconds. For the very worst odors, such as burned popcorn, place vanilla extract in a bowl and microwave for at least 30 seconds. Leave the door closed for 12 hours, remove the vanilla, and wipe down the inside of the microwave.

The Smoking Oven

When something runs over in the oven and starts smoking and smelling, grab the salt. Sprinkle on a heavy layer of salt and continue cooking. The smoke and odor will stop immediately. When you're done cooking, close the oven and leave it closed overnight. The next day you will be able to lift out the spill with a pancake turner!

To clean the oven, preheat it to 200°F and leave on for 15 minutes. Shut it off and leave the door closed. Fill a 9 x 9-inch glass cake pan with 2 cups of ammonia and place on the top shelf. On the lower shelf place a pan filled with 2 cups of boiling water. Close the oven door and leave the pans inside for 2 hours or overnight. Remove the ammonia and the water. Make a paste of ammonia, ½ cup of baking soda, and 1 cup of white vinegar. Spread the paste over the oven walls and leave it on for about 15 minutes. Scrub with a sponge and steel wool pad (if necessary), then rinse well. This even works on heavily soiled ovens.

Make Your Own Castle Cleansers

For a great nonabrasive scouring powder for disinfecting, combine:

4 parts baking soda
1 part borax

Store the powder in a shaker container.

For a nontoxic, grease-cutting scouring powder, combine:

4 parts baking soda
1 part washing soda

Store the powder in a shaker container.

Cleaning and Protecting Cooktops

I receive so many questions about cleaning cooktops that I decided to devote a section just to that. Actually, glass and smooth-top ceramic surfaces are fairly easy to clean if you follow a few rules when dealing with them.

- Clean the surface only when it is cool, with either dishwashing liquid, a paste of baking soda and water (3 parts baking soda to 2 parts water), or a specially formulated cooktop cleaner. Apply this with a paper towel or soft cloth. Rinse the cooktop thoroughly and towel-dry. Do not use a soiled dishcloth or sponge to wipe the top; it may leave a film, which can cause discoloration the next time it is heated. If this discoloration occurs, remove it with a specially formulated cooktop cleaner.

- Burned-on soil can be removed with a razor-blade scraper. Avoid abrasive cleaners and pads.

- If your cooktop is in really bad shape, you will have to take more drastic action before you can have cleaning ease. You can try a product called Bon Ami, which comes in a can and is much like cleanser. This product can be used safely on mirrors, windows, and windshields. It has a mild pumice action. Use it very carefully with a soft, wet rag to remove heavy soiling. You can also use a mild ammonia solution along with a scrubbing-type sponge for heavily soiled cooktops, or try nongel toothpaste, applied with a soft cloth, to help remove stains and burned-on food. Follow up these cleaning procedures by washing with dishwashing liquid and water and rinsing well. Rinsing with club soda will put a nice shine on the top surface.

• I discovered a wonderful product called Clean-X Clean Shield Surface Treatment (formerly called Invisible Shield) for cooktop cleaning. Using this allows you to do what I call "preventive cleaning." You apply this treatment, and in the future when you clean, spills and burned-on food bead up. It makes your stovetop surface react as if it were nonstick cookware—spills wipe off with nothing more than a damp cloth. You can safely use this on glass and most surfaces (except wood and paint). Call (800) 528-3149 to find out where the product is sold in your area.

QUEENLY COMMENT: To remove stains from nonstick cookware, boil 2 tablespoons of baking soda, ½ cup of white vinegar, and 1 cup of water for 10 to 15 minutes in the pan. Re-season the pan with salad oil.

Refrigerator Odors and Spills

When you wipe out the refrigerator, always use a sponge moistened with white vinegar. It leaves a clean, fresh scent and helps prevent mildew.

A dab of vanilla, lemon, or orange extract on a small pad of cotton will keep the refrigerator fresh smelling without a perfume odor.

Many common refrigerator odors may be removed by placing a small tub filled with charcoal in the middle rack in the refrigerator. I use the charcoal made for fish tanks.

If you are shutting off a refrigerator, be sure to prop the door open a crack for air circulation. Put a container of fresh coffee grounds inside to ward off unpleasant odors. For strong odor removal, a container or nylon stocking of coffee grounds placed on a refrigerator shelf works wonders.

For cleaning ease, wipe the inside of the refrigerator, including the shelves, with a cloth dipped in glycerin, available in the hand cream section at the drugstore. This light coating will keep spills from sticking. Even milk or sticky substances will wipe right out.

The Chill on Freezers

Try using the glycerin in freezers, too. That way spills, even though frozen, can be wiped right out.

Wash out the freezer with a solution of 1 gallon of warm water and ¼ cup of borax to clean and deodorize. Rinse and dry before turning the freezer back on.

Cleaning Cutlery

You really can tell the difference between silverware that's been properly cleaned and cared for and silverware that's seen the worst food battles. Here's how to keep cutlery looking spiffy.

Stainless Steel Cutlery

This is such an easy way to clean your stainless steel cutlery (forks, knives, and spoons). Mix the following ingredients in the kitchen sink or any nonaluminum container:

¼ cup chlorine bleach
¼ cup Calgon Water Softener
1 gallon very hot water

Immerse stainless steel cutlery in the solution for 30 minutes and wash as usual. This is not for use on real silver. To remove stubborn spots from stainless steel, use a little nongel toothpaste or some silver polish in a separate container with a little ammonia added to it. Apply this to each piece of cutlery with a soft cloth; wash, rinse well, and dry.

Silver Cutlery

Wash silver cutlery as soon as possible after using. This prevents tarnish-causing stains. To clean a lot of silver cutlery quickly, put strips of aluminum foil in a large bowl. Place the silver cutlery on top. Cover the cutlery with boiling water and add 3 tablespoons of baking soda. Soak the silverware for 10 minutes, and then rinse and dry it. Use care on hollow or glued pieces. (This also works on silver jewelry.)

You can also make your own silver-cleaning cloths. Saturate cotton squares in a solution of:

2 parts ammonia
1 part silver polish
10 parts cold water

Let cloths drip-dry and use as silver polish cloths.

Stainless Steel Sinks

So much of my mail asks about cleaning and keeping up the appearance of stainless steel sinks. One such writer suggested using the sink as an ugly planter and using nothing but paper plates and plastic silverware! Take heart—you can keep stainless steel sinks clean and actually enjoy them.

SPOTS & SPLATTERS

A Soft Solution for Hardened Grease

Dear Queen:
How can I clean greasy buildup on kitchen cabinets that appears to be old? It won't come off with regular wiping. There's also a greasy buildup on the stove hood and screen.

The Queen Responds:
Pick up some Avon Skin-So-Soft in the original formula. Put some on a cloth and wipe the grease away, then wipe down the entire cupboard. Buff with a soft cloth. It is amazing!

For regular cleaning: Clean with a paste of baking soda and water and rinse well. Drying the sink helps to prevent water marks and rust.

To polish a sink: Put a tablespoon of flour in a dry sink and rub with a soft cloth. Then rinse and dry. Another polish method is club soda. Put the stopper in the sink, pour in some club soda, and rub with a soft cloth. Again, dry to prevent water spots.

To remove rust and water spots: Use white vinegar on a soft cloth or sponge. It will not only erase the spots but also brighten the sink. Rubbing alcohol or lighter fluid will remove rust marks, too. Remember: Lighter fluid is flammable, so use it with care and never use it near an open flame or candle. Wash and rinse the sink well if you use the lighter fluid as a rust remover, and have the room well-ventilated while using the lighter fluid.

To remove rust from fixtures: Rub the rust spot with salt and lemon juice until the rust disappears. Then rinse and polish.

To remove stains: Prepare a paste of 3 parts cream of tartar to 1 part hydrogen peroxide and apply it to the stains. Allow it to dry and then wipe with a wet cloth or sponge.

To shine a sink: Coat the sink with a few drops of baby oil. Wipe it off with paper towels. If it doesn't seem shiny enough, repeat the procedure.

To erase hairline scratches: Using very fine steel wool, gently give the entire sink the once-over to obliterate hairline scratches. Then wash and buff with a soft cloth.

Metal Cleaners You Can Make Yourself

Here are some fast and easy homemade metal cleaners. Always test these metal cleaners in an inconspicuous spot before using them.

For brass, use a mixture of lemon juice and salt. Wipe on until the piece is clean, then rinse and dry. This is not for use on brass-plated pieces.

For copper, use ketchup or Worcestershire sauce. Wipe it on, rub until clean, and then rinse and buff.

(continued on page 110)

THE QUEEN'S QUICK KITCHEN TIPS

Smells and stains are the hallmarks of most kitchens. Even a Queen has to deal with them occasionally! They may be a fact of life, but that's no reason to live with them. Here's what to do.

- To remove food odors from plastic containers, fill the containers with warm water and add a little dry mustard; ¼ teaspoon is plenty for an average-size container. Let the mustard mixture soak for an hour or so and then wash the container.

- To remove stains from plastic, put the open container in the sun. For stubborn spots, brush with a little lemon juice first.

- To chase away the odor of burned foods, boil some lemon slices or 1 tablespoon of bottled lemon juice in a saucepan for a few minutes.

- To chase away the odor of fried foods, even fish, place a small bowl of white vinegar next to the stove as you are frying.

- Clean porcelain pieces and the sink by filling the sink with warm water and adding several denture-cleaning tablets.

- Remove stains from the countertop by massaging a paste of cream of tartar and lemon juice into the stain, let it soak, and then rinse the countertop.

- Clean and sanitize your sponge and dishcloth by wedging them into the dishwasher and washing them along with a load of dishes. You can also wet the sponge or dishcloth and put it in the microwave for 30 seconds.

- To remove grease from wooden cupboards, apply a very thin coat of car wax, let it dry and buff.

- Do not wash silver and stainless steel together in the dishwasher. The stainless steel may stain the silver.

- Remove plastic stuck to the outside of toasters with a little nail polish remover. Be sure the toaster is unplugged, and be sure to wipe and rinse the area.

- Store your steel wool pad in the freezer each time you finish with it, and it will never rust. Just tuck it into a sandwich bag.

- Remove rust from baking pans by rubbing with cleanser and a cut raw potato.

- To clean a scorched pan, fill with warm water and add several table-spoons of baking soda. Boil until the scorched parts loosen and float to the surface.
- Spray a grater with nonstick cooking spray before using it, and cleanup will be a breeze.
- Clean the outside bottom of a cast-iron pan with oven cleaner, being sure to keep the cleaner away from the surfaces that will come in contact with food and washing the pan well after applying the cleaner. Clean the inside of the pan by boiling a solution of water and a couple of tablespoons of white vinegar in it. Re-season with cooking oil and store with a piece of waxed paper in it after each use. Never wash the inside of a cast-iron pan with soap.
- To clean the inside of a thermos, fill with warm water and add 1 teaspoon of chlorine bleach. Let soak 30 to 60 minutes and rinse well to remove all traces of the bleach.
- Preserve wooden salad bowls by wiping them with a paper towel soaked in cooking oil. This prevents drying and cracking. Do not immerse them in water for more than just a few seconds to clean. Always dry them thoroughly.
- Remove rust from a knife or other kitchen utensil by sticking it in an onion for about an hour. Move the piece back and forth to help the onion juice do its work.
- Always put glass dishes into hot water sideways, and they will never break from the expansion and contraction. Be sure to avoid putting cold glassware into hot water, too.
- To remove rust from countertops, such as Formica and plastic laminates, make a paste of cream of tartar and either lemon juice or hydrogen per-oxide, apply it to the rust spot, and allow to sit for about 30 minutes. Scrub the countertop with a nylon-type scrubbing sponge and rinse. If necessary, reapply the paste.
- When using your double boiler, drop several marbles in with the water. If the pan should start to boil dry, the marbles will rattle, alerting you to the problem before the pan is ruined.

For gold, you can use nongel toothpaste and a soft brush (such as a toothbrush) on small gold pieces. Rinse well. You'll find that any household ammoniated cleaner mixed 50/50 with water also works well.

For chrome, rub with aluminum foil wrapped around your finger or hand, or wipe with a dry, used dryer fabric softener sheet to bring back the shine.

Hot Tips for Irons and Ironing Boards

If you look around, you can tell who's a wash-and-wear kind of person, and who goes the extra mile and presses their clothes before they head off to work in the morning. While I'm the Queen of Quick and Easy, I do feel there's a need to pick up an iron from time to time. Here's how to keep your iron moving along smoothly.

Cleaning Irons without a Nonstick Surface

Heat the iron to the hot, nonsteam setting. Run it over table salt sprinkled on a brown paper grocery bag.

You can also use nongel toothpaste. Apply it to a damp cloth and rub the cloth over the soleplate on a cool iron until starch buildup and ironing residue are removed. Rinse the soleplate well.

For terrible buildup or burned-on fabric or starch, take the iron outside and cover all parts of the iron except soleplate with paper (and sealed with masking tape). Spray oven cleaner directly onto the soleplate of a cool iron. Wait several minutes and then rinse off well with cool water and an old rag or sponge. Be sure to iron on a clean, old white rag or old T-shirt before ironing clothing to be sure that all oven cleaner residue has been removed. Be sure to use the steam feature, too, so that the oven cleaner is removed from the steam vent holes.

Cleaning Irons with a Nonstick Surface

Use a laundry prespotter. Rub it on, and then rinse it off well.

Aftercare for Irons

After cleaning your iron with any of these methods, remember to rinse it well and then fill it with water. Turn the iron on to the heavy steam setting and iron over old fabric prior to using on clothes. This will remove any residue remaining in the vent holes—otherwise, it could be deposited as a nasty spot on your new silk blouse!

Cleaning the Vent Holes

Many times the vent holes in the bottom of the iron will become clogged. With the iron unplugged, take a pipe cleaner and clean out each vent hole individually.

ROYAL DECREE: Always empty steam irons after each use to prevent clogging.

Cleaning the Internal Parts

Fill the steam iron with equal portions of water and white vinegar. Let it steam for several minutes. Disconnect the iron and let it sit for 1 hour. Empty and rinse with clear water using the same process. Be sure to iron over old fabric prior to ironing clothes.

Keeping Ironing Board Covers Clean

To make covers last longer and stay clean longer, spray them with spray starch once the cover is on the board and iron the starch in well. You may need to clean the iron's soleplate after ironing the starch into the cover.

Energy-Efficient Ironing

Put aluminum foil under the ironing board cover when you put it on the board. It will reflect heat onto the garments as you iron and cut ironing time.

Taking Charge of Electronic Equipment

We're using telephones, TVs, cameras, and other gadgets almost 'round the clock, and guess what? They accumulate lots of dust and grime. Here's how to send a clear signal about keeping your electrical equipment clean.

ROYAL DECREE: Never clean any electronic equipment without unplugging it first!

Telephones

To clean and disinfect telephone receivers, apply Listerine mouthwash with a soft cotton pad or rag. Do not rinse off. This is great advice for offices during cold and flu season.

Television Screens

Denatured alcohol (available at hardware stores) makes a great cleaner for many pieces of electronic equipment. To clean the TV screen, turn off the power to the TV. Apply alcohol to a rag or paper towel and wipe the screen thoroughly, then buff.

Stop Dust from Settling on Televisions

Apply an antistatic product to a rag and wipe the screen and cabinet, or mix 1 part liquid fabric softener to 4 parts water and apply with a soft cloth and buff. Be sure the TV is off when you do this.

Radios

These need to be dusted often because of all the tiny crevices that attract dust. Clean them occasionally with denatured alcohol applied with a cotton ball. Do not use alcohol on wood.

Cameras

Cameras should always be stored in their cases when not in use. This prevents them from becoming dusty. Except for wiping off the outside of the lens with a cotton ball and a little alcohol, leave camera cleaning to the professionals.

Videocassette Recorders

These need to be kept free of dust to stay in good working order. It is best to cover them with a plastic cover when not in use. If the room is damp, keep silica packets (available from florists or many times found in new leather shoes or purses) on top of the VCR. (Keep these packets away from children.) Clean the VCR occasionally using a cleaning tape to ensure good-quality pictures on playback. Store videotapes in cardboard or plastic cases to keep them clean and in good condition for playback and recording.

Answering Machines

These need to be dusted with a lamb's-wool duster, particularly inside the machine. You can use an aerosol cleaner, but make sure that the machine is dry before you replace the cassette.

Fax Machines

These also need to be dusted and occasionally wiped with denatured alcohol.

Compact Discs

To keep your compact discs clean, mix 2 tablespoons of baking soda and 1 pint of water in a spray bottle. Shake well to mix and spray on the disc, wiping with a soft cloth. Do not wipe in a circular motion; wipe from the center hole in the disc out to the outside edge.

Computers

To avoid costly problems with computers, it is important that they be kept dust-free. Dust between the keys of your keyboard with a cotton swab, or vacuum with the duster brush on your vacuum or with a special computer vacuum that helps you get between the keys.

To clean the keys, mix 1 part water and 1 part alcohol and apply the solution to the keys with a cotton swab. Don't overwet. Undiluted denatured alcohol may also be used in the same manner.

Make sure that computers are situated out of direct sunlight, which can cause overheating. Sunlight also makes it difficult for the user to see the computer screen clearly.

Dust the screen and spray with an antistatic product.

Care and Control of the Washing Machine and Dryer

How difficult can it be? You add water and detergent, drop in the clothes, select the cycle, and walk away. When you come back the clothes are clean. It's almost like magic! Okay, but have you ever considered how clean your washing machine is after all that hard water and *all* those dirty clothes?

The Best Way to Clean a Washer

Your washer needs some tender loving care from time to time, especially if you have hard water in your area. So if your clothes start to seem dull and gray, maybe you don't need to run out and buy that new and improved detergent. Maybe all you need to do is clean the washing machine.

Here's the easiest way I know to clean a washer: Fill the washer with hot water. Add 1 quart of chlorine bleach (no detergent, please). Run the washer through the longest wash cycle. When the washer is still wet—this should be immediately after the bleach cycle—add 1 quart of white vinegar and run the washer through the same cycle again. This will clean out soap scum and mineral deposits from the spin basket and also from the hoses. If you live in an area with hard water, you really need to do this every 3 months; otherwise, every 6 months will do. You'll be amazed at the difference it will make.

If you start to notice little brown spots that look like rust on clothes when they come out of the washing machine, you can probably guess that it is rust! (For information on removing rust stains from clothes, turn to page 353. It's easier than you think.) Carefully look over your spin basket when this occurs, and check for any chips in the finish. Chipped areas rust and transfer rust to clothes. The only way to remedy this problem is to replace the spin basket. Check with your appliance dealer, and be sure to get the right basket for your machine.

ROYAL DECREE: And a word of caution: Take care when using detergent or fabric softener balls. They can chip the spin basket with their weight.

The Quick-Clean Method for Washers

When you don't have time to give your machine a really thorough cleaning, just fill the washer with hot water and pour in 1 gallon of white vinegar. Run through the entire wash cycle.

Cleaning the Fabric Softener Dispenser

Clean the automatic fabric softener dispenser every month to every 6 weeks to keep it working well and to prevent it from leaving softener stains on clothes. (Liquid softener can leave blue spots on clothes; marks from dryer sheets can look like small grease patches.) To clean the dispenser, warm 1 cup of white vinegar (I use the microwave) and pour it into the dispenser as you would softener. Make sure you use warm vinegar, and make sure you do this when the washer is empty. Large pieces of sticky fabric softener will occasionally be flushed out during cleaning, and they could adhere to clothes; believe me, it's not a pretty sight. I suggest cleaning the fabric softener dispenser when you are cleaning the machine with one of the methods recommended in this chapter.

Cleaning the Bleach Dispenser

It is equally important to keep the bleach dispenser clean. Clean any removable parts by washing with hot water and dishwashing liquid. When you clean the washer with white vinegar, be sure to add some to the bleach dispenser, too.

👑 **QUEENLY COMMENT:** If you use less detergent than normal, you will have less soap buildup on clothes *and* in the washing machine. Use ½ cup of Arm and Hammer Washing Soda and about half the amount of detergent you would usually use. Adjust this formula by increasing or decreasing detergent for your individual washing needs.

Tips on Buying and Placing a New Washing Machine

- If you don't have space for a washer and dryer to sit next to each other, remember that you can buy some very efficient stackable units. Just make sure to measure the area *before* you buy.

- A front-loading washer is definitely a space saver—the top makes a great work space for spotting clothes. You'll need to protect the top of the washer if you are going to work off it, though. A plastic breadboard is ideal.

- Another good feature of front-loading washers is the way they tumble clothes. They generally tumble clothes the way a dryer does, and that's gentler on fabric than agitating. It is also less wobbly when spinning. The downside is that front loaders generally have a smaller capacity than top loaders, and they're usually not as good at cleaning heavy, ground-in dirt.

- There are many top loaders to choose from. Consider your needs carefully. You may want an extra-large capacity washer if you wash large loads of towels and sheets—but don't "overbuy." It's a waste of money to buy bells and whistles that you don't need—and there's more to go wrong, too!

- Give your washing machine plenty of room to vibrate. Allow an inch of space all the way around the machine.

- To keep the exterior of your washer and dryer clean and shiny, apply a coat of Clean-X Clean Shield (formerly called Invisible Shield) as soon as you buy your machine. This will put an invisible nonstick finish on the surface that will keep it looking like new. Water will bead up and wipe off, as will detergent and spotters. Reapply as needed.

- If your washer's power cord does not reach the outlet, have the outlet moved or the power cord replaced with a longer one. Absolutely *never* use an extension cord between the washer's power cord and the outlet. If water touches the connection between the extension cord and the power cord, you could be electrocuted.

- Do not install your washer in an unheated garage or utility room. Water that is trapped inside can freeze and severely damage the machine.

- One last installation tip: If you are installing a washing machine in a vacation home that is not heated during cold weather, have it drained completely by an appliance service technician before shutting up the home for the winter. Again, trapped water can freeze and damage the machine.

- If I can leave you with a final piece of advice concerning washing machines it would be this: *Never* leave home when the washing machine is running. It only takes seconds for a hose to break or a malfunction to occur, and that can cause flooding and damage in your home. I cannot tell you how many water damage cleanups we did when I owned my cleaning and disaster restoration company in Michigan. The amount of water that can pour from a small hose is unbelievable. So is the damage that can be done—not only to things that can be cleaned or replaced but also to precious treasures that can never be saved. It's heartbreaking.

Drying: How to Succeed without Really Trying

Now that the clothes are washed, they're ready for the dryer, so let's talk dirty dryers!

Keeping the dryer clean is important: A clean dryer will work more efficiently, saving you time and money. A clean dryer will also help to prevent dryer fires. Dryer fires are much more common than you might think, so let's find out how to keep dryers clean to prevent fires and other drying disasters.

The Basics

If you have a lint-clogged dryer venting system, your clothes will not dry properly, and you will waste time and money running longer cycles to get the clothes completely dry. Turn the dryer on, and go outside and hold your hand under the dryer vent hood—you know, that metal thing on the outside of the house. If you don't feel a strong flow of air, it's time to clean.

Clean the dryer vent pipe or flex exhaust hose once a year to prevent lint buildup. Try to lock a date in your mind and do it every year. I like Halloween because you can extract the lint and create a dust bunny costume at the same time! Remove the duct or hose from the dryer back and the exhaust mounting, and shake it out. It may be necessary to run an old cloth through the hose to dislodge any lint that is unwilling or unable to leave the vent. Be sure to reseal the joints, using a fresh piece of duct tape if necessary.

On the outside of the vent, clean the hood and vent by using a straightened wire coat hanger or bottle-type brush. Push it back and forth in the vent to remove accumulated lint.

Always make sure that your vent is straight. Kinks will block the airflow.

The Lowdown on Lint

The lint filter in the dryer is no less important than the vent. Keeping it clean is vital. A clogged lint filter allows lint to accumulate and can eventually start a fire. A dirty lint filter also blocks airflow, so your clothes will take longer to dry. And that means extra money on your gas or electric bill.

To clean the filter, remove it, wipe off the lint, and replace. You can do this easily by wiping the filter with a used dryer fabric softener sheet, which will collect the accumulated lint so that you can dispose of it without additional mess.

It's important to vacuum the filter periodically. Use your vacuum attachments to clean the area where the lint filter is installed (this is the opening on the dryer that the filter slides into).

ROYAL DECREE: If you have a gas dryer, always use caution not to kink or damage the gas line when shifting or moving the appliance.

Cleaning around and under the Dryer

While you have the dryer out, vacuum and wash the floor area underneath the unit. If you see any grease or oil leaks on the floor, it's time to call the appliance repairman.

Fine Furnishings and Furniture

When you spend princely sums to furnish your castle, you want to be sure that your beautiful furnishings stay as handsome as they were the day you purchased them. I've cared for many fine pieces over the years and can offer many useful tips for quick and easy cleaning and upkeep.

Today's Wood, Tomorrow's Heirlooms

Wood furniture in a home is a big investment. Properly cared for, it will last and keep its new appearance for years, eventually to be called "antique" by our grandchildren and great-grandchildren. Here are some tips to keep your furniture looking great, advice on fixing problems that arise, plus my recipe for making your own furniture polish.

Water Marks, Heat Scars, and White Rings

Massage mayonnaise into the marks and leave it on overnight. The next morning, wipe off the mayonnaise, and the marks should be gone. You

MAKING YOUR OWN FURNITURE POLISH

There are several great furniture polishes that you can make at home with ease. The general rule for homemade polish is to rub it in with a soft cloth and wipe it off and buff with another clean, soft cloth.

- Combine ¼ cup of white vinegar and 1 cup of olive oil in a clean container. Shake before each use.
- Combine 1 cup of mineral oil and 3 drops of lemon extract. Shake before each use.
- Grate 2 ounces of beeswax (available at drugstores) into a jar and cover it with 5 ounces of natural turpentine. Shake occasionally until dissolved, or stand in a bowl of hot water. Apply to furniture with a soft cloth (just a small amount is all that is needed) and buff with a clean, soft cloth. If it becomes hard over a period of time, set it in a bowl of hot water. This formula seems to work especially well on unvarnished furniture.

can also use petroleum jelly, butter, or margarine. If you have a really stubborn spot, mix cigarette ashes or rottenstone (available at the hardware store) with the mayonnaise and repeat the procedure above.

Nongel white toothpaste is also effective in removing white water rings. Dab toothpaste on a damp cloth and gently massage the ring in a circular motion until it's gone. Wipe and buff with a soft cloth. Apply furniture polish if necessary.

Remove Old Polish and Dirt

Put two tea bags in a pot with 1 quart of water and bring it to a boil. Cool to room temperature. Dip a soft cloth in the solution, wring it until it is just damp, and wipe furniture with it. Buff it dry with a soft cloth, and then decide if the furniture requires polish.

(♛) **QUEENLY COMMENT:** To restore dried-out furniture, dab petroleum jelly on a soft cloth and polish furniture to help feed and restore dry wood. You will be amazed to see the wood grain and natural luster appear.

Cleaning Very Dirty Wood Furniture

Mix a solution of 1 quart of warm water and 3 or 4 drops of dish-washing liquid. Wash the furniture with a soft cloth wrung out until it is damp. Rinse the piece and buff it dry.

Covering Scratches

To cover scratches on wood furniture, use a crayon the color of the wood. Apply the crayon to the scratched area, heat the area with a blow-dryer, and buff the crayon into the scratch with a soft cloth.

For darker woods, rub the meat of a pecan or walnut into the scratch and buff well.

To cover scratches on mahogany or cherry wood, use iodine.

Removing Stickers from Wood

To remove a price tag, identifying label, or decal from wood, pull up as much of the sticker as possible, then dip a cloth in vegetable oil or baby oil and gently scrub the area until the sticker and adhesive are gone. Finish by buffing well with a soft cloth.

Eliminating Odors

Many times old wooden trunks and dressers will have a musty mildew or stale odor. To eliminate this, take a slice of white bread (yes, it really has to be white), put it in a bowl, and cover the bread with white vinegar. Leave the bowl inside of the trunk or dresser drawers for 24 hours. If the odor remains, repeat the process. If mildew odor persists in dresser drawers, shellac or varnish the inside of them; the odor will be sealed in.

Taming Dust Bunnies without a Whip

Dusting is one of those thankless jobs that we all have to do. No matter how many times we do it, we still have to do it again and again. Here are things that you can do to make the job easier and faster.

Lamb's-Wool Dusters

For dusting hard-to-reach and high areas, use a good lamb's-wool duster. Do not use a feather duster; it simply shifts the dust around. A lamb's-wool duster attracts dust, is easily washed, and can be used for years. Look for these at janitorial supply stores and home centers, in mail-order catalogs, and on Web sites that sell cleaning supplies.

Dust Repellent

To keep dust off blinds, refrigerators, and glass-top tables, mix a solution of 1 part liquid fabric softener to 4 parts water. Spray on or apply with a soft cloth and dry with a soft cloth. This will repel the dust.

Dusting Prints

Use cornstarch to remove extra furniture polish and wipe fingerprints off wood furniture. Shake a little on the surface and polish with a soft cloth.

HOME-TREATED DUST CLOTHS

There are many dusting products on the market that you can buy, but you can easily make your own treated dust cloths for just pennies. Here's how.

- Use your favorite cleaning product to make up a bucket of hot, sudsy water. Add a couple of teaspoons of turpentine. Throw in some clean, cotton dust cloths, stir so that they get saturated, and let them soak for 8 to 10 hours. (I usually leave them overnight.) After they have soaked, wring them out and air-dry them. As soon as they are dry, they are ready to use.
- Mix together 2 cups of hot water and 1 cup of lemon oil. Dip lintless cloths into the solution. Squeeze thoroughly and air-dry. Store in a covered metal can—an old coffee can works great.

Upholstery Cleaning Made Easy

This section will give teach you how to choose upholstered furniture wisely, spot-clean it, handle emergency spills, and clean it thoroughly.

Cleaning Codes and What They Mean

One of the first things everyone should know about upholstery is that there are different cleaning methods for different types of fabric. By knowing which cleaning method is preferred before you buy a piece of furniture, you can make good decisions on wearability and cleanability before you decide whether or not to take the piece home.

Upholstery is supposed to be marked with a code that allows the consumer to know in advance what type of cleaning the manufacturer recommends for that particular piece of furniture. These instructions, known as cleaning codes, are generally found under the seat cushions on the platform of the furniture (the part that the cushions sit on). I will discuss each cleaning code individually below. If you do not find the code under the seat cushions, check all tags for instructions and never buy any upholstered furniture without knowing how it can be cleaned. This information is essential. Here are the three codes you'll find.

W: If you find a W on your furniture, it means that it can be cleaned with water. This would mean that you could rent an extraction carpet and upholstery cleaning machine from a home center or hardware store, or you can use one that you have purchased to clean the fabric. You can also use water in spotting spills. This is the most durable and cleanable fabric you can buy. It is ideal for dining chairs, family room furniture, anything that gets heavy use or on which spills might occur frequently.

S: If you find an S on your furniture tag, it means that it must be cleaned with cleaning solvents (dry-clean only), and you cannot apply water to it. This would eliminate spot-cleaning with water-based products. Dry-clean-only fabrics are generally not as durable and also do not clean as well. If you have a piece with this code, do not allow it to become heavily soiled before calling in a professional cleaner, or you will be disappointed with the results. If you need to spot-clean a dry-clean-only fabric, try using Energine Cleaning Fluid, available at grocery and hardware stores. Test it first in an inconspicuous spot to be sure that it doesn't damage the fabric. Apply with a clean, light-colored cloth and blot continuously. Once you have removed the spot, use a blow-dryer to dry the spot quickly so that it doesn't leave a noticeable ring on the fabric.

S/W: This code means a combination of solvents and water can be used to clean the upholstery. It does not appear on many pieces. I think furniture labeled with this code should be cleaned by professionals. I would suggest using furniture with the S/W code in low-use areas of your home so that cleaning doesn't become a big issue. The S/W code does not appear on furniture as much any more, but it does appear frequently on fabric blinds and shades. It means that the item is not cleanable and is a vacuum-only piece. Beware!

Don't Undress Your Furniture

Many people have asked me about taking the covers off the foam cushions and washing them in the washing machine. *Don't do it!* If you remove the cushion covers and wash them, they may shrink and not fit back on the foam correctly. No matter what, it is virtually impossible to get them back on the foam forms evenly and correctly. Plus, the covers will be noticeably cleaner than the rest of the sofa and will fade and wear out more quickly.

In case you're wondering why there are zippers in the backs of cushions if you're not supposed to use them, the zippers are there in the event that professional upholstery cleaners need to change the foam cushions. The furniture industry never intended for consumers to remove the foam cushions from the covers.

Spot Cleaning

If you need to spot-clean a cushion, unzip the zipper and put a pad of paper towels or a folded white rag between the foam and the cushion

CANDLE WAX MEETS UPHOLSTERY

If you have the misfortune of having candle wax come in contact with your upholstery, don't despair. First, put a large quantity of ice in a plastic bag and lay it on the wax long enough to allow the wax to freeze. Remove the ice and immediately chip up any wax that you can.

Next, take a brown grocery bag and, using only the part without writing, lay it over the wax. Using a medium to hot iron, press over the wax, allowing it to absorb into the paper bag. Move the bag continuously to a clean area. Once you have absorbed as much of the wax as possible, use Energine Cleaning Fluid to spot-clean the area, remembering to use a blow-dryer to dry the spot when you are done.

If any staining remains, use 3 percent hydrogen peroxide from the drugstore applied with a spoon to bleach out the wax color. Apply peroxide, wait 15 minutes, and blot, continuing until the color from the wax is gone.

covering. Apply your spotter, carefully following the directions. Try not to rub the area, as it causes abrasion on the fabric surface; instead blot, blot, blot. I have had great success with Spot Shot Upholstery Stain Remover. It is easy to use and works on a wide variety of spills and soiling. It can be used on many different fabrics, and it works well on the sofa or chair body as well as on the cushions. It is great for food spills on dining chairs, too.

ROYAL DECREE: Remember, whatever spotting method you choose, always test the spotter in an inconspicuous place first.

The Leather Report

Many of us have leather furniture, car interiors, clothes, and accessories. Unfortunately, along with wearing leather and using it in our homes comes the frustration of cleaning it.

Cleaning Leather Furniture

Keep leather furniture out of direct sunlight, otherwise it may crack and dry out. You should apply hide food once or twice a year to ensure that the leather remains supple. You can purchase it in hardware stores and home centers and where leather furniture is sold. Make sure that you rub it in well so that it does not come off on clothes. I like to apply it, rub it in well, let it sit for 12 hours, and then buff again before using the piece. Dust or vacuum leather regularly. Clean leather furniture with saddle soap or wipe it with a damp cloth rubbed across a wet bar of glycerin soap or moisturizing facial soap, such as Dove. If the leather piece is tufted and has buttons and piping, use a soft-bristled toothbrush or paintbrush moistened and rubbed across the soap. Always dry leather with a clean, lint-free cloth.

If you have a sealed leather table or desktop, clean, polish, and seal it with paste wax once or twice a year.

Keeping Leather Apparel Looking Spiffy

If you have dirty leather shoes, purses, coats, or accessories, you can treat them much the same way that you do your furniture. For cleaning purses and shoes, a damp, soft cloth rubbed across a bar of moisturizing facial soap, such as Dove, works well. You should always use care to not overwet the article. Do not rinse after washing; instead, allow to dry naturally, then polish as usual.

Removing Water Spots

Simply run a damp sponge over the area and allow to dry.

MAKING HIDE FOOD

Make your own hide food by mixing 1 part vinegar to 2 parts linseed oil in a jar with a lid. Shake well and apply it to leather with a soft cloth, changing cloths frequently as they soil. Buff well so that the oil won't transfer to clothes. Test in an inconspicuous area before using on light-colored leather.

Treating Salt Stains

Dab on a solution of 3 parts white vinegar to 1 part water.

Making Ink Stains and Spots Disappear

To remove ink stains and spots from leather, apply a little cuticle remover. Dab it on the spot, rub gently with a soft cloth, and then wipe and buff. For difficult stains, you may need to allow the cuticle remover to sit for 10 minutes or so before rubbing. Reapply if necessary.

Removing Dark Stains

If you have light-colored leather furniture or apparel with dark stains on it, try wiping gently with a thin paste of lemon juice and cream of tartar. Gently massage in, and then finish off with a soft, damp cloth. Be sure to rinse the leather well and follow up with one of the cleaning methods above.

Removing Mildew

To remove mildew from leather, apply a coat of petroleum jelly, allow it to sit for 4 to 5 hours, and then rub it off.

Meticulous Marble—Leave No Stone Unturned

Marble used in living room and other furniture is usually true marble, while bathroom and kitchen countertops are usually synthetic, or cultured, marble. True marble should be sealed with a stone sealer because it is very susceptible to stains, so always be sure to wipe up spills quickly.

Maintaining Marble

Dust or wipe marble with a damp cloth as needed. Sprinkle caked-on spots with borax or baking powder and rub with a damp sponge or cloth. You can also use a commercial marble polish.

Bathroom or kitchen marble can be cleaned with 1 part liquid fabric softener to 2 parts water. Clean thoroughly and polish with a soft cloth.

Fine Scratches

Use extra-fine steel wool to apply baking soda and water mixed to a paste. Flush the marble with water and let it dry; repeat if necessary. Buff with a dry cloth or use the buffing wheel on your electric drill.

Removing Stains

If marble isn't properly sealed, it can stain easily. Here are tips for the most common stains.

Grease Stains

Grease stains usually appear as circles and are often dark in the center. Wash the surface with ammonia, rinse with plenty of water, then repeat. Or cover the area with a ½-inch-thick paste of 20 percent hydrogen peroxide and powdered whiting from the paint store. Keep the area damp by covering it with plastic wrap sealed with masking tape. After 10 to

SPOTS & SPLATTERS

Removing Super Glue Spills

Dear Queen:
I was working on a wooden project when I goofed and got super glue on my Formica countertop (along with a little piece of the wood). How can I remove the glue and wood, or is it stuck there permanently?

The Queen Responds:
Try using straight acetone (from the beauty supply store) on the super glue. This should break the seal of the glue without damaging your Formica countertop. Keep a single-edged razor blade handy when you do this, and very gently pry up the glue and the piece of wood, dabbing more acetone on the spot until the glue is removed.

15 minutes, rinse with water, avoiding any wood trim. Repeat if necessary. Buff the area and then polish it.

Rust

Rub with a rough cloth or make a mix of commercial liquid rust remover and whiting and then follow the directions for grease stains. After removing the paste, rub marble with a dry cloth.

Tea, Coffee, and Ink

Use the hydrogen peroxide/whiting method described in the grease stains method above.

Water

Use hydrogen peroxide, applied with a medicine dropper, followed with a drop or two of household ammonia. After 20 minutes, wash the area.

Wine

Use hydrogen peroxide.

Mystery Stains

To remove stains of an unknown origin, try hydrogen peroxide mixed with cream of tartar or nongel toothpaste, rubbed in with a soft cloth and rinsed off.

Restoring the Polish

To restore the polish to marble, rub with a cloth dampened with turpentine.

QUEENLY COMMENT: Warming marble with a blow-dryer or setting the marble piece in the sun will make stain removal quicker and easier.

Outside the Castle

Keeping the palace porches and grounds in tidy shape is just as important as taming the imperial dust bunnies inside. Whether you need to polish the patio furniture for afternoon guests, clean the grill for the next royal feast, or spiff up the car for the King, you'll be pleased to know that I have a shortcut or tip for every outdoor surface! Why not involve the whole royal family in outdoor cleanup? Little princes and princesses will enjoy the together time, and you'll enjoy all the extra help!

Everything under the Sun for Patio Furniture

No matter what part of the country you live in, at some time you have to clean the outdoor furniture. Follow this advice to make the job go faster.

QUEENLY COMMENT: To maintain the shine on plastic, resin, and metal furniture, apply a good-quality paste car wax just as you would when waxing a car.

Furniture Cushions

There are several ways to clean outdoor furniture cushions. You can use Spot Shot Upholstery Stain Remover or Spot Shot Instant Carpet Stain Remover. Follow the directions on the can. Or mix your own solution: In a spray bottle, combine 1 teaspoon of dishwashing liquid and 1 teaspoon of borax per quart of warm water. Spray this on both sides of the cushions and let it sit for about 15 minutes. Then take out the hose and, using a strong spray, rinse the solution and the dirt off the cushions. Put them back on the chairs and set them out of the direct sun to dry. Vacuum the cushions as needed to remove dust between cleanings.

Aluminum

Although it doesn't rust, aluminum can become dull and pitted when left outdoors. To clean and restore the shine, scrub with a plastic scrubber soaked in detergent or a soap-filled steel-wool pad, then rinse and dry.

Aluminum with Baked-Enamel Finish

Use a sponge soaked in detergent and wash well, then rinse and dry. To protect, apply a coat of good-quality car wax. This will make cleaning easier and will maintain the shine. The wax can be used on tables with a baked-enamel finish, too.

Canvas

Soiled canvas seats and chair backs are usually machine washable, but be sure to put them back on the furniture when they are still damp to maintain their shape. To clean canvas that you cannot put in the washing machine, such as large seats, seat backs, or awnings, run a scrub brush back and forth across a bar of Fels-Naptha Laundry Soap. Rub this back and forth across the canvas and then rinse well. This will even remove bird droppings and, many times, the staining, too.

Plastic

Wash with a good all-purpose cleaner and water, then rinse with water and dry. An alternative for white furniture is automatic dishwasher detergent and warm water (1 gallon of warm water to 3 tablespoons of automatic dishwasher detergent). Wash and let the solution sit on the furniture for 15 minutes or so and then rinse and dry.

The Grill Drill

Let's talk about ways to make cooking on the grill easier and more fun for palace chefs.

Prevent Sticking

Before you light the barbecue, spray the grill rack with nonstick cooking spray. (Never spray an aerosol can near an open flame, or your kingdom will come to an end with a big kabang!) Nonstick cooking spray works great on gas or charcoal grills. Apply a liberal coat and food won't stick, making cooking and cleanup a lot easier.

Cleaning the Grill

To clean the grill surface when it is heavily caked with baked-on food, follow this procedure: Simply wrap the rack in a piece of heavy-duty aluminum foil, dull side facing out. Heat the barbecue to high heat and place the rack over the coals or flame for 10 to 12 minutes. When you remove the foil after it has cooled, all the burned-on grease and food drippings will fall off and your rack will be spotless and ready to grill again.

ROYAL DECREE: Immediately after cooking on a grill, make a ball of aluminum foil and "scrub" the warm grill rack surface with it, taking care not to burn your fingers.

Coming Clean on Grill Racks

Many people recommend putting the grill rack in the bathtub filled with hot water, detergent, and ammonia. I find this a particularly messy way to do it because you have to clean the tub when you're done. If you do use this method, be sure to lay old rags or a garbage bag in the tub to prevent scratching the tub surface with the grill rack.

I suggest you try this easier method instead: Lay some paper towels moistened with undiluted ammonia on both sides of the rack. Put it in an appropriate-size plastic bag and seal. Leave it overnight, and the next day open the bag (away from your face because it stinks). Wipe down the rack with the paper towels in the bag, wash it well with soapy water, and rinse it.

Keeping Pan Bottoms Clean

Before setting a pan on the grill rack to warm barbecue sauce or marinade, or to cook additional foods, rub the pan bottom with bar soap. The soap makes it easier to clean off the soot when you are done cooking.

Cleaning Permanent Briquettes

Flip the briquettes and ignite the grill. Close the cover and allow it to burn at a high setting for about 15 minutes; this will burn off previous food drippings. Before you use the grill the next time, flip the briquettes onto another side and repeat the procedure, then grill as usual.

Grease Splatters

For cement or wood patios, keep a container of salt nearby when barbecuing. Should grease spatter or drip, immediately cover with salt. Sweep up and reapply until grease is absorbed. Scrub the spots with dishwashing liquid and rinse.

Keeping the Outside of the Grill Clean

This is such a fast, easy way to clean the outside of the grill. It works well on charcoal and gas grills and will make them look almost like new. Take some GOJO Waterless Hand Cleaner (available at grocery stores, hardware stores, and home centers) and rub it on the outside of a cool grill with an old rag or paper towel. Work it into the metal well, paying special attention to any grease or barbecue sauce spots. Do not rinse; instead, take paper towels and buff the grill surface and watch as the dirt is replaced by a great shine.

Cleaning the Glass Grill Window

Many gas grills have glass windows in them. Of course, once you use the grill a few times, you can no longer see through the window! To clean the windows, spray the inside of the glass with oven cleaner. Wait a few minutes, and then scrub and rinse well. On the outside of the glass, use GOJO Waterless Hand Cleaner and buff well.

All Hands on Deck

A certain amount of routine maintenance is required to keep your backyard deck structurally sound, safe, and looking its best.

Though other types of lumber may have been used, chances are that your deck is built of cedar, redwood, or pressure-treated yellow pine. These are the most commonly used materials for decks because they are resistant to rot and insect damage. When exposed to the elements for extended periods of time, any wood will show signs of weathering. Even if the deck was originally treated with stain or a preservative, this treatment eventually needs to be renewed.

Inspect and Protect Your Investment

The first thing you need to do once the weather turns nice is inspect the deck surfaces for any splintering, which you will need to sand. Pay special attention to the railing.

You'll find many stains and sealers designed for decks. Several manufacturers now offer products called deck brighteners, which actually bleach the surface to remove stains and weathering on wood surfaces. Apply these products carefully, following the instructions. Usually, you will brush the product on with a stiff bristle brush, and rinse off thoroughly prior to applying any finish coating.

Sealers protect the deck from moisture and are available in clear or tinted varieties to act as a stain. Sealers require periodic renewal to maintain protection.

Go over the actual decking to be sure it is tight and in place, fixing whatever is required. Finally, if no repair or staining is needed, follow some of these suggestions to give the deck a good cleaning.

If there are leaves and other yard debris on the deck, either sweep or use a blower to clean off the surface.

Hose Off the Deck

With a garden hose and a strong and preferably long-handled brush, use the strongest spray setting on the nozzle to break up dirt on the surface. Follow this with the brush to loosen any stubborn soil. This works especially well with two people, who can take turns hosing and scrubbing.

Kill Mildew

Check the condition of the wood. Green or black areas indicate mold and mildew. To remove mold and mildew from the wood, you will need either a commercial deck-cleaning product (which may be purchased at your local home center), or you can prepare your own using a mixture of 1 cup of trisodium phosphate (available at janitorial supply stores and home centers), 1 gallon of oxygen-type bleach (safer to use than chlo-

PROTECTING PLANTS AROUND YOUR PALATIAL DECK

After you have washed your deck, I recommend that you hose down the grass and any plants surrounding it to remove any cleaning solution that has dripped on them. No damage should be done to plants from your washing and cleaning tasks, but rinsing is a good precaution. If you have used a garden sprayer, be sure to wash it out well and rinse the brush before storing, too, to remove any cleaning solution residue.

rine bleach), and 1 gallon of hot water. The bleach will kill the mildew, and the trisodium phosphate will thoroughly clean the wood surface. You can apply this with a garden sprayer or mop it on.

Wet down the deck with the hose and then apply the cleaning solution. Spread the solution evenly and scrub with the brush you used earlier. Let the solution sit for about 15 minutes and then hose off. Repeat the wetting, bleaching, and rinsing process as necessary until the entire deck is clean. Make sure you do the stairs, handrails, and any other deck parts.

Quick Cleaning

To give the deck a quick cleaning during the in-use season, mix up a gallon of hot water and ¼ cup of any good-quality household cleaner, or mix 1 gallon of hot water, 1 tablespoon of dishwashing liquid, and ¼ cup of borax. Mop the deck down with one of these solutions and rinse well. Be sure to rinse plants and grass down.

Removing Sap from an Unfinished Wood Deck

Tree sap can be a problem on wood decks. To remove it, apply mineral spirits with an old rag, rub, and wash off with dishwashing liquid and water (1 teaspoon of dishwashing liquid to 1 quart of hot water). Rinse well.

Do Away with Window Pains

If you want the job done right, you need to have the right equipment at hand, the right cleaners in the bucket, and the right attitude. Remember, cleaning a window a day keeps the sun shining in!

The Right Tools

To achieve professional results, you need to use the same tools the professionals use. You can find all of these things at either a janitorial supply store (look in the yellow pages) or a hardware store.

Squeegee. A good squeegee is an absolute must. Don't be fooled into thinking that a cheap plastic squeegee or a car windshield squeegee will do the job—they won't! The best size to start with is a 12- or 14-inch squeegee. This will work well on most windows, and once you have mastered this size, you can move up to an 18-inch for large-paned windows and down to a 6-inch for small French panes.

ROYAL DECREE: No matter what you have heard about cleaning windows with newspaper, don't do it! It is a dirty, messy method and leaves newsprint all over white window trim and paint.

Scrubber. A good scrubber is a plus. This tool looks like a squeegee wearing a fluffy coat. It is used to wet and clean the window prior to using the squeegee. If you do not want to invest in this, be sure you buy a good natural sponge.

Rag or chamois. Use a dry rag or chamois for drying the squeegee rubber (blade) and the edges of the glass.

Scraper. Use a window scraper for removing paint, concrete, and other stubborn debris. If you don't purchase a scraper, you can use a good medium- to fine-grade steel wool pad, but be sure the pad and the window are soapy wet. Never use one of those scrub pads that you use on dishes; this will scratch the glass, and never use steel wool on tinted glass.

Extension pole. If you have difficult, high, hard-to-reach windows, consider an extension pole made for a squeegee. This will enable you to stand on the ground and reach the high windows without a ladder.

Bucket and trisodium phosphate. You'll need a bucket of water and trisodium phosphate (TSP) or dishwashing detergent (two or three squirts to a bucket). Add the TSP or dishwashing detergent after you have filled the bucket with water.

QUEENLY COMMENT: Use a dry blackboard eraser on a dry window or mirror after cleaning it to banish any streaks you've left behind. Works like a charm!

Let's Get Started

Getting started is the hardest part. Once you're on your way, you may find you actually enjoy doing windows. Follow the steps listed below, in order. You'll be cleaning like a pro in no time!

- Fill your bucket with warm water and add the TSP or dishwashing liquid.

- Be sure you have all the necessary equipment laid out and ready for use.

- Dip your scrubber or sponge into the cleaning solution and wash the window thoroughly, using a very wet steel wool pad to remove any stubborn spots, such as bug stains. You do not have to press very hard on the steel wool pad. Rewet the window so that you'll have time to squeegee the window before it dries. Try not to clean in the direct sunlight, because the sunlight dries the window too quickly, and you'll end up with streaking and spotting.

- Tilt the squeegee at an angle so that 2 inches of rubber blade touches the glass. Start at the top corner and draw the squeegee along the top edge of the window.

- Wipe the squeegee blade on a sponge. Starting on the dry surface close to the frame, draw the squeegee down to within about 3 inches of the bottom of the glass.

- Repeat this stroke until you have squeegeed all of the glass. Be sure you overlap each stroke and wipe the squeegee blade after each stroke.

- Soak up excess water with a well-rinsed sponge.

- Tilt the squeegee at an angle again so that 2 inches of rubber blade touches the glass. Start at the bottom corner and draw the squeegee along the bottom of the glass.

- Have your rag or chamois handy to wipe the window edges if needed. If you see a streak on the window, let it dry, then use a poly/cotton rag, such as an old T-shirt, to polish it out.

SPRAY-AND-WIPE CLEANING SOLUTIONS

If you prefer to wash your windows the spray-and-wipe way, here are a couple of good cleaning solutions.

Glass Polishing Paste and Screen and Bug Stain Remover

Baking soda

Water

Make a thin paste of baking soda and water and rub it onto the glass or screen. Rinse the glass or screen well, and dry it with a soft cloth.

Easy Window Cleaner

2 quarts warm water

½ cup cornstarch

Combine the warm water and cornstarch. Apply the cleaner to a window with a sponge. Buff the window dry with paper towels or soft, lint-free rags.

Tough-Job Window Cleaner

1 pint rubbing alcohol

2 tablespoons clear ammonia

2 tablespoons dishwashing liquid

Apply to the window using a nylon-covered sponge, rinse, and buff dry. This cleaner is great for hard-water spots.

Screen Savers

Most people just hose screens down to clean them. This just moves the dirt from one part of the screen to the other. Here's a better way: Soap the screen with a sponge that's been dipped in a pail of warm water containing 2 tablespoons of dishwashing liquid, ¼ cup of ammonia, and 2 tablespoons of borax. This solution really suds up the screen. Lay a rag on the ground and gently tap the screen on it. Most of the soapy water containing the dirt will come off this way. To finish, rinse the screen with the hose and stand the screen to dry, or dry the screen with a rag.

Concrete Solutions
for Cleaning Cement Driveways and Patios

One question everyone asks is how to clean cement driveways, garage floors, and patios. The best time to clean cement is when the temperature is between 50° and 75°F and the direct sun is not shining on it. Take this into consideration when using the cleaning methods in this chapter.

Grab the Dust on Cement

To make quick work of sweeping a cement garage floor or patio, pick up some sweeping compound at either a janitorial supply store, hardware store, or home center. The sweeping compound will "grab" the dust instead of spreading it in the air as you sweep. When you're done, just sweep it into a dustpan and throw it out.

A Garage Floor's Best Friend

Cat-box litter, either regular clay or clumping, is wonderful for absorbing liquid spills, especially oil of any kind. Simply pour it on the spot and then—the secret to success—grind it into the spot with your foot. Leave it and allow it to absorb all of the oil that it can. Then sweep up. Repeat the process if necessary.

Old Stains on Cement

Apply a spray-and-wash product and leave it on for 5 to 10 minutes. Sprinkle with laundry detergent, scrub with a stiff brush or broom, and then rinse the floor.

Another good method is to make a paste of hot water and automatic dishwasher detergent. Scrub it into the spot and let it soak for at least 1 hour, preferably overnight. Add additional water and scrub the stain, then rinse well.

Removing the Toughest Stains

Use oven cleaner to remove the toughest spots. Spray it on, keeping your face well back from the nozzle spray. Let it stand for 15 minutes, scrub stains with a stiff brush or broom, and hose off. Repeat if necessary. Rinse cement and brush with plenty of water. Do not combine other cleaning products with the oven cleaner, and do not use other products on the spot until the floor has been rinsed well with water.

ROYAL DECREE: Do not allow children or pets in the area when using this method.

Removing Rust from Concrete

Wet the concrete and sprinkle with lemon Kool-Aid. Cover with plastic and soak for 15 minutes. Remove the plastic, scrub with a brush, and rinse well.

Another method that may work for you is applying ZUD Heavy Duty Cleanser. This can be purchased in the cleanser section of most

SPOTS & SPLATTERS

Cleaning Oil off Asphalt

Dear Queen:
Can you tell me how to get an oil slick out of my asphalt driveway?

The Queen Responds:
Cat-box litter is just what you need for that oil stain, whether it's on cement or asphalt. Both the clay and clumping litter will work for this job. Just pour it on the spot, and then grind it into the spot with your foot. (The "grinding it in" is the important part.) Leave the cat-box litter on the spot for a few hours, and then sweep it up. Repeat the procedure as necessary until the spot is gone. After you have removed as much oil as you can, wash the driveway with a solution of trisodium phosphate (available in hardware stores and home centers) and hot water.

grocery and department stores. Make a paste with warm water and work it in well with a brush. Let it soak for 30 minutes and then scrub with additional hot water and rinse well.

If the rust stain is really bad, you will have to use a solution of 10 parts water to 1 part muriatic acid. Let this sit for 2 to 3 hours and then scrub with a stiff (nonmetallic) brush. Use extreme caution if you use this method. Wear goggles, gloves, and old clothes, and rinse, rinse, rinse!

ROYAL DECREE: Keep children and pets away from the area while using the acid and while the floor is drying.

At the Car Wash

While there are some folks who take care of their cars as if they were fine pieces of porcelain, there are others whose cars get a little cluttered and, shall we say, dirty inside and out. My quick tips for car care can make the cleanup of your cruiser as fun as a drive down Pacific Coast Highway. Well, maybe not that fun, but at least you'll get the job done right!

Stain Guard

Before long trips, spray the front of your car, where the bugs collect, with nonstick cooking spray. This will stop bugs from sticking, and dirt can be easily washed off.

Cleaning the Windshield

Clean your windshield with baking soda and water prior to washing the car. Add white vinegar to a wet, lint-free rag to remove grease film and give you a streak-free shine.

Bug Scraper

Save the plastic net bags from your produce purchases (onion bags are ideal) to scrub the window when it is spattered with bugs. Keep a couple

> # MAKE YOUR OWN WINDSHIELD WASHER SOLVENT
>
> This can be used in the windshield washer container in your car—winter or summer. It's a great cleaner and cheaper than commercial windshield washer fluids. Combine 1 quart of rubbing alcohol, 1 cup of water, and 2 tablespoons of liquid dishwashing detergent or laundry detergent. This should not freeze even at −30°F.

in the car to use at the gas station when washing your windows, then throw them away after use. These are great for traveling.

Removing Tar

Saturate tar spots with linseed oil. Let the oil soak in, and then rub with an old rag or paper towel moistened with the oil.

Removing Bumper Stickers

Use a blow-dryer to heat the sticker, then use a flat edge, such as an old credit card, and start peeling. Continue to heat and peel. Remove any glue residue with nail polish remover (test a spot to make sure you don't remove paint or the finish from the bumper).

Shining Chrome

If you have dirty chrome on your car, simply dampen a piece of aluminum foil and rub. This is a great way to remove rust, too.

Stopping Battery Corrosion

Scrub the battery terminals and the holder with ½ cup of baking soda combined with 2 cups of warm water. When dry, apply petroleum jelly to the area.

Preventing Doors from Freezing

Spray the rubber gaskets around the door and trunk with nonstick cooking spray. This will keep water out and also keep the gaskets supple. Remember this trick if you plan on having the car washed in cold weather.

Removing Salt Residue from Carpet

Combine a 50-50 solution of white vinegar and water. Apply to carpet and blot the area to remove excess liquid. Reapply as necessary.

Cleaning the Interior

For spots on carpet and upholstery, count on a good carpet cleaner such as Spot Shot Instant Carpet Stain Remover. Use as directed on the can.

Keeping Leather Upholstery Clean

Wet a soft cloth with warm water and rub it across a wet bar of Dove Moisturizing Soap several times. Wash the seats thoroughly, rinsing out the cloth and reapplying the soap as it becomes soiled. Do not rinse; instead, dry with a soft cloth.

Eliminating Smoke Odors

If you smoke in the car, put a layer of baking soda in the bottom of the ashtray to absorb smoke odor. Empty it frequently. Dryer fabric softener sheets placed under the seats also help to keep the smoke smell under control. For musty smells, put cat-box litter in a nylon stocking and tie the top shut. You can place several of these odor-absorbing stocking under the seats or in the trunk.

Calling in a Professional, So to Speak

If your car is really in need of a complete interior cleaning, rent an extraction machine at the hardware store or home center and clean upholstered seats and carpet thoroughly throughout the vehicle. Be sure to leave the windows down to allow the interior to dry completely.

Kids, Pets, and Other Messy Subjects

Pests, plants, pets . . . In every palace, the daily itinerary includes coping with or cleaning up after them. Not to mention any future crown princes and princesses! Whether you need to get the pests out of your pantry, keep a vase of cut flowers fresh longer, get the stain off the rug when Precious misses the litterbox, or remove crayon from your newly painted wall, you'll find safe, effective techniques in this chapter. All Queen-tested and approved for your palace!

User-Friendly Palace Pest Control

Are the bugs bugging you? Are the pests pestering you? You can control bugs without chemicals—the safe, environmentally friendly way. When planting flowers or controlling insects inside the house, keep this guide handy.

Try Vinegar

A wonderful substitute for insect repellent is white vinegar. Apply it liberally to your skin with a cotton ball. Bugs will hate the way you taste, and the smell of the vinegar disappears once it dries. Great for kids!

Aphids

Mix nonfat dry milk with water according to the directions on the box, then put it in a spray bottle and apply it to the leaves of your plants. As the milk dries, the aphids get stuck in the milky residue and die. You can rinse the plants from time to time with the hose. This will not harm your plants, and it offers an inexpensive solution to a big problem.

Aphids and Spiders

Wash off the plant with a mild solution of dishwashing liquid and water. Try a ratio of ½ teaspoon of dishwashing liquid to 1 quart of water. Flush leaves, including the undersides, with the solution. Do not rinse off.

Aphids and Whiteflies

These bugs are attracted to anything that's bright yellow and can be trapped by placing a yellow board (or other yellow objects such as yellow poster board, margarine lids, or sticks painted yellow), coated with petroleum jelly or Tack Trap near susceptible plants. Recoat when the traps dry out.

Aphids on Roses

Use 1½ teaspoons of baking soda per pint of water and apply every 7 days. This method is user-, child-, and earth-friendly.

Grasshoppers

To deter grasshoppers, plant basil around the flowerbed borders. Grasshoppers will eat the basil and leave the plants alone.

Ants

For ants on the counter, wipe down the counter with undiluted white vinegar.

To prevent ants from coming in the house or getting into cupboards, sprinkle dried mint or red pepper where they are entering the house and in the cupboards.

To get rid of anthills, pour 3 gallons of boiling water down each one. This is best done when the ants are active and near the surface. Do not do this close to flowers, or the flowers will die, too.

Another way to kill ants is to mix a combination of 50 percent borax and 50 percent confectioner's sugar. Place this on cardboard or a piece of board near the anthill. The ants are attracted by the sugar and carry the fatal borax/sugar combination back to the nest to feed the queen and other ants. Soon all are dead.

ROYAL DECREE: Do not place the borax/sugar powder where children or pets may ingest the mixture.

Borax is sold in the laundry aisle at the grocery store as a laundry additive, not as a pesticide.

Cockroaches

To keep cockroaches out of the cupboards, place bay leaves on the shelves.

Kill cockroaches with a mixture of ⅓ borax, ⅓ cornmeal, ⅓ flour, and a dash of powdered sugar. Sprinkle this in crevices under sinks and vanities, where cockroaches love to hide. Remember, keep this away from children and animals.

You can also try this formula for cockroaches: Mix powdered boric acid with sugar and powdered nondairy creamer. I use a mixture of 50 percent boric acid to 25 percent each sugar and creamer. This is inexpensive and relatively safe, but it should be kept away from children and pets. Sprinkle the mixture in all the dark, warm places that cockroaches love under sinks and stoves, behind refrigerators, in cabinets and closets, and so on. The roaches will walk through the powder and then clean themselves, much the way a cat preens. Once they ingest the powder, they die.

Flower Power

Flowers are a natural part of Queenly festivities—they add beauty and fragrance all over the palace. Here are my favorite ways to keep cut flowers fresh longer and vases, flowerpots, and artificial flowers clean.

Making Fresh Flowers Last Longer

To make fresh flowers from your garden or floral arrangements from the florist keep longer, use the following recipe. Remove any foliage below the waterline, trim the stem ends periodically, and keep the solution fresh—your flowers will last longer.

Royal Flower Fluid

  1 quart water
  2 tablespoons lemon juice
  1 tablespoon sugar
  ½ teaspoon liquid bleach

Add the solution to the flower container and enjoy fresher flowers longer. If you have an arrangement from the florist, add this solution each time you add water.

   If you don't have the ingredients above on hand, add 2 ounces of Listerine mouthwash per gallon of water.

   To make cut flowers last longer without shedding, spray with hair spray. Hold the spray can about a foot away from the flowers and spray it in an upward direction to prevent the flowers from drooping.

Cleaning Vases

To easily clean a flower vase, fill it with warm water and add one or two denture-cleaning tablets, depending on the size of the vase. Let it soak at least an hour or overnight. Wash, rinse, and dry well. If you don't have any denture-cleaning tablets, throw in a handful of dry rice and some white vinegar and shake, shake, shake. Let the vase soak with vinegar and warm water if necessary. Wash and rinse the vase well.

Transporting Fresh Flowers

If you are taking fresh flowers from your garden as a gift, or to the office, fill a balloon with water, put the stems in, and secure the neck of the balloon to the stems with a rubber band, twist tie, or ribbon. Poking the stems through a paper doily will also hold the stems in place and make an attractive presentation. Your flowers will arrive at their destination looking fresh with no spilled water to worry about!

The Dirt on Flowerpots

When planting flowers in a pot that has a drainage hole in the bottom, line the bottom of the pot with enough coffee filters to cover it. Add a few pebbles, and then add the soil. When you water the plant, the dirt won't run out the bottom.

Flowerpot Filler

When planting shallow-rooted flowers in a large pot, line the bottom with coffee filters and pebbles, fill the pot ⅓ full of packing peanuts and then fill with soil. The pot will be much lighter to move, and you won't require as much soil to fill the pot.

Healthful Water

When you boil eggs, save the water to water your plants. The water is full of minerals.

Cold coffee or tea combined with water provides an acidic drink for your plants. (Be sure it doesn't run out on the carpet.)

Water from an aquarium provides excellent fertilizer for plants, and club soda that has lost its fizz is good for plants.

QUEENLY COMMENT: Visiting royal relatives for a few days? Going on vacation? Stand plants in the sink or bathtub, depending on the number you have. Be sure they are in pots with a hole in the bottom. Add a few inches of water to the tub, and plants will be automatically watered while you are gone. To preserve the tub finish, lay an old towel in the bottom to set the plants on.

Let Them Shine

To shine indoor plant leaves, wipe gently with glycerin. Another great way to add shine is to wipe leaves with a mixture of half milk and half water. Do not use oil on plant leaves, as it attracts dust and dirt.

Window Boxes and Patio Flowerpots

Container gardens dress up even the most regal palace. Window boxes and flowerpots are easy to keep clean. After you plant the flowers in the pots, put a layer of gravel or marbles on top. When you water or it rains, the dirt won't splash all over the plants, pots, patio, or porch.

Hanging Plants

To water hanging plants with ease and without the mess of water running all over, use ice cubes. The cubes melt slowly so water won't run out onto the floor or patio.

Weed Prevention

To prevent the weeds from growing in the cracks of sidewalks, promenades, and patios, sprinkle salt into the cracks.

To kill weeds already growing in sidewalk cracks, pour boiling salt water on them. Use a mixture of ¼ cup of salt to 2 quarts of water. Avoid getting the hot salt water on any prize plants, or they, too, will succumb.

Cleaning Artificial Flowers

To really clean and remove soil from artificial flowers and arrangements, whether they're dried silk or polyester, place them in a bag with table salt. Add salt in proportion to the size of the flowers. Close the bag and gently shake the flowers in the salt for several minutes, or shake longer if the flowers are heavily soiled. Shake gently to remove the salt. The salt won't look dirty when you are done, but if you run water into it, you will be surprised how much dirt it has removed from the flowers.

You can also place silk flowers in a pillowcase, tie a knot in the pillowcase, and put it in the clothes dryer on the air fluff or air only cycle for 15 to 20 minutes.

Spray polyester flowers with acrylic spray from the craft store, and they will resist soiling. If they get very dusty, wash under a mild stream of running water, shake, and stand up to dry.

Future Rulers: Babies and Kids

Kids are life's reward and add great joy to our lives. They also test all of our patience and cleaning skills. If you have children, large or small, or you have grandchildren, you need to memorize this section, or at least know where this book is at all times!

Bath Helpers

Put small slivers of mild soap into the open end of a small sock and tie it shut, or make a small slit in a small-size sponge and insert soap. These won't slip out of small hands (or yours when washing the baby).

For a great, safe way to bathe a toddler, put a plastic laundry basket with mesh openings in the tub and put the child in it.

ROYAL DECREE: Remember to *never* leave a child alone in the bathtub.

Baby Shoes

To make baby shoes easy to polish, rub them with the cut side of a raw potato or some rubbing alcohol prior to polishing. After polishing, spray with hair spray to keep the polish from rubbing off so easily. Put a little clear nail polish on the areas that are always scuffed, and the shoes won't wear as much in those areas. And remember to keep baby from chewing on her shoes if you've used any cleaners, sprays, or polish!

Diaper Pins

If you are using cloth diapers, you know the misery of a dull diaper pin. To keep pins safely in one place where you can easily grab them and make them slide through fabric easily, stick them into a bar of soap.

Meal Mess Helper

To avoid those messy spills under baby's high chair, put a plastic tablecloth under it at mealtime. Cleanup will be a breeze, and you can even put the tablecloth in the washing machine with an old towel, detergent, and warm water. Hang to dry. This is a great tip when your toddler eats in Grandma's dining room!

Cleaning Stuffed Animals

Dust heavily with baking soda or cornstarch and work in well with your fingers. Roll the toys in towels or place in a plastic bag and leave overnight. The next day, use a clean brush to brush the toys thoroughly after removing from the bag. Doing this outdoors saves cleanup.

Rattles and Teethers

A great place to wash these is in the dishwasher. Tie them in the top basket and wash with the dishes.

Formula Stains

On white clothes, apply undiluted lemon juice and lay the garment in the sun.

On colored clothes, make a paste of unseasoned meat tenderizer and cool water or use an enzyme product from the laundry section at the grocery store. Apply and let it sit for at least 30 minutes prior to laundering. Rubbing with a bar of wet Fels-Naptha Laundry Soap will also help.

Cleaning Training Pants

To keep training pants white and odor-free, soak in a solution of 2 tablespoons of borax (available in the laundry section at the grocery store) and 1 gallon of hot water. Soak 1 hour prior to laundering.

To Remove Gum or Silly Putty from Hair

Rub cold cream or petroleum jelly into the gum. Use a dry Turkish towel (or cotton terry cloth rag) to pull down on the hair strands and petroleum jelly. Work until all is out, then double shampoo.

QUEENLY COMMENT: That old reliable peanut butter also works great when you discover your little prince has a big wad of gum in his curly locks. Massage the gum and peanut butter together between your fingers until the gum is loosened and can be removed, taking care to apply peanut butter only where it's needed. Freeze the area with ice cubes in a plastic bag and then pick out the gum. You'll have to shampoo at least twice to get out the peanut butter.

Crayon on Walls

Spray with WD-40 lubricant. Wipe off with a paper towel. Wash with hot water and liquid dishwashing detergent, working in a circular motion. Rinse well.

Crayon on Fabric

Place the stained surface down on a pad of paper towels and spray with WD-40, let it stand a few minutes, turn over, and spray the other side.

Again, let it sit a few minutes. Apply dishwashing detergent and work into the stained area, replacing the toweling as it absorbs the stain. Wash in the hottest water for the fabric you are working with, using your regular laundry detergent and all-fabric bleach.

Watercolor Paint on Fabric

Brush and rinse as much of the watercolor from the surface as possible. Apply a soft-scrubbing product with a damp sponge and rub in a circular motion, working toward the center of the spot. Rinse and dry. If any stain remains, apply nail polish remover to a cotton ball, blot the stain, and rinse thoroughly. Repeat as needed.

Watercolor Paint on Carpet

Apply rubbing alcohol with a sponge, blotting the stained area lightly. Turn the sponge as the stain is absorbed. Repeat until no more stain is being removed. Most of the remaining stain can be removed with a damp sponge and soft-scrubbing product. Rinse carpet well.

Marker Marks on Appliances, Wood, or Hard Plastic

Wipe all stains with a damp sponge. If any stain remains, apply a soft-scrubbing product with a damp sponge, working in a circular motion, and rinse. If the stain remains, saturate a cotton ball with nail polish remover, blot the remaining stain, and rinse well. This works on paneling, painted wood, tile, and no-wax vinyl floors.

Marker on Carpet

Dampen a sponge with rubbing alcohol and use a blotting motion to absorb the marker, changing the sponge as needed. Apply a good carpet stain remover, such as Spot Shot Instant Carpet Stain Remover, as directed on the can.

Marker on Clothing

Rinse the stain from the fabric with cold water until no more color is being removed. Place the fabric on paper towels and saturate with rubbing alcohol, using a cotton ball or small cloth to blot the stain. Replace the paper towels as often as needed to prevent restaining the fabric. Treat the stain with a lather from a bar of Fels-Naptha Laundry Soap and launder as usual.

Chalk on Hard Surfaces

For colored or white chalk on masonry, painted surfaces, vinyl flooring, tile, plastic, or glass, brush and rinse as much of the chalk from the surface as possible. Remove the remaining stain with a damp sponge or cloth dipped in a soft-scrubbing product. Rinse surface well.

Chalk on Carpet

Vacuum the area well, using the attachment hose to concentrate the suction over the chalk. If stain remains, use a good carpet-spotting product.

Colored Chalk on Fabric

Place the stained area on a pad of paper towels and blot the spot with rubbing alcohol. Work in a lather of Fels-Naptha Laundry Soap and launder as usual.

Glue on Carpet and Fabric

For water-based glue such as Elmer's School Glue, fold a paper towel to overlap the glue spot and saturate to almost dripping with warm water. Place this on the glue spot and leave on for 45 minutes to an hour to allow the glue to soften. Rub the glue spot with a wet rag in a circular motion to remove all the glue you can. Repeat this procedure until glue is removed. Follow with a good carpet stain remover like Spot Shot.

Silly Putty and Similar Products on Carpet and Fabric

Scrape off what you can with the dull edge of a knife. Spray with WD-40 lubricant and let stand for 10 to 15 minutes. Scrape again. Respray as required, wiping up the stain with an old rag. Once you have removed the residue of the product, apply rubbing alcohol to the stain and blot, blot, blot. Reapply as necessary.

Silly Putty and Similar Products on Hard Surfaces

To remove Silly Putty and similar products from hard surfaces, spray with WD-40 lubricant and wipe with a paper towel or old rag. Use a cloth saturated with rubbing alcohol to wipe up any remaining stain. Wash with a solution of dishwashing liquid and hot water, working in a circular motion. Rinse well.

Writing on Plastic Toys and Doll Faces

Ink and marker are very difficult to remove from plastic surfaces. Try applying a cotton ball saturated with rubbing alcohol. Let sit for 15 minutes and then rub. Sometimes using the pressure of a cotton swab dipped in alcohol helps. You can also try rubbing with a little cuticle remover on a soft cloth. Apply the cuticle remover, wait 10 minutes, and then rub gently with the cloth. Rinse well.

The Palace Pets

Do your pets have accidents in the house? Did you have a pet-sitter while you were on a trip, and when you returned you found that the cat didn't use the litter box and the dog didn't go outside? Do you know what to do when the cat leaves you a hairball surprise on the carpet or the spaghetti didn't agree with the dog? Help is on the way! Here's all the information you need to clean up pet accidents and keep them from happening again.

Pet Odor

Pet odor caused from urine or feces is one of the toughest deodorizing problems you will face, whether you live in a castle or not. The stain from the problem is only a small part of the dilemma. Unless you completely deodorize the area where the pet accident occurred, the animal, especially cats, will return to the spot and resoil it.

Pet odor is a protein-based problem and cannot be eliminated by normal spotting procedures. In order to remove odor, you must use an enzyme product to digest the protein, particularly in urine. If you do not use the correct cleaning procedure, the cat or dog will locate the smell and reuse the area.

Enzyme products may be purchased at pet supply stores, veterinary clinics, and janitorial supply stores. There are many enzyme products available. Two that I particularly like that are available nationwide are Outright Pet Odor Eliminator made by the Bramton Company and Nature's Miracle.

I have had experience with both products and find that they both work well. I tend to favor Outright because I successfully used it in my former business and have used it personally (thanks to Zack, the Palace Pussycat, my 17-pound Bengal cat) for 15 years.

Do not be fooled into believing that you can spray on a deodorizer and the odor will magically disappear. It won't happen, and you will have wasted time and money on a product that doesn't work. Now let's get to the four basic steps of pet odor removal.

1. Remove and Blot

You must remove any solid waste from the area and blot up any liquid residue using a heavy pad, paper towels, or old rags. Lay this pad on the carpet and stand on it to absorb as much liquid as possible.

2. Treat the Stain

Now you are ready to treat the accident with the enzyme product of your choice. Read the directions on the product carefully, following them exactly. Do not be afraid to really saturate the carpet. Generally, pet accidents soak through the carpet back and into the pad, so the enzyme treatment needs to soak in just as deeply. Water will not hurt your carpet; it is dipped in water numerous times during the dyeing process. If you don't put the enzyme in deeply enough, you will not eliminate the odor. This is the most important step, so be sure to saturate the entire area, covering the circumference of the stain thoroughly, too. Remember, not only does the urine go deeply into the carpet, it also spreads.

Want to know Zack, the Palace Pussycat's secret in this process? Cover the treated area with a plastic garbage bag or a dry cleaner's bag. If there is any lettering on the bag, do not let it touch the carpet or it will transfer to the carpet. Weight the plastic down with something heavy—the idea is to keep the enzyme from drying out until it can do its job, which is digesting the protein in the urine or feces. Leave the plastic in place at least 24 hours, preferably 48 hours. Resist temptation and don't peek!

3. Allow Adequate Drying Time

Uncover the area and allow it to dry thoroughly. This may require as much as a week to 10 days, depending on how deeply you treated the spot. To speed drying, let a fan blow across the area.

4. Clean the Spot

Once the area is completely dry (and only when it *is* completely dry), check for odor. If there is still odor, treat it again as directed above. If the odor is gone, clean the area with a good-quality carpet stain remover that specializes in pet stains. I like Spot Shot Instant Carpet Stain Remover. I have used it for years. It works quickly and efficiently and won't leave residue in the carpet to encourage resoiling.

If you have pets, keep some enzyme cleaner and carpet stain remover on hand for pet accident emergencies.

Don't Panic If You Have No Enzyme Product or Carpet Stain Remover!

There is hope even if you don't have an enzyme product on hand. First, soak up as much liquid as possible from the carpet and remove any solids. If you have club soda on hand, pour that on and blot by standing on paper towels or rags (if you have no club soda, then use cold water). Do this repeatedly to remove as much urine as possible. Mix a mild solution of white vinegar and water (⅓ cup of vinegar and 1 quart of cool water) in a spray bottle and spray onto pet stains to help remove the smell. Rinse with clear water and blot. Buy an enzyme product and a carpet stain remover at your earliest convenience and use them as directed above.

Oops! The Carpet Changed Color

Urine spots may change the carpet color. The carpet may be lightened or bleached. Many times this is not obvious until the carpet is cleaned for the first time after the accident. It is more common when the stain has not been treated in an appropriate manner. If this happens, try sponging the area with a mild ammonia solution. This will sometimes return the carpet to its original color or at least make the color change less noticeable.

Pet Accidents on Upholstered Furniture

When pets have accidents on upholstered furniture, you must first be sure that the fabric can be cleaned and treated with water. Check the platform of the sofa or chair under the cushion to determine the cleaning code. It should be listed on a tag. W indicates that the piece can be cleaned with water, so it can be treated as described on page 124. Clean the area using a good-quality upholstery spotting product. If the code is an S, this means solvent must be used in the cleaning process, which must be done by a professional. Do not apply an enzyme product or spotter. Call a professional. In this instance, the foam in the cushion may require replacing after cleaning.

If a pet urinates on a mattress, treat it as described on page 158 with the following exception: When you're done treating with the enzyme, cover the spot with plastic and stand the mattress on edge to expedite drying. If possible, leave the enzyme on for 12 hours. Remove the plastic and sprinkle the area with borax. Let dry thoroughly and vacuum well. If necessary, follow by cleaning with a good-quality carpet stain remover.

When the Cat Leaves You a Hairball or the Spaghetti Doesn't Agree with the Dog

If you have pets, you know what it's like when your cat or dog suffers a digestive upset. You hear the problem begin and run to move the dog or cat off the carpet (which seems to be their favorite place to leave "gifts"), but you're too late and faced with a mess to clean up.

First, resist the temptation to wipe up the mess. If there are solids that can be picked up with a paper towel, do so, but do not smear the accident into the carpet. Trying to immediately wipe up more liquid messes will only make the mess worse. Instead, sprinkle a heavy coating of baking soda on the area and allow it to dry. The baking soda will absorb moisture and digestive acids. Once the area is dry, remove with paper towels or vacuum the area, removing all of the mess that will come up. Vacuum very thoroughly to remove the baking soda. Then and only then, you should grab the rag and the cleaner. Use your favorite carpet stain remover, following the directions carefully. Remember to blot rather than rub.

If any discoloration remains after cleaning, try applying either undiluted lemon juice or hydrogen peroxide from the drugstore. Let it soak into the stain for 15 minutes and then blot. If the spot is still visible, apply again, watching carefully to be sure that there are no changes in carpet color.

A WORD FROM ZACK, THE PALACE PUSSYCAT: If you need a more aggressive treatment, mix lemon juice and cream of tartar into a thin paste. Apply to the spot, let dry, and then vacuum up. When done with any of these procedures, rinse the carpet with cool water.

Removing Pet Hair from Fabric

Sometimes the vacuum cleaner isn't enough to remove pet hair from upholstered furniture. If this is true in your case, try one of the following methods.

- Dampen a sponge and wipe over the furniture, rinsing the sponge as necessary.
- Wipe in a downward motion with your hands while wearing rubber gloves.
- Wrap tape around your hands, sticky side out, and swipe over the hair, changing the tape as needed.

- Wipe with a dampened body-washing puff.

- Wipe with a used dryer fabric softener sheet.

Keeping Cats from Digging in Your Houseplants

To keep your cat from digging in indoor flowerpots, place cotton balls dipped in oil of clove just below the soil lines.

If your pet is eating your houseplants, here's a great product to try: It's called Bitter Apple and is simply sprayed on the plant leaves. It won't hurt the plant or your pet. Its bitter taste will immediately stop the pet from chewing on the plants. Try your local pet store.

Keeping Fleas Out of Doghouses

To deter fleas, sprinkle salt in the crevices of the doghouse.

If Your Pet Meets the Wrong End of a Skunk . . .

If your pet meets the smelly end of a skunk, apply Massengill douche, mixed as directed on the box. Do this outside your home, and do not rinse the dog. To avoid getting the product into the dog's eyes, apply a little petroleum jelly around the eye area.

3
Royal Robes and Related Matters

Laundry Matters in the Palace

A Queen and her court always need to look their best, and taking proper care of clothing is one of the most time-consuming duties a Queen undertakes each week. Once you're loaded with helpful tips and tricks for getting and keeping clothes clean, though, the job will go much quicker.

Clothing Care Labels: What Are They Good For?

When you examine a label, do you look at the size and nothing else? Well, you're missing out on a lot of valuable information. Care labels are very important. You should read each and every one of them before you purchase a garment and each time you have it cleaned.

The Federal Trade Commission (FTC) requires manufacturers to attach a permanent label to textile garments indicating directions for care. This label must be easily located. It should not separate from the garment, and it should remain legible during the life span of the garment. The label must warn about any part of the recommended care method that could harm the garment or other garments being laundered or dry-cleaned with it. It must also specify if a garment cannot be cleaned without damage.

Symbols may also appear on a care label to supplement written instructions. When a garment carries an international symbol tag, all care methods will usually be listed.

May I Remove the Care Label?

Garments are required by law to have a care label attached at the time of sale. Of course, no law can take into account a woman wearing a little black dress with a big white care label hanging out the back. Removing the care tag does entail some risk, though; you may forget the proper cleaning instructions, and your dry cleaner will not have access to some valuable information.

If you do remove care labels, mark them with a description of the item and put them in a safe place where they can be easily located. You might remember today that your favorite summer dress should be washed in cold water and laid flat to dry, but by next summer you may have forgotten this entirely. A corkboard in the laundry room is wonderful; you could staple the care label to a small index card and identify the garment by describing the color and type of garment it is. Tack the card on the corkboard, and you'll have care directions at your fingertips. Other family members (who might surprise you by doing the laundry sometime) can always "check the board" before throwing your little black sequined dress in the washing machine. Remember to remove labels or cards from the board when you no longer have the item.

Cleaning Instructions

It takes only a few seconds to glance at the care label inside your garment, and those few seconds of time will determine if your clothes will successfully make it through their trip into the washing machine or if they are better off being dry-cleaned. Read, read, read care labels; your clothes will thank you!

Dry-clean. A garment marked "dry-clean only" can be cleaned using normal dry-cleaning fluid found in any commercial or coin-operated dry-cleaning establishment. Be aware that dry cleaning, despite its name, is not necessarily dry. Water may be involved in the process, whether by moisture added to the fluid or by steam press or steam air-form finishing.

Professionally dry-clean. If your garment is marked "professionally dry-clean," then it is restricted to the dry-cleaning methods possible only in commercial dry-cleaning plants. A label marked "professionally dry-clean" must be accompanied by further information, such as "use reduced moisture," "low heat," or "no steam finishing." Your dry cleaner should be alert to these labels, but there's no harm in pointing them out.

Machine-wash. This indicates use of either a commercial or home washing machine. Other information may be included, such as specific washing temperatures, size of load, or drying instructions.

Does "Washable" Also Mean Dry-Cleanable?

If a garment care label says "washable," it may be safely dry-cleaned . . . or it may not be safely dry-cleaned! Unfortunately, there is no way of telling from the label. A manufacturer is required to list only one safe method of cleaning, no matter how many other methods can be safely employed. And be warned: Manufacturers are not required to alert you to care procedures that may *not* be safe.

Doing the Laundry-Sorting Boogie

Now it's time to actually do the laundry! Make it easy on yourself. Sort *before* you start to wash. Some people like the grab-and-stuff laundry method: they grab the clothes—no matter what fabric or color—and stuff them into the machine, as many as they can at one time. These people are easy to recognize. They're the ones with pink underwear, color-streaked clothes, shrunken sweaters, short pants, and clothes that are otherwise "challenged." Sort your laundry for best results. You'll thank me for this advice, I assure you.

Sorting Clothes

Here's how you should separate wash loads.

- Dark fabrics from white and light-colored fabrics
- Lightly soiled clothes from heavily soiled garments, such as work clothes
- Fabrics by water temperature (hot, warm, or cold)
- Fabrics that will shed lint on other fabrics (terry cloth, corduroy, flannel, and so forth)
- Lingerie, hose, and delicate fabrics that should be washed in a mesh bag
- Clothes that may have fugitive color and bleed onto others

Do This *Before* You Wash

Remember the old adage: A stitch in time saves nine. Avoid snags, tangles, tears, and trouble by following these quick steps.

- Button buttons.
- Hook bras.
- Zip zippers.
- Tie sashes, cords, and straps to prevent tangling.
- Check pockets for coins, tissues, pens, and other laundry nasties.
- Remove anything on the garment that cannot be washed.
- Repair tears so that they don't become larger while agitating.
- Secure hems if they're starting to fall so that you won't have to resew the entire hem after the wash cycle.

Time to Pretreat!

Even if a garment looks as if it might be better on the rag pile, give pre-treating a chance! You may be able to save it with just a little care. Here's what to do.

- Check for spots, spills, splatters, and stains before putting a load of clothes into the washer.

- Pretreat these with one of the spotters you'll find on page 24, or go to the A-to-Z Palace Spot and Stain Removal Guide on page 327 for help and advice.

- Soak heavily soiled garments before laundering. Do *not* soak wool, spandex, silk, or fabrics that are not colorfast.

Mark the Spot

Use a brightly colored clothespin to mark the stain, or use a rubber band and wrap it around the area that needs to be spotted prior to laundering. Have family members do this *before* they put their clothes into the hamper. This will make spots and stains easier to locate and easier to treat. Spots will be obvious, so you don't need to examine each article as you sort.

Now You're Ready to Wash!

Add detergent to the washer as it fills up with water. If you are using cold water and powdered detergent, you can be sure that all the detergent dissolves by mixing it with a little hot water before adding it to the machine. If you still find powder residue on your clothing, consider switching to a liquid detergent. Add additional laundry aids such as bleach, water softener, or laundry booster as the washer fills so they'll dissolve or be thoroughly mixed in before you toss in your favorite blouse or comfiest pair of jeans.

Load the machine with dirty clothes, but do not overload it. If you stuff too many garments into the machine, the clothes will not get very clean and will have more wrinkles, too.

Make sure your load is balanced—not all bunched on one side of the agitator—especially if you are washing one large or heavy item, such as a blanket or bath mat.

ROYAL DECREE: Don't leave the house while you're doing laundry. If the washing machine malfunctions or a hose breaks, you'll come home to a disaster.

If you have room in your laundry or closet areas, provide several different colored laundry baskets so that family members can sort dirty clothes as they take them off. Try having a basket for whites, colors, jeans (if your family wears a lot of them), and delicates. You'll be off to a good start if most of the laundry is presorted. I like to say that the whole laundry-sorting boogie will go faster if you're organized! Use these colored baskets to hold clean clothes that are ready to be folded and to carry clothes that can be put away.

Dryer Dilemmas

It's time to talk about some quick, easy tips to make the job of drying wet clothes a lot easier. Anyone who does laundry knows how a little "Oops!" can happen and how frustrating it can be. So let's de-oops the clothes dryer!

The Lowdown on Lint

If you're drying clothes that have lint (or a big "Oops!"—a tissue in the washing machine), put a piece of nylon net in the dryer along with the clothes. The net will catch the lint so you won't have to drag out the lint roller or, worse still, pick off all of the fuzz by hand. I buy cheap nylon net from a fabric store and throw it out when it's full of lint.

The Wrinkle on Clothes

We all know that if you take items out of the dryer as soon as it shuts off, you can fold or hang your clothes with little or no ironing. But you can't always get to the dryer immediately. Let's be honest: How many times have you gone to the dryer and found a load of clothes that were forgotten? Another "Oops!" The clothes are a mass of wrinkles! Don't go to the trouble of rewashing the clothes, and don't iron them either. Just toss a damp towel in the dryer and rerun the load for a few minutes. The wrinkles will release, and you can hang up the clothes. Be sure not to use a white towel with dark clothes, or you will give yourself another problem—lint!

Accidental Messes in the Dryer

To remove crayon, lipstick, or Chap Stick from inside the dryer, turn off the dryer and spray a paper towel with WD-40 lubricant. Wipe out the dryer until all of the mess is removed. Wash the dryer out with warm water and dishwashing liquid, then toss in a load of old wet rags and dry them.

Try Carbona Stain Devils to remove chewing gum and glue. For ink, use rubbing alcohol or Ink Away by the makers of Goo Gone.

Dryer No-Nos

Don't put stained or spotted clothes in the dryer. The heat will set the stain, making it next to impossible to remove. Instead, treat the stain with one of the appropriate methods mentioned in this book, and launder again. (See chapter 14 and the A-to-Z Palace Spot and Stain Removal Guide on page 327.)

ROYAL DECREE: Do not put anything in the dryer that has come in contact with paint, gasoline, oil used on machinery, or any flammable fluids. These things are fire hazards, and the fumes they give off can ignite. If they are heated in a dryer, you could start a fire or create a hazardous situation in your home. Be sure to line-dry these items instead, even after repeated washings. Trust me—you do *not* want to have to refer to "Dealing with Household Damage," on page 365!

GETTING THE MOST OUT OF YOUR DRYER

Let your dryer work more efficiently by following these guidelines.

- Clean the dryer lint filter after each use.
- Always check to see that the dryer is empty before using it.
- Avoid drying extremely small loads or crowding the dryer with extra-large loads. Very small loads can clump, and very large loads don't tumble well. Both waste time and energy.
- Dry lightweight fabrics together and heavy fabrics together for more efficient drying.
- Dry loads one after another. That way, you can utilize the heat already in the dryer.
- Don't add wet clothes to clothes that are almost dry. This wastes energy and money!

Getting the Hang of Line-Drying

We have come full circle. For years it seemed as though the dryer had taken over and that clotheslines were obsolete. Now, we are returning to the days of natural fabrics, with drip-dry clothes, clothes that need to be laid flat to dry, and clothes that cannot be put in the dryer for any reason. Don't worry. You don't need a clothesline in the backyard to care for some of these hang-to-dry clothes.

The Basics

As your grandma will tell you, don't spin out too much water from clothes that you are going to hang to dry: spinning sets in the wrinkles. Instead, shut off the washer halfway through the spin cycle and hang the clothes on a clothesline, allowing for plenty of air circulation between clothes. Dry colored clothes out of direct sunlight (the sun fades them), but hang white clothes in the sun—this will bleach them to an incredible, eye-popping white. They'll smell great, too.

Hanging clothes on plastic hangers with sloped ends will allow them to dry without those awful "shoulder dimples." You'll avoid rust that way, too!

Line-Drying Special Garments

I've line-dried many royal robes in my day and have a few tricks up my velvet sleeve when it comes to line-drying. Here they are.

Trousers. Hang these by the cuffs. The weight of the trousers will usually keep the legs wrinkle-free, which means less or no pressing. We like that!

THE QUEEN'S BEST DRYING TIPS

Whether you're drying your special occasion clothes, your work-around-the-palace clothes, or your luxurious linens, these handy hints will keep your things looking magnificent.

- If you use a clothesline outside, keep it clean by wiping it down periodically. Wet an old rag and run it over the line before hanging clothes.
- Strong sunlight will eventually weaken fibers, so keep an eye on the clothes and bring them in as soon as they are dry.
- Bedding washed and hung out to dry occasionally will be crisp and fresh-smelling. White linens will be brighter!
- Do not air-dry down comforters. They dry slowly, and mold or mildew may form in the process. Follow the instructions on the care label.
- A tension curtain rod hung in a laundry room makes a great place to hang clothes to dry. A piece of chain also works well, and you can hook hangers through the links.
- If a garment label says "hang to dry," don't put it in the dryer. It may shrink, or the fibers may distort.
- If clothes are wrinkled after line-drying, putting them in the dryer on the "no heat" or "air fluff" setting may save you from ironing them. (Do not use a fabric softener sheet, though. Without heat, fabric softener sheets can stain clothes.)

Sweaters. To prevent sweaters from having shoulder dimples or "clothespin points," thread the legs of an old pair of panty hose through the arms of the sweater, and pull the waist out through the neck opening. Attach clothespins to the feet and waist of the panty hose instead of to the sweater. Just make sure to remove the panty hose before you put on the sweater—unless you plan to rob a bank . . .

Dresses and coats. When hanging heavy dresses and coats to dry, use two hangers to absorb the weight. If hanging dresses or coats outside to dry, hook the two hangers in opposite directions to keep the breeze from blowing the garment off the line.

Lingerie and panty hose. These are better dried in the house over the shower bar, on a small bathroom clothesline, or from plastic hangers with clips.

Know When to Hold 'em, Know When to Fold 'em

Normally, I don't like to use the F-word—folding, that is. But yes, it's sad but true, there are some clothes that simply cannot be hung on a hanger; they must be folded. Don't worry, though. You don't have to be the Empress of Elbow Grease to quickly fold clothes and put them away.

It's best to hang items that wrinkle easily, such as cotton and rayon. Blouses, dress shirts, and dresses (that aren't knitted) are best on a hanger as well. It's best if you fold knits because they can easily stretch out of shape.

Consider the space your clothes have to fit into before you fold them. If, for example, drawer space is at a premium in your house, consider rolling things such as underwear, T-shirts, socks, and towels. You can fit more rolled clothes into a drawer or cupboard than if they're folded flat, and wrinkles will be minimal. Rolled clothes also save lots of room in your suitcase—an added bonus for frequent travelers.

Sweaters and sweatshirts are best folded, and you will never have shoulder dimples either. To fold, lay the garment facedown and fold each side to meet in the middle at the back. This will avoid a line running down the center of your garment. Fold the sleeves down the back of the garment, and then fold the garment in half lengthwise. These items can also be rolled effectively.

Socks can be rolled toe to top. You might also want to consider investing in drawer dividers made specifically for socks and hose. You will never find your socks in a tangled mess—or, worse still, missing—with sock dividers. Colors will be obvious and easy to pick out, too.

Fitted sheets can be tamed. Fold them in half lengthwise, and then fold each curved end into the middle. Now you have a square end to work with. Fold in half again and then either roll or continue to fold to the size that best fits your storage area. If you don't mind the same sheets on the bed each week, wash them, dry them, and put them back on straightaway—you will never have to fold them again!

Fold rubber- or latex-backed rugs with the fabric side in to prevent the backing from sticking together during storage.

Consider using hooks on the back of the closet doors for robes and nightclothes. Don't use suction hooks, though. They're not strong enough to hold clothes.

If doing underwear for multiple family members together, consider buying different brands for each person to make sorting and folding go faster. Try this with socks, too.

THE ELUSIVE SOCK MONSTER

Just to set the record straight, washers and dryers positively do *not* eat socks. Nor is there a sock monster in your utility room that steals them! Missing socks can sometimes be found wedged between the drum and the machine. Check your pant legs and shirt sleeves, and check the dryer hose, too. I once found a lonely sock on the driveway—it had tried to escape by shimmying out the dryer hose and up through the vent!

Keeping a tension curtain rod or shower rod set up in the laundry room makes it easy to hang clothes as you remove them from the dryer. Let each person claim his or her own hanging clothes and basket of ready-to-fold or folded clothes. This will cut your laundry time way down.

QUEENLY COMMENT: If the kids have to fold their own clothes, don't let them dress out of the laundry basket all week; make sure they put away their things. If the basket stays full of clean clothes, you might just discover that they're throwing the dirty clothes on the floor all week!

Ironing and Ironing Boards: Taking the Heat

Nobody likes to iron, but occasionally, no matter how carefully you launder and dry your clothes, you're going to have to iron them, too. Ironing can be a nasty chore, but I have some ways to make it easier. Just think of me as Chairman of the Ironing Board!

First of all, if you have to iron, do it in a place you enjoy. Set up the ironing board in the family room or somewhere you can watch television as you work, or near the stereo where you can listen to some music or a book on audiotape. You might even like to set it up in a room where the family is gathered so that you can all visit as you work. You can also enlist family members to hang up and put away their clothes as you iron them. (And don't assume I'm talking to Mom. Dad should be able to do the ironing just as well!) Now to the basics.

Make the Most of Your Time at the Board

Even though some folks find ironing to be a stress reliever or a great place to think through the mysteries of life, many others probably just want the job done—and done quickly. Either way, my methods are efficient and easy to use.

Energy-efficient ironing. Put aluminum foil—shiny side up—between the ironing board and the ironing board cover. The aluminum foil will reflect the heat upward onto the garments you are ironing, so it will take less time to iron.

Keeping ironing boards clean. To keep your ironing board clean longer, spray the cover with spray starch and iron over it.

Ironing delicate fabrics. The secret to ironing these fabrics is to lay a "press cloth" over them and iron on that. A man's handkerchief (white is ideal) or any piece of lightweight white cotton will work fine. Never lay a bare iron on delicate fabrics.

Ironing collars. Iron both sides of the collar for a crisp, smooth finish. Start at the point and iron inward to the center to avoid pushing creases to the tip.

Seams and hems. To avoid creating a line over seams and hems, iron the garment inside out and stop just short of the seam or hemline.

Pressing embroidery. Lay the piece of embroidery facedown on a towel, and iron it on the reverse side. That way, you won't flatten the embroidery.

Handling large items. Before you start ironing, turn the ironing board around so that you are using the wide end rather than the point. You can cover more area if you iron this way. Fold items, such as large tablecloths, in half and iron one side, then fold in half again and iron the both sides.

Dampening clothes. Our moms use to sprinkle clothes with water to help release the wrinkles and make ironing easier. This is still a good idea, especially with all the natural fibers we are wearing. Items that are too dry are very difficult to iron, so use a spray bottle to mist clothes that have dried. If clothes are heavily wrinkled, lay a damp towel on the ironing board and iron *with steam*. This works remarkably well on heavy trousers and jeans.

The shoulder pad challenge. Try not to iron over shoulder pads, or they will leave ugly rings on the fabric. Just an additional note: Before you launder shoulder pads, tack the filling and the cover of the shoulder pad together so that it will not shift during the laundry and ironing process.

IRONING DO'S AND DON'TS

You may not want to go back to basics, but it's always good to take a refresher course. Who knows? You just might learn a little something from the Queen!

- Do clean the iron if it sticks, jerks, or leaves a film on the ironing board cover. Never iron clothes with a dirty iron soleplate. The iron needs to be cleaned before you iron clothes.
- Do use only a cool iron on synthetic fibers.
- Do start with a cool to warm iron if you're not sure what the fabric is.
- Do test-iron in an inconspicuous area. If in doubt about the fiber content, use a press cloth to avoid "shine" on the fabric surface.
- Do empty the water from the steam iron when you are done using it to prevent mineral buildup in the water reservoir.
- Don't iron over zippers, buttons, or any lumps.
- Don't iron rubber, suede, leather, or stretch-type fabric.
- Don't iron dirty clothes or clothes that you have perspired in. It will set the stains and damage the fibers.

Right Side, Wrong Side, Which Side?

Iron cotton, net, or silky rayon right side up. These fabrics tend to wrinkle more than others, and ironing them on the wrong side will not get all the wrinkles out.

Iron polyester on either side. Iron other garments on the wrong side of the fabric for best results. You'll avoid scorch marks, shiny spots, and other fabric damage.

Yikes! The Iron Was Too Hot!

If you've scorched something with a too-hot iron, try soaking the fabric in cold water overnight. That may remove the scorch mark.

On white fabrics, try saturating a cloth with 3 percent hydrogen peroxide. Lay the cloth over the scorch and iron over it until the mark is removed. Do *not* use this method on colored fabric.

Refer to the A-to-Z Palace Spot and Stain Removal Guide on page 327 for more ways to treat scorch marks.

Taking the Dread Out of Dry Cleaning

Not everything we wear can be laundered, and that means a trip to the dry cleaner and the dreaded game of "Will that spot come out?" Most people end up at the dry cleaner because they have clothing stains they can't get out themselves. Luckily for us, professional dry cleaners, with their special solvents, equipment, and training, can remove some of the most disastrous-looking stains rather simply. Successful stain removal depends on three things: the nature of the stain, the type of fabric, and the colorfastness of the dye. Remember to check your care labels. Not all fabrics and dyes are made to withstand the use of cleaning or stain removal agents. Here's what to do with a couple types of stains.

Invisible Stains

Many stains that are caused by food, oily substances, or beverages may become invisible when they dry. Later on, with exposure to heat or the passage of time, a yellowish or brownish stain will appear. You have probably seen this on clothes you have hung away and pulled out months later. This is caused by the oxidation of the sugar in the staining substance. It is the same thing that makes an apple turn brown once it is peeled and exposed to the air.

You can be a better dry-cleaning customer and help your dry cleaner do a better job for you by pointing out such stains when you take a garment in to be cleaned. The cleaner often treats these stains prior to cleaning, much as you prespot your laundry at home. This pretreatment is vital since the heat of drying or finishing may set the stain, making it impossible to remove.

When an oily substance is exposed to heat or when it ages in a piece of clothing for a long period of time, it oxidizes. You can recognize this type of stain by its irregular shape on the fabric. Oily stains can be removed easily during the dry-cleaning process, provided they have not been there for an extended period of time. Once they are yellow or brown, they are almost impossible to remove.

Perspiration Stains

Perspiration can also cause problem stains, especially on silk and wool clothes. Perspiration left in a silk garment can eventually cause deterioration of the fibers.

Repeated exposure to perspiration and body oils can leave clothing with a permanent yellow discoloration and even an offensive odor. Perspiration can react with the dye in the fabric, making it even more difficult to remove the stain.

If you perspire heavily, have your clothes cleaned more frequently, especially in the warmer months.

Important Reminders

Make sure that you point out any unusual care instructions to your cleaner, and make sure that you point out spots and spills, identifying them wherever possible.

Whether you are doing the cleaning yourself or a professional is doing it, treatment of spots and spills with the right spotter is essential.

If you remove the care tag, it's a good idea to label it clearly—that is, identify the garment to which it belongs—and pin it to a corkboard in your laundry room for future reference.

Dry cleaners attempt to remove stains in accordance with professional practice. Sadly, not all stains can be removed, despite the dry cleaner's best efforts. The more information you give to your dry cleaner and the sooner a garment is brought in, the greater the chance of success in stain removal.

Queenly Care for Fabrics and Clothing

Even if you read fabric care labels, it's helpful to have a friend (a Queen in this case!) who can give you extra advice on keeping your special fabrics and clothes looking their best. From preserving wedding wear and furs to getting the grime out of work clothes, you've come to the right chapter for handy tips and tricks.

Cleaning Guide for Fabric Types

I am the "stain stalker," and in these next pages I am going to walk you through laundry procedures for certain fabric types and unusual items.

Acetate. This is a temperamental fabric. Do not allow it to become heavily soiled, and do not use an enzyme detergent when laundering. Acetate is commonly used for curtains, brocades, taffetas, and satin.

(Think "evening wear"!) It's also a popular lining. You can machine-wash acetate in cold water, or you can hand-wash it. Be sure not to spin or wring acetate, because this will set in wrinkles. Rinse extremely well and press with a cool (low setting) iron on the wrong side of the fabric.

Acrylic. This fabric should be laundered frequently since it can retain perspiration odors. Acrylic is usually machine washable in cool water. Check the care label. Dry flat or hang to dry, being sure to reshape the garment while it is still damp.

Angora. This wool is made from rabbit fur or goat hair. Angora sheds a lot—although if it's blended with nylon, it will shed less. Wash angora in warm or cool water, using a very mild soap or a little shampoo. Do not rub, twist, or lift the garment up and down in the water, because this may cause it to stretch. Washing in a sink is best. Let the water run out and then press the liquid out of the garment. Rinse well again, pressing the water out. Roll the garment in a towel and then reshape. Dry flat out of the sun. Do not press angora; instead, hold a steam iron just above the garment to remove any wrinkles.

Blends. Blends, such as cotton/polyester, are made from combined fibers. To launder these fabrics, follow the guidelines for the most delicate or the most prominent fiber. The most common blends are cotton/polyester, cotton/linen, and silk/polyester.

Brocades. Use care when laundering brocades. You don't want to crush or flatten the pile design. Hand-wash in cool water or dry-clean according to the care label. Do not wring. Iron on the wrong side of brocades, using a press cloth or towel between the fabric and the iron.

Canvas. A heavy, firm, very tightly woven fabric, canvas was originally made from cotton or linen, but now it comes in synthetics or blends. Machine-wash canvas in cold water and tumble dry on a low setting. Test for colorfastness before washing. If it's not colorfast, have it dry-cleaned.

Cashmere. This is an expensive fiber that comes from the undercoat of cashmere goats. Treat it with respect. Dry-clean these prizes or hand-wash with care in cool water and well-dissolved gentle soap. Rinse well, and do not wring. Dry flat, reshaping the garment as it dries. Iron on the wrong side while still damp with a cool iron, if necessary.

Chiffon. This is a very thin, transparent fabric, made from silk or synthetic fibers. Hand-wash as you would silk.

Chintz. Chintz is actually glazed cotton and is often printed with a pattern. Dry-clean this fabric unless the label states that it can be washed. Follow the care label instructions carefully.

Corduroy. Take care when washing corduroy. It wears well, but care is needed to avoid crushing and distorting the pile. Turn corduroy inside out and launder using warm water. Dry at a normal setting. Remove from the dryer while still damp and smooth the seams, pockets, and cuffs. Hang garments to complete drying, and iron on the wrong side of the fabric. The pile may be restored by brushing it gently.

Cotton. This natural vegetable fiber is woven and knitted into fabrics in all weights and textures. Hand-wash lightweight fabrics, such as

SPOTS & SPLATTERS

Crown Jewels

Dear Queen:
How can I clean marks from gold and silver jewelry off cotton, silk, and wool? I have coated the back and sides of gold and silver jewelry with clear nail polish, but I still end up with black marks at the necklines of my clothing.

The Queen Responds:
Prevention is the best answer in this case. Purchase some of the ACT Natural microfiber cloths from www.euronetusa.com. Wipe your jewelry with a damp ACT Natural cloth, and then buff jewelry pieces with a dry cloth each time you wear them—that should keep the jewelry from creating stains on your clothes.

organdy and batiste, and hang them to air-dry. Iron cotton clothes when damp with a hot iron to remove most wrinkles.

Machine-wash light-colored and white medium to heavyweight cottons in warm water. Use cold water for bright colors that may bleed. Dry on a low dryer setting. Remove from the dryer while still damp, and iron with a hot iron right away.

Damask. This is a jacquard-weave fabric. It may be made of cotton, linen, silk, wool, or a blend of fibers. Hand-wash lightweight fabrics and be sure to check the individual fiber listings and care label. Dry-clean silk, wool, and all heavier weight fabrics.

Denim. If you have jeans, you know this strong fabric is prone to shrinking, streaking, and fading. Machine-wash denim in warm water. Blue and other deep colors bleed the first several washings, so be sure to wash these separately. Washing older, faded jeans with the new ones will restore some of their original color. Dry at low settings to avoid shrinkage. Iron while damp, if necessary, and be aware that jeans may bleed color onto your ironing board.

Down. Down is the soft underfeather of waterfowl that is often combined with adult feathers. It is machine washable *and* dry-cleanable. Just be sure to follow the care label closely. Much of the treatment will depend on the fabric covering the down, so pay attention to manufacturer's directions.

Do not air-dry down. It dries too slowly, and mold or mildew may form in the process. Dry down items in your dryer, or use a large-capacity dryer if needed. Set temperatures low (under 140°F), fluffing and turning the item often. Make sure to dry the item thoroughly. This can take time.

👑 **QUEENLY COMMENT: Want really fluffy duvets and pillows? Putting a clean tennis shoe or tennis ball in with the item will fluff it up!**

Flannel. Flannel is actually a napped fabric, and it comes in a plain or twill-type weave. Cotton and synthetics should be washed according to the care label, but when in doubt, use cool water and mild detergent.

Dry at a low dryer setting, and remove flannel while damp to avoid wrinkles. You may also line-dry this fabric. Wool flannel should be dry-cleaned.

Gabardine. Gabardine is a firm, tightly woven twill fabric, often made of worsted wool, but sometimes made of cotton and synthetic fibers. There are large amounts of synthetic fibers sold as gabardine in trousers and blazers for men and women. Follow your label directions—many synthetics are machine washable and dryable. If the care label says to dry-clean it, be sure to do so.

Lace. An extremely delicate fabric, lace may be made of cotton, linen, or synthetic fiber. Wash using a mild soap or detergent intended for delicates. Avoid rubbing since it will distort the fibers. Rinse well without wringing, shape by hand, and hang to air-dry or dry flat. Delicate lace pieces may need to be reshaped and pinned down to dry. If you must iron lace, do so over a terry cloth towel. (White is best.) Never put lace in the dryer.

Leather and suede. Generally, leather and suede are not washable. Check your care label carefully. If you have washable leather items, wash them by hand and be sure to protect them with a leather spray protectant. To clean suede, rub it with another piece of suede or a suede brush (not any other kind of brush) to restore the nap and keep it looking new.

Remember, leather needs to breathe, so do not cover it with plastic or store it in a tightly enclosed area. If you are looking for a dust cover for leather or suede, use cloth—an old pillowcase is ideal.

To remove spots from leather (don't try this on suede!), try using cuticle remover. Rub it into the spot, wait 10 minutes, and then massage the area with a cloth dipped in the cuticle remover. Wipe down thoroughly.

To remove spots from suede, try dabbing them with white vinegar.

Linen. A tough fabric that withstands high temperatures, linen is a favorite in hot climates. It is made of natural flax fiber and comes in light to heavyweight fabrics. Hand-wash or machine-wash linen in warm water (again, read your care label). If the fabric is colorfast, you may remove stains and brighten the fabric with an oxygen bleach or Brilliant Bleach from Soapworks. Do not use chlorine bleach.

Iron linen while it is still damp. To help prevent creasing, you may treat it with starch or sizing. Press heavyweight linens with a hot iron; press lighter weight linen and linen blends (linen, plus other fibers) with a warm iron.

Linen is also dry-cleanable.

Mohair. An oldie but a goodie! Mohair fiber is taken from Angora goats. When cleaning mohair, follow the directions for cleaning wool.

Nylon. This is a durable synthetic fiber that comes in varying weights and is often blended with other fibers. When used alone, it is machine washable in warm water. It can also be dry-cleaned. When cleaning a nylon blend, check the care label.

Dry on a low setting or hang to dry using a nonmetal hanger. Do not dry nylon in sunlight, because it may yellow. Nonchlorine bleach is best for nylon.

Organdy. Think "party dress"! Sheer and lightweight, organdy is actually a cotton fiber. Hand-wash organdy, and iron it with a hot iron when it's damp. Use starch as you iron to give organdy a crisp look. May also be dry-cleaned.

Polyester. This strong synthetic fiber won't stretch or shrink, which is probably why it's so popular. It comes in various weights and textures, and it is often found blended with cotton and wool.

Wash polyester in warm water. Tumble dry, but don't let it sit in the dryer, because that will encourage wrinkles. Remove it immediately, and you may not need to iron it. If ironing *is* necessary, make sure to use a low setting.

If the polyester is blended with another fiber, just follow the washing instructions for the more delicate fiber.

Ramie. Very similar to linen, ramie is a natural fiber made from—what else?—the ramie plant! It can be used alone or blended with other fibers; you'll often see clothes with the fiber content marked as ramie/cotton.

Machine-wash in warm water, tumble dry, and iron while damp with a hot iron. Avoid twisting the fibers, or they will become distorted. May be dry-cleaned, too.

Rayon. This is a synthetic fiber that is sometimes called viscose. Follow the care label directions closely, but for the very best results, have this fabric dry-cleaned. Dry-cleaning not only cleans well but also gives rayon the crisp pressing it needs to maintain its shape and good looks.

Satin. Originally made only from silk, this shiny fabric is now available in acetate, cotton, nylon, and even polyester.

Dry-clean satin made out of silk and acetate. You may wash cotton, nylon, and polyester satins, as long as you follow the washing instructions for those fibers.

Seersucker. You've seen this fabric in shirts, blouses, and nightwear. It has puckered stripes that are woven in during the manufacturing process. Seersucker is most frequently made of cotton, but it's also available in nylon and polyester. Check the fiber content and then follow the washing and drying instructions for those fibers.

Drip-dry or tumble dry and iron on low heat if necessary.

Silk. This is a natural fiber made by the silkworm. It is a delicate fabric that requires special care to avoid damage. Check the care labels, but you may be able to hand-wash crepe de chine and lightweight and medium-weight silk in lukewarm water with mild soap or detergent. You can also use cold water with cold-water detergent.

Do not use chlorine bleach. You may use Brilliant Bleach by Soapworks without damaging the fibers.

Rinsing silk well is important. Rinse several times in cold water to remove all suds. Towel blot and dry flat. Do not wring or rub silk. Iron on the wrong side of the fabric with a warm iron.

If your care label indicates that the garment is machine washable, follow the directions with the utmost care. Dry cleaning works best for suits, pleated silks, and silks that are not colorfast. Do not use strong spotters or enzyme spotters on silk.

Spandex. Spandex is added to other fibers to give them stretch and elasticity. Machine-wash spandex garments in warm water on the delicate or gentle cycle. Do not use chlorine bleach. Do not put them in the dryer, or iron them; high heat will break down spandex fibers. Line-dry or dry flat, following directions on the care label.

If you have exercise clothes containing spandex, be sure to launder them each time you wear them. Body oil can also break down spandex fibers.

Terry cloth. A toweling-type of fabric, terry cloth has a looped pile made of cotton or cotton/polyester blend. You find it in towels, of course, and even sleepwear.

Machine-wash terry cloth in warm or hot water. Tumble or line-dry. Add softener for a softer texture.

Velour. This is a napped fabric that is available in wool, cotton, silk, and synthetics. Dry-clean unless the care label indicates it can be washed and dried.

Velvet. A beautiful soft pile fabric, velvet comes in silk, rayon, or cotton. Dry-clean for best results.

To raise the pile on velvet, steam from the wrong side over a pot of boiling water. Hold the fabric at least 12 inches from the water, and be careful not to allow the fabric to come in contact with the water. This works well for creases in the back of dresses.

Wool. This is a natural fiber made from the fleece of sheep. Hand-wash sweaters and other knits in cold water with cold-water detergent. Rinse several times, and do not wring or twist. Towel blot and dry flat, reshaping as needed.

Perspiration Stains: They're the Pits!

Perspiration will weaken fabrics, so treat vulnerable areas with care, following my surefire methods for removing perspiration stains.

Don't Wait!

The best time to treat those invisible perspiration problems is right after you wear a garment for the first time, and *before* you toss it in the washer.

The No-Sweat Solution

Moisten the underarm area—or any other spot where perspiration stains are a problem—and work in a lather of Fels-Naptha Laundry Soap. Once you've worked up a good lather, toss the garment in the machine, and launder as usual. If odor is present, apply warm water to the area and work in 20 Mule Team Borax. Let sit for 30 minutes or so, then launder.

You can also work Biz Activated Nonchlorine Bleach into the stained fabric for an effective solution to perspiration stains. Just make sure to wet the offending area first.

(crown) **QUEENLY COMMENT: Odorzout is also an extremely effective odor eliminator. Use it dry on those smelly areas. You can leave it on overnight—you can even put some in your clothes hamper.**

Stain, Stain, Go Away

If you discover stains on a recently washed garment, don't despair! Try dampening the fabric with warm water and working in laundry detergent and Biz. Let that soak for about 30 minutes and launder as usual.

I have found that soaking garments (whites or colors) in Brilliant Bleach from Soapworks is very effective for removing underarm stains.

You can also try to clean existing stains with heated white vinegar. Spray it on the fabric and then work in 20 Mule Team Borax. This works well on odors as well as stains.

If the fabric has changed color from perspiration stains, try spraying with sudsy ammonia, let sit about 15 minutes, then launder as usual. Bear in mind that yellowed or discolored fabric may be damaged. The garment may not be salvageable.

Beads and Sequins: Let's Face the Music and Dance

To live like a queen, you must know how to get your sequins shimmery and keep your beads beautiful. You just never know when you'll be invited to another grand ball or celebration.

Laundering Beads and Sequins

Some sequined and beaded clothes can be washed. Here's how to keep them looking great.

- Button all garments completely prior to laundering.

- Turn clothes inside out prior to laundering.

- If the garment is machine washable, use only the gentle cycle and set the machine for a 2- to 3-minute wash. Use only cold water and mild detergent.

- If the item is hand washable, use mild laundry soap or a little shampoo and cold water.

- Put a little hair conditioner in the final rinse if the garment is knitted.

- Always hang beaded or sequined garments to dry or lay them flat—never dry them in the dryer.

Freshening Up Fancy Clothes

Spritz lightly with undiluted vodka under the arms and around the neck and cuffs. Hang the garment to dry.

Spills, No Thrills

Many beaded outfits are labeled "spot-clean only." Use a little club soda or Energine Cleaning Fluid. Apply any moisture sparingly and then use a blow-dryer to dry the spot quickly to avoid a moisture ring.

Furs: Real and Synthetic

If you have a fur coat (I'm sure you know who you are!), I promise I won't lecture—at least not in these pages.

Regular Cleaning Is Key

Any fur garment that is worn regularly should be cleaned regularly, too. This means that you should have the fur cleaned once a year by a professional cleaner who specializes in fur. It's best to have your fur cleaned just prior to storing it for the summer—this also applies to synthetic furs. Keeping your fur clean will also deter moths. It's a good idea to wear a soft scarf around the neck to keep stains and body oil away from a fur collar.

Removing Spots and Stains

A professional cleaner will remove stains, such as makeup, food, and beverages, that can ruin fur. Treat small stains with a little Energine Cleaning Fluid; you can use this on the fur and on the lining. Follow the directions on the can, and make sure to dry the areas that you spot-clean with a blow-dryer in order to keep moisture rings from forming. Always test cleaning products in an inconspicuous spot first.

The Last Few Words

Hang furs and synthetic furs on well-padded hangers in a cloth bag; don't use plastic dry cleaner or garment bags. Shake the fur well when you take it from storage. You should air it out before you wear it.

Preserving Your Wedding Gown

Wedding gowns are expensive investments, but with so much excitement leading up to the big day, cleaning the dress afterward rarely crosses our minds. Often the dress is quickly discarded in favor of more comfortable travel attire, then it's left to lay while we trip off on our honeymoon. Yet, with just a little bit of care, you can preserve the dress, for sentimental reasons perhaps, or for your own daughter to wear someday.

Before the Big Day

First, don't leave the store without a care label. If a care label is not sewn into the gown, be sure to get written cleaning instructions from the store clerk or seamstress.

Once you have chosen your gown, it's best to leave it at the store until the last possible moment. You'll avoid wrinkling that way. If you bring your dress home prior to the big day, decide where you are going to hang it to avoid wrinkling—perhaps an over-the-door hanger in a spare room. Do not hang your precious dress in the attic or the basement. You'll only be inviting dust, dirt, bugs, dampness, and water damage.

The Day after the Big Day

Don't just throw your dress down after the wedding. Hang it on a padded hanger. Assign someone to pick up the dress within a day or two after the wedding and transport it to the cleaner you have chosen. Those spots and spills and lipstick smudges from all those happy kisses will come out much more easily if you have the dress cleaned sooner, *not* later. Ask your mom, sister, or best friend to help out.

Whatever you do, don't come home from your honeymoon to a dirty dress lying in a pile on the floor. Even if it never is worn again, you can have beautiful pillows made from the fabric and veiling to use on a bed. That's what I did!

The Best Way to Clean Your Dress

Always have the dress professionally cleaned *before* you put it into storage. Your dress may have invisible stains from food, beverages, perfume, and body oil. If these stains are not properly cleaned, they can

STORING YOUR GOWN

Sadly, no cleaning process or storage method can guarantee against yellowing and deterioration of the fabric in your gown. There are steps that you can take, however, to ensure the best possible results. Follow my wedding gown cleaning tips, and your dress will have a happy future.

- Have your dress packed in a special heirloom storage box. You can have your cleaner pack the dress, or you can buy the box and pack it yourself. Remember to use nonacid tissue paper.
- Wrap the dress in a sheet if it is not boxed. Do not store it in plastic, or it will yellow.
- Stuff the bodice and sleeves with white, nonacid tissue paper to prevent permanent wrinkles.
- Store headpieces, veils, shoes, and other accessories separately. A box or bag will be fine. No plastic, though.
- Store in a cool, dry place. The basement and the attic, though popular, are not good choices.
- If you decide to store your dress on a hanger, hanging it from the sewn-in straps will prevent damage to the shoulders.
- Look over your gown once a year—Valentine's Day is a memorable date—to be sure that no spots have been overlooked. If you find any spotting or discoloration, have the dress treated by a professional cleaner as soon as possible.

become permanent. Try to point out stains or spills to your cleaner *before* he whisks your dress away for cleaning.

A lot of wedding gowns are beaded or lavishly trimmed. Inspect these trims with your cleaner prior to cleaning, since many of them are not made to withstand the dry-cleaning process. Beads, glitter, and pearls are made of coated plastic and may be attached to the dress with adhesives that will not weather cleaning chemicals. Some trims may yellow during the process. Some items "dyed to match" may not be colorfast and may not match after cleaning. Look for a qualified, experienced cleaner in your area who will discuss all these things with you.

Off-to-Work-We-Go Clothes

Dirty, greasy work clothes should never be washed with other clothes, because soil may transfer to the other clothes, and you'll have more of a mess than what you started with.

Prespotting Stains

Prespotting is essential. Treat spots with a good spotter or Spot Shot Instant Carpet Stain Remover. It's very effective on grease and oil. Launder in the hottest water you can for the fabric type, using a long wash cycle and adding ½ cup of washing soda along with your detergent.

Grease and Oil Be Gone!

If grease and oil are major problems, spray the areas with WD-40 lubricant and wait 10 minutes. Work in undiluted dishwashing liquid and launder as usual.

GOJO Waterless Hand Cleaner is also an effective degreasing agent. Work it into the spot and then launder as usual.

Wash Away Dust and Mud

If dust and mud are concerns, prewash the clothes with the hottest possible water, ½ cup of washing soda, and ½ cup of 20 Mule Team

Borax. After the cycle is complete, add laundry detergent and launder as usual.

A Magic Elixir?

For heavily soiled, greasy work clothes, try pouring a can of Coke in the washer with your detergent and launder clothes as usual. The combination of cola syrup and sugar works like magic!

👑 **QUEENLY COMMENT:** Good water and detergent circulation is important, so don't overcrowd the clothes in the washer.

Getting in the Swim

Swimwear is expensive, but correct care, washing, and storage will ensure a long life for your swimsuit or teeny Queeny bikini! Always read the care label before buying swimwear.

After the Pool

After swimming in a chlorinated pool, soak your suit for 15 minutes or so in cold water with a little liquid fabric softener. Rinse your swimwear in cold water, then wash it in cool water with mild detergent. Rinse it well again, and dry it in the shade. Chlorine is very hard on fabrics, weakening them and changing the color, so be sure to rinse the suit as soon as you can. Never put your suit away without rinsing it out first.

After the Beach

If the suit has been worn in salt water, soak it for a few minutes in cold water to remove the salt, and then wash it in cold water with mild detergent. Rinse it well, and dry it in the shade.

After the Swimwear Is Dry

Fold the suit once it's dry. Store it in tissue or in a perforated plastic bag for winter (to allow the fabric to breathe).

The Spit and Polish for Wardrobe Accessories

There's a bit of folklore for everything, even socks and nylons: *If the legs of stockings, panty hose, leggings, or socks intertwine on a clothesline or in a dryer, the owner of the garment is assured of joy and happiness.* Isn't that splendid?

Socks It to Me!

You may not give much thought to socks until you have to take off your shoes. Here's how to keep socks clean and fresh so you're not embarrassed.

Getting Socks Back to White

To get white socks really clean, soak them for an hour in 1 gallon of hot water and 2 tablespoons of automatic dishwasher detergent. Pour the socks and soaking solution into the washer and launder them as usual. They'll be clean and bright like you've never imagined.

You can also whiten socks by soaking them in hot water with slices of one lemon or ½ cup of lemon juice. Soak socks several hours or overnight, then put the socks in the washer and launder them as usual.

Stomping Out Foot Odor

Turn your socks into sweet-smelling odor beaters by adding ¼ cup of baking soda to 1 gallon of water. Spin the socks in the washer without rinsing out the baking soda solution. Dry as usual.

Panty Hose Primer

Panty hose can be a big investment, so taking care of them properly will let you get the most out of your purchase.

Making Them Last

To increase the life of your panty hose, dip them in water, wring them out, put them in a plastic bag, and freeze them solid. When you remove them from the freezer, let them thaw and dry completely. They'll be ready to wear, and they'll last longer! Do this before you wear them for the first time. To increase the elasticity in panty hose, add 2 tablespoons of white vinegar to the rinse water when you wash them.

Washing Hosiery

To wash panty hose with ease in the washer, place a pair of good panty hose inside the leg of old panty hose—the old panty hose "covering" will protect the good panty hose from snagging or abrasion in the wash. Just knot the end of the old panty hose leg at the top so that the good panty hose won't come out during washing. Adding some fabric softener to the rinse will lubricate the fibers and make the hose last longer, and it will cut down on static electricity. Out of softener? Use some hair conditioner!

Putting Your Best Foot Forward

What article of clothing gets more wear and tear than our shoes? Many of us have a favorite pair of tennis shoes that we live in. When we come home, we take them off after a hot day at work, and our family leaves the room making comments about a skunk smelling better. There is a quick, easy answer to shoe odor, though. Taking good care of shoes will make them look better, of course, but it will also extend the life of the shoes, too.

Cleaning and Deodorizing Shoes

This method will work with any shoe. First, sprinkle some baking soda in the shoe, and then place it in a plastic bag and freeze it for a night or two. Allow the shoe to come to room temperature (unless you want to cool your feet) and then shake out the baking soda and wear. It is a good idea to leave the baking soda in the shoe until the next wearing.

Stretching Shoes

Here's another freezer tip for the pair of shoes that pinches your toes. For each shoe, use a heavy-duty zip-closure bag, or double up two of them and put them in each shoe. Carefully pour water into the bags, until the toe area is full. Close the bags securely so that the water doesn't seep out and wet the shoes. To help prevent the outside of the shoes from getting wet, put each shoe in a plastic bag. Place the shoes in the freezer for at least 24 hours. As the water freezes, it expands. And as it does, the shoes will expand and stretch. You will need to allow the shoes to defrost enough to remove the bags of water when you take them out of the freezer.

Sneaks and Cleats

To keep the shoes looking new, set them on paper and apply several coats of spray starch or fabric protector when you first buy them. They will stay clean longer, and soil will wash out more easily.

To clean white canvas shoes: Apply a paste of automatic dishwashing detergent mixed with hot water to the shoes. Keep the paste on the shoes at least 30 minutes, and then scrub the surface with a nail brush or toothbrush. Rinse the shoes well and allow them to dry out of direct sunlight. You can also put the shoes in the washing machine with several old white towels and launder them as usual after soaking and brushing.

To clean white athletic shoes: Use whitewall tire cleaner. Take the shoes outside and put them on newspaper. Spray them with the tire cleaner, and let them sit for 2 to 3 minutes. Wipe them with paper towels or old rags. Remember, whitewall tire cleaner is a bleaching product, so rinse shoes thoroughly before wearing them in the house on carpet. Pay special attention to rinsing the soles clean to avoid any problems.

Keeping Dress Shoes Dressy

Special-occasion shoes deserve special attention. You may not wear them often, but I know you'll want them to look great when you have to make an impression!

Polishing White Leather

Before polishing white leather, clean the shoes well. To remove scuffs, try an art gum eraser or a paste of baking soda and water. To cover scuffs that won't come off, use liquid typewriter correction fluid prior to polishing. Prep the shoes for white polish by rubbing them with the cut side of a raw potato. The potato will help the polish go on smoothly and cover scuff marks.

KEEPING CHILDREN'S SHOES TIED

Dampen the laces of children's shoes with a spray of water before you tie them. This allows you to tie the bows tighter, and the laces will stay in place when the water dries.

QUEENLY COMMENT: When you're out of shoe polish, reach for the furniture polish. Take a rag and spray it liberally with furniture polish. Rub the shoe well and buff. In a real hurry, you can use baby wipes, too! Rub the shoes with the baby wipes and buff them.

Fixing Scuffs and Tears on Shoes

If there's a black mark on dress shoes, try a dab of nail polish remover, rubbing alcohol, or lighter fluid on a clean cloth. For areas where the color is removed because of a scuff or tear, try using a marker in the same color. Wipe the shoe immediately with a paper towel after applying the marker, and then polish.

Scuffs on Gold or Silver Shoes

Use an old, dry toothbrush with white toothpaste to remove the scuff; polish with clear polish or furniture polish.

Polishing Patent Leather

Rub petroleum jelly into patent leather and buff with a soft cloth. It not only polishes but also prevents cracking.

Scuff Marks on Vinyl or Plastic Shoes

Use lighter fluid to remove the marks, then buff with a soft rag. Be sure to dispose of the rag or paper towel that you used to apply the lighter fluid outside.

QUEENLY COMMENT: If the plastic tips fall off your shoelaces, twist the ends of the shoelaces and dip them in clear nail polish.

Handbag and Hat Heaven

We don't have purses to match every outfit the way ladies did a few decades ago, but we do need to take care of the handbags we have since they get used heavily. And you may not even own a fancy hat, but I can bet you have a baseball cap (or 2 or 3 or 20) in your home if any males are in residence! You can't toss handbags and hats in the washing machine, but you can still get them clean.

Bagging It!

For people on the go, I'm sure keeping handbags clean is a low priority. But I guarantee you that when your accessories and clothes look great, you'll feel great, too. It's worth the few minutes it takes to keep bags and purses clean.

Leather Bags

Clean leather bags quite easily with a cloth that you have wrung out in warm water and lathered with a bar of moisturizing face soap, such as Dove. Rub the leather well, rinsing the cloth as needed and working in the soap until all dirt has been removed. Buff well with a soft cloth.

You may also polish the bag with leather cream or polish, following the directions on the container. Laying the bag in the sun for 15 minutes or so will allow the polish to absorb better.

ROYAL DECREE: Never store leather bags in plastic; wrap them in cloth or tissue instead. Never store leather bags with plastic or vinyl ones either. The leather will bleed color on to the other bags, ruining them.

Patent Leather Bags

Use a little petroleum jelly on a soft cloth to buff patent leather bags to a brilliant shine. Buff once more with a clean, dry cloth.

Plastic or Vinyl Bags

These bags should be washed with a soft cloth or sponge and a mild soap or all-purpose cleaner. Rinse them well and buff them. If you want to restore the shine, apply a little spray furniture polish to a soft cloth and buff.

(♕) **QUEENLY COMMENT:** Use your vacuum attachments to remove lint from the lining of your handbag, and spot with Energine Cleaning Fluid where necessary. Use the blow-dryer to dry the wet spots to prevent moisture rings.

Suede Bags

Brush suede bags frequently using a suede brush. Grease marks can be removed with a little dry-cleaning fluid, such as Energine, or try a little undiluted white vinegar on a soft cloth. Brush the nap into position and allow it to dry out of direct sunlight, and then brush it again. If the nap is severely flattened, steam the bag lightly over a pan of boiling water, but do not allow the bag to become too wet. Air-dry the bag and then brush it well.

Evening Bags

Clean elegant evening bags with a soft cloth and some dry-cleaning fluid. Dry well by blotting or using a blow-dryer. Beaded bags can be lightly dusted with talcum powder to absorb dirt. Enclose the talcum-dusted bag in a towel, wait 24 hours, and then gently brush it. Use care to avoid loosening threads holding the beads.

Heads Up

Hats off to you! Hats are your crowning glory (at least they are mine!), so follow my easy tips for keeping them clean.

Baseball Caps

Clean soiled baseball caps the easy way by putting them in the dishwasher on the top rack. Run through the entire cycle, take out the hats, and allow them to air-dry. Washed this way, baseball caps will retain their shape. (Works well for Queenly crowns, too!)

SPOTS & SPLATTERS

Baseball Cap Quandary

Dear Queen:
What can I do to prevent sweat stains on baseball caps?

The Queen Responds:
Try a product called Hat Saver. Spray it on the outside of base-ball caps; one application will protect caps and keep them looking like new for months. Order it online at www.hatsaver.com or call (888) SAVE-HAT.

Hard-to-Clean Hats

Clean hats that are not washable, such as felt and cowboy-style hats, by using a soot-and-dirt removal sponge, available at hardware stores and home centers. Rub the dry sponge over the soiled areas of the hat, as if you were erasing with a large eraser. Do this outside or over a trash container or sink. Continue to work until you have removed all the soiling you possibly can.

Nylon and Knit Hats

Cool water and shampoo work well on nylon or knit caps. Add a few drops of hair conditioner to the rinse water to soften and condition the fibers. My Canadian friends will be pleased to know that this method works well on toques!

Ties—Don't Let Them Tie You in Knots

Ties are generally not washable—a real shame because nothing suffers more food spills or accidental gravy dippings than ties. This does not mean that you can't successfully spot clean them, though!

Despotting and Despilling

If you have a tie with a food stain or beverage spill, first slip a pad of paper toweling in the opening between the front and the back of the tie. This will prevent the spot from forcing its way through the tie. Using Energine Cleaning Fluid, moisten a soft, light-colored cloth (think "washcloth") and blot the spotted area. As the paper-towel pad absorbs the spot and the Energine, move the paper towel to a clean, dry section to keep up the absorption. Continue to blot until the spot is removed; and then—*this is important*—use your blow-dryer to dry the spot quickly to avoid a moisture ring.

Smoothing the Wrinkles

When ironing a tie, lay it flat on the ironing board, cover it with a press cloth (a lightweight towel or man's handkerchief will work), and press it with steam. Hang the tie to dry completely.

QUEENLY COMMENT: When storing ties, hang them to prevent wrinkles and creases. When you travel, roll them in your suitcase, and you won't have to worry about wrinkles.

Snap, Zip, and Hook
(No, It's Not a New Breakfast Cereal!)

The best advice I can give you while caring for clothing and fabrics is to zip your zippers, snap your snaps, hook your hooks, and button your buttons. If you don't, you run the risk of catching, pulling, or tearing fabric; damaging the interlocking mechanism (such as zippers); and pulling off buttons during the washing process.

Just Zip It!

If you have a zipper that sticks and doesn't want to pull up, rub it with a little soap, paraffin, or candle wax. Zip the zipper up and down several times. This will lubricate the teeth and get it moving again. To give your zipper a little extra "stick," spritz it with hair spray.

QUEENLY COMMENT: If the zipper on your slacks or skirt really wants to slide down, add a button, snap, or some Velcro just above it. The extra fastener will decrease the tension on the zipper and help it stay zipped!

Button Bonus

To keep buttons from falling off, dab a little clear nail polish on the thread in the center of the button. This will keep the thread from wearing through so easily; you may need to reapply the polish after repeated washings. For buttons that get hard wear, sew them on with dental floss. It may not be as pleasing to the eye as thread, but the buttons won't fall off!

Linens and Things in the Palace

There's nothing like a fluffy bath towel after a luxurious mineral bath or a crisp, clean bed sheet when the Queen needs to rest her royal crown! Don't you love it when you pamper yourself? But I'll bet most royal family members could use a reminder about keeping bedding, household linens, and decorative accessories looking marvelous, so check out my best tips and queenly tricks.

Don't Throw in the Towel!

It's lovely to step out of the shower and wrap yourself in a clean, fluffy towel—what I call a *warm fuzzy*. Towels are pretty low maintenance; nevertheless, there are some things you can do to keep them at their best. Read on . . . what follows is absorbing!

Coming Clean

Washing towels in hot water with your favorite laundry detergent or soap will remove normal soiling. Add ½ cup of washing soda to a full load of towels if you want to kick your detergent up a notch and clean more effectively.

Presoaking heavily soiled towels is always a good idea. Soak them in hot water and ½ cup of 20 Mule Team Borax, and you will deodorize them as well!

Fabric softener will provide you with soft, fluffy towels, but overuse will make the towels less absorbent. Use softener every second or third time instead of every time you launder them. You can also use ½ cup of white vinegar as a softening agent. And no, the towels will not smell like vinegar!

Running for Color

Dark-dyed towels will lose a considerable amount of dye during their first several washings. If you have faded towels the same color as the new ones, wash them together to restore some of the color to the old batch. Adding 1 cup of table salt to the wash water the first time you launder dark towels will keep them from fading so quickly.

Do not wash dark towels and light towels together—ever! The light towels will pick up the color and fuzz from the dark ones, and the dark towels will end up with light-colored lint all over them.

Always wash new towels before you use them to remove the sizing and make them more absorbent.

Where, Oh Where Has the Absorbency Gone?

If you find yourself with towels that are slick and will not absorb, here's what to do:

- Soak them overnight in the washer in cold water with ¼ cup of Epsom salts. Add detergent and wash as usual the next day.
- Wash nonabsorbent towels several times in a row and do not add fabric softener.

- Sometimes hanging these towels to dry instead of drying them in the dryer for a couple of washings works well.

The Final Fluff

Do not wash anything else with towels. Washing things together transfers lint from item to item.

If your towels have a mildew odor, sprinkle them lightly with Odorzout and let them sit for a day or so, then dump everything into the washer (towels *and* Odorzout) and launder as usual.

(♛) QUEENLY COMMENT: **Always wash towels in the hottest possible water.**

Bedtime at the Castle

We're going to wash those pillows, sheets, blankets, and comforters. No sleeping on the job!

Pillows

To freshen pillows, tumble them in the clothes dryer set on air or warm for 30 minutes with several barely damp, light-colored towels and a dryer fabric softener sheet. Don't use the fabric softener sheet if you have fragrance allergies.

Fiber-filled pillows. These flatten with use, so chances are you'll want to restore their bulk and softness. Clean them in your washing machine every couple of months, and choose a windy day if possible. Wash the pillows in cold or lukewarm water with a mild detergent, and use a short cycle. If you have allergies, try Fresh Breeze Laundry Soap by Soapworks. Make sure the pillows are rinsed well, and then spin them dry.

If you are washing pillows by hand, use cool water and mild suds, and press out all the water you can. Rinse several times to remove all the soap, then press and roll out the water.

Hang pillows to dry in a shady, breezy location if possible, and turn them frequently. Finally, place pillows in the dryer on the lowest setting to fluff the filling. Adding a new tennis ball or clean tennis shoe in the dryer will help to pump up the volume!

Place pillows inside zippered pillow covers to keep them clean and fresh longer.

Feather pillows. Wash these in cool suds and dry them in the shade. Heat can release traces of oil in the feathers and cause them to give off unpleasant odors.

Make sure you allow plenty of time for the feathers to dry. Fluff and shake the pillow frequently to rearrange the feathers for better drying.

You may put feather pillows in the dryer on the air setting to reposition the feathers and add bounce to the pillows. Again, putting in a couple of tennis balls or clean tennis shoes will beat up the feathers and add fluff. Keeping feather pillows in zippered pillow protectors is also a good idea.

Other pillows. There are a lot of different pillows on the market these days, including specially formed cervical pillows. Wash them according to the care label so you don't damage the filling.

Sheets

Always wash sheets before using them for the first time. Use warm water for polyester and blends; use hot water for 100 percent cotton sheets. Dry sheets according to care label directions (most sheets require the medium dryer setting).

Wash dark sheets separately from white or light-colored sheets to avoid color runs.

ROYAL DECREE: Mend tears in sheets before laundering or they will become huge holes from the agitation in the washing machine.

Flannel Sheets and Pillowcases

Launder these in the washing machine with warm water, and always make sure to wash them before using for the first time. Bear in mind that

SPOTS & SPLATTERS

Dear Queen:
I need some help. I bought blue flannel sheets. I washed them before I put them on the bed, and they have been washed three or four more times since then, but I still have a blue body when I get up in the morning. I tried both hot wash and cold wash, but I'm still seeing blue dye everywhere. Can you help?

The Queen Responds:
Try soaking the sheets in the washing machine in warm water and 1 to 2 cups of salt, depending on the size of the load.

---

flannel sheets have an enormous amount of lint, so they may not be suitable for people with allergies (although the more they are laundered the less severe the lint will be). Rinse them in warm water and a cup of white vinegar to help with the lint problem, and make sure you clean the lint filter frequently during the drying cycle the first few times you wash and dry the sheets. Wash flannel separately from all other fabrics.

Blankets

If the care label indicates that your blankets are machine washable, which most are, make sure the machine has plenty of room for movement between the folds of the blanket. Wash blankets with mild soap in cold water and add 1 cup of white vinegar to the final rinse to remove any soap residue and keep the blankets soft. If the care tag indicates the blanket can be machine dried, dry it in a warm dryer. Or hang the blanket to dry out of direct sunlight over several clotheslines strung at least 12 inches apart to avoid stretching the blanket. Store blankets by wrapping them in plastic, or inside a clean pillowcase.

For electric blankets, follow the care label directions carefully to avoid damaging the wiring and creating a possible fire hazard.

Bedspreads

Washable spreads should be laundered according to the care label directions. Nylon, polyester, polyester blends, and cotton bedspreads all wash well. Rayons, silks, and acetates should be dry-cleaned.

Chenille spreads, which are quite popular again, are easily laundered in the washing machine. Use warm water and mild detergent and rinse well. Dry chenille bedspreads in the dryer and shake them well to restore the nap. Linting, which is common in these types of spreads, will stop after a few washings. Be sure to clean the dryer's lint filter a few times as you're drying these spreads.

For heavily quilted spreads, you can use tennis balls or a clean tennis shoe in the dryer to give the quilting extra loft.

Down Comforters

I find that it's best—and also easiest—to have these cleaned professionally. If you do decide to launder yours, use a commercial-size washer, using the shortest possible cycle.

Do not wash these more frequently than you have to. Air the comforter frequently instead, and use a duvet cover or comforter cover that can be laundered as needed.

Feather Beds

Follow the directions that come with your feather bed and accessories. Be sure to read all of the cleaning information and follow care instructions carefully.

Mattresses

It's important to turn your mattress every 3 months to allow for even wear. Alternate between turning it end to end and side to side.

Covering a mattress with a pad or a plastic zip mattress protector is your best defense against stains, especially on a child's bed. A cloth pad is much cooler than plastic.

If you are faced with cleaning up a wet spill, such as urine, absorb all the moisture you can with paper towels or rags, applying pressure as you blot. Clean the area with Spot Shot Instant Carpet Stain Remover and stand the mattress on its side against a wall to speed drying and keep moisture from going deeper into the mattress. Once the mattress is dry, apply a layer of Odorzout to absorb the odor. Odorzout is an odor eliminator, not a cover-up. If you can, lay the mattress out in the sun to dry, it will speed up the process.

The Wonderful World of Window Treatments

Without question, reading the care label and closely following care instructions are the most important things you can do to keep window treatments looking crisp and clean. Window treatments are huge investments so taking care of them is worth your time.

Cleaning and Caring for Curtains

You can extend the life of window coverings by vacuuming them frequently with the upholstery attachments on your vacuum cleaner. You may also take them down and shake them, or tumble them in the dryer on the air setting.

ROYAL DECREE: Never try to wash curtains that should be dry-cleaned.

YOU ARE MY SUNSHINE

Even when skies are gray, curtains deteriorate when exposed to light for prolonged periods of time. Sunlight weakens and damages fibers and fades colors. If your curtains or drapes are covering a particularly sunny window, hanging a blind or shade to protect the fabric might be a wise idea.

Do not allow draperies to become heavily soiled before cleaning, especially if they are labeled "dry clean only." Dry cleaning does not clean as well as wet cleaning, and all soil may not be removed.

Remove all drapery hooks, drapery weights, and hardware from curtains prior to washing them. Be sure to follow the directions for the type of fabric on the care label.

Drying Curtains

Some curtains can be dried in the dryer. Check the care label. Just be sure not to overcrowd the dryer, and remember to rearrange the draperies often during the drying cycle. Remove the curtains while they are still slightly damp to avoid heat-setting any wrinkles.

Pressing and Hanging Curtains

If pressing is required, remove the curtains from the dryer while they are still damp and press out any wrinkles. For a crisp finish, use spray sizing or starch. When spraying sizing or starch, two light sprays are better than one heavy one and will prevent white "flaking" on the fabric. Sizing and starch will help to repel dirt as well.

If you've washed sheer or lace-type curtains, pressing them gently while damp and hanging them slightly damp will encourage them to fall into gentle folds at the window.

Giving Slipcovers the Once-Over

Some slipcovers can be laundered in the washing machine. Just make sure to wash unusually large or bulky covers in a large, commercial washing machine.

Washing Slipcovers

Test for colorfastness (see page 41) before washing slipcovers. Shake out or vacuum the slipcovers before washing them, and remember to follow the instructions on the care label.

Pretreat any spots or spills before laundering. Fels-Naptha Laundry Soap worked into the arms and headrest will remove a lot of the greasy soiling. Wash slipcovers in cool water and mild detergent and make sure to rinse them well—twice if necessary. Do not overcrowd the slipcovers in the machine, or you will be disappointed with the results.

Drying Slipcovers

Dry slipcovers following the directions on the care label. Slipcovers are heavy, so if you're going to hang them to dry, make sure to spread them over several lines, spaced at least 12 inches apart. If you're using the dryer, you should rearrange, untangle, and fluff the covers frequently as they're drying.

Pressing and Redressing Slipcovers

Press slipcovers with an iron heated to the appropriate temperature for the fabric type, and fit the covers back on the furniture while they are still slightly damp. Not only will they stretch more readily when damp, but they will also shrink slightly as they dry, and that will draw out wrinkles and creases.

Let the Light Shine: Cleaning Lampshades

Most of you probably ignore lampshades when you're cleaning, but take it from me—lampshades are loaded with dust and dirt. You need to treat each type of lampshade differently when you're in cleaning mode so you don't damage it.

Fabric-covered and stitched shades. I find the easiest way to wash these shades is in the bathtub! Put enough cool water in the tub to allow you to roll the shade on its side. Add some mild soap or detergent. Gently swirl the shade in the water-and-soap combination. Drain the soapy water and rinse the shade with cool water, using the same swirling method. Shake the shade gently to remove excess water and allow it to dry upright. Drying can be speeded up by using the blow-dryer. This works particularly well on thick and corded areas that dry more slowly.

Paper shades and shades with glue. You can't wet paper shades or shades with glue, so your best bet is to vacuum them frequently with the duster brush on your vacuum. You can also purchase a soot-and-dirt removal sponge at the hardware store or home center. It's basically a big block eraser that you use dry to erase the dirt away. It works beautifully, just as long as you don't allow the shade to become heavily soiled. This eraser can also be used on washable shades. Make sure the soot-and-dirt removal sponge is used dry on a dry object. You may wash the sponge, but be sure to let it dry before using it again.

ACT Natural microfiber cloths also work well on lampshades. Dampen the cloth (only slightly damp, please) and wipe down the shade. It will remove dirt and hair without harming the shade.

A DIAMOND IS FOREVER, AND SO ARE SCORCH MARKS

Unfortunately, scorch marks on lampshades are not removable. Scorch marks are generally caused by bulbs that are too large for the shade. The bulb's intense heat weakens the fabric or shade material, which then turns yellow or brown. To your horror, scorch mark damage is permanent. My only advice is to use care when choosing bulbs, and follow the wattage guidelines on the lamp.

Parchment shades. Dust or vacuum parchment shades regularly. You can use the soot-and-dirt removal sponge on these too. Even a slice of white bread with the crust removed will work! Rub the bread over the shade, preferably on the outside, and watch the dirt fall away with the crumbs.

Plastic shades. Wash these in warm water and mild soap. Dry them well and then restore the shine with spray furniture polish.

Palace-Perfect Table Linens

Nothing makes a table look better than a beautiful tablecloth and napkins, but cleaning up after the meal can be a bit of a chore. Here are some foolproof ways to make the cleanup fast and easy.

Removing Stains from Tablecloths

Bleach white cotton and linen items. For white linens, you can also dissolve 2 denture-cleaning tablets in warm water. Spread out the stained area in a tub or sink. Pour on the solution and let it soak for 30 minutes, then launder as usual. Soak colored items in heavy-duty detergent solution.

Soaking stained table linens in Brilliant Bleach (from Soapworks) produces beautiful results. Soak until the stain is removed—even if it takes several days—without harming the fabric.

Red wine stains. These methods will work on any type of red stain, including red soda, cranberry juice, and fruit punches. Always keep some white wine handy for red wine spills. Pour the white wine on the red wine and it will remove the stain. Do this as soon as you can. Keep club soda on hand for red stains too. Pour the soda through the stain, preferably over the sink. Pretreat and launder as usual.

One of my very favorite products is called Wine Away Red Wine Stain Remover, but don't let the name scare you—it works great on red soda, Kool-Aid, cranberry juice, grape juice, red food coloring, and even tea and black coffee. It is made of fruit and vegetable extracts, so is totally nontoxic and easy to use.

Dried tea and black coffee stains. For tea stains, drape the stained item over a bowl or sink. Sprinkle with 20 Mule Team Borax until the entire stain is covered. Pour a kettle full of hot water around the stain, working toward the center. Repeat if necessary and then launder as usual. For dried coffee stains, treat with a solution of 50 percent glycerin and 50 percent warm water. Rinse and blot well. Treat with laundry presoak prior to laundering.

Stains on cloth napkins. The most common stain on cloth napkins is lipstick. To remove this, spray the area with WD-40 Lubricant, wait 10 minutes, then work in undiluted dishwashing liquid and launder as usual. As an alternative, you can work in GOJO Crème Waterless Hand Cleaner, then launder as usual.

For food and beverage stains on cloth napkins, treat with a commercial prespotter or one of the ones we made on page 24, or use Spot Shot Instant Carpet Stain Remover. Be sure not to let the spotters dry on the napkins before laundering them.

You can also soak both white and colored napkins in Brilliant Bleach without damaging the fabrics or colors.

Storing Tablecloths Wrinkle-Free

Instead of folding tablecloths into small squares, fold them minimally lengthwise and then roll them. They'll take less room to store, and they won't wrinkle as easily as folded tablecloths will. Hang tablecloths that wrinkle easily over a hanger covered with a fabric cover, such as a towel.

ROYAL DECREE: Never starch tablecloths before storing them or they will yellow. If storing tablecloths on a fabric-covered hanger, cover them with a sheet or cloth to keep them dust- and dirt-free; don't cover them with plastic because plastic causes yellowing.

Caring for Plastic and Vinyl Tablecloths

Clean plastic and vinyl tablecloths by wiping them with a clean damp cloth and rinsing them well. For stubborn stains, make a paste of lemon juice and cream of tartar and work it into the stain. Allow the paste to sit on the stain for a few minutes, then rinse. Let the tablecloth dry completely before folding it.

Sprinkling clean plastic tablecloths with a little talcum powder before storing them will prevent stickiness and mildew.

The Shear Delight of Sheepskin

Luxurious sheepskin can turn into a royal disaster if it gets heavily soiled. Most sheepskin rugs or throws are not machine washable. You could consult a professional cleaner to get your sheepskin clean, or you can give one of my cleaning methods a try. My best advice, though, is to always read the care label carefully *prior* to purchasing sheepskin so you know what you're up against should the rug or throw need to be cleaned.

Light Cleaning

For lightly soiled sheepskin, use a carpet cleaning powder, such as Host or Capture. Both of these are excellent. They come with a machine to use on carpets, but you only need the chemical powder for sheepskin.

Sprinkle the cleaner onto the fleece and work it in well with your fingers, wearing rubber gloves. Roll up the sheepskin, slip it into a plastic bag, and leave it for at least 8 hours, then shake or vacuum to remove the powder. Brush or comb the fleece and shake again before using.

Washable Sheepskin

If your sheepskin has a treated back and can be washed, follow the manufacturer's directions with care. Always use cool water and hang it to dry out of the sun. If you choose to dry it in the dryer, make sure to use the lowest possible heat setting.

Dry-Cleaning Household Linens

I am asked frequently about dry-cleaning items such as drapes, bedspreads, comforters, upholstered cushion covers, slipcovers, and antique linens. Here are my recommendations.

Draperies

Dry cleaning or professional laundering can prolong the life of your draperies and valances. With proper care, draperies can be expected to last from 3 to 5 years. Unfortunately, environmental conditions such as humidity, exposure to sunlight, and water damage from rain and condensation can discolor and weaken fabric, leaving draperies vulnerable to shredding when they are agitated during the cleaning process. Age, moisture, light, heat, and nicotine can also damage draperies and turn them yellow.

Shrinkage is a big concern for draperies that have not been preshrunk, especially cottons and rayons. Your dry cleaner has stretchers to help eliminate this problem.

Distortion and fabric stiffening can also occur during the cleaning process—how much damage will occur depends on the fiber, weave, and design of your drapes. Some draperies may even have a reflective coating that may not make it through the dry-cleaning process.

ROYAL DECREE: Talk with your dry cleaner *before* you have your draperies cleaned. Examine your draperies together. Be clear in your expectations and be honest as to the age of your drapes. Otherwise . . . it's curtains!

Bedspreads and Comforters

Many bedspreads and comforters should be dry-cleaned or professionally laundered. Check for care instructions at the time of purchase so you know what is recommended. It's best to have tailored and quilted pieces cleaned professionally.

Be sure to include all matching pieces when you have the bedspread or comforter cleaned—that way colors will remain uniform and you won't have one piece more faded than another.

Upholstery and Slipcovers

Upholstery is usually cleaned in place by professional cleaners, such as those who do carpet cleaning. These professionals will be able to maintain the color of your upholstery so that it matches the rest of your furniture.

So why do cushion covers have zippers if we can't take them off and dry-clean or launder them? It is to allow for foam replacement, *not* home cleaning. Once you remove these covers, it is almost impossible to put them back on evenly with the seams straight. My best advice? Never remove and launder cushion covers.

If slipcovers are removed for dry cleaning or laundering, you need to be aware of whether they were preshrunk and what the shrinkage factor is. Check at the time of purchase.

It's a good idea to have slipcovers cleaned by professionals. They can ensure that the proper size washing machine is used because overcrowding in the machine can set in wrinkles. They also have the right equipment for touch-up pressing.

Antique Fabrics

These are your treasures. They belonged to your mom, your grandmother, or your favorite aunt; you love these linens, you treasure them, and now they're dirty and need to be cleaned. Antique quilts, linens, and fabrics require great care during the cleaning process. Not every cleaner is equipped to handle antique and fragile linens, so you may have to check around. Let your cleaner know right away that the item is very old and treasured. Proper cleaning might restore an aged, discolored piece.

Word of mouth is the best great way to find a good-quality dry cleaner. Don't be afraid to ask around. Ask, too, what the cleaner's policy is on damaged items.

PROLONG THE LIFE OF YOUR FABRICS

Keeping house is as much about avoiding potential pitfalls as it is about cleaning. Smart buying and routine cleaning practices will help to keep your furnishings in great shape. Consider these things when buying and caring for household linens.

- Bear in mind that closely woven fabric is more durable than loosely woven fabric, so if the item will get a lot of use be sure the fabric will stand up to the punishment and use it will receive.
- Consider sun exposure when selecting fabrics. If you are putting drapes at a sunny window, consider acrylic, polyester, and glass fibers; they'll hold up longer.
- Read all the care instructions *before* you buy. If you don't want to be bothered with a lot of care, select another item.
- Rotate drapes at windows that are the same size to vary exposure to light.
- Be sure your cleaner knows what your care label recommends.
- Regular cleaning can prolong the life of all fabrics. Clean your household items on a regular schedule.

4
Seasonal Palace-Cleaning Program

Spring

It's spring! The flowers are blooming, the birds are singing, everything's fresh and new, and you can't wait to get started with your spring cleaning. Yikes! Did I say spring cleaning? That has no part in my spring fantasy. How about yours? Spring cleaning was a necessity a long time ago when log cabins were boarded up to keep out the winter cold. The arrival of spring presented the first opportunity to clean out all the soot and grime that had accumulated during the long winter months, hence the phrase "spring cleaning." Those of you living in log cabins may want to continue this practice, but for the rest of us, well, there are better things to do.

That's not to say that there aren't certain times of the year when you'll want to clean a little more thoroughly. It may be just after Christmas, it may be right before Aunt Martha's next visit—who knows, it might even be in spring! When you do it is entirely up to you. As for *what* to do, read on. And if you're not ready to clean, you'll

225

also find tips on getting out grass stains, dyeing Easter eggs—even doing your taxes!

March Cleaning Madness

Feeling like spring cleaning is a royal pain in the palace, but your formerly beautiful castle is starting to look more like *Animal House* than *your* house? It's time to spring forward and take a stab at straightening up. I'll show you how.

Don't Clean Your Clutter

The hardest part of cleaning is working around the accumulation of all those things you've somehow acquired. If you *really* want to streamline your cleaning process, take a few minutes, go room to room, and take stock of what's in sight, as well as what's hiding in your cupboards. I'll bet my crown (the cheap cardboard one) that you have things that haven't been used in 3, 5, 10 years or more.

SPOTS & SPLATTERS

Smoked Stuffed Animal

Dear Queen:
I was given a very large white stuffed animal (a cat) for my bed, but the lady who gave it to me is a smoker. Therefore the white cat is a little yellow. I heard you can put stuffed animals in a pillowcase and wash them on the gentle cycle, but this one is too big for that. How can I get it clean?

The Queen Responds:
For large stuffed animals, take them to a reputable upholstery cleaner. (In Arizona, I like Carpet One Carpet Cleaning.) You will be amazed at how beautifully stuffed animals can be cleaned.

Think carefully. Do you really want to keep that purple giraffe? Do you really want to clean it? If you can't bear to part with your collectibles (I love cats and pigs—don't ask), consider storing some and displaying others, rotating your selection from time to time. You'll have less to clean.

If you have a lot of treasures, think about investing in a glass-fronted display cabinet. The glass will protect your ornaments from dust, and you shouldn't have to clean them more than once a year.

Are you really going to read all those back issues of *National Geographic*? Don't be timid. Throw them out or donate them.

If that cat figurine that Aunt Lucille gave you 10 years ago is missing a paw and part of its tail, look at it, smile at the memories, and then say "good-bye." Don't keep things that are broken and can't be repaired.

Think before you purchase the latest gadget. If you don't buy it, you won't have to clean it—or store it.

A Word about Cleaning Products

Gather all your cleaning products together in one container before you start your rounds—something with a handle is ideal. If you have more than one bathroom, think about purchasing a set of cleaning products for each. It may cost more at the time, but you'll save yourself the aggravation of toting products from one floor to the next.

QUEENLY COMMENT: Can't find any twist ties and the trash bag is full? Just use dental floss or a rubber band. Both are tough and water resistant, so you don't have to worry about the rain.

Make sure you have plenty of clean cloths and vacuum bags. If you anticipate throwing out a lot of garbage, make sure you have lots of good, strong trash bags. Check supplies of soaps and any all-purpose cleaners that you may use. There's nothing worse than starting a task only to have to stop halfway because you don't have what you need at hand.

The most expensive products are not always the best. Try store brands and homemade solutions—they can work just as well as their more expensive counterparts.

Try not to depend on harsh chemicals. I will thank you, and the environment will thank you. Things like baking soda, white vinegar, 20 Mule Team Borax, Fels-Naptha Laundry Soap, lemon juice, salt, and club soda work just as well and aren't harmful to your family or the environment. Baking soda is a great deodorizer and a wonderfully mild abrasive. White vinegar is a terrific cleaner, especially for soap scum and mildew. Borax is a never-be-without laundry additive, and Fels-Naptha Laundry Soap is great for stubborn stains. And let's not forget the club soda, lemon juice, and salt. Club soda works on all sorts of spills; lemon juice is a great natural bleach; and salt can be used on just about everything, from artificial flowers to clogged drains. (See chapter 2 for more on these great cleaners and how to use them.)

👑 **QUEENLY COMMENT:** **Be wary of using too many antibacterial products. Unless you're prepping for surgery, good old soap and water work just fine.**

Look for odor eliminators instead of cover-ups. Make sure to purchase products without scent. Try using baking soda or a good, natural odor eliminator such as Odorzout.

Don't forget to change that little box of baking soda in your fridge. Pour the old box down the drain and chase it with ½ cup of white vinegar, and you'll create a little volcano to naturally clean and freshen drains.

Eliminate smells in old trunks and drawers with a slice of white bread placed in a bowl and covered with white vinegar. Close the trunk or drawer for 24 hours, and when you remove the bread and vinegar, presto—the odor will be gone!

Here are four more of my favorite Queenly tricks for keeping your palace smelling fresh.

- Fresh, dry coffee grounds will remove smells from refrigerators.

- A pan of cat litter will remove musty smells in closets and basements.

- Crumpled newspaper will remove musty odors from drawers.

- Dryer fabric softener sheets will leave a clean, fresh scent in luggage, storage containers, closets, and drawers.

First Things First

Decide on your approach and be consistent. If you decide to clean for an hour, stick to it. If you decide to clean one room now and another tomorrow, stick to that. Indecision and distraction can really affect how well you clean. If you start out doing one thing and end up doing another, you'll have a houseful of half-finished projects, and you won't feel as if you've accomplished anything. That can be very frustrating, to say the least!

I like to start with the room that requires the least amount of effort, and that's generally the one that's used the least. It may be the guest room, the living room—it may even be the kitchen. Hey—no judgments. Think of it as a sort of warm-up. Start with the lightest task, and you'll see results fast. That will motivate you to keep going!

Generally speaking, work from top to bottom. Dust from the light fixtures, tops of furniture, etc., will fall onto the carpet and floors. So do floors last and you'll know that your house really is clean.

Don't backtrack. Finish one task before moving to another. Put on some high-spirited music to set the pace and keep you going.

ROYAL DECREE: If it isn't dirty, don't clean it!

Let's Get Started

Dusting comes first. But don't just pick up any old cloth, and don't, for heaven's sake, use a feather duster. They may be some man's fantasy, but they just scatter the dust all around. Really, they're worse than useless.

I strongly recommend washable lamb's-wool dusters. Lamb's wool both attracts and contains dust, so it won't whisk the dust around from one surface to another. Lamb's wool is also washable, so it lasts for years and years. And there's another benefit: In a pinch, a good lamb's-wool duster looks like a Queenly scepter! Just hold one aloft and see for yourself. . . . (You can buy lamb's-wool dusters in many sizes and varieties, including dust mitts and telescoping dusters, which are great for those hard-to-reach corners.)

Use a telescoping lamb's-wool duster to clean ceiling fans.

Don't just move ornaments while you're dusting. Make sure to dust them, too!

After you've dusted your electronic equipment, it's a good idea to give it a wipe with some rubbing alcohol. Apply with a clean, soft cloth, then buff dry. Make sure to turn the power off first, though!

Once you've dusted, give the upholstery a good going-over. Use the appropriate attachment on your vacuum cleaner: the small brush for cushions and arms, the long nozzle for crevices and hard-to-reach areas. If you own a sofa bed, make sure to open it up and vacuum the mattress. (Most sofa-bed mattresses are one-side-only, so don't try to flip it.) Don't forget to vacuum scatter cushions.

Climb the walls, I mean *clean* the walls, by tying a towel over the head of a broom and pulling it down the wall. Shake out the towel as necessary, and change it when it becomes soiled. Work up and down the wall—not side to side—and use strokes that are comfortable for you. Complete one room at a time.

Walls don't need to be washed every year unless you're a smoker. So don't wash walls that don't need it. If, however, a room looks grimy, a good wall wash could save you the effort of painting.

Don't Forget These Queenly Tactics

- Give the inside of kitchen cupboards a wash with a simple solution of warm, soapy water. Anything sticky can be removed with a little baking soda.

- Vacuum your mattress with the upholstery attachment, then flip it for even wear. A plastic bag, such as a dry cleaner's bag, placed between the box spring and mattress will help ease the strain of this task. (Best not to take any chances, so if you have young children, skip the bag and let your muscles do the work.)

- Since you're flipping your mattress, don't forget to wash your mattress pad, blankets, and pillows before putting the bed back together.

- Yes, even that self-cleaning oven needs to be cleaned.

- Draperies should be cleaned once a year. Please read the care label carefully, and don't try to wash curtains that should be dry-cleaned.

QUEENLY COMMENT: You can extend the life of your window coverings by vacuuming them frequently.

- Not every room requires the same amount of effort or attention, so decide before you begin what *clean* means to you. If it's a light dusting, that's fine. If it's a spic-and-span day, that's fine as well.

- If you use the space under your bed for storage, remove the storage containers, vacuum the carpet, and clean the containers before you put them back.

- If the woodwork on your walls is dirty, you should carefully wash it even though you might not wash the walls.

- Take down the globes from overhead light fixtures, wash them, and put them back up. While you're at it, when the lightbulbs are cool, dust them, too.

- If hinges are squeaking every time you open a door, lubricate them with a quick spray of silicone.

- Don't overlook door handles! Wash and polish them. They get used constantly and seldom get washed.

April: Bustin' Out All Over

Allergy season *and* tax time? If it weren't for Easter, April really would be the cruelest month. Don't fret. You can shorten the sneezin' season by allergy-proofing your home. (See chapter 4 for some really effective allergy busters.) As far as taxes are concerned, well, I can't tell you how to pay less, but I can help with things like pencil marks and sweat stains. So turn your attention to Easter and the beauty of the month—those blue skies that remind us that the best things in life are free.

Taxing Times

Once you've dealt with allergies, it's time to deal with those other seasonal irritants: taxes! Read on to find out how to deal with those stains and other little annoyances that come up at this time. Just think of me as your own personal support group!

QUEENLY COMMENT: No, I'm *not* going to tell you how to launder your money!

First, stock up on aspirin. You can use it to treat underarm stains as well as that tax-season headache! (What do you mean, you're not sweating?) For underarm stains on T-shirts and other cottons, dissolve 8 to 10 aspirin tablets per cup of warm water, then saturate the underarm area of the garment. Allow to sit for 30 minutes, and then launder as usual. If you're wearing the same tee night after night (hey, no judgments), rub the underarms with a bar of Fels-Naptha Laundry Soap—then go change your shirt!

Pencil marks? Just take a nice, clean, soft eraser and gently rub the mark away.

If you're one of those confident types who prepare their taxes in pen, treat ink stains by soaking the garment in milk for several hours before laundering. You can also blot with rubbing alcohol or Ink Away, available at office supply stores.

Paper cut? After disinfecting, secure it with a piece of Scotch tape. The tape will protect the cut from the air and will also help to ensure that it doesn't get pulled farther apart. And if it doesn't get pulled farther apart, it won't hurt!

If you don't have any tape on hand, even a dab of superglue will help. Really! It's a great little healer. A little dab on the paper cut and no more pain! Is it dangerous? No. Just don't use it on deep cuts, and please, don't glue your fingers together. Uncle Sam will not accept that as an excuse for late filing! You did glue your fingers together? A little acetone polish remover will unstick you fast!

Okay, you're almost done. You've prepared your return, made out your check, sealed the envelope, and are just about to leave the house for the post office when you realize you've forgotten to enclose the check. Dang! Don't despair. Reach for Un-Du. It will open the envelope right up. No tears, no muss, and you'll be able to reseal it safely. Un-Du is available in home centers, drugstores, hardware stores, and discount stores. It has such a wide range of uses. Use it to remove kids' stickers from walls, price stickers from anything but fabric, and bumper stickers when you change party affiliations. No home should be without it.

If you don't have any Un-Du, try putting the envelope in the freezer for an hour or so, then roll a pencil under the envelope flaps. With a little bit of care, that envelope will open right up faster than you can say "Mata Hari!"

You don't owe? You're my hero! You say you're getting a refund? Give me a call. . . .

It's Easter

Now it's time to turn our attention to something more cuddly than the taxman! I have such fond memories of gathering around the table to dye Easter eggs with Dad and the Queen Mother. It's something the King and I love to do, too, and we include as many friends and family members as possible. The Queen Mum always insisted on covering the kitchen table with an old plastic tablecloth to protect it from stains and spills (where did you think I got it from?) so that our creations wouldn't harm the table. Here's what else you can do.

Place a clean washcloth or potholder in the bottom of the pot and add cool water. Gently place the eggs in the pan, being careful not to overcrowd them. The cushion on the bottom of the pan will help prevent cracks, and you can add a tablespoon of white vinegar for extra insurance. (Vinegar will seal any cracks and help the egg to congeal.) Turn the heat on to medium and bring the eggs to a gentle boil. Continue to boil gently until they are done—about 20 minutes.

👑 **QUEENLY COMMENT:** **Check your eggs for freshness by placing them in a bowl filled with cold water. Eggs that float to the top are old and should be discarded.**

- Keep raw eggs fresh in the refrigerator by applying a light coat of solid vegetable shortening. The shortening seals the egg, which keeps the air out and helps the egg last longer.

- If you drop a fresh egg during any of the dyeing process, just sprinkle the splat with a heavy layer of salt, wait several minutes, then wipe up with a dry paper towel. The salt will "cook" the egg so that it is easy to remove.

- Prepare for coloring by putting out several glasses of hot water (plastic will stain). Add 1 tablespoon of vinegar to each cup. The acid in the vinegar will help the dye adhere to the eggs.

- You can use natural things to make great Easter egg dyes. Mustard and turmeric create a wonderful yellow shade, coffee and tea turn eggs tan to brown, red onion skins soaked in water create a purple dye, hot cranberry and cherry juice make vivid reds, and heated orange soda gives you orange! Use your imagination and create additional colors or mixtures.

- Remember: If you plunge hard-boiled eggs into cold water as soon as they are cooked, you won't be bothered with that gray ring on the inside of the egg white.

- Need to know which eggs are boiled and which are raw? Just give them a spin on the counter. A hard-boiled egg will spin easily, whereas a raw egg will wobble.

ROYAL DECREE: If you are going to allow your colored Easter eggs to sit out in baskets, don't eat them! Eggs spoil rapidly at room temperature and can cause anyone who eats them to become very sick.

The Merry Month of May

May is one of my favorite months. The uncertain weather of early spring is a thing of the past, and the whole summer seems to stretch out before us. What better time to get reacquainted with the garden? I came by my love of gardening naturally: I inherited it from my mom! The Queen Mother taught me to garden the natural way, with minimum fuss and *no* chemicals. I'm going to pass that along to you! I'm also going to share some recipes for homemade personal care products, because there's nothing nicer than pampering yourself after a warm afternoon in the garden. And because May is the month of Mother's Day, why not treat her, too?

A Garden of Ideas

Get a head start on summer! Plant seeds in an egg carton to which you have added a small amount of soil. (Don't pack it too hard, and don't let it spill out over the sides.) Keep the soil moist, taking care not to overwater. When you've seen the last frost, it's time to pop the seedlings out of the egg container and plant them in the ground. Still impatient? Speed up germination by laying a piece of plastic wrap over the seedlings to keep them moist and warm. Leave the plastic in place until the plants start to poke their heads through the soil. Here are some more of my favorite gardening tips.

- Try latex gloves in the garden instead of cloth. They're easier to clean—you can just rinse them under the hose and let them air-dry—and they don't stiffen up like canvas gloves do.

- For a moisturizing treat while gardening, rub your hands with hand cream or petroleum jelly before donning your gloves.

- Don't like to wear gloves? Scraping your fingernails over a bar of soap before you get started will prevent dirt from collecting under your nails and will protect them from breaking.

- Tie a used fabric softener sheet around your belt to keep mosquitoes away while you garden.

- Use a little wagon to haul your supplies around the garden. Check garage sales for good deals.

- Carry a quart-size spray bottle filled with water and a squirt of liquid dish soap. If you see bugs attacking your flowers, just give them a squirt and they'll vamoose!

- Need a kneeling pad? Take a 2- or 3-inch piece of foam, wrap it in plastic or put it in a large resealable bag, and you're all ready to go.

Fabulous Fertilizers

I love these natural fertilizers. You probably already have most of them somewhere inside the palace. Just take them outside and give them a try!

- Crushed eggshells worked well into the soil make a wonderful fertilizer. Terrific for gardens and houseplants, they aerate the soil, too.

- Bury some used coffee grounds in your garden to provide much-needed acid to soil that has a high alkaline content. You'll notice much greener greens!

- Fish-tank water is loaded with nutrients. Use it for gardens and houseplants.

- Plants love starch, so save the water each time you boil noodles or other pasta. Just make sure to let the water cool down before pouring it on your plants!

- Dampened newspapers placed on the ground around plants will help keep the soil moist and hold weeds at bay. Wet the newspapers well—you need the weight of the water to hold them down—then sprinkle lightly with soil. The papers are biodegradable, so they will eventually dissolve.

Palace Grounds Pest Control

No need to resort to toxic sprays and dusts when these safe, effective, all-natural remedies work just as well. If you have a Palace Pussycat or Pup who enjoys strolling the grounds, he'll thank you for keeping his good health in mind, too!

- Keep pests such as aphids, mites, and whiteflies off roses, geraniums, hibiscus, and other plants by spraying them with a combination of 1 quart of water and ½ teaspoon of liquid dish soap. Reapply the solution every 2 weeks.

- Dissolve 1 to 1½ teaspoons of baking soda in 1 quart of water to kill bugs on flowering plants. Spray every 7 to 10 days.

- Powdered milk can kill aphids on roses. Mix ⅓ cup of powdered milk in 1 quart of warm water and spray. The aphids will get stuck in the milk and die. Hose the roses down occasionally, and reapply as needed.

- Here's a great natural way to control black spot on roses. Add 1 tablespoon each of baking soda and vegetable oil to 1 gallon of water. Then add 1 drop of liquid detergent and shake well. Spray directly on the foliage, and spray every 5 to 7 days during humid weather. Make sure to wet both sides of the leaves.

- Chase away pests that feed on your tender plants by mixing 1 tablespoon of hot mustard or red pepper with 1 quart of water. Spray directly on the foliage. One hot taste and the pests will be gone!

QUEENLY COMMENT: Ever tried one of my favorite techniques, companion planting? Planting garlic, parsley, or basil among your flowers will deter bugs. Marigolds also work well. Just plant them as an edging around the garden.

QUEENLY COMMENT: Here's a nifty trick! You can cut grass that's still damp with morning dew by spraying the blades of your mower with vegetable oil. The wet grass won't stick, and you can get on with the rest of the day. Car wax works well too, but it's probably best to skip the drive through the car wash!

Keep on the Grass

Morning is the best time to water your lawn. Grass that's damp with dew will absorb water better than grass that's fully dry. Parched grass can be resistant to moisture, so don't wait until your lawn is dehydrated before you bring out the hose or sprinkler. And try not to water your lawn at night if you can avoid it. Night watering can encourage fungus.

WHO KNEW THEY WORKED?

Here are some great garden ideas that are positively ingenious. Try them around your palace grounds and see for yourself!

- Old panty hose make great ties for plants and tomatoes. They're strong and flexible, but soft enough so that they won't cut into the plant.
- Cutting roses and trimming bushes can be a prickly job, but if you grip thorny stems with barbecue tongs or clothespins . . . no more pierced fingers!
- Tuck a bar of soap inside a mesh bag and tie it around the outside faucet. After gardening, cleanups will be a breeze.
- Hands that are very dirty can be cleaned with a thick paste of oatmeal and water. Rub well into hands before rinsing and washing as usual.
- Kill weeds with a natural toddy of 1 ounce of white vinegar, 1 ounce of inexpensive gin, and 8 ounces of water. Pour on the weeds and say "good-bye."

How do you know when it's time to water the lawn? I like the bare-foot test. If you feel comfortable walking across the grass barefoot—and if the lawn isn't crackly and springs back up when you walk across it—there's no need to water. But if the grass feels unpleasantly spiky and lays down flat after you've left the area, it's time to water.

A good soaking of water will promote a healthy lawn. That means strong roots and good color. I put a small empty can of Zack's cat food

THE CAT'S MEOW

Hi, it's Zack, the Palace Pussycat, checking in with a few words on critter-safe animal control. Nobody wants unwanted critters in their gardens—but that's no reason to get nasty! Use these safe, effective techniques instead.

Bothered by moles and gophers? Some people swear by castor bean plants, but the leaves, seedpods, and shiny red seeds are poisonous to kids and pets—yikes, that's me! Try human hair instead. Hair is an irritant to these small mammals, but it won't harm them or anyone else. Ask your hairdresser for a bag of clippings, and stuff the hair into the hole. It won't be long before these little critters move on. (If you have extra hair left, you could try knitting a toupee for your Uncle Jack.)

If dogs, raccoons, or other animals are tipping your garbage cans over, tie a couple of rags soaked in ammonia to the handles. All it takes is one sniff, and your garbage can will no longer be attractive to marauding critters. (Those dogs—sheesh!)

Discourage fleas and flies from gathering around your pet's outside sleeping and eating area by planting rue (*Ruta graveolens*) nearby. You can also rub rue on furniture to keep cats (like me) from scratching. Just use care so you don't discolor the upholstery.

Keep the neighborhood dogs and cats out of your flowers by mixing crushed red pepper (cayenne) in and around the flowerbeds. No more four-legged visitors! Not, of course, that *I* would ever do such a thing . . .

—Zack

on the grass when I water the lawn. When the can is full, I know I've given the grass about an inch of water, and that's plenty.

Try not to cut grass too often. A closely manicured lawn may be fine for the golf course, but longer grass is actually healthier because it holds moisture longer. Use the high setting on your mower for best results.

Just Tooling Around

Take good care of your garden tools, and they'll last you a lifetime. Keep a container of sand in the garage or shed, and push your shovels and trowels into it when you've finished your chores. Sand is a wonderful natural abrasive. It will clean your tools and stop them from rusting. Not only will this tool-time sandbox prevent dirt from spreading around the garage area, but you'll always know where to find your garden tools!

QUEENLY COMMENT: Spray your garden tools with nonstick cooking spray each time you use them. The dirt will be easy to remove when you are through. In fact, it should fall right off.

Paint the handles of your yard tools a bright color, and they will be easier to spot among the green of your yard. Not only that, you'll be able to identify your tools if you loan them out.

If rust has disfigured a metal tool, try rubbing it with a stiff, wire brush. Scrape a metal file across dull edges, and they should come back to life if they're not too dull. Naval jelly, which is sold at hardware stores, is also a good alternative for rust on metal. Follow the directions on the container.

You can help protect your tools by applying Clean-X Clean Shield or a thin coat of paste wax to the metal. The wax will form a barrier between the metal and the elements and should retard the growth of rust.

Rough handles mean rough hands, so make sure to take care of your tools. Wood handles that have become jagged and coarse can be made smooth again with a good rubbing of some light-grade sandpaper. Apply a generous coat of linseed oil when you've finished sanding, and you'll protect the wood from cracking and splitting.

If you still find the handles too difficult to hold, try wrapping them in tubes of foam insulation, the kind used to insulate water pipes. Slit the foam lengthways, slip it onto the handle, and wrap lightly with heavy-duty tape. Not only will the foam protect your hands from the wood, it will also protect the wood from the elements.

ROYAL DECREE: Don't forget to store your tools out of the elements.

A Mom for All Seasons

When you hear the words "Mother's Day," I'm sure you think of your Queen Mother just as I do mine. Naturally, we all want to do something nice for our mothers—and naturally is what it's all about. So read on to find out how you can make your own collection of personal care products that are easy to make, and natural too. Give these to your own Queen Mum, and every day can be Mother's Day!

Let's Face It

An oatmeal scrub will treat dry skin and draw impurities from your complexion. Mix ¼ cup of oatmeal, 1 teaspoon of honey, and enough milk, buttermilk, or plain yogurt to make a paste. Apply liberally to your face—making sure you avoid the delicate eye areas—then gently massage in small circular motions. Allow the mask to dry before you rinse with warm water. Once the mask has been removed, give your face an invigorating finish by splashing with cool water. Apply your favorite moisturizer, or for a more thorough facial, follow with the tightening oatmeal mask.

Grandma loved this tightening oatmeal mask, and you will, too. Mix 1 tablespoon of oatmeal with the white of 1 egg. Apply the mixture to your face and allow it to dry. Rinse off using cool water.

Very dry skin? A little mayonnaise added to the tightening oatmeal mask will give you a smooth finish.

Prone to breakouts? Apply a thin mask of milk of magnesia once a week. Allow to dry and rinse with cool water.

👑 **QUEENLY COMMENT:** Need a four o'clock revival? Try witch hazel. Keep a small bottle in your desk at the office along with some cotton balls. Dampen the cotton balls with the witch hazel, then blot your face and neck . . . and prepare to be revived! It's that easy. Keep the witch hazel in the refrigerator if you can. And for an extra treat, pour some in a spray bottle for an after-workout spritz!

The Eyes Have It

These remedies aren't new, but they're worth repeating.

- A slice of chilled cucumber on each eyelid will relieve tired eyes. And that 15-minute rest won't do you any harm, either!
- Cold tea bags are great for puffy eyes, so keep some on hand in the refrigerator. Put your feet up and place one on each eyelid.
- A little bit of Preparation H helps keep puffy eyes at bay. Just make sure to avoid tear ducts and the eye itself.
- Dab some castor oil on the skin around your eyes before going to bed at night to moisturize the area. Stay well away from the eyes, and make sure not to use too much oil.

Your Crowning Glory

Restore luster to dry hair with a light, natural oil such as corn oil or sunflower oil. Those of you with very dry hair may like to use olive oil, but make sure to use a light touch. Olive oil can be extremely difficult to wash out. Warm the oil before you use it. But heed this warning: Oil heats up very quickly and can cause severe burns, so avoid the microwave. The best and safest way to warm oil for a scalp treatment is to place the oil in an egg cup, then put the egg cup inside a mug or small bowl that you have filled with hot or boiling water.

Heat about 1 teaspoon of oil to lukewarm and apply it to dry hair with the palms of your hands. Make sure that the shaft and ends are well-coated (not saturated, though), but avoid getting oil on your roots, which will weigh hair down. Cover your hair with a plastic bag and try to leave it on as long as you can—overnight is best. Finish with a thorough shampoo, lathering twice. Skip the conditioner and get ready for the compliments!

Mayonnaise also works well—it's a combination of egg and oil. Don't heat the mayonnaise, or it will separate. Just remove a quantity from the jar—a couple of tablespoons should be fine, unless you have very long hair—and let it stand at room temperature for a few hours. Rub on just enough mayonnaise to soak the hair thoroughly (remembering to avoid the roots) and comb through. Leave on for 30 minutes, shampoo well, and rinse with water and lemon before that final rinse of cool water.

Let's See a Show of Hands

Make your own hand cream by mixing 2 parts glycerin to 1 part lemon juice. Massage a little into your hands after washing and at bedtime. This easily-absorbed cream works well and smells lovely!

Soften hardworking hands and feet by rubbing with equal proportions of cooking oil and granulated sugar.

Cuticles may be softened by soaking in a bowl of warm olive oil. Push them gently back with a cotton swab. If cuticles are really dry, coat them with olive oil at bedtime.

Lemon juice is great for removing stains on hands. Bottled or fresh-squeezed, just massage it into hands before washing with good old soap and water.

Your nail polish will last longer if you apply a little white vinegar to each nail. Just coat each nail with a cotton swab prior to applying your nail polish. The acid in the vinegar encourages the polish to stick to the nail so you get better coverage and longer-lasting wear.

Speed up the time it takes to dry nail polish by plunging freshly-polished nails into cold water. Shake hands to dry. And to prevent nicks and chipping, brush baby oil on just-polished nails!

LET'S DISH!

Of course, nothing says "Mother's Day" like breakfast in bed. So give yourself (or your Queen Mum) the royal treatment and ask The King—or the kids!—to cook.

Orange Blossom French Toast

12 slices bread

6 egg yolks

½ cup half-and-half or whole milk

⅓ cup orange juice

1 tablespoon grated orange peel

¼ teaspoon salt

¼ cup butter

Leave bread out to dry overnight.

Next morning, in a medium bowl, slightly beat egg yolks, then mix in half-and-half or milk, orange juice, orange peel, and salt. Dip bread in batter, turning to coat both sides.

Heat butter in skillet and cook bread on both sides until golden.

Serve with syrup and love.

Makes 6 servings

18

Summer

The lazy days of summer are perfect for lounging around the pool, having weekend barbecues, and stopping to smell the roses. They're also perfect for grass and perspiration stains, sunburns, and insect bites. Read on for my Queen-tested tips for summer vacations, camping, picnics, and coping with the day-to-day disasters of indoor-and-outdoor living. Even a palace is not exempt!

June: A (Crown) Jewel of a Month

Summer! It's finally here. The kids are out of school, and it's time to hit the road on the family vacation. Frightened of an endless chorus of *Are we there yet?* It doesn't have to be that way. The kids don't have to be bored—and neither do you. There are many things you can do to make that trip a good one: enjoyable *and* safe. So let's put our imaginations to work and have some fun. I've even included a few regal ideas for reviving your car when you return. And let's not forget the King! Father's Day *is* coming. . . .

Hit the Road, Jack

You're going on a family trip in the car. You may be in there for hours. If that strikes fear in your heart, you're not alone. Hit these pages before hitting the road.

(👑) **QUEENLY COMMENT:** **If you've read about it in a book or newspaper column, chances are it's *not* a safe place to store your valuables! Burglars read, too. Use your imagination *and* your discretion.**

Before You Leave

It's fun to take a little time away from the palace. And if you take some time to prep the house before you leave, your homecoming will be that much sweeter. Here's what to do.

- Lock the doors and windows, but leave the shades up and curtains open. Put the lights on an automatic timer.

- Clean out the refrigerator and remove any perishables.

- Want to know if your freezer has shut off while you've been away? Take a child's ice pop—the ones that come in the clear plastic push-up wrapper—and lay it flat to freeze, then prop it upright on the rack inside the freezer door. If the freezer goes off while you're away, the pop will be hanging over the inside of the door instead of standing straight up. You'll know then that the freezer food *isn't* safe to eat.

- Store your valuables in a safe place. The freezer, jewelry box, and lingerie drawer are not secure choices.

- Turn off small electrical appliances. Unplug decorative lights and fountains.

- Smokers will want to make sure that ashtrays are empty. Odor from cigarette butts can linger long after the cigarette has been extinguished, and there's nothing worse than coming home to a house that smells like a stale ashtray!

- Suspend delivery of the newspaper and the mail.
- To keep plants watered when you're not at home sit them in the bathtub in about an inch of water. The plants will absorb the water gradually, so an inch is enough to last a week or two. For those plant pots that don't have a hole in the bottom, fill a glass with water, insert one end of a coarse piece of string in the glass, and bury the other in the plant. Believe it or not, this homemade water wick will keep most plants moist while you're away!
- Leave a key and contact number with a trusted neighbor.

What to Pack

No two vacations are alike, so consider what you want from your trip *before* you start to pack. If your weekday routine dictates that you wake at 6:30 to head off for work each morning, then chances are the last thing you want to hear is the ringing of your alarm. If, however, you want to be first in line at Disneyland, you're going to need that clock.

Here's a sample list to get you started.

- Small sewing kit
- Travel hair dryer
- Umbrella or raincoat
- Hunting or fishing license
- Alarm clock
- Swiss army knife
- Small fold-up tote for all those extras you'll buy
- Small amount of laundry detergent for those "oops!"
- Exercise gear
- Camera and film

- Batteries
- A few plastic garbage bags for holding dirty laundry
- Bathing suits
- Plenty of T-shirts
- Tweezers—they come in very handy
- Gallon-size Ziploc bags for damp swimsuits, etc.
- A few clothespins and some safety pins

ROYAL DECREE: Take along an almost-empty liquid soap container filled with water. It makes a handy cleaner for all those little emergencies.

Don't Forget These Necessities

If you're going on a road trip in your car, you'll always need to take these useful items along.

- Personal medicines and spare eyeglasses
- Children's pain relievers and remedies for upset tummies
- Sunglasses, suntan lotion, insect repellent
- A first-aid kit, some paper towels, and tissues
- Proof of insurance—auto *and* health
- A duplicate set of car keys
- A spare tire, car jack, flashlight, windshield scraper, and emergency repair kit
- A few gallons of fresh water for you and your radiator
- Maps
- 1-800 numbers for credit card companies
- A small notebook and pen
- Picture ID

HOME ODORS

Want to make sure the palace smells minty fresh on your return? Wintergreen oil is a wonderful deodorant. You can purchase some at a health-food store. Put a few drops on cotton balls, and stash in plants, decorative pieces, etc., all over your castle.

Backseat Drivers

Traveling with children requires special care and preparation, not to mention a good dose of imagination and patience. So plan ahead. Keep children occupied and try to avoid mishaps *before* they happen. You'll be glad you did.

👑 **QUEENLY COMMENT:** Spray the front of the car with nonstick cooking spray before you hit the road. Bugs and grime will wash right off.

Do's and Don'ts for a Safe Trip

Boredom's not the only potential disaster when traveling with kids. Let's not forget about safety! Here's how to make sure your little crown princes and princesses reach their destination safely.

- Do lock all doors and teach your children not to play with the door handles.
- Do set a good example for your children by buckling up each time you enter the car.
- Do make sure that children sit in the backseat.
- Do make sure to take plenty of cold water.
- Do make frequent stops so that children can stretch their legs.
- Don't permit children to ride with their heads, arms, or hands sticking out of the car through open windows.

- Don't leave children or pets in the car alone—even for a short time.

- Don't allow children to suck on lollipops while riding. A sudden stop could be disastrous.

ROYAL DECREE: Keep sugared snacks to a minimum! Children energized with sugar are *not* good travelers.

We're Not Finished Yet!

Children are resilient, but their little bodies can be especially sensitive to the environment. Keep a close eye on small passengers, and be on the lookout for any signs of car sickness and upset tummies. Sometimes a quick stop for some fresh air is all it takes to avoid a problem.

- Keep a new toothbrush in the glove box, along with a small tube of mint toothpaste. If a little one does get carsick and vomit, brushing his teeth afterward will make him feel much better. Just make sure to stay away from sweet or flavored toothpastes, which may aggravate nausea.

- When preparing snack foods for a car journey, make sure to avoid small foods a child could choke on, such as hard candy and peanuts.

- Baby wipes are great for wiping sticky hands and faces (both yours *and* your children's). They're terrific for cleaning hands after pumping gas at the self-serve, too.

- Little ones will need a change of clothes. Everybody will benefit from having a spare, fresh T-shirt. And don't forget the diapers!

- Water bottles with pop-up openings and spill-proof cups will keep liquid messes to a minimum.

- Invest in lap-top traveling desks so little ones have a hard surface to color or play games on.

Now for the Fun Stuff

Once you've gotten all the safety and practical stuff down pat, it's time for the games and toys. These are all Queen-tested, and are guaranteed to be royal entertainment!

- Children love to play with office supplies such as Scotch tape, paper, and Post-it notes—and they can't hurt themselves with any of them, either. Don't give children pens or pencils, though, or scissors.

- Play money is great fun. Your child can set up her own mall in the backseat! Just make sure to avoid giving coins to small children.

- Squares of aluminum foil are great for making sculptures and jewelry, and they can be used again and again. (Don't give foil to young children, who may be tempted to put it in their mouths.)

- High-tech kids can still enjoy singing songs and reciting rhymes. Encourage children to make up their own verses. Don't be afraid to get creative!

- Paint books—the kind that already have the paint on the page— are very popular with young children. All you need is a little brush and an inch or so of water in a cup. No fuss, no spills.

- Don't forget the classics. Hangman, tic-tac-toe, and "I Spy" are great, and so are crossword puzzles.

- Pack the bubbles!

- Have your child make some paper-bag puppets before you leave. They'll be distracted with their craft, and that will give *you* some uninterrupted time to prepare for the trip. Children will be pleased to take their new creations with them in the car.

- Children love to use binoculars.

- Tattoos, the kind that press on with a wet cloth, are lots of fun.

- Go Fish card games are great. Even children too young to know the game will enjoy playing with the cards. Fifty-two pickup, anyone?

- Everyone knows that books on tape are great for long trips, but small children can get bored just listening. So why not let them record their own books? Many inexpensive cassette players have record buttons, so why not pick up a few tapes at the dollar store and let your child try his on-air talents? He can describe the scenery, make up stories and songs, record a letter to Grandma—he could even interview you!

(continued)

THE CAT'S MEOW

Cats (and, I guess, even—yikes—dogs) have rights. This is Zack, the Palace Pussycat, here with a few words on keeping your pets safe and comfortable while you're off gallivanting around on vacation. And incidentally: Come back soon!

- Please make sure that I'm well cared for while you're away. I need food and water, of course, but I need some company, too. I get *awfully* lonely when you're gone! And please put a note on the door or window that lets people know I'm inside. Pets can get lost or overlooked in the commotion of a fire. I shudder to think what could happen. . .

- If you're taking me with you, please make sure that I have a place of my own in the car, as well as food and water. Bring my bed if at all possible. And please—keep me out of the sun!

- Give dogs frequent potty breaks and some exercise. Always keep them on a leash. (You *know* how they are about running away. . .)

- Don't forget my litter tray. A disposable one will be fine. Just don't expect me to go potty at 70 miles per hour with trucks speeding by! I need my privacy.

- Make sure that we're wearing our tags, just in case we become lost or disoriented.

—Zack

- Kids love disposable cameras. Consider giving one to each child.

- Toddlers can use licorice laces and Cheerios or Fruit Loops to make necklaces and bracelets. When they get bored, they can eat their creations!

- Buy some small, inexpensive toys at the dollar store—things like plastic dinosaurs and little trolls. Wrap them up with brightly colored paper and dole them out as after-snack goodies. Children love unwrapping toys almost as much as the toys themselves. But keep small toys away from little ones, who may put them in their mouths.

- Cookie sheets and breakfast-in-bed trays make great portable workspaces for children. Just make sure you don't give little ones sharp and potentially dangerous objects, such as pens and pencils. The slightest bump can mean disaster when these items are at hand. Crayons and jumbo markers are best.

- Yahtzee is still a great traveling game.

At the Car Wash

A long trip can take its toll on your car. Here's what to do to get it looking good again fast!

- Use a paste of baking soda and water to clean the outside windshield so that it shines.

- Put some baking soda in your car's ashtray. It may not discourage smokers, but it will help neutralize the odor.

- Keep some used fabric softener sheets in your glove box. Use them to wipe the dashboard, clean the air vents, and polish the rearview mirror. Store them in a Ziploc bag, and you'll still have room for all those maps and fast-food coupons!

- If birds leave you unwanted gifts on the car, simply take some waterless hand cream and work it in well with an old rag. Let sit for several minutes and it should rub right off.

- Remove road tar by saturating it with linseed oil. Apply the oil liberally to the tarred area, let soak for a while, and then wipe with an old rag that has been dampened with more linseed oil. Be sure you dispose of the rag outside in the trash.

- Make your own windshield-washer fluid by mixing 2 quarts of rubbing alcohol, 1 cup of water, and 1 teaspoon of liquid dish soap. This will not freeze at −30°F. In summer, add 1 pint of rubbing alcohol and 1 teaspoon of liquid dish soap to the car washer container and fill with water. This will keep the windows clean in rain and warm weather.

- Baking soda on a soft, wet cloth is great for cleaning chrome, headlights, and enamel.

- Wipe down windshield wiper blades from time to time to remove road film.

- Wash the car in the shade to prevent streaking.

- Use a couple of squirts of liquid dish soap in a bucket of warm water to wash the car. Start at the roof and wash and rinse in sections so that the soap doesn't dry on the car.

- Dry the car with an old bath towel, then for a super shine rub down with a good-quality chamois.

MAKE YOUR OWN AIR FRESHENER

If you return from a vacation to a musty-smelling palace, don't despair. Instead, whip up a batch of this homemade air freshener, and you'll be breathing easy in no time!

In a gallon jug, combine 1 cup baking soda, ¼ cup clear ammonia, and 1 tablespoon scent (use your imagination—any scented oils or extracts work). Slowly add 16 cups of warm water, label, and store. To use, pour well-shaken solution into a spray container and mist air as needed.

QUEENLY COMMENT: Want to treat Dad to an extra special Father's Day? Use elbow grease to tackle his car! Rust spots can be removed from car bumpers quite easily—just rub with a ball of tinfoil! If the rust is stubborn, try dipping the foil in a glass of cola! (Don't ask. . . .)

Father's Day: A Royal Event

You don't think we'd let the month go by without celebrating Father's Day, do you? (What would the King think?!) I always think that the best gift is a gift of time. So why not give your father—or your own personal King, the father of your crown princes and princesses—the day off, and let him wander the links for a lovely game of golf. And when he comes home, treat him like a king (of course!), and treat his clubs to some tender, loving care. . . .

Fore!

Clean golf clubs by lightly rubbing the head and shaft with dry, fine-grade (0000) steel wool. Don't wet the steel wool. Dust with a dry cloth, then use a damp cloth to give the club a final wipe before buffing dry with another clean, soft cloth.

Cleaning the grips is as easy as using soap and water—but the kind of soap you use makes a big difference. Dampen a soft cloth with warm water, then work up a lather with a moisturizing bath bar, such as Dove or Caress. Don't use a deodorizing soap, as that will dry out the leather. Rub well to remove the dirt, rinsing the cloth each time it becomes grimy. Repeat until the grip is clean, then reapply the soap and water one last time. Don't rinse: Buff with a soft cloth instead. This will keep the grip moist and prevent it from drying out and cracking. For really stubborn dirt or older clubs, work in a little GOJO Crème Waterless Hand Cleaner and wipe until clean. Then wash with the soap formula and dry well.

Here's how to care for the King's golf glove. Keep the golf glove in a self-closing plastic bag to maintain softness between games. If you need to clean the glove, use the bar soap method prescribed for grips, keeping the glove on your hand to preserve its shape during the process. Work only with a damp cloth, and make sure not to saturate the glove. Finish by buffing with a soft cloth that's clean and dry, and then allow the glove to dry naturally, out of direct light. To restore a dried-out glove, try rubbing a little hand cream into it while you're wearing it!

Golf shoes need attention, too. Brush the bottoms of the shoes with a firm brush to remove any dirt and debris. If the King has been playing on a wet course, don't do this until the shoes are dry. Wash leather shoes as needed with Dove Moisturizing Bath Bar, removing scuff marks with a little nongel toothpaste or rubbing with a little cuticle remover. For fabric-type shoes, brush well and spot with a damp microfiber cloth. Always keep the shoes treated with a good-quality water repellent for those rainy days and dewy mornings. Got a little odor problem? Put some Odorzout in the toe of an old nylon or sock, and keep it in the shoes when you store them to eliminate odor.

Clean golf balls by soaking them in a solution of 1 cup warm water and ¼ cup ammonia. Rub lightly, rinse, and lay out to dry. Store extra golf balls in an egg carton. The compartments are the perfect size!

QUEENLY COMMENT: Having trouble identifying your golf and tennis balls? A tiny drop of colored nail polish is just as good as any monogram.

July: Jumpin' for Joy

Even the most devoted couch potato ventures out of the house in July. So haul out the baseball equipment, hop on that bike, put on the skates, or go for a dip in the pool to cure those summertime blues. Sound too energetic for you? Then how about becoming a chaise lounge or hammock potato at a beautiful campsite for a week or so? That can be a wonderfully relaxing way to recharge your body, let the kids run off some steam, and have some quality family time, too.

Let the Games Begin!

Take me out to the ball game . . . just make sure the equipment is clean and in good working order before you do. Otherwise, it's one, two, three strikes you're out!

Wash your baseball glove with a damp cloth and Dove Moisturizing Bath Bar. Buff with a soft cloth—no rinsing necessary. Keep the leather soft and supple by rubbing with a little petroleum jelly from time to time. Store your ball in the palm of your glove to help keep its shape.

Want to know the best way to clean your bike? Treat it like a car! Wash the frame with some hot water and a little dishwashing liquid. Rinse well, dry, then apply a coat of car wax to prevent rust. Wash the seat with a little bit of bar soap on a soft cloth and buff dry.

Dented Ping-Pong balls? Just drop them into a bowl of hot water and let them float for a few minutes. Dings should pop right out. Sorry—balls that are cracked or have large dents can't be repaired.

Give your skateboard an occasional wash with good old soap and water. Pay special attention to the wheels by scrubbing with a brush to remove any embedded soil and stones that may slow you down.

QUEENLY COMMENT: Wearing petroleum jelly under your socks can prevent blisters. Apply a thin layer on tender parts *before* you exercise. And never wear sports socks more than one day running.

Odor can be a problem with skates—both inline and ice. I recommend sprinkling with Odorzout, a first-rate odor eliminator. Shake some into the boot, leave overnight, then gently shake out the following morning. Odorzout is an odor eliminator, not a perfumed cover-up, so your skates will stay fresher longer. Don't have any? Try baking soda instead.

To clean skate boots, try using a microfiber cloth such as ACT Natural. The ACT Natural cloth can be used on its own—there are no harmful chemicals to damage those expensive skates.

SPOTS & SPLATTERS

Clean, Not Green

Dear Queen:
I have our dog's water container out on our back porch. It's one of those big plastic bottles you fill with water and turn upside down, and it fills the dish. My problem is that it gets green fungus in the plastic bottle, and the opening isn't big enough to get your hand in to clean it out. I have tried soaking with soapy water and swishing a rag around in it, but it doesn't get it all out. Is there anything I can safely pour into it that will dissolve the fungus? Please help if you can!

The Queen Responds:
Fill the bottle with hot tap water and then add 1 to 2 teaspoons of liquid chlorine bleach. Let it soak, then shake and rinse well several times to remove the bleach water before filling with fresh water.

Before you exchange that hockey equipment for baseball gear, make sure to store your pucks in the freezer. They'll stay harder and more resilient that way!

Who Says There Ain't No Cure?

Summer isn't all fun and games. There are hot nights and insect bites, sunburns to soothe, and lawn furniture to clean—what we in the trade commonly refer to as *the summertime blues*. Read on for some handy cures.

- Remove dirt and mildew from a child's wading pool by flushing with warm water and baking soda.

- Sprinkle baby powder on sandy beach bodies, and the sand will fall right off.

(continued)

- A hot night and no AC? Baby powder on your sheets will absorb moisture and give you a more comfortable night's sleep. What, no baby powder? Use cornstarch instead!

- Wipe exposed skin with undiluted white vinegar to discourage biting insects.

- Apply a compress of warm salt water if you're bitten by a mosquito or chigger. For long-lasting itch relief, mix a little salt and solid shortening, such as Crisco, and dab it directly on the bite.

👑 **QUEENLY COMMENT:** That frosty film on the carton of ice cream is *not* a protective coating, and it *can* be prevented. Just cover the top of the ice cream with waxed paper and press firmly. No more "protective crystals!"

- Deodorant that contains aluminum (and most do) can be put on a bite to control the itch.

- Sliding doors get a lot of use in the summer, so be sure to keep tracks clean and well-lubricated. The easiest way? Spritz tracks with furniture polish, then wipe with a dry cloth or paper towel. The polish will pick up grime and keep the tracks better lubricated than a cleanser would. If you want to add some glide between cleanings, just wipe the tracks with a square of waxed paper. Works every time!

- A plastic shower liner makes a great tablecloth. It's inexpensive and washable.

- Sheets make better beach blankets than blankets. They don't hold sand, and they're easier to launder when you get home. Pick up some spares at a thrift store.

- Black pepper will deter ants. Just sprinkle under rugs or cupboard liners. Silverfish can be kept at bay with Epsom salt: Just shake some in cupboards and under lining paper in drawers.

I Hate It When That Happens...

Tar on bare feet? Remove it by rubbing vigorously with toothpaste.

- Put sunburned kids in a cool (not cold) baking soda bath for half an hour. This also works well for chicken pox and mosquito bites.

- No need to use chemicals or expensive products to clean lawn furniture. Just rinse with warm water and baking soda. Sprinkle dry baking soda directly on stubborn marks—this natural abrasive will take them right off!

Camping

If slow room service is your idea of camping, you may want to skip this section. Otherwise, read on for tips on how you can have a royally good time on every camping expedition.

The Necessities

The King and I never head for the hills without these camping essentials.

- Campsites can be very dark in the evening, so make sure to bring along a flashlight. And don't forget the batteries!

- Remember that Swiss army knife you got for Christmas 3 years ago? Now's the time to use it. You'll need some good kitchen knives, too, so don't forget to bring those as well.

- Take along toilet paper in a lidded coffee can to keep it dry. Need I say more?

- Bring a few candles, a votive, or a tea light.

- Make sure to bring along a little dishwashing liquid, a scouring pad, and some absorbent towels.

- A cooked breakfast is one of the joys of camping, but bacon and eggs are *not* finger foods! Don't forget the cutlery, cooking utensils, a pot to boil water in, and a frying pan.

QUEENLY COMMENT: Rubbing two sticks together to make a fire is highly overrated. Don't try to be macho. Bring along matches or a lighter.

- Bring along a length of nylon rope. You can use it for dozens of things, such as drying clothes, elevating food so that animals don't get at it, and setting up an emergency shelter. You can even use it to replace those lost guy ropes. Use your imagination . . . just don't tie up the kids!
- Bandannas are wonderfully versatile. They make good napkins, facecloths, bandages, and slings. Tuck one under the back of your crown—I mean, baseball cap—to keep the sun off your neck, foreign-legion style!
- A first-aid kit is a must. Make sure yours is stocked with bandages, antiseptic, tweezers, a thin needle for splinters, Imodium for those tummy troubles, aspirin or aspirin substitute, sunscreen and sunburn relief, insect repellent, and a whistle to call for help in an emergency.

QUEENLY COMMENT: Cell phones are great, but the batteries on whistles never run down.

- Bring soap. You can find the water when you get there.
- Dental floss and a darning needle will come in handy for quick repairs to holes in clothes and tents.
- Duct tape is indispensable.

Fire Starters

There's an easy way to dry out wet kindling. Construct a small tepee out of your kindling, making sure to leave an opening into which you can insert a tea light or votive candle. Insert the lighted candle, then watch as the kindling crackles and dries. You should have a fire under way by the time the candle has burned down.

QUEENLY COMMENT: Pinecones make great kindling. They heat up fast and burn for a long time.

Bring along a few cardboard tubes from paper towels or toilet paper. Twist a few sheets of newspaper to fit inside the tube (I find the business section works best), making sure to leave some paper hanging out the ends. Toss a few of these in with twigs and wood, and you'll have a roaring fire in no time!

My dad and I learned quite accidentally that grease from cooking pans makes a great fire starter! Use paper towels to wipe up the grease from pots and pans, then store them in self-closing plastic bags. The next time you need to start a campfire, wrap some twigs in the paper and set them alight!

Keeping matches dry can be a challenge, but if you dip the match head and part of the matchstick into some candle wax, it will resist water. Light as usual—the act of striking the match will remove the wax. (This only works on wooden matches, not cardboard.)

Rub the outside of pots and pans with a bar of soap before you use them. Do this to both the bottom and sides of the pan, and soot will wipe right off along with the soap.

Loitering within Your Tent

Well, your tent may not be exactly palatial, and it may not be as comfortable as curling up in your cozy castle, but here's how the King and I make roughing it less rough.

- Rocks, twigs, and other sharp objects may damage your tent, so make sure the ground is clear before you set up camp.

- Avoid wearing heavy shoes inside the tent.

- Use extreme caution around open flames. Nylon tents melt easily.

- Pack tent poles carefully to avoid punctures.

- Prolonged exposure to direct sunlight can weaken tent fibers, so wherever possible, set up the tent in a shaded area.

- A strip of glow-in-the-dark tape wrapped around tent stakes will ensure that you never trip over them again!

- Drive tent stakes 12 inches into the ground to provide adequate stability. Your tent will even stay up in the wind. The stakes should be at a 45-degree angle, slanting *away* from the tent. Paint each stake at the 12-inch mark and you'll never have to guess again!

Cleaning Your Tent

Make sure to store your tent correctly—that means cleaning it first! With proper care, your tent can last for years.

Shake off all loose debris before packing and storing the tent. Clean any spots with a wet brush rubbed over a bar of Fels-Naptha Laundry Soap, then rinse. Air-dry thoroughly. A damp tent is a breeding ground for mildew.

Stakes should be stored alongside the tent, but make sure you put them in a canvas bag or even a few old pillowcases—something to ensure that the stakes will not tear or puncture the tent itself.

Take action at the first sign of mildew: an organic rotting odor, black spots, or a powdery white smudge. Sponge the tent with a solution of ½ cup of Lysol and 1 gallon of warm water. Allow the Lysol to dry on the tent (think *leave-in conditioner*), and air-dry thoroughly prior to storing. For advanced mildew, use a combination of 1 cup of lemon juice (fresh or bottled) and 1 gallon of warm water. Rub onto visible mildew and allow to dry facing the sun.

Spray zippers with a silicone lubricant to ensure smooth action and prevent freezing. Rubbing with paraffin or candle wax works well, too.

(W) QUEENLY COMMENT: Never underestimate the power of a large darning needle and dental floss.

Repairing Your Tent

Stakes and tent poles cause the majority of tears in canvas tents. Either the pole slips and tears the fabric next to the eyelet, or the canvas itself is tied too tightly to the ground stakes. Bear this in mind when setting up your tent.

Canvas is too heavy for most home sewing machines, so if your tent is generally in good condition, you may want to consider getting it repaired by a tent or sail maker.

For a cheaper alternative, glue an appropriate-size square of canvas to the tent. Make sure you overlap the tear by about 1 to 2 inches. Putting a patch on both sides of the tent will reinforce the repair. Use fabric glue or even a hot glue gun, and remember to waterproof the repair once the glue is dry.

IT'S IN THE BAG

Keep your sleeping bag clean and mildew-free by washing it in a large-capacity machine. Add ½ cup of 20 Mule Team Borax to the water along with your detergent and ½ cup of white vinegar in the rinse instead of fabric softener.

Make sure that the sleeping bag is totally dry before storing to prevent mildew. When ready to store, place about ¼ cup of Odorzout in a nylon stocking and tuck inside the sleeping bag to prevent odors. A good sprinkling of baking soda will help to keep it fresh, too. Store your sleeping bag inside a king-size pillowcase to keep it clean.

Duct tape is great for making emergency repairs. Just make sure to tape both sides of the tear. And remember: This is just an interim measure! Have your tent properly repaired once you get back home.

Nylon or cotton hiking-type tents can be repaired on a home sewing machine. Look for patch kits, available where tents are sold.

August: Going All Out

Where did the summer go? Seems like only yesterday we were preparing the garden for spring, and now we're thinking about how to make the most of this final summer month. I hate to be a drag, but it's time to give your house the once-over before autumn starts. That means paying attention to those tasks that everybody seems to ignore: cleaning the driveway and the gutters. It's not all chores, though. We still have some time for that last summer picnic!

Driveway Dilemmas

Driveways take quite a beating, but we never seem to pay much attention to them until they're covered with oil spills and weeds. Put off caring for your driveway, and like most jobs, it will become more difficult and time-consuming when you finally do get around to it. So sweep your driveway regularly—say, once a month in the summer—and wash it thoroughly once a year. You'll be glad you did.

Give your driveway a good sweep. Use a stiff push broom or long-handle brush, and make short, brisk strokes to direct debris away from the center of the driveway. Here are more ways to give your driveway the royal treatment.

- Wash concrete driveways with a simple solution of water and washing soda. Dissolve 1 cup of Arm & Hammer Washing Soda in a bucket of warm water and apply it to the driveway with a long-handle brush or a stiff push broom. Scrub well, then rinse the driveway with clear water.

- Oven cleaner works well for those really tough stains. Spray it on, let sit for a few hours, and then rinse well. Just make sure to keep the kids and pets a good distance away.

- For old marks and blotches, apply a heavy layer of a good laundry stain remover, such as Zout, and allow it to sit for 5 minutes before sprinkling with powdered laundry detergent. Apply a small amount of water to get a good lather going, then scrub with a stiff broom and rinse well.

- Cat-box litter is good at absorbing oil. Just make sure to grind it into the stain with your feet.

- Patio blocks can be cleaned with washing soda or laundry stain remover. Don't use the oven cleaner method, though. It can remove color and damage the blocks.

- Kill weeds that grow through the cracks in driveways and patios by saturating them with 1 gallon of warm water to which you have added ¼ cup of salt.

- Prevent weeds from growing in these cracks by sprinkling salt directly into the crevices. That's all there is to it—just let nature do the rest.

Get Your Mind *into* the Gutter!

Gutters are designed to carry rainwater and melting snow off your roof and away from your house. They are not storage places for leaves, Frisbees, and tennis balls. Keep them clean.

Check your gutters to see if they're in good working order by spraying a hose directly into the trough. If the water runs through the trough and out the spout, you're in good shape. If, however, the water flows over the sides, it's time to give those gutters a good cleaning.

Use a ladder to clean gutters. Never approach them from the roof. That's asking for trouble. If the ground beneath your ladder is soft, sit the legs of the ladder in a couple of small cans, such as those from tuna fish. The cans will help distribute the weight, and the ladder won't slope or sink into the ground at uneven levels.

Once you're confident that the ladder is secure, climb to the height of the gutters and, wearing rubber gloves, scoop out the debris that's collected there. Hang a couple of shopping bags on your ladder and use them to hold the debris. When one is full, just toss it to the ground and start filling the next. (Just don't forget to shout, "Look out below!")

Once you've removed the debris, flush the spout with water to make sure it flows freely. Usually, a forceful stream of water directed down the spout will be strong enough to push out anything that's blocking it. If that doesn't work, try inserting the hose *up* the spout. That should loosen the debris. One final blast of water from the top down should then be enough to dislodge whatever is blocking it.

You can avoid a lot of this hassle next year by placing a screen or netting over the gutters, which will prevent leaves and other debris from settling.

Time for a Picnic

A sunny day, a brightly colored checkered tablecloth, something good to eat . . . sounds like heaven to me! There's nothing quite like a picnic to round off an afternoon of outdoor fun, but insects and food poisoning can ruin the day. Read on to find out how to ward off those uninvited guests, as well as for advice on how to relieve that burn from the last of the summer sun. Oh, and let's not forget how to care for and clean that barbecue grill!

Don't Bug Me

Nothing spoils a good picnic faster than bad bugs. (And the Queen Mum and I tend to feel that *any* bug that's trying to spoil our picnic is bad!) Keep them away, and enjoy your royal repast in peace, with these tips.

- Insects are attracted to intense colors—bright *and* dark. Bear this in mind when selecting tablecloths and paper plates, as well as your clothes for the day. This is not the time to be bold!

- Citronella candles are great standbys. No picnic should be without them.

- Insects love grapes, melons, and sweet fruit drinks, as well as strongly-scented foods, such as tuna, strong cheeses, and meats. Think about this as you prepare your picnic.

- Choose a picnic site that's away from rivers, lakes, and streams. Insects tend to gather around water.

QUEENLY COMMENT: Flies ruining your picnic? Keep them away by wiping the table with some **undiluted white vinegar** or laying some **citrus peels** on the tablecloth.

- Odors can broadcast mealtimes to insects, so keep foods sealed in plastic containers until you're ready to eat.

- Make sure to cover serving plates so insects can't touch down on your meal—even for a moment. Domed food covers are great, as are pieces of inexpensive nylon netting. Don't have either? Try turning a large bowl upside down over platters.

- Don't let a bug surprise you in your soda or juice. Cover the glass with a piece of aluminum foil and then push a straw through it.

- Ants can't make it through water, so the best way to deter them is by sitting the legs of your picnic table in tin cans filled with water. Disposable pie tins or old Frisbees work well for tables with thicker legs.

- Entice insects away from your picnic by giving them a picnic of their own. Put a pie plate filled with water and sugar several yards away from your eating area. The bugs will rush to their meal, leaving you alone to enjoy yours! (Don't forget to pick up the pie plate before you leave.)

QUEENLY COMMENT: Outdoor fun may come with cuts and scrapes, but the *ouch* that comes with bandage removal doesn't have to. Just rub some baby oil around the bandage before pulling it off.

Food for Thought

Picnics may be the ultimate in casual eating, but that doesn't mean you should be casual about the way you prepare and store the food. Bacteria thrive in hot weather; that's why it's easy to become sick from food poisoning. So take a few precautions and have a lovely, stress-free day.

- Keep hot foods hot and cold foods cold. That means making sure you have one cooler set aside for cold foods, and one for hot.

QUEENLY COMMENT: A tear or hole in a picnic cooler can be repaired with candle wax. Gently warm the bottom of a candle over a flame, then rub it on the tear until the seam can no longer be noticed. A wax scar will form, and that should prevent further splitting.

- Insulate foods by wrapping them in layers of newspaper or brown paper grocery bags.

- Large blocks of ice keep food colder and last longer than their smaller counterparts, so use your imagination when choosing containers for ice. Milk cartons, for example, do a great job! Rinse out the carton (no need to use soap), fill it with water to about 2 inches from the top, then pop it into the freezer until you're ready to go. Don't cut the top off, and don't tear it open, either. Resealing the spout once you're ready to go will ensure that this ice block stays cold a long time.

- Think of that foam cooler as your "hot chest." Put all of your hot foods together, wrap them well in layers of paper, and the combined heat will create a Thermos to keep everything hot for a few hours.

- Add mayonnaise to foods when you're ready to eat them, not before. It's not the mayonnaise that's the problem; it's usually the foods you mix with it that carry bacteria. Mayonnaise deteriorates quickly in warm conditions, and can act as a host for bacteria.

I Hate It When That Happens...

Ketchup too slow for your liking? Tap firmly on the *side* of the bottle, and the ketchup will come right out.

- Ketchup and mustard deteriorate in hot weather, so leave the big bottles at home. Now's the time to use up all those extra packets of ketchup and mustard you picked up at fast-food restaurants.

- Don't eat picnic leftovers or food left out for more than 2 hours.

- If it smells or looks bad, throw it out. Don't take chances.

The Grill Drill

Never use gasoline or kerosene to start a fire! These substances are extremely flammable and very difficult to control. And they're not safe to use around food, either.

Don't try to revive a smoldering fire with a squirt of charcoal lighter fluid. The fire could flare up, and you could be engulfed in flames. Revive a fire by dampening a few fresh pieces of charcoal with lighter fluid and carefully placing them one at a time in with the old coals.

Dispose of ashes with care. Douse them with water, stirring them with a metal fork, then douse with yet more water. You can also dispose of ashes by dumping them into a metal can. Wait at least 24 hours before putting them in with other garbage.

Clean the exterior of gas and charcoal grills with GOJO Crème Waterless Hand Cleaner. Dip a paper towel into the GOJO, work it into the outside of the grill, and watch the dirt, grease, and barbecue sauce come right off! Buff with a clean paper towel and the grill will sparkle like new—with the added benefit of a nice protective coating.

The easiest way to clean a grill rack? Lay the cool rack upside down on the grass and leave it overnight. The dew will work to soften any burned-on food, and the next morning you can simply wipe it off!

Place a layer of sand in the bottom of a charcoal grill to prevent the charcoal from burning through the bottom.

Remove burned-on foods with black coffee. Just pour the coffee over a hot grill rack and wipe with aluminum foil.

The Hot News on Sunburns

Ouch! You forgot the sunscreen—and now the damage has been done. It happens to the best of us. Sunburns hurt. Bad. But there are some steps you can take to cool the heat and soothe the pain. Read on!

- A cool bath helps. Shake in some baking soda or about ½ cup of salt. Soak for about 30 minutes or so, then apply aloe gel to still-

THE CAT'S MEOW

Zack, the Palace Pussycat, here, with a few thoughts on making summer more bearable for all of us. (Not that you'll find *me* complaining about lolling in the hot sun!)

Don't you hate it when pet food gets dry and sticks to the bowl? I know I do—and *I'm* not the one who has to clean it out! There is a solution, though: Give the bowl a quick spritz of nonstick cooking spray before dishing out the food. No more stuck-on food. No more difficult cleaning jobs.

A little bit of oil in my food will also help with that bowl cleanup. And it's also good for my coat!

A lot of people like to use DustBusters to clean up scatterings of cat litter (apparently not all kitties are as fastidious as I am), but not many of them know that a used fabric softener sheet makes a great addition to the filter. Easy to clean and fresh smelling, too!

—Zack

damp skin to keep the temperature down. (Works on mosquito bites and chicken pox, too!)

- A thin layer of Preparation H is soothing to hot, itchy skin, and is especially good on delicate facial areas. Yes, I am serious!

- Make up compresses of 1 part milk to 3 parts water, then lay on burned areas for soothing relief. The protein in the milk will draw out the heat.

- Moist tea bags can offer much-needed relief to eyelids that are burned and swollen. Lay the cold bags over closed eyes, then relax for 30 minutes or so.

- Heavy lotions can trap heat rather than soothe it, so try gels instead, particularly those containing aloe.

- Your grandmother may remember this old-fashioned remedy: Whip 1 egg white with 1 teaspoon of castor oil, then apply to affected areas. Let dry. Rinse off with cool water.

- Spraying on a 50/50 solution of cider vinegar and tepid water will cool the burn on contact.

- Vitamin E is a wonderful moisturizer for burned skin.

19

Fall

Ah, fall. It's a good time to be a Queen. The days are still long, but now the air is cool, not drenched with summer's heavy humidity. The sky's a brilliant blue, and the trees are starting to flame into their glorious fall foliage colors. It's time to pick up the pace and get ready for this time of year's round of activities: school for your little crown princes and princesses, getting ready for the holidays, and—yikes!—winter looming in the distance.

September: School Time

Children are grumbling. Parents are rejoicing. It must be September and back to school! It doesn't matter if you're dealing with a first grader or a high school senior (or whether you yourself are heading back to college), going back to school can be both exhilarating and stressful. So get organized. Plan ahead. Establish rules. Consider your schedule and your family's needs, and with a little bit of imagination, you can get the school year off to a good start.

School Daze

This year, take care of your crown princes' and princesses' school needs *before* the school rush. Here's my best Queenly advice for getting the royal family ready to go.

First Things First

Try not to buy any new clothes for your kids without taking stock of what you have on hand. Go through their closets first, *then* hit the back-to-school sales.

Take an afternoon—a rainy one, if you can—and sift through your children's closets. If they're at an age when they're interested in what they wear, enlist their help and consider it a joint project. This is a terrific opportunity to show them the benefits of being organized. Come armed with a few large plastic bags and some silly jokes. Let them pick the music to play and let them decide (with your help) what stays and what goes. The more you involve your children in the process, the more likely they are to cooperate. And if there are any squabbles down the road; well, remind them that the choices were made by both of you!

The first step to an organized closet? Get rid of anything that's too small or that you know won't be worn anymore. If repairs are needed, now's the time to do them. Hem hems, fix zips, sew on buttons, and tend to any other mending that you can. Then make use of those large plastic bags and get rid of whatever can't be used. Can't find a mate to that sock? Get rid of it. Elastic gone on those underpants? Use them as cleaning rags. Be ruthless. If an item of clothing is not up to the task, throw it out. Those torn jeans may be old favorites, but if they're ripped beyond repair, let your son say farewell to them and put them in the trash. That pink blouse may have been your daughter's favorite, but if it didn't fit her last year, it's not going to fit her now. Donate the blouse to a thrift shop and move on to the next item. This is no time to be sentimental. You've got a closet to organize!

Now look into that pared-down closet and see what you've got left. At this point, I like to remove everything so I can organize it anew. Take all the clothes out of the closet and put them on the bed. You might find it easier to make separate piles: one for shirts or blouses, one for pants, one for skirts, one for sweaters, and so on. Your child's style will dictate how many different mounds of clothes you have. You don't have to be precise with your categories—just separate clothes into logical groups so they're easier to put back.

Now comes the fun part. There's only one rule when it comes to organizing: It has to work for you, and you have to be consistent. (Well, I guess that's two, but who's counting?) So, if your daughter wants to organize her closet by colors, let her. If your son wants to organize his clothes by day of the week, let him. Just make sure your child knows that he or she will be responsible for the upkeep of the system, *every single day*.

Take the time to talk to your child. Offer her some choices. Blouses here, T-shirts there, skirts over here, and pants down there. If your daughter rarely wears those two blue dresses and is keeping them for special occasions, you may want to suggest that she keep them near the back of her closet and bring more frequently worn items to the front. If your son wears mostly tees and sweatshirts, ask him if he'd rather keep these items in baskets. (Do you know a child who *likes* to hang up his clothes?)

Talk about the best ways of organizing, and you may come up with some nifty ideas that will suit your child well. Be imaginative and flexible. The more realistic you are in planning the closet, the more likely your child is to keep it tidy. And isn't that what it's all about?

Here are a few suggestions.

- Make it easy for your child to put his clothes away by installing hooks at easy-to-reach levels.

- Install low bars so that little ones can hang up their own clothes.

- Baskets and buckets are great for holding children's socks and underwear.

- Let your child select some bright hangers in her favorite colors. Clothes are less likely to end up on the floor that way.

- A baseball-cap holder is great for that Little League enthusiast.

- Everyone knows that an over-the-door shoe rack is great for shoes. It's also great for T-shirts, gym clothes, swimsuits, and dance gear.

- Use plastic storage bins to hold clothes that aren't used daily. And make sure to label them well. If your child is too young to read, let him draw pictures so he knows what's inside.

- Encourage children to make use of all of the racks and shelves in their closets (the ones they can reach, anyway!).

- Give each child a colorful laundry hamper, and let older children know that they're responsible for taking their laundry down to the laundry room.

One last thing: Now that your children know the work that goes into organizing a closet, you might want to remind them of that old adage: *Work saved is work done.* Encourage your children to keep their closets organized and their clothes clean. Remind them to put away their school clothes when they remove them, not several hours later when the wrinkles have had time to set. Who knows . . . they might even listen!

Clothes Calls

You've mended, handed down, donated, and tossed. But of course you still have to buy your crown princes and princesses some new school clothes so they don't have to go to class looking like paupers. Try these simple tips to make the process of clothes shopping more painless.

- When hitting back-to-school sales, remember to save some money for new fads that show up the first few weeks of school—those things the kids "just can't" do without.

- Read the care labels on new clothes. Make sure you know whether an item has to be hand-washed or dry-cleaned *before* you buy it.

- If your child is having problems with a zipper, try rubbing a pencil over it a few times. The graphite will help the zipper to glide as smooth as if on ice!

- If new school clothes are too stiff—a problem with jeans especially—break them in by throwing ½ cup of table salt in with the wash. They'll come out nice and soft!

(♛) **QUEENLY COMMENT:** If new school shoes are causing your child to slip, score the soles with the tines of a fork.

Just 5 More Minutes!

I wish I could give you more time in the morning, but I'm a Queen, not a magician. There are, however, some things you can do to make your mornings less hectic.

The school bus leaves in 10 minutes, and all across the country kids are screaming, "I can't find it!" Don't let this happen to you. Help each child select a designated spot for books, homework, and sports equipment—plus anything else they need to take to school in the morning. Baskets are great, as are bright plastic buckets. Canvas bags hanging on coat racks are good, too.

Designate another safe place for report cards (did I just shiver?), notes from teachers, and permission slips that need to be signed. And let your children know, firmly, that the morning something's due is *not* the time for signatures.

An over-the-door shoe rack in see-through plastic can be great for holding those small items that kids never seem to be without (and never seem willing to leave the house without). Label a few pockets for each child and tell them it's their own little holding bay. These pouches can be used to hold skipping ropes, GameBoys, caps, and small toys, not to mention hats, scarves, and mittens. Give top pockets to older kids and save the easy-to-reach pouches at the bottom for the little ones.

If kids want to agonize over what goes with what (not to mention who's *wearing* what), that's fine. Just remind them that 7:00 in the morning is not the time to be doing it. Save yourself a headache and let the kids select what they want to wear to school—but get them into the habit of setting out their clothes the night before.

(👑) QUEENLY COMMENT: Television is a great distraction. Keep the TV off in the morning and you'll all save time.

Who's on First?

A large family calendar is a must. Keep it displayed in a location that's prominent *and* convenient. Older children can be taught to log in their own events (just make sure they tell you first!). Use the calendar for school functions, sports events, doctor's appointments, and birthday parties. Keep a bulletin board nearby. You can use that to hold any relevant papers, like invitations, cards, and notes.

A daily visit to your family calendar is not a bad idea. It just takes a minute or so to prevent overlaps that may lead to conflicts.

Get your children in the habit of looking at the calendar, too. Show them how their week is shaping up *before* they enter into it. Let your children know that four busy days in a row might not be such a good idea, and encourage them to use their calendar to make choices. Everybody needs to be reminded that they don't have to say yes to *everything*.

(👑) QUEENLY COMMENT: If nothing's scheduled on a particular day, why not use the calendar for other things? Jot down a knock-knock joke or an encouraging word about a child's performance. An organized life doesn't have to be boring!

Accept the fact that things don't always run smoothly. Some days *are* better than others. Take a deep breath and don't sweat it. Tomorrow offers another chance to get it right.

Get It Off Your Chest

Now that you're in the mood to get organized, why not extend the project for just a few more minutes and tidy up your medicine chest? This small but important project could mean a lot to your family's safety.

Remove everything from the cabinet and place the contents on a large flat surface, such as a table. Again, organize the contents into logical groups. Medicines here, bandages there, and so on. Now:

- Toss out anything that doesn't have a label.

- Get rid of any medicines that have passed their expiration dates.

- Take note of any duplicates you may have but don't, for heaven's sake, combine them. You may have two half-empty bottles of aspirin, but putting them together in the same bottle to save space is a bad idea, especially if they have different expiration dates.

- Blister-pack pills are often separated from their boxes. If you aren't certain of the medication or if you don't know the date of expiration, get rid of them. This is no time to be frugal.

- Chances are, you have at least one tensor bandage that's lost its elasticity. Get rid of it.

QUEENLY COMMENT: Cleaning out a medicine chest is similar to cleaning out a closet, except you don't have to sew on any buttons!

- Unwanted medications can still be dangerous, so make sure to dispose of them safely. Flushing them down the toilet may be satisfying in a dramatic sort of way, but that can be bad for the environment. Don't just toss pills in the garbage, either. They can be deadly to children and animals. The best way to get rid of medication is to put it in a childproof container, then in another jar (which you seal), and then safely in the garbage. Don't take any chances.

- Take this time to clean the shelves of your medicine chest. Metal shelves can be cleaned with a little bit of baking soda and water. Glass shelves can be cleaned with vinegar. Make sure that surfaces are dry before restocking, and take this opportunity to be a rebel and store anything *but* your medicines in your medicine chest. That's right!

- Store your medication in a place that is clean, dry, and safe from curious youngsters. Save the medicine chest for the cotton balls.

👑 **QUEENLY COMMENT:** Despite its name, the medicine chest is probably the *worst* place to store medicines. Not only does it suffer fluctuations in temperature, but it's damp and steamy, too!

Before You Fire Up That Stove . . .

Carbon monoxide is a tasteless, odorless killer. It can be released by wood-burning stoves, fireplaces, furnaces, kerosene lamps, and gas-fired heaters, and it occurs when these items burn without enough oxygen. When fresh air is restricted, carbon monoxide can build up in your home and cause an irregular heartbeat, headaches, and fatigue. In very high amounts, it can cause death.

So make sure your furnace, woodstoves, and other heating appliances are cleaned, serviced, and in good working order before you fire them up for the cold months ahead. And please, take the following precautions against this silent killer.

- Ensure that adequate air is available in any room that contains a gas-burning appliance.

- Have your furnace, chimneys, and flues checked regularly for cracks and leaks.

- Make certain that door and stovepipe connections fit tightly on all old wood-burning stoves.

- Use a range hood and fan with a gas stove.

- Keep a window slightly open when using a space heater that operates on oil, gas, or kerosene.

- Never barbecue in a house or closed garage.

- Always make sure the garage door is open when running the car.

(👑) **QUEENLY COMMENT:** The most important thing to do to protect yourself and your family is to purchase a carbon monoxide detector. They are not expensive but may turn out to be priceless.

October: What a Scream

The days are getting shorter. The nights are getting longer. And that nip in the air tells us without a doubt that the seasons are changing. I hate to be the one to mention this, but it's time to get ourselves and our castles ready for the colder months. So, let's store our summer clothes and soon-to-be-out-of-season sports and gardening equipment. Then let's move inside and turn our thoughts to brighter things, like lighting fixtures. Once we've done that, we can get dressed up in costumes and scare the living daylights out of the neighbors. What else is Halloween for?

Storing Summer Clothes

Hot weather is finally over, and now it's time to store your summer clothes. Try to avoid the temptation to just push them to one side of your closet. You'll feel better organized all year long if you make the effort to adjust your closet to the seasons. You won't have so many items to sift through when looking for something to wear, and your clothes are less likely to become wrinkled in the crush.

Clothes should be washed before storage; otherwise, stains will have a nice long time to set, and you'll never get them out. It's best to have everything laundered (or dry-cleaned, as the case may be), even if they seem to be clean. Some stains are hard to detect and only materialize over time, like a rash. Best to tackle them right away.

Another good reason to launder clothes before storing them? Moths are attracted to your scent.

(👑) **QUEENLY COMMENT:** **Try to avoid using fabric softener on clothes you're about to store. Fabric softener can leave grease spots, which can attract undesirables and weaken fibers. Best to forgo the softener, or use a vinegar rinse instead.**

For surprise spots on washable clothes, try using ½ cup of hydrogen peroxide and 1 teaspoon of ammonia. Saturate the stain and allow to sit for 30 minutes. Then launder. Zout stain remover is also great on old stains; use as directed.

Make sure that swimsuits are washed before storing them. Chlorine residue can damage fibers and may give you a nasty shock when you head to the beach next year. It's best to wash swimsuits using your

RE-PEEL THOSE MOTHS!

Don't forget to protect your natural fibers from those natural predators, moths. Cedar chips work well. Just slip the chips into a sachet so the cedar oils won't touch your clothing then insert a handful into the container with your clothes.

Perhaps the best deterrent, though, is this lovely homemade citrus remedy: Take some oranges, grapefruit, lemons, or limes. Remove the peels and cut them (the peels, that is) into thin strips. Place the strips on a cookie sheet (making sure it's clean) and leave in a warm place to dry. You can also speed the drying process by placing the tray in a 300°F oven. Preheat the oven, then turn it off before putting in your citrus tray. Prolonged heat will burn the peels.

Once the peels are dry and cool, put them into clothes pockets, storage drawers, or boxes. No nasty smells, and no damage from moths, either.

machine's gentle cycle and cold water along with your favorite laundry detergent. (If you have been swimming in salt water, soak the suit in cold water for 15 minutes *before* washing.) If you hand wash your suit, make sure to rinse well to get rid of all detergent. Air-dry your suit out of the sun. Don't put it in the dryer. Heat can break down the elastic and spandex that keeps the shape of your swimsuit.

Suitcases come in handy for storing seasonal clothes, but I like under-the-bed storage boxes best. Choose between cardboard or plastic, whichever suits your space and budget. I like the transparent plastic boxes because they allow me to see at a glance what's inside. Nevertheless, I also tape a list of the contents to the top of the box so I can get to things in a hurry, if need be. (I *am* an organized Queen!)

Be creative as to *where* you store your boxes. Under-the-bed storage boxes don't have to go under the bed. Look at the unused space in children's closets, for example. And who says that the linen closet it strictly for linens? Just be careful of storing clothes in the basement, attic, or other places where mold and mildew can damage clothes.

Give some thought to how you want to pack the boxes *before* you start the process. Use separate storage receptacles for each person, try not to overstuff boxes, and be sure to group types of clothes together. You'll be glad you did when, next summer, you find how easy it is to unpack boxes that have already been organized with care.

ROYAL DECREE: Don't store clothes in plastic dry-cleaner bags. They can cause yellowing.

Bringing the Outdoors In

Now that summer is drawing to a close, it's time to take a few steps to make sure that your tools and summer gear are safe and dry for the winter ahead. A word of caution: If you store your seasonal equipment in the garage (and most of us do), don't forget to leave room for your car!

- Lawn chairs and summer gear can be suspended from the ceiling of your garage with sturdy hooks.

- Open rafters make great storage space, too. Secure items there with bungee cords.

- Don't overlook the simple solutions. A shopping bag hung on a nail can be great for storing small and medium-size balls.

- An inexpensive string hammock, the type you might use to display a child's collection of stuffed animals, makes a great home for soccer balls and other large items.

- Peg-Board is endlessly versatile. Use it to hold hand tools and other small equipment. There's a reason it's stood the test of time!

- Sand doesn't freeze, so store your small gardening tools in the same container of sand that you've been using all summer.

- Garden hoses can crack and split in severely cold weather, so store them inside. Just make sure they're empty first. Pockets of water can collect and freeze in cold weather, and that can result in a tear.

- Take steps to ensure that your lawn mower will start in the spring. Old, unleaded fuel can solidify over winter, and that will clog up the workings on your mower. Empty the gas tank, and then run the mower till it stops. Only then should you store it for the winter.

Let There Be Light

Now that it's too cold for outdoor lanterns and citronella candles, let's turn our attention to indoor lighting, namely, the main light in your dining area. It may not be the chandelier from *The Phantom of the Opera*, but the light over your dining room table is still important. Keep it clean and sparkling—it will reflect well on you.

QUEENLY COMMENT: Use a premoistened alcohol wipe to quickly shine chandelier crystals for no drips and lots of sparkle!

Chandeliers have a reputation for being difficult to clean, but it doesn't have to be that way. First, turn off the light and give the bulbs a chance to cool down—don't start until they're cool to the touch. Place a small, plastic snack bag over each bulb and secure with a twist tie to prevent moisture from seeping into the socket. Next, position a table directly under the chandelier, covering it with a sturdy plastic table cover and a good layer of old rags (towels work well). This will give you a work base and will also catch the cleaning solution as it drips off the chandelier.

Now for the cleaning solution: Make a mixture of 2 cups of warm water, ½ cup of rubbing alcohol, and 2 tablespoons of an automatic dishwasher spot stopper, such as Jet Dry. Pour the solution into a spray bottle—you can pick them up quite cheaply at a dollar store—then spray the chandelier liberally. Allow it to drip-dry. Pour the leftover solution in a cup and use it to hand-dip the crystal teardrops or other decorative hanging pieces. No need to remove them from the chandelier; just dip them and let them drip-dry. The chandelier will be sparkling.

But wait: You're not finished—not until you clean the bulbs themselves. Lightbulbs collect dust, and that prevents the beauty of the light from shining through. Make sure that the bulbs have had a chance to cool down, then wipe them with a soft, dry cloth. Don't apply much pressure to the bulb, or it may break.

Of course, not all overhead lights are chandeliers, even in my palace. You may have traditional fixtures with a flat base attached to the ceiling.

I Hate It When That Happens...

If a lightbulb breaks off in the socket, first unplug the light, then grab a bar of soap and push it into the jagged edges. Turn the soap counterclockwise and presto! You've safely removed the broken bulb.

You may have track lighting or lights connected to a fan. The glass may be clear, frosted, or colored. No matter, it still needs to be cleaned. Remove fixtures carefully. If the light is hard to reach, make sure you use a step stool or ladder to remove it—it's easier on you, and easier on the light. Keep one hand firmly on or under the fixture while you undo the screws or brackets that hold the fixture to the ceiling, and remove with great care. You don't want to chip the edges.

Now, place an old towel in the bottom of your sink so you can wash the fixture. That should prevent the fixture from hitting the hard bottom and breaking. Fill the sink with warm water and a bit of dishwashing liquid. Wash the fixture gently, remove it from the water, and set it safely to one side on another towel. Empty the sink, then fill it up again with warm water, this time adding ¼ cup of white vinegar. You'll need to put another towel in the water, too. Place the fixture in the sink one last time and leave it there for a minute or so.

Gently remove excess moisture with a soft, lint-free cloth, then allow to air-dry thoroughly. Use this dry-time to gently wipe down any metal components with a damp cloth. Buff well with a dry cloth, and wipe down the lightbulb(s) with a soft cloth. Be sure the fixture is shut off and the bulb and metal are cool. Now you can put the fixture back in place and let the light shine through!

Trick or Treat

Okay, the chores are done and now it's time for fun. And because it's October, that can mean only one thing: Halloween!

The Treat

Make sure your little crown princes and princesses have a great time with these royal tricks.

- Makeup is much safer for children than masks, which can obscure their vision.
- Remove glitter makeup and heavy dark makeup from kids' faces with petroleum jelly. Gently work in the jelly (use care with glitter

makeup not to get it into the eye area), then tissue away the makeup. Wash the child's face well when done.

- Make sure to leave plenty of room for your child's clothes under the costume. And make sure the costume isn't trailing on the ground. You don't want your child to trip!

- Check your children's candy before you let them eat it. If little ones are impatient, give them a piece of the candy you bought until you've had time to check the bounty.

- Put some reflective tape on costumes and shoes so that your child will be visible. Consider making a cute flashlight part of the costume.

- Did you color your hair green for Halloween, only to discover that the color won't come out? Don't give up hope. Reach for the baking soda, liquid dish soap, and shampoo. Make a paste the consistency of thick shampoo, work it well into your hair—concentrate on your hair, not your scalp—then rinse thoroughly. No more green!

The Trick

Sometimes those little pirates and ghosts come home with a lot more than candy. Here's how to treat those muddy problems.

- Wet mud on clothes can be treated by flushing the wrong side of the fabric with lots of cool water. Hold the garment under a faucet and direct a forceful stream of water at the clean side of the garment. (Flushing the dirty side with water will only grind the mud into the fabric.) Once the water runs clear, work some Fels-Naptha Laundry Soap into the area and launder as usual.

- Muddy shoes should be allowed to dry, then vigorously brushed with a shoe brush. Use fast, downward strokes rather than circular motions, which could grind the mud into the shoes. If mud remains on leather shoes, clean with a bar of soap (Dove moisturizing bath bar works well) and a soft cloth. Clean canvas or athletic shoes using Fels-Naptha Laundry Soap and a nailbrush.

- Mud on car upholstery, whether fabric or leather, should be allowed to dry before treating. Use the attachment hose on your vacuum to remove all the mud you can. For fabric upholstery, use your favorite carpet and upholstery cleaner (I like Spot Shot Instant Carpet Stain Remover), following the directions on the container. On leather, wash the area using a moisturizing bar soap, such as Dove, and wipe with a clean soft cloth.

The Pumpkin Patch

Pumpkins mold and decay quickly, so make sure to put something under your pumpkin, such as a couple of paper plates or a plastic tablecloth. You don't want to have a black stain as a reminder of the holiday!

If you already have a black stain, you may be able to remove it with one of the following remedies.

For pumpkin mold on a porch or concrete, try cleaning the area with oven cleaner. Spray the area with the cleaner and allow to sit 10 minutes, then agitate with a brush and rinse well. Do this on a cool day, and make sure to keep kids and pets away.

For wooden tabletops, use a little nongel toothpaste on a damp cloth and rub in a circular motion. You can also try some 0000 steel wool dipped into turpentine. Do this in a very small, inconspicuous spot first. Apply some lemon oil to the area when you are finished, let it soak in, and buff with a soft cloth.

Just remember: You can avoid that stain altogether by making pumpkin pie out of that pumpkin. See "Let's Dish!" on page 290 for my dad's all-time favorite pumpkin pie recipe. The Queen Mum never let a holiday go by without it!

November: Let's Give Thanks

It's November, and the year is almost over! Where did it go? Thank heavens for Thanksgiving and the time to pause, to give thanks for what we have. Thanksgiving is a time of tradition—a big turkey dinner with

LET'S DISH!

I love pumpkin pie, and I confess, I think the one the Queen Mum whipped up for my dad every Thanksgiving is the very best. Try it and see if you agree!

Dad's Favorite Pumpkin Pie

2	cups canned pumpkin
1	can evaporated milk and ⅓ cup regular milk to equal 2 cups
1	cup granulated sugar
2	eggs, well-beaten
½	teaspoon ginger
1	teaspoon cinnamon
½–¾	teaspoon nutmeg
½	teaspoon salt
1	deep 8" or 9" pie shell

Using a mixer, combine all ingredients thoroughly.

Pour into pie shell. Bake for 15 minutes at 425°F. Then turn down temperature to 350° and bake until a knife pushed into the center of the pie filling comes out clean, approximately 30 minutes. Serve with whipped cream or nondairy topping.

Makes 8 servings

all the trimmings, Grandmother's silverware, Aunt Jean's china, and Uncle Jim's bad jokes.

Nobody wants to keep Jim's bad jokes, but the silverware and china, well, that's something we hope to have for a good long time. That's why proper cleaning and maintenance is a must. Take the time to care for these precious heirlooms, and not only will you enjoy them for years to come, but you'll be able to pass them along to your children, your grandchildren, and perhaps even your great-grandchildren!

Oh, and when you're finished with the china and silverware, take a moment to get ready for the snow. November is the gateway to winter, after all.

Traditions at the Table

As we Queens know, everybody loves a beautifully set table. It can transform any home into a palace—at least for one night! But that sparkling crystal, elegant china, and heirloom silver needs special care. Here are my best Queenly tricks of the trade.

The China Syndrome

First things first. You'll need to evaluate what you have, so remove everything from the cabinet and place it on the dining table. Don't put the china on a bare table (you could scratch the finish), and don't put it on the floor where you might break something—those *I Love Lucy* situations are best avoided!

Now it's time to get tough. If you're *really* going to repair that teacup—you know, the one that's been broken since the Carter administration—now's the time to do it. If it can't be repaired, and if it doesn't really have any sentimental value, throw it out. Bear in mind that cracked dishes can be unsafe to eat on because food and debris can settle in the cracks and not come out during washing. If in doubt, throw it out!

If you have a piece of china that has great sentimental value but is broken beyond repair, consider putting it in a sturdy paper bag and giving it a good whack. Collect the pieces (there won't be a million—trust me) and glue them around a picture frame or on a trinket box. Add some jewels, pearls, or artificial flowers, letting your imagination run wild. You'll end up with a lovely keepsake.

ROYAL DECREE: *Never* use the dishwasher to wash antique china, **china with metal trim, or hand-painted china. It's just not worth the risk!**

Dishes that don't get regular use should be cleaned before use. Soap and water will generally do the trick. Just make sure to rinse well. For special challenges, like black cutlery marks on china plates, use nongel toothpaste on a soft cloth to rub the marks away. If you have fine, hairline cracks in old china, soak it in warm milk for 30 to 60 minutes. The cracks should disappear when you remove the plate from the milk. Wash as usual and dry well. If food has left any stains on the china, make a paste of lemon juice and cream of tartar, and rub gently. Rinse the piece well when you're done.

The next step is to dust the cabinet shelves with a soft cloth. Then wash them with a cloth that has been immersed in a mild, soapy solution (1 teaspoon of liquid dish soap to 1 gallon of warm water) and then wrung out until just damp. Wash well and dry thoroughly with a soft, lint-free cloth. You may prefer to wash the shelves with a solution of brewed tea (1 quart of warm water and 1 tea bag). Allow the solution to cool to room temperature and wash the shelves using a soft cloth. Then dry thoroughly. You may also use a damp microfiber cloth instead.

Glass doors should be cleaned with a solution of 2 parts warm water to 1 part rubbing alcohol. Apply the solution directly to the cloth, then wipe gently in small circular motions. Make sure to clean the corners of the glass, too. Buff with a dry, lint-free cloth.

ROYAL DECREE: *Never* **spray glass cleaner directly onto glass doors, picture frames, or mirrors. The solution can seep into the wood and can cause damage to the surrounding areas.**

Sliding doors have tracks that need to be cleaned from time to time. The crevice attachment on your vacuum cleaner is perfect for this. After you've vacuumed, wash the track with a damp, soapy toothbrush, and dry with a soft cloth. Keep the track and doors running smoothly by rubbing them with a little lemon oil or spraying with some furniture polish.

Okay. You've cleaned your cabinet and evaluated its contents. Now's the time to put everything back. Take stock of what you have before returning items to the shelves. What are your favorite pieces? What do you want to display, and what would you rather conceal? Bear this in mind as you arrange your cabinet. Put larger pieces at the back of the cabinet, smaller items in front. Create groupings. Keep one set of china together, silver together, and crystal together, and so on. Put the things you seldom use in the back or on the shelf that's most difficult to reach, and keep them clean by covering with plastic wrap. Always empty sugar from the china sugar bowl.

Stack dinner plates, dessert plates, saucers, and other flat items together, and insert a napkin or paper towel between each one to avoid scratches. Sit groups of these flat items on each other to make the most of your space. Cups are more delicate and easily broken, though, so don't stack them more than two high. Be creative with your groupings. Try putting some of your old and new pieces together. You may just see things in a whole new light!

If you plan to wash your china in the automatic dishwasher, take one piece (say, a cup) and wash it over the course of a month to determine if it's dishwasher safe. Just leave the cup in the dishwasher and let it run through the wash with your everyday dishes. Take a look at the piece every few days or so. If it appears that the trim is changing color, the pattern is fading, or small cracks are occurring, you'll want to stop the experiment. If the piece remains unharmed, you can follow with the rest of your set. For best results, use the "china" or "short" cycle, as well as the "energy saver" or "no heat" drying cycle. (You'll save energy and money, too!) I wish I could tell you another test you could try, but there isn't one. If you are buying china, you might want to consider buying one extra, inexpensive piece to try this dishwasher experiment.

Crystal Clear

Crystal that stands up securely in the rack can be washed in the dishwasher. It should not lean, lay sideways, or hook over the prongs on the dishwasher rack. Don't allow crystal pieces to bump against each other during washing—they'll chip. Avoid water spots on crystal by adding 1 teaspoon of 20 Mule Team Borax to your automatic dish-washing detergent.

ROYAL DECREE: Place a towel in the bottom of the sink when hand-washing crystal. The towel will cushion the crystal and prevent breakage.

When hand-washing crystal, wash only a few pieces at a time, and make sure not to overload the sink. Crystal should be cleaned in hot water—but not too hot. As a general rule, if the water is too hot for your hands, it's too hot for the crystal. Sudden changes of temperature can cause crystal to crack, so place it sideways into the water instead of bottom first. For a squeaky clean finish, add 1 tablespoon of white vinegar to the water along with your liquid dish soap.

Crystal should be stored upright, as you would drink from it. A lot of people like to store glasses upside down to prevent dust from accumulating in the goblet or flute, but it's not a good idea. Moisture can be trapped inside the glass, causing damage to the crystal and the shelf on which it's stored.

QUEENLY COMMENT: Cranberry stains on that tablecloth? Remove them with a little Wine Away Red Wine Stain Remover. Works like a charm.

Hi Ho Silver

Acidic foods and their residue can tarnish silver and may even cause it to pit. Salt, egg yolk, fish, broccoli, mayonnaise, and mustard are the biggest offenders. Get into the habit of rinsing your silver right after you clear the table. You may not be able to wash the dishes right away—I know it's not *my* idea of an after-dinner treat!—but a thorough rinsing will go a long way to prevent permanent damage.

Wash silverware in hot water and mild dishwashing liquid. Rinse well, and dry with a soft, lint-free cloth. Don't allow silver to air-dry, as this can result in water spotting. Silver *must* be dry before storing, so make sure to dry well.

👑 **QUEENLY COMMENT:** **Rubber causes silver to tarnish, so don't dry pieces on a rubber mat or store it wrapped in rubber bands.**

- Silverware washed in a dishwasher should never be mixed with stainless steel cutlery. Pitting may occur.
- Never store silver in plastic bags or plastic wrap. That traps condensation and can encourage tarnish.
- Store silver in a tarnishproof bag or wrap it in acid-free tissue paper. If you wear clean, soft gloves when doing this task, you won't leave finger marks—that's where tarnish can begin.
- For quick silver cleaning, put strips of aluminum foil in a large bowl, place the silver on top of the foil, pour boiling water over the silver, and add 3 tablespoons of baking soda. Soak for a few minutes, then rinse and dry. Don't use this method on hollow or glued pieces.
- Rubbing silver with a damp cloth dipped in baking soda will also remove tarnish. Or try a little nongel toothpaste on a soft, damp cloth. Rinse and dry thoroughly before using.

👑 **QUEENLY COMMENT:** **Just boiled some potatoes? Let the water cool and then pour over silver. Allow it to soak for 30 minutes. Wash, rinse, and rub with a soft cloth. The starch in the potato water will clean the silver.**

- Never store salt in silver saltshakers. This could lead to tarnish.
- Remove tarnish and other stains from the inside of silver coffeepots by rubbing with a fine piece of steel wool dipped in white vinegar and salt. Use grade 0000 steel wool.

- Place several sugar cubes in a silver coffeepot before storing, and it will never have an old, musty smell. The Queen Mum taught me that one!

- Store silver teapots and coffeepots with the lids open or off so that moisture is never trapped inside.

- Clean the inside of silver teapots by filling with water to which you have added a small handful of Arm and Hammer Washing Soda. Let soak overnight, rinse, and dry well.

- Clean silver-plated items as you would real silver, but be gentle—silver plating can rub off.

- Cleaning silver is important, but be careful not to rub too hard on the hallmark. If you wear it off or distort it, the value of the set will be reduced.

Silver takes on a beautiful patina with age and with use—rather like a Queen!—so don't just keep it stored away in a drawer. A beautifully set table is an important part of a holiday meal, and your silverware is a meaningful part of that setting. So use your silverware, treat it well, and each time you set the table you'll have beautiful memories to enjoy.

QUEENLY COMMENT: If someone spills gravy on your tablecloth during dinner, sprinkle the spill with baking soda or salt to absorb it, and enjoy the rest of the meal. After dinner, treat with Zout stain remover and launder as usual.

There's No Business Like Snow Business

So you're thinking, *What does a woman—even a Queen!—in Arizona know about snow?* Well, I lived in Michigan for more than 40 years (we don't have to go into details here), so believe me, I know what I'm talking about when I talk snow!

Give Snow and Salt the Boot

Your footwear really takes a beating from snow and ice combined with road salt. Here's how to keep it looking good.

- Keep boots looking their best by applying a good coat of quality paste polish and following up with a spray of water protectant.

- Damp or wet boots should be dried standing up. A roll of cardboard or a bent wire hanger will help them keep their shape. Never allow boots to dry on a heat register—the leather could crack.

- Remove salt stains by wiping with a mixture of 1 part water and 1 part white vinegar.

QUEENLY COMMENT: Buttons on winter coats do double duty, what with that heavy fabric and the constant on-and-off as you go from indoors to out. Try sewing them on with dental floss. If your coat is dark, just finish off with dark thread to avoid an ugly contrast.

SHOVEL IT

Every year, hundreds of people suffer heart attacks from shoveling snow. Follow these simple rules to minimize the hazards.

- Never shovel snow after a heavy meal or after drinking.
- Dress in layers and always wear a hat.
- Don't overload your shovel—snow can be very heavy.
- Always bend from the knees.
- Make sure someone knows where you are.
- Pace yourself. Take frequent breaks.

Give your snow shovel a coat of nonstick cooking spray before you start to tackle the driveway and those annoying clumps won't stick to the shovel!

Car Detail

For many of us, winter driving can be a scary experience. Snow, ice, freezing rain—ecch! It's enough to put a crimp in your crown. But if you take care of your car and use some common-sense precautions, you can drive with more confidence on those inevitable trips away from the castle.

- Don't wait until it's too late. Schedule a tune-up and winterizing appointment for your car.

- Give your car a thorough cleaning before the winter sets in. Don't forget to vacuum the carpet and upholstery, and treat it with a good-quality fabric protector.

- Make sure the dashboard and defroster are clear from obstructions.

- Rubber mats with deep, diagonal grooves really help to capture melting snow. They're a good investment.

- Locks frozen in your car? If your car is in the garage near an electrical outlet, use a blow-dryer on the low setting to direct warm air into the lock, from a distance of about 6 inches. That should do the trick! If your car is outside, heat your key with a match or lighter and insert it into the lock. Leave it there for a few minutes, and then gently turn the key. You may have to do this a few times, but it should work. *Don't try this method if your lock has an electronic device!* You could damage the chip.

- Rub Vaseline on the gaskets so doors don't freeze.

QUEENLY COMMENT: Prevent frozen locks in your car by covering the lock with a couple of layers of masking tape. The tape will keep the lock free from moisture, which is what causes the ice to form.

- Getting stuck in the snow can be a real pain in the radials, so keep a bag of cat-box litter in your trunk for some much-needed traction. A few layers of newspaper work well, too.

- Don't run out of windshield washer fluid. One part rubbing alcohol to 1 part water, and a few drops of liquid dish soap, work well on winter windshields. And if you treat them first with Clean Shield protectant, they'll be that much easier to clean. Snow and grime will wipe right off.

- You can shave a few minutes off your morning snow detail if you place an old beach towel on the windshield the night before a forecast snowfall. Tuck the towel beneath the windshield wipers before the snowfall, pull it off afterward, and you won't have to scrape your windows. Just give the towel a good shake and dream of sunnier days. A mitten placed on your sideview mirror will save you time, too!

- It's always a good idea to keep an emergency kit in your car during winter. Nobody leaves the house saying, "I think I'll get stuck in the snow today," so be prepared. Take along the following:

  ❑ Blanket

  ❑ Flashlight and some extra batteries

  ❑ Two bottles of water

  ❑ Chocolate bar (for emergencies only!)

  ❑ Piece of red cloth to tie to the car

Winter

Winter—Brrrr! It's cold enough to make even a Queen want to exchange her crown for some warm earmuffs. (Or at least it was before the King and I moved to Arizona!) No season mixes good and bad together as much as winter. It's a time of colds and Christmas; of frozen toes and family gatherings; of New Year's parties and post-party cleanups; of short, dark days and Valentine's Day. Read on for some royal ideas on how to make the best of the bad parts and get the most from the good parts!

December: Family, Friends, and Fun

Christmas comes but once a year, which is a good thing if you're the one who has to do all the work. Try to make Christmas as stress-free as possible by planning ahead and enlisting what help you can. Don't be a holiday hero. Involve even the youngest members of your family. Make lists. Plan ahead, and try to not abandon your family's routine. The closer you follow your normal routines—regular mealtimes and bedtimes, for example—the more you'll be able to enjoy the excitement of Christmas without the chaos. So go ahead and deck those palace halls . . . just don't forget to dust them first!

HOLIDAY HINTS

Here are 10 ways to guarantee that your holidays will be a whole lot happier!

1. Tell your children that Santa only comes to a clean house (or palace, as the case may be). Don't laugh—the Queen Mum tried it, and it worked on me for years!

2. Take the time to clean your house *before* you bring in the tree and all the decorations. Sure, you'll probably need to do a quick vacuum once you have the tree in place, but it's easier to clean a house when you don't have to maneuver all those holiday adornments around. Trust me on this one.

3. Make lists and stick to them. It's amazing how much time and effort you'll save.

4. Never say no to those offers of "Can I bring something?" or "Can I help?"

5. Shop early in the morning or late at night when stores aren't as crowded. Make use of the Internet and catalogs whenever possible.

6. Consider these quick gifts: a phone card, a wine club membership, a framed photo of a special time, this book, a gift certificate for a favorite coffeehouse, and pretty stationery with stamps.

7. Use gift bags instead of wrapping paper.

8. Make your own frozen dinners by preparing extra portions when you're cooking a big meal. Great for dinner when you're rushed, and great for the kids when you're on your way out to a party.

9. Get your holiday clothes cleaned and ready in advance. Hang the clothes and accessories together, and you'll have time for a leisurely bath, too!

10. Remove the word *perfection* from your vocabulary.

It's a Family Affair

You'll have more fun—and a whole lot less stress!—if you let the crown princes and princesses assist with the holiday preparations. Here are some kid-friendly activities where little hands can help a lot.

- Enlist the whole family in a quick cleanup. Small children can dust, older ones can vacuum, your spouse can do the dishes, and you can tidy up and put things away. It's amazing what you can accomplish together in 30 short minutes.

- Involve children in sending out Christmas cards. Older ones can address the envelopes, and little ones can lick the stamps!

- Let your children bake some Christmas cookies. They're easy to prepare and require little supervision—just make sure to keep small hands away from the oven. You can make things easier by giving cookie cutters a quick spritz of nonstick cooking spray to prevent dough from clinging. And for those stubborn cookies that won't come away from the baking sheet? Slide a length of dental floss under each cookie, and they'll glide right off.

- Children love to make pictures with artificial snow, but it can be difficult to wash off windows and surfaces. Prevent snow from sticking by preparing the surface with a light misting of nonstick cooking spray. If you forget this step, you can still remove it easily: Just rub with a little bit of white nongel toothpaste.

- Let the kids wrap some gifts. The outcome may not be just as you'd like, but the kids will have fun, and they'll be proud of their accomplishment.

(♛) **QUEENLY COMMENT:** Nourish your Christmas tree with a mixture of 1 quart of water, 2 tablespoons of lemon juice, 1 tablespoon of sugar, and ½ teaspoon of liquid bleach. If you want a simpler solution, try 2 ounces of Listerine or 1 tablespoon of maple syrup.

Oh, Christmas Tree

Do you dread the holidays because of the needles you still seem to be stepping on the following summer? Here's how to keep your castle carpet virtually needle-free and your tree fresh until you take it down after the holidays.

- Know the height of your living room before you select your tree. Make sure to allow for the stand (about a foot) and the treetop. Size *does* matter!

- Older trees are dry and will drop needles when shaken, so make sure to shake the tree before you buy it. Choose one that has sturdy, flexible needles and a strong, fresh scent.

- The first thing to do when you bring your tree home is to cut off a small diagonal section at the base of the trunk. Trees need a lot of water, and this small act will help them to absorb it.

- Pine tree needles will last longer if spritzed first with fabric sizing or spray starch. Just make sure to do this *before* you put the lights on.

- Put a plastic tablecloth under the base of your tree to help protect your carpet from spills.

- If you do have a spill from your Christmas tree, clean it up as soon as possible, or you'll have mold on the carpet. Slide the tree carefully to one side and blot up all of the water by standing on some heavy towels placed on the carpet. Absorb all you can. Clean the area with your favorite carpet cleaner, and let a fan blow across the area until it is thoroughly dry, at least 24 hours.

- Add water to the reservoir of a Christmas tree with a turkey baster, and you'll keep spills to a minimum, and be sure to water your tree daily.

- Rub a little petroleum jelly on the trunk of your artificial tree before inserting the branches. They'll be easier to remove.

- Put lights on your tree before adding any other decorations. And when choosing your lights, remember that white bulbs give off more light than colored ones.

- Run out of hooks and hangers? Use paper clips, bobby pins, twist ties, pipe cleaners, or dental floss. These makeshift hooks work well, but they're not very attractive, so try putting these ornaments deeper in the tree, where you're less likely to see the fasteners.

THE CAT'S MEOW

It's Zack, the Palace Pussycat, here to remind you that we cats (and even—yikes!—dogs) should get to enjoy the holidays as much as the rest of the family. Christmas may be an exciting time for people, but it can be a little nerve-wracking for those of us with four legs. Here are a few things to watch out for.

- Holiday plants such as holly, poinsettia, and mistletoe can be toxic. Please keep them away from us—and from small children, too!

- Cats love to play with tinsel, but we also like to eat it. This can wreak havoc on our intestinal tracts. Please keep the tinsel and other stringy decorations out of our reach. If you want to put tinsel on the tree, avoid the lower branches.

- We may like to eat rich foods, but they're not good for us and can make us sick—especially chocolate! If you can't resist our soulful faces staring up at you while you're eating dinner, give us some carrots and a small piece of turkey (without the gravy). Of course, it's best not to feed us from the table at all, but don't ever say *I* told you that!

- Bear in mind that I may not be the party animal you think I am. If you're having lots of company, please put me in a room by myself, with my food, water, and litter box. And better include a chew toy for the dog. You know how they get!

—Zack

QUEENLY COMMENT: Protect your door from scratches by securing a piece of weather stripping under your wreath.

At the Table

Here are some of my favorite tricks for making sure the palace table is beautiful and shiny for the festivities (or reviving it after the guests have left).

- Finding your good napkins wrinkled from storage can be frustrating. Don't despair. Just throw them in the dryer along with a damp towel. After 10 minutes or so, the creases will relax, and you won't have to iron them.

- Don't throw away those empty rolls of wrapping paper. If you make a slit down the side of the roll and slide it over a coat hanger, you can use it to hang tablecloths without worrying about creases.

- Clean your dining table the natural way, with tea! Make a pot of tea. Sit down, have a cup yourself, and wait until the tea is cool to the touch. Pour the liquid into a small container, saturate a clean, lint-free cloth, and wring it out till barely damp. Then wipe the table and leaves in the direction of the wood grain. Buff dry with a soft, dry cloth.

- Remove white marks from your table with a little bit of mayonnaise. Just make sure it's regular mayonnaise—low-fat won't do the trick. Mix the mayonnaise with table salt or cigarette ash. Massage the mixture into the mark for about 45 minutes. Yes, 45 minutes! It's a long time, but it's the massaging that gently buffs the mark away. Allow the mixture to sit for several hours, preferably overnight. Linseed oil and rottenstone (both available in hardware stores) work well, too.

- Use wax sticks or crayons to cover scratches. Make sure you get these from the hardware or furniture store (your child's crayons won't work here), and take care to match the shade of the stick to the table. Once you've applied the crayon according to the manufacturer's instructions, heat the area with a blow-dryer and buff firmly with an old rag for an almost invisible repair.

QUEENLY COMMENT: Put a few layers of foil in the basket before you add the napkin and rolls. Your bread and buns will stay warmer longer. And just about everybody likes warm buns!

It's a Wrap

There's nothing as delightful as a nicely wrapped gift. But that doesn't mean you have to bust your Christmas budget on wrapping paper. Be creative instead! Once you start looking at (practically) *everything* as wrapping paper, your options expand dramatically. Here are some more tips for royal gift wrapping.

- Keep rolls of wrapping paper handy by standing them up in a wastebasket or in a small, clean garbage can.

- Empty wrapping paper rolls can also be used as kindling. Slide small twigs, dried leaves, and broken bits of pinecones in the tubes to make the foundation of a wonderful, crackling fire for those chilly, winter evenings.

- Run out of wrapping paper? Recycle some old gift wrap by spraying the back with spray starch. Press with a warm iron, and you're ready to go!

- Keep the end of the tape from disappearing by folding it over a paper clip. You'll never have to pick at bits of tape again while trying to wrap gifts.

- Don't burn foil wrapping or magazines in a fireplace—they emit noxious, dangerous gases.

- Recycled Christmas cards make great gift tags.

QUEENLY COMMENT: Be creative when wrapping packages. Fabric, wallpaper, maps, T-shirts, and sheet music all make great gift coverings.

That Oh-So-Common Cold

Christmas may be a time of giving, but nobody wants to get a cold. Here are some ways to minimize your chances of getting this seasonal nuisance. If you *do* get a cold, look here for some comforting remedies . . . and some solutions for the stains those remedies can cause on your soft flannel sheets!

QUEENLY COMMENT: Help prevent colds by washing your hands for as long as it takes to sing "Happy Birthday". . . twice! That's the amount of time you'll need to wash your hands properly.

An Ounce of Prevention

Because colds linger for so long, they can really make the holidays a drag. Try not to let them get a foothold by following these preventive tactics.

- Contrary to the old wives' tale, you can't catch cold from being out in the cold weather. Colds are caused by viruses. Avoid the virus, avoid the cold.
- Wash your hands frequently, and wash them well. Use water that is comfortably hot. *Always* use soap.
- Avoid touching your eyes, nose, and mouth.
- Use tissues instead of handkerchiefs, if at all possible. Tissues are more easily disposed of, along with their germs!
- Don't leave tissues in an open trash can. Dispose of them in a plastic bag kept just for that purpose. You don't want anyone else picking up your germs!
- Try not to share things with someone who is ill. That includes towels, glasses, and utensils.
- Continue to share kisses—there's nothing like a little love when you're sick! Just confine it to the cheeks.

ROYAL DECREE: Be particularly vigilant about sharing phones especially at the office. Use a soft cloth dipped in Listerine mouthwash or rubbing alcohol to swab down phone mouthpieces, door handles, and computer keyboards. Alcohol wipes work well, too. It's a good idea to do this twice a week during cold season.

Cold Care

Once a cold's got hold of you, give yourself the royal treatment. You should start by getting some rest.

- Keep your feet warm. Believe it or not, cold feet can cause your nostrils to become cold and dry, and that can aggravate your cold.

- Wash bedding and pajamas in the hottest possible water.

- The fragrance of fabric softener can irritate delicate noses, so soften flannel sheets and cotton towels with ¼ cup of white vinegar when you have a cold.

ROYAL DECREE: Make sure you check the date on those cold medicines *before* you take them!

- Rubbing some Vicks VapoRub on the outside of your throat and chest will soothe that congestion, no matter how old you are.

- Put a dash of wintergreen oil in a basin of hot water, lower your face to the water (no closer than 12 inches, though), and put a towel over your head to create a tent. Breathe deeply for some much-needed relief.

QUEENLY COMMENT: Prone to cold sores? Dab on some Pepto-Bismol when you feel that first tingle, and chances are the sore won't make an appearance!

Humidifier Heaven

Moist air is heaven to dry throats and nasal passages, but if you don't keep your humidifier clean and free from mold, you may find your cold aggravated by airborne pollutants. Here's how to keep it clean and running smoothly.

Remove mineral deposits from detachable parts, such as the plastic rotor tube and locking ring, by submerging them in a pot of hot white vinegar. Bring a pot of vinegar to a boil, remove it from the stove, and then immerse the tube and ring in the vinegar for about 5 minutes. Rinse well in clear water, and make sure that all parts are dry before returning them to the unit.

Clean a humidifier by swishing around a solution of 1 cup of bleach in 1 gallon of water in the container that holds the water, allowing it to soak for a few minutes, if necessary. Scrub any mineral deposits with a brush and then rinse. Make sure the humidifier is cool and empty before you start.

What to Do for Those Cold Medication Stains

Rubs, liniments, eardrops, and ointments are all oil-based, so you should treat any stains from them as soon as you can. Rubbing the stain with a good waterless hand cleaner such as GOJO Crème Waterless Hand Cleaner is your best bet. Apply directly to the stain, and rub it in well with your thumb and forefinger. Wait 10 minutes, then apply a good stain remover, such as Zout, before laundering in the hottest possible water.

QUEENLY COMMENT: Baby wipes are great for removing stains caused by medicated ointments. Rub the stained fabric firmly with the baby wipe, then pretreat and launder as usual.

Cough syrups and other red-based stains can be removed quite effectively with Wine Away Red Wine Stain Remover or Red Erase. Apply liberally as directed on the container, then launder as usual. Alternatively, soak the stained area in 1 cup of warm water and 1 tablespoon of salt.

LET'S DISH!

Mom made these cookies every year for as long as I can remember. When I got old enough, I got to "help"—I loved the decorating part best. And I admit to sneaking a bite of the dough, not a healthy thing to do.

The Queen Mother's Christmas Cookies

2 cups flour

1 teaspoon baking powder

½ teaspoon baking soda

½ teaspoon salt

½ cup shortening

1 cup sugar

¼ teaspoon nutmeg

¼ teaspoon lemon extract or grated rind

2 eggs

In a bowl, mix together the dry ingredients.

Using a mixer, cream together the shortening, sugar, nutmeg, and lemon extract until well blended and light in color. Beat in the eggs and add the dry ingredients a little at a time, beating between additions.

Chill the mixture in the refrigerator for an hour or so, and then bake in one of the following ways:

- Roll out the dough, cut with cookie cutters, and place on a greased cookie sheet.
- Drop by rounded tablespoons onto a greased cookie sheet and flatten with the bottom of a drinking glass dipped in flour.

Decorate the cookies by placing a raisin or nut in the center of each cookie. Sprinkle with granulated sugar (colored granulated sugar is nice for Christmas).

Bake in a 375°F oven for 10 to 12 minutes. Do not overbake.

Think I'll go call my mom . . .

Makes about 3 dozen cookies

Fabric stained from hot toddies and medicated drinks should be flushed under cool, running water as soon as possible. Be sure to direct the water to the *wrong* side of the fabric. Next, make a paste with 20 Mule Team Borax and cool water. Use about 2 parts borax to 1 part water, adding more water as needed to create a pastelike consistency. Apply to the fabric, then have a cup of tea and watch your favorite sitcom. Once 30 minutes have passed, it's time to loosen the mixture by applying more cool water. Work the loosened mixture between your thumb and forefinger, then launder as usual in the hottest possible water for the fabric type.

QUEENLY COMMENT: Americans suffer from more than one billion colds a year. That's nothing to sneeze at!

January: A Royal New Year

It's January, a time of good intentions and new beginnings. We've made our resolutions and, with any luck, have recovered from our seasonal indulgences. We're ready for a fresh start. But first, we have to clean up from last year. That means putting away the Christmas decorations and taking down the tree, and storing the lights and all that half-price wrapping paper that seemed like such a good idea at the time. So let's get to it. If we start now, we'll still have time to enjoy that Super Bowl party!

Let's Un-Deck the Halls

Putting up decorations can be a lot of fun, what with all the excitement of the holidays to look forward to. But there are few surprises after Christmas—unless, of course, you're talking about that mystery stain you've just discovered on the hall carpet! The best way to clean up after the holidays is to take a deep breath, roll up your sleeves, and get down to it. The sooner you start, the sooner you'll be finished. And isn't that what it's all about?

SPOTS & SPLATTERS

Sticky Lights

Dear Queen:
What can I use to remove the tape that I used to put up my Christmas lights on the windows? Window cleaner doesn't work.

The Queen Responds:
Try Un-Du Adhesive Remover, made by Doumar Products. It is great for removing stickers, and so on, from everything from glass to wallpaper. It works on contact and won't leave residue or a stain behind. Pick it up at drugstores, hardware stores, and office supply stores.

Lights

If you just whip the lights off the house and tree and toss them in a box, you'll hate yourself come next December when you find them twisted, tangled, and broken. Wrap them around an empty paper roll instead. Take a large paper roll—one from wrapping paper will do fine—and cut a notch at one end. Tuck one end of the lights in the notch and start rolling them around the tube. When you get to the end of the tube, make another notch to fasten that end of the lights. Do this to each strand, clearly labeling the tubes as you go: indoor or outdoor lights, tree lights or decorative strands, and so forth. Make sure you separate any lights that aren't functioning properly and mark those too, either for repair or scavenging.

Large lights or extra-long lengths can be rolled in a circle, the way a cowboy loops a rope. Delicate, expensive, or special light strands can be stored in the type of inexpensive plastic food bowls that come with covers. The lights won't get crushed or broken, and they can be stacked for storage without damage.

Christmas Trees

Taking down the tree is really a two-person job, so try to enlist some help. A tree bag is your best bet, as it will prevent pine needles from being trailed through the house. Just make sure to buy a bag large enough to cover the base of the tree and long enough to cover the height. The first step is to siphon off all the water that you can—a turkey baster works great. Next, lay a large covering, such as a plastic shower curtain, on the floor. Take a good look around to ensure that breakables are safe, and make sure you're well out of range of any hanging light fixtures. Loosen the tree stand, and gently tip the tree onto the covering, being careful not to shed too many needles or spill any remaining water left in the reservoir. (Remember the first rule of cleaning: If you don't make a mess, you won't have to clean it up!)

Don't pull the bag up haphazardly, and don't tug. Be gentle and gradually unroll the bag up the length of the tree, something like putting on a pair of panty hose. (If you wear panty hose, that is . . .) Once you have the tree into the bag, tie the bag tightly and drag it outside. You can, of course, carry the tree, but there's always the chance that you'll drop it, and that may cause damage.

Artificial trees can be stored fully assembled in Christmas tree storage bags. Simply open the bag, "fold" up the limbs on the tree as directed (you did keep the booklet that came with the tree, didn't you?), place the tree carefully into the bag, and zip it up! Lack of storage space may dictate that you dismantle the tree and keep it in a box. If that's the case, just make sure to identify the branches, base, and stem—unless, of course, you like jigsaw puzzles.

Ornaments

First, make sure to dust the ornaments before you store them. Used fabric softener sheets are great for this job, but you will need rather a lot. Wipe the ornament with the used dryer sheet, then cover it so that the *other* side of the sheet touches the ornament. The fabric softener sheet will protect the ornament during storage, and the residue of softener will help to repel static electricity—and therefore, dust—when you hang it on the tree next year! Once you've wrapped the ornament, place it gently in a storage container, such as a shoe box or plastic storage carton. Those large metal canisters that once held popcorn are great, too.

👑 **QUEENLY COMMENT:** Decorative candles can be cleaned quite easily with a cotton ball moistened with rubbing alcohol.

Whatever container you use, make sure not to overcrowd it or force the lid down, and try not to use tape to secure the box. Tape can ruin the box for future use and, if stored in an attic, can get sticky and gummy during the hot summer months. That can cause a real mess! A bungee cord hooked around the ends of the container will keep the lid firmly closed. Try that instead.

Once again, make sure to mark the storage container, and make sure to separate ornaments that were expensive or have sentimental value. Delicate elongated ornaments can be stored inside toilet paper tubes, and smaller items can be placed safely in egg cartons. Save silk balls that are starting to unravel by giving them a spritz with some hair spray or spray starch.

Wrapping Paper
The most important thing about storing Christmas paper is to actually remember that you have it so you don't go out and buy more next year! Either put the paper in an obvious spot so that it's the first thing you see as you start to take out the decorations, or make a note that you have X number of rolls on hand. It's not a bargain if you buy it twice!

I store my wrapping paper under the bed. Long plastic storage containers meant for this purpose work exceptionally well and can be found quite inexpensively in dollar and discount stores. If you don't have a storage container, lay the rolls of paper on the floor and tie them together with some string or an elastic band. A bungee cord hooked into the ends of the rolls will hold the paper in a neat bundle.

Just make sure to slip them into a large garbage bag to keep them clean during storage.

Some people like to store their wrapping paper and ribbons in an old suitcase. That can work well, just as long as you remember which suitcase you've used. You don't want to end up in the Bahamas with nothing to wear but Santa Claus wrapping paper and a big red bow!

Ribbons and Bows

If you're like me, you'll have leftover ribbons and bows when you've finished wrapping all those presents. I've discovered a few tricks to keep them from getting all snarled and crumpled—and how to bring them back to life if they do get crushed. Read on . . .

- Store premade bows in a plastic storage or shoe box to prevent them from getting scrunched up. If you've bought an assortment of bows, tip them out of the bag and into the box. Those bags always seem to be too small to hold the bows, and so many of them wind up flattened and bent.

- Keep rolls of ribbon tidy by putting a rubber band or ponytail holder around the roll. You'll prevent unraveling that way.

Baubles, Bangles, and Beads—In Other Words, Miscellaneous!

When you think about it, there are so many bits and pieces associated with the holidays—almost enough to fill a small palace! Here's how to keep them safe and sound until next year.

I Hate It When That Happens...

You've just found the perfect color bow at the bottom of the bag, and darn if it isn't crushed! Not to worry. Crushed bows can be brought back to life by putting them in the dryer on air fluff (no heat) for a few short minutes. Presto! Good as new.

- Garland is usually too lush to be wrapped around just one paper roll, so fasten a few tubes together with a rubber band and wind the garland around that. Make sure you wrap the garland around the roll like a candy cane, side to side, and secure it in notches that you've cut in each end. Don't draw the garland from top to bottom—the strand could stretch or break.

- Dust silk flowers before storing them with a blow-dryer set on cool.

- If you store Christmas dishes in plastic wrap or stacked in Ziploc bags, you won't have to wash them before using them next year.

- Make sure to launder Christmas tablecloths and napkins prior to storing. Old spills will oxidize during storage and can be difficult, if not impossible, to remove.

(👑) QUEENLY COMMENT: Save those empty baby wipe boxes. They come in handy for storing gift tags and those slivers of ribbon that are so handy for decorating small packages.

- Take care when storing the nativity scene. Wrap each figure separately, either in tissue paper or a used fabric softener sheet. Paper towels don't work well for this job because their fibers can catch on any rough edges. If you scratch a figurine, try touching it up with a child's colored pencil.

(👑) QUEENLY COMMENT: Delicate Christmas knickknacks can be stored in egg cartons.

- Artificial wreaths can be stored year to year in a large pillowcase (depending on the size of the wreath) or in a large plastic bag. Wrap some tissue paper around the wreath first, but be gentle when removing it—you don't want to damage any of the branches. If the ribbon on the wreath is flattened, just plump it up with a curling iron.

- Many charities make good use of discarded Christmas cards. St. Jude's Ranch, for example, is a nonprofit youth home that teaches kids an art and a way to earn money by cutting off the verse and making the fronts into new cards. Entire cards are welcome, as are cards with the backs cut off. For more information call (800) 492-3562, or visit St. Jude's Web site at www.stjudesranch.org.

Making a List, Checking It Twice

Make a note of what seasonal items you've stored, and *where* you've put them. If you make a list of what you think you'll need next year—wrapping paper, Christmas cards, extension cords, larger-sized pants—you'll be in a good position to pick up bargains. More importantly, you'll save yourself that last-minute flurry of panic when you realize that your tree lights don't reach the outlet. Remember, excitement is good. Panic is bad.

It's Time for That Super Bowl Party!

I love Super Bowl parties. Everybody seems to be in such great spirits. Good friends, good food, and good fun. What could be better?

Touch-Ups after Touchdowns

Well, the game may have been good, but the post-party cleanup can be something else. Here's how to minimize the damage.

- Beer stains on clothes? Flush with cool water, work in a few drops of liquid dishwashing soap, and launder as usual.

- If you end up wearing a guacamole stain, treat it with Zout Stain Remover or rubbing alcohol. Gently dab the alcohol on the stain, and let sit for 15 minutes before pretreating and laundering as usual.

- If your house has that smoky, day-after smell, bring some white vinegar to a boil, then reduce to a simmer for about 30 minutes, being careful not to let the pan boil dry. Let the vinegar stand, and after a few hours unwanted odors will be absorbed.

QUEENLY COMMENT: Simmering orange or lemon peels can give your castle a fresh, natural scent.

- If the upholstery smells like smoke, lay a clean sheet on the furniture and sprinkle it with Odorzout. Let sit overnight, then remove the sheet and shake outside. Odorzout is all-natural and won't stain.

- Spilled ashtray? Don't reach for the vacuum—at least not right away. You could have a nasty vacuum fire on your hands, at which point you'll be wishing that a spilled ashtray was your *only* problem! Pick up any butts and dispose of them in an empty can until you're sure they are cool. If you're sensitive to cigarette odors, you may want to dispose of the vacuum bag or empty the canister.

ROYAL DECREE: Never apply water to an ashtray spill! You'll have a black, gooey mess on your hands that's far worse than anything you started with.

February: Hearts and Flowers

This is the month of cold weather and high heating bills. Thank goodness, it's also the month of love! Offset the winter cold by snuggling with your honey. Let the Valentine's flowers remind you of spring, and brighten those long winter nights with some sparkling jewelry. And if Cupid does leave his mark, well, look no further for some quick cleanup tips.

Happy Valentine's Day!

Flowers, jewelry, candy? I'd love Valentine's Day even if it *wasn't* the day the King proposed!

Petal Pushers

We all love getting flowers—and we love it even more if we can keep them alive for more than a few hours! Here's how to enjoy *your* King's bounty as long as possible.

- Do your best to select the freshest flowers available. Look for healthy stems with unblemished leaves and petals. Flowers that are in bud and just beginning to open will last longer than those already in full bloom.

- Be sure to remove leaves that fall below the waterline. They can contaminate the water.

- Cut stems on an angle while holding them under running water, then immerse in fresh water. It's best to do this in the early morning when it's coolest.

- Coarse, heavy stems (you'll find them on flowers such as glads, mums, pussy willows, forsythia, and even roses) should be split with a sharp knife before placing in water. This will encourage the stem to drink up the water. Pounding the base of the stem with a wooden spoon works well, too.

- Change the water every day. And for a longer life, add one of the following mixtures:
    - A teaspoon of sugar and about a ¼ teaspoon of lemon juice
    - Several aspirin tablets that have been dissolved in a little warm water
    - A tablespoon of liquid bleach. That will stop the water from clouding—particularly useful when using a clear vase.

- Prolong the life of flowers by keeping them cool and displaying them out of direct sunlight.

- Remove anthers from lilies. Those long, pollen-bearing shoots can rub off on clothes, carpeting and walls, and the stains can be extremely difficult to remove.

QUEENLY COMMENT: Clean pollen stains from clothing by sponging with rubbing alcohol. Don't use anything with ammonia. That will set the stain.

Artful Arrangements

Arranging flowers doesn't have to be hard—even when they refuse to cooperate! Here's how to create arrangements worthy of a palace.

- Flowers too short for the vase? Place stems in plastic drinking straws before arranging them.

- Vase too deep? Fill it with marbles prior to adding water and flowers.

- Wilted flowers? Snip about an inch off the ends and stand them in hot water for 20 to 30 minutes before returning to a vase of clean, cool water.

- Make sure that floral foam is saturated with water before adding flowers.

- Arrange large flowers first, then follow with smaller blossoms and greenery.

QUEENLY COMMENT: Tulips are the only flowers that continue to grow *after* they've been cut!

- Coffeepots, teapots, and milk bottles make lovely, imaginative vases.

- Plastic hair rollers are great for arranging flowers. Stand them upright in the bottom of the vase and place stems in the cylinders to keep them in position.

- Try to match the flowers to the vase. Hourglass shapes are good for single-bloom flowers such as tulips, and urns are great for flowers that droop easily. Slim, cylindrical vases are best for tall flowers such as glads.

- Placing your arrangement in front of a mirror will double the impact of your flowers.

Diamonds Are a Queen's Best Friend

Who doesn't love to get a gift of jewelry? Who doesn't want to know how to care for it?

- Rubbing alcohol is great for cleaning costume jewelry. Pour a little rubbing alcohol over the piece—place the jewelry in a shallow dish or small container first!—and gently brush with a soft toothbrush. (A word of caution: Many costume pieces are glued, and soaking can loosen the glue, so try not to saturate it.) Finish with a quick rinse in cool water and wipe dry.

- Costume jewelry that doesn't contain glue can be cleaned with denture-cleaning tablets. Drop a few tablets in a cup of warm water and allow the jewelry to soak for 5 minutes or so. Rinse and dry well. For intricate pieces, dry with a blow-dryer.

- Remove dirt from intricate pieces by brushing with a soft-bristle toothbrush and some white nongel toothpaste. Rinse by brushing with a clean toothbrush and just water, and dry well.

QUEENLY COMMENT: Restore the luster to pearls by buffing gently with a soft cloth moistened with olive oil.

- Clean diamonds by placing in a tea strainer and dipping them in a pot of boiling water into which you have added several drops of ammonia and a drop or two of dishwashing liquid. Immerse for a few seconds and then rinse in cold water. For extra sparkle, dip the diamonds in a little bit of undiluted vodka or alcohol for a minute or two, then rinse and pat dry. This may be used for hard stones such as diamonds, rubies, and sapphires. *Do not* use this method on emeralds.

- Emeralds are extremely soft. They can crack easily and absorb water, so buff them with a soft toothbrush or an ACT Natural

I Hate It When That Happens...

Tangled chains got you in knots? Place a drop of baby oil on the chain, then gently untangle by pulling the links apart with two sewing needles.

microfiber cloth. Don't soak them or immerse them in water, and if you want a thorough cleaning, take them to a professional.

- Remove tarnish from silver with a paste of lemon juice and baking soda. Apply the mixture with a soft toothbrush, then allow to dry. Remove with a clean, dry toothbrush and polish with a clean, soft cloth.

- Jade can be washed in mild, soapy water. Dry immediately.

- Opals and turquoise are porous stones that should not be washed. Brush settings with a dry, soft toothbrush, and shine with chamois-type leather or an ACT Natural microfiber cloth.

- Wash gold in a bowl of soapy water. A soft, gentle stroke with a soft toothbrush will help clean crevices, details, and links. Dry with a soft, lint-free towel, and then buff with a chamois or microfiber cloth.

- Always fasten a chain-link necklace before storing it to prevent tangles. Chains that tangle easily can be slipped through a drinking straw. Cut the straw to half the length of the chain, drop the chain through and fasten the clasp on the outside of the straw. No more tangles.

The Valentine's Day Stain Chain

Love should last forever, not that chocolate stain.

- Chocolate on clothes requires special treatment. Scrape off all you can with a dull straight edge, taking care not to force the chocolate more deeply into the fabric. Gently apply some Zout Stain Remover, allow it to sit on the fabric 5 minutes or so (don't let it dry), and then flush under a forceful stream of warm water. If a grease mark is still visible, sponge with any good dry-cleaning solution such as Energine Cleaning Fluid. For really tough stains, soak in Brilliant Bleach by Soapworks. Follow package directions carefully.

QUEENLY COMMENT: You can keep the fizz in champagne for hours if you slip the handle of a metal teaspoon down the neck of the bottle. I don't know why it works, but it does!

- Dried alcohol stains will turn brown as they age, so quick removal is important.
- Champagne spills on clothes should first be blotted with club soda, then pretreated with a good laundry stain remover.

SPOTS & SPLATTERS
Yesterday's News

Dear Queen:
Will anything keep newspaper articles from turning yellow? I have a few articles with great sentimental value, and quite a few other articles I would like to store.

The Queen Responds:
Believe it or not, milk of magnesia does the trick to keep newspaper clippings from yellowing! Follow the procedure used by experts at the National Archives: Mix 2 tablespoons of milk of magnesia in 1 quart of club soda, then refrigerate overnight. Pour the mixture into a shallow pan and submerge the clippings for 1 hour. Dry overnight, then store with confidence. (And don't forget to date and label your clippings for easy reference.)

- Stains from pink champagne can be removed with Wine Away Red Wine Stain Remover.

- Perfume stains can be avoided if you apply your fragrance *before* you get dressed. Make sure it's dry before putting on your clothes.

- Perfume is a combination of alcohol and oil—deadly to fabrics. Treat perfume stains with Zout Stain Remover and launder as soon as possible. If the fabric is dry-clean only, be sure to point out the stain to your dry cleaner.

- Never iron an area that has been sprayed with perfume. You might set the stain, or worse, remove the color from the fabric!

- Perfume stains can be removed from sturdy fabrics with a lather of Fels-Naptha Laundry Soap and warm water. Work well into the stain, let sit 15 minutes, and launder as usual.

- Stains from massage oil can be removed with a good waterless hand cleaner, such as GOJO. Rub it well into the fabric—*massage* it in if you'd like!—then flush with warm water. A paste of liquid dish soap and 20 Mule Team Borax will also work. Launder as usual, using your normal detergent and the hottest possible water for the fabric. One-half cup of 20 Mule Team Borax will ensure that all residue is removed.

5
Everything You Need
to Be a Queen

A-to-Z Palace Spot and Stain Removal Guide

I am so glad that you feel safe airing your dirty laundry (and all the other dirt) with me. I am, after all, the Babe of Borax, one of the original Mold-Diggers, the High Priestess of Household Chemicals, the Vixen of Vinegar, the Deaconess of Dry Cleaning, the Goddess of Grease Stains, the Sultaness of Soap, Solvents, and Solutions—and of course, the Queen of Clean®! And you know what else? I'm not finished yet . . . not until I give you this, my all-you-need-to-know spot and stain removal guide, straight from the palace!

Now, a few words of caution before we begin. *Don't* go trying any of these spot removal methods *without* paying heed to my Royal Rules of Stain Removal on page 328. Promise?

Finally, let me remind you not to let a stain spoil your day. Stains happen! Just look 'em up and get 'em out.

The A-to-Z Guide

Acid. Acid can permanently damage fabrics, so it must be treated immediately. Neutralize acid by flushing the area with cold running water as soon as possible. Next, spread the garment over a pad of paper towels and moisten with ammonia. Dab the spot several times, then flush again with cold water. If you do not have ammonia on hand, apply a paste of cold water and baking soda, then flush with water. Repeat this several times, then launder as usual.

Do not use undiluted ammonia on wool, silk, or any blends containing these fibers. If you have gotten acid on silk or wool, you may dilute ammonia with equal parts cold water and apply as directed above.

Adhesive tape. Sponge adhesive tape with eucalyptus oil, baby oil, or cooking oil. Allow to soak 10 minutes or so, then work in undiluted dishwashing liquid and rinse well. Pretreat and launder as usual.

You may also consider using De-Solv-It, Goo Gone, or Un-Du to remove adhesives from fabric and hard surfaces. Un-Du is so great, it will remove a stamp from an envelope!

Alcoholic beverages. These stains will turn brown with age, so it is important to treat them as soon as possible. First, flush the area with cold water or club soda, then sponge immediately with a cloth barely dampened with warm water and 1 or 2 drops of liquid dish soap. Rinse with cool water and dry the area with a hair dryer set on medium.

Alcohol is often invisible when it is spilled, but it can oxidize with heat and age, which makes it impossible to remove. Presoak dry alcohol stains in an enzyme solution such as Biz All Fabric Bleach, and launder as usual.

If you spill alcohol on a dry-clean-only fabric, sponge with cold water or club soda, and then take the garment to the dry cleaner as soon as possible. Make sure to point out the stain.

For beer spills, sponge with a solution of equal parts white vinegar and dishwashing liquid, then rinse in warm water.

For treating red and white wine spills, *see* **Wine.**

Animal hair. Removing pet hair from clothes and bedding can be a challenge. Try using a damp sponge and wiping over clothes and bedding, and so forth. Rinse the sponge frequently to keep it clean. You can also remove hair by putting on rubber gloves and dipping them in water. Simply dip and wipe, dip and wipe. The hair will rinse off easily.

Antiperspirants and deodorants. Antiperspirants that contain aluminum chloride are acidic and may interact with some fabrics. If color changes have occurred, try sponging fabric with ammonia. Rinse thoroughly, and remember to dilute ammonia with an equal portion of water when spotting wool or silk.

If you want to avoid yellow underarm stains and prevent color removal, take a bar of Fels-Naptha Laundry Soap and work it into the underarms of clothes *before* you launder them for the first time, even if you see no visible stain. Work up a good lather between your thumbs and then launder as usual.

You can also try applying rubbing alcohol to the stain and covering the area with a folded paper towel dampened with alcohol. Keep it moist and let it sit for a few hours prior to laundering.

To treat yellowed areas that have become stiff, apply an enzyme-soaking product. Biz All Fabric Bleach is a good one to try. Make a stiff paste of the powder by mixing it with cold water. Rub it into the stained areas. Next, put the garment in a plastic bag and leave it there for 8 hours or overnight. Wash in very hot water. If dealing with fabrics that can't withstand hot water, drape the underarm area over a sink and pour 1 quart of hot water through the fabric. Launder as usual.

Don't iron over a deodorant stain, or you will never be able to remove it.

I have also had success soaking garments with underarm stains in a solution of 1 quart of warm water and 3 tablespoons of Brilliant Bleach. Soak up to several days if necessary. Brilliant Bleach is safe for whites and colorfast garments.

Last-ditch effort: Spray the stained area heavily with heated white vinegar, work in 20 Mule Team Borax, roll up in a plastic bag and leave overnight, then launder as usual.

Baby formula. For white clothes, try applying lemon juice to the stains and laying the garment in the sun. Pretreat and launder as usual.

Unseasoned meat tenderizer is also great for removing formula and baby-food stains. Make a paste of the tenderizer and cool water, rub it into the stain, and let sit for an hour or so before laundering. Meat tenderizer contains an enzyme that breaks down protein stains. Just make sure to use *unseasoned* tenderizer!

Soaking colored clothes and whites in Brilliant Bleach is also effective, although you may have to soak for several days to achieve perfect results on difficult stains. Remember, this bleach is nonchlorine, so it's totally safe for baby things.

Barbecue sauce. *See* Tomato-based stains.

Berries (blueberries, cranberries, raspberries, strawberries). There are many complex ways to deal with berry stains, but I've had great success with one of the simplest, a product called Wine Away Red Wine Stain Remover. Don't be fooled by the name—it works on red fruit stains and juices, too.

Just spray Wine Away straight on the fabric, and watch in amazement as it breaks down the stain. Follow the directions on the container carefully and launder immediately after use. Totally nontoxic, Wine Away is safe on all washable surfaces.

Beverages. Blot beverage spills immediately until you have absorbed all you can, then sponge with clean, warm water and a little borax. (Use about ½ teaspoon of borax to ½ cup of water.) Sponge and blot repeatedly and launder as usual.

Also see information under specific beverage stains.

Blood (fresh and dried). If you have blood all over your clothes, laundry may not be your biggest problem . . . but for those little accidents, try the following techniques.

For washable fabrics, soak as soon as possible in salt water or flush with club soda. You can also make a paste of unseasoned meat tenderizer and cold water, and apply it to the stain for a few hours. Wash in cool water and detergent, by hand or machine.

Pouring 3 percent hydrogen peroxide through the stained area can be effective in many instances. The sooner you do this, the more success you will have. Make sure to try this only on washable fabrics, please. Pour the peroxide through the stain, then flush with cold water, pretreat, and launder as usual.

Biz All Fabric Bleach and Brilliant Bleach both work well on blood. When using Biz, make a paste with cold water and apply to the stain, allowing it to sit for several hours. With Brilliant Bleach, soak the garment for a significant period of time—anywhere from 1 to 24 hours. Neither of these products will harm colorfast fabrics.

For dry-clean-only fabrics, sprinkle with salt while the blood is still moist, then take to a dry cleaner as soon as possible.

Human saliva will break down fresh bloodstains, so try applying a little of your own saliva to a small spot of blood—this may do the trick.

For a quick fix for fresh bloodstains, apply cornstarch to the surface and then flush from the wrong side of the fabric with soapy water. Pretreat and launder as usual.

Blood on leather can be foamed away with 3 percent hydrogen peroxide. Dab on the peroxide. Let it bubble and then blot. Continue until the blood is removed. Wipe the surface with a damp cloth and dry.

Butter or margarine. Scrape off any solid concentration of butter with a dull edge, such as the back of a knife.

On washable fabrics, work in undiluted dishwashing liquid, wash, and dry.

If the stain is old, spray it with WD-40 lubricant to regenerate the grease, then work in undiluted dishwashing liquid and wash in the hottest water possible for that fabric type.

Sponge silks and delicate fabrics with Energine Cleaning Fluid. Allow to air-dry. Repeat if necessary.

Do not iron the fabric until all traces of the grease have been removed. Ironing will set the stain and make it impossible to remove.

Take dry-clean-only fabrics to the dry cleaner as soon as possible. Be sure to identify the stain and its location on the garment.

Candle wax. For candle wax on clothes and table linens, place the article in a plastic bag, place the bag in the freezer, and let the wax freeze. Scrape off what you can with a dull, straight edge—the back of a knife or an old credit card works well. Lay a brown paper bag (with no writing facing the fabric) on the ironing board. (Grocery store bags work well. Just make sure that the writing is facedown on the ironing board *away* from the fabric—otherwise you may transfer lettering to your garment.) Cover with a similar bag (again, with the writing *away* from the fabric) and press with a medium/hot iron, moving the paper bag like a blotter until you have absorbed every bit of wax you can. Be patient! Blot with Energine Cleaning Fluid to remove the balance of the grease from the wax.

Wieman Wax Away also works beautifully on any kind of wax. Follow the directions on the product label carefully.

Candy. To remove candy from fabrics, combine 1 tablespoon of liquid dish soap with 1 tablespoon of white vinegar and 1 quart of warm water. Soak the stain in it for 15 to 30 minutes, then flush with warm, clear water. Pretreat and launder as usual.

For chocolate stains, *see* **Chocolate.**

Chewing gum. *See* **Gum.**

Chocolate. Scrape off all that you can, then soak washable fabrics for 30 minutes in an enzyme prewash solution such as Biz. Rub detergent into any remaining stain and work well between your thumbs. Rinse the area under forcefully running cold water. If a grease spot remains, sponge the area with dry-cleaning solution such as Energine Cleaning Fluid. Any residual stain should come out during normal washing. If the stain is still visible after washing, soak in Brilliant Bleach, or combine ½ cup of 3 percent hydrogen peroxide and 1 teaspoon of clear ammonia and soak the stain for 10 minutes at a time, checking every 10 minutes and resoaking if necessary. Remember, fabrics need to be tested for colorfastness before using peroxide.

For dry-clean-only fabrics, flush the stain with club soda to prevent setting, then sponge the area with Energine Cleaning Fluid. If the stain persists, take it to your dry cleaner.

Coffee and tea (black). Blot up all that you can and, if the garment is washable, flush immediately with cold water. Rub detergent into the stain and work well between your thumbs before laundering as usual. If the stain is still visible and you can use hot water on the fabric, spread the stain over the sink, or stretch the stained part of the fabric over a bowl and tie or rubber-band it in place (like a little trampoline), then set the bowl in the sink. Cover the stain with 20 Mule Team Borax and pour boiling water through it, spiraling from the outside of the stain until you have reached the center. Let soak 30 minutes to an hour and launder.

For more delicate fabrics, soak in Brilliant Bleach.

For sturdy whites, such as knits and T-shirts, dissolve two denture-cleaning tablets in warm water and soak the stain for 30 minutes. Check the garment. If the stain is still visible, soak again and launder as usual.

Out at a restaurant? Dip your napkin in water and sprinkle it with salt, then blot the offending stain.

For stains from lattes and cappuccinos, *see* **Milk**.

Cola and soft drinks. Sponge these spills as soon as possible with a solution of equal parts alcohol and water. On washable clothes, bleach out remaining stains with an equal mixture of 3 percent hydrogen peroxide and water. Saturate the stain and wait 20 minutes. If the stain is gone, launder as usual. Repeat if the stain remains. You can also soak the fabric in a solution of Brilliant Bleach as directed on the container.

Borax is also effective in soft drink/cola removal. Moisten the spot thoroughly and sprinkle with borax, working well between your thumbs. Flush with water and treat again if necessary.

Getting the stain out as soon as possible is important: Cola and soft drinks will discolor fabrics as they oxidize.

Collar stains. This is for those women whose husbands won't share laundry duty and the women who didn't know that the wedding ring came with a ring around the collar! It's easy to remove, though. Just use some inexpensive shampoo! Shampoo dissolves body oils, so it works great on that collar ring. Keep some in a bottle with a dispenser top in the laundry room. Squirt on enough to cover the offending stain and work it in well, then launder as usual.

Copier toner (powder). First, carefully shake off any loose powder and brush lightly with a soft brush. An old, soft toothbrush works well. Pretreat with your favorite spotter, or try Zout Stain Remover or Spot Shot Instant Carpet Stain Remover and launder as usual, using the hottest water for the fabric type. Don't rub or brush with your hand. The oil in your skin will spread and set the stain.

Cosmetics (foundation, blusher, eye shadow, eyeliner, and mascara). Bar soap, such as Dove, Caress, and other such beauty bars work well on cosmetics spots. Wet the stain and rub with the soap, working it in well. Flush with warm water and, once the stain is removed, launder as usual.

Sometimes just working in laundry detergent will be all you need. For difficult cases, add some borax to the area and work well between your thumbs.

If your garment is dry-clean-only, try some Energine Cleaning Fluid directly on the spot. Make sure to use a cool blow-dryer to keep a ring from forming on the fabric. You'll need to take the garment to a professional cleaner if the stain doesn't come out. (*See also* **Makeup.**)

Crayon and colored pencil. Place the stained area on a pad of paper towels and spray with WD-40 lubricant. Let stand for a few minutes, then turn the fabric over and spray the other side. Let sit for 10 more minutes before working undiluted dishwashing liquid into the stained area to remove the crayon and oil. Replace the paper-toweling pad as necessary. Wash in the hottest possible water for the fabric, along with your normal detergent and appropriate bleaching agent (depending on whether the clothes are white or colored). Wash on the longest wash cycle available, and rinse well.

Another way to remove crayon from washable fabrics such as wool, acrylic, linen, cotton, and polyester is to lay the offending stain between two pieces of brown paper and press with a warm/medium iron. A grocery bag works well—just remember to keep any ink that may be on the bag away from the fabric. The paper works as a blotter to absorb the crayon, so keep changing it as the wax is absorbed. If any color mark remains, soak the garment in Brilliant Bleach or flush with Energine Cleaning Fluid.

Note: Don't panic if the crayon has also gone through the dryer. Simply spray an old rag with WD-40 lubricant, then thoroughly wipe down the drum. Make sure the dryer is empty when you do this—no clothes, no crayons. Place a load of dry rags in the dryer and run through a drying cycle when you're through. This will remove any oily residue.

Dye (*see also* Hair Dye). Dye stains are difficult if not impossible to remove. Try one or all of these methods.

Spread the stained area over a bowl and put a rubber band around the fabric *and* the bowl to hold the fabric taut, like a trampoline. Sit the bowl in the sink with the drain in the open position to allow the water to run freely away. Turn on the cold water faucet to a nice steady drip and let it drip through the dye spot for 3 to 6 hours. Monitor the sink to be sure the water is draining. This treatment is effective in many cases.

You can also try saturating the dye spot with a combination of equal parts 3 percent hydrogen peroxide and water. Sit the fabric in the sun, keeping it moist with the solution until the spot completely disappears. Rinse well and launder as usual. Use only on colorfast clothes.

If your dye problem is caused from fugitive color—that is, color that has run from one fabric to another during the wash cycle—all the bleaching in the world won't help. Try Synthrapol or Carbona Color Run Remover instead.

Quilters have used Synthrapol for years to remove color that runs in homemade quilts and hand-dyed fabrics. Make sure to read *all* the directions on the bottle prior to using.

Carbona Color Run Remover is extremely effective on cotton fabrics. It is not for delicates or some blends, so do follow the directions on the box carefully. It may also cause damage to buttons and, in some cases, zippers. You may want to remove these prior to treating.

Egg. First scrape off any solid matter. Then soak the fabric in a glass or plastic container with any enzyme-soaking product, such as Biz

Nonchlorine Bleach. Soak for at least 6 hours or overnight. If a stain remains, work in powder detergent, rubbing vigorously between your thumbs. Rinse and wash as usual. Check the garment carefully for any remaining stain when you remove it from the washer. Don't apply heat until all of the stain is removed, or the stain will become permanent.

You can also try treating the area with cool water and unseasoned meat tenderizer. Work this into the area well and allow it to sit for a few hours, being sure to keep the area moist. Continue treating until no stain remains.

Take nonwashables to the dry cleaner as soon as possible. Quick treatment is important. Make sure you identify the stain to your cleaner so it can be treated properly and promptly.

Eyeliner and eye shadow. *See* **Cosmetics.**

Fabric softener spots. For the greasy spots that sometimes appear on clothes after drying with dryer fabric softener sheets, dampen the spot and rub with pure bar soap, then relaunder.

For spots from liquid fabric softener, rub with undiluted liquid dish soap and relaunder.

Felt tip marker. *See* **Marker.**

Food dye. Fruit juices, gelatin desserts, fruit smoothies, and frozen fruit sticks all contain food dye that can leave a nasty stain on clothes.

Treating the stain while it is still fresh is the very best thing you can do. If you are out in public and don't have access to any cleaning supplies, wet the spot with club soda or cool water and blot, blot, blot. If you are at home, treat the spot with 1 cup of cool water to which you have added 1 tablespoon of ammonia. Once you have flushed the spot well with this solution, grab the salt shaker and rub salt into the wound . . . I mean, stain! Let this sit for an hour or so, and then brush off the salt. If the stain is still visible, treat again the same way.

You can also try stretching the fabric tight and holding it under a forceful stream of cold water. This will flush out much of the spot without spreading it. Next, rub in your favorite detergent, scrubbing vigorously between your thumbs. Rinse again in cool water. Do not apply heat to the stain until it is completely removed.

I have had great success soaking food dye spills in Brilliant Bleach (follow the directions for hand-soaking on the container).

If you are dealing with a red, orange, or purple stain, try Wine Away Red Wine Stain Remover, used according to directions. Don't be fooled by the name—it's great for all red-type stains. You will be amazed!

Remember, if the stain is not removed during the spotting process, it will not come out in the laundry!

Fruit and fruit juice (*see also* Berries). These stains absolutely *must* be removed before the fabric is washed. The combination of heat and age will set fruit stains, and they will be impossible to remove, even for the Queen.

Sponge or spray the area immediately with soda water or seltzer. If these products aren't available, use cold water. *Do not use hot water.* Rinse the offending spot as soon as possible while it is still wet. Rub in your favorite detergent and scrub the area between your thumbs. *Now* rinse under hot running water—as hot as the fabric can tolerate. Pull the fabric taut and allow the full force of the water to flow through the area. The stronger the flow, the better.

If the stain is still visible after this treatment, make a paste of 20 Mule Team Borax and warm water, and work it into the stained area. Let this dry and brush off. Repeat as needed. You can also try pulling the fabric tight over a bowl, using a rubber band to secure it. Sprinkle 20 Mule Team Borax over the stain and, using the hottest water possible for the fabric type, start at the outside edge of the stain and pour the water through the borax in circles until you are pouring through the center of the stain.

Fresh fruit stains, if treated promptly, will usually come out. Quick treatment is especially important for fruits such as peach and citrus.

Fruit stains, old. Before you can remove the stain, you must reconstitute it. You can do this by applying glycerin to the area. Rub it in well and allow it to soak for 30 minutes. Then treat as above.

For nonwashable fabrics, gently sponge the stain with cold water as soon as it occurs, and then take the garment to a dry cleaner as quickly as possible. Be sure to identify the stain so it can be treated properly.

If the stains are red, use Wine Away Red Wine Stain Remover as directed in the section on berry stains.

Furniture polish. Furniture polish is usually an oil-based stain, so it must be reconstituted. Restore the oil in the polish by spraying with WD-40 lubricant. Allow the lubricant to soak for 10 minutes, then work in undiluted dishwashing liquid. Work this in well between your thumbs to remove the grease. Flush with a forceful stream of the hottest water you can for the fabric type. Pretreat with a product such as Zout, which is great for grease spots, and launder as usual.

You can also try cleaning the area with Energine Cleaning Fluid, used according to directions on the can.

If the furniture polish has color in it, *see* **Dye.**

Glue, adhesives, mucilage. Modern adhesives and glues are very hard to remove. You may have to use a special solvent. Take the garment to the dry cleaner and be sure to identify the spot.

Here's a rundown of glue types and how to remove them.

Model glue. Can usually be removed with nail polish remover containing acetone, although you may need to purchase straight acetone at a hardware or beauty supply store. Always test the acetone in a small area first.

Plastic adhesives. For best results, treat these stains before they dry. Try washing in cool water and detergent. If the stain remains, bring 1 cup or so of white vinegar to a boil, and immerse the stain. Have more vinegar boiling as you treat the stain so that you can switch to the hot vinegar as soon as the first cup starts to cool. Continue reheating the vinegar and treating for 15 to 20 minutes.

Rubber cement. Scrape off all that you can with a dull, straight edge that you can throw away. (Don't use a credit card for this—unless it's over its limit!) Treat with Energine Cleaning Fluid as directed.

You can also try working petroleum jelly into the glue until it pills into balls that you can then scrape from the fabric. Treat the area with undiluted liquid dish soap and launder in the hottest water the fabric will tolerate.

Miscellaneous glues. Sponge or rinse the fabric in warm water. Work in your favorite powdered detergent or liquid detergent along with some 20 Mule Team Borax. Rub vigorously between your thumbs. Rinse and wash in the hottest water you can for the fabric type.

Remember, soap and water will remove most synthetic glue when the spot is fresh. Acetone will remove most clear, plastic cement-type glues. Make sure to test acetone in an inconspicuous area, and never use on acetate fabrics—it will dissolve them!

For old, dried glue stains, soak the fabric in a solution of boiling hot white vinegar and water. Use 2 parts white vinegar to every 10 parts of water, and soak for 30 to 60 minutes. You may need to scrape off the glue as it softens. Then pretreat and launder as usual.

Grass, flowers, and foliage. There are several ways to remove grass stains from fabrics. Pick one and try it. If it doesn't completely remove the stain, try another. Just don't put clothes into the dryer until the grass stain is removed.

First, a word of caution: Avoid using alkalis such as ammonia, degreasers, or alkaline detergents. They interact with the tannin in the grass stains and may permanently set the stain.

Okay—first, washable fabrics: Sponge on rubbing alcohol, repeating several times. If the stain persists, sponge with white vinegar and rinse. Work in your favorite laundry detergent and rinse well.

Rubbing white nongel toothpaste into grass stains will often remove them. Rub well, then rinse and wash as usual.

For jeans, apply undiluted alcohol to the area and allow to soak 15 minutes before laundering as usual.

Zout Stain Remover and Spot Shot Instant Carpet Stain Remover also work very well on grass stains. Follow the label directions. Biz All Fabric Bleach made into a paste with cold water is effective in treating stubborn grass stains, too.

For grass on white leather shoes, rub the grass stain with molasses and leave it on the shoe overnight. Wash the molasses off with hot soap and water, and the grass stain should be gone.

For grass on suede fabric, including shoes, rub the stain with a sponge dipped in glycerin. Then rub with a cloth dipped in undiluted white vinegar, brush the nap gently to reset, allow it to dry, and brush again. Remember, test in an inconspicuous spot first.

Gravy. With gravy, you need to remove the starch used to thicken it, so you will want to soak the garment in cold water long enough to dissolve the starch. It may take several hours.

Pretreat prior to laundering with a good spotter, such as Zout Stain Remover or Spot Shot Instant Carpet Stain Remover. Launder in the hottest possible water for the fabric type.

You can also soak the garment in Brilliant Bleach, for days if necessary.

Grease and oil (including cooking oil and salad dressing). Grease and oil must be removed thoroughly, otherwise a semitransparent stain will set and will turn dark from all the soil it attracts.

To treat a grease stain, it helps to know whether it is from animal oil, vegetable oil, or automotive oil.

To remove a grease stain, first remove as much of the greasy substance as possible without forcing the grease farther down into the fabric fibers. Use a paper towel to blot and absorb all the grease that you can. Next, apply a drawing agent such as baking soda, cornstarch, or talcum powder. Rub it in gently, and let it sit for 15 to 30 minutes to allow the agent to absorb and draw the grease out of the fabric. Brush the powder off thoroughly and check the stain. If it looks like you can absorb more grease, repeat the process.

Next, lay the fabric over a thick rag or a heavy fold of paper towels. Working from the back of the fabric, blot with Energine Cleaning Fluid. Change the pad under the fabric as needed and repeat if necessary.

When grease stains are stubborn, we need to fall back on the idea that grease removes grease. Spray the grease spot with WD-40 lubricant and let it soak for 10 minutes. Then work in undiluted dishwashing liquid and work well between your thumbs. Flush with the hottest water you can for the fabric, pretreat, and launder as usual. Do not use this method on silk or crease-resistant finishes.

Many grease stains will eventually turn yellow when set with age and heat. Treat these stains by soaking in diluted hydrogen peroxide or Brilliant Bleach. Don't use this process unless you know that the clothes are colorfast.

Use Energine Cleaning Fluid on dry-clean-only fabrics, or take to a professional dry cleaner.

For heavily soiled, greasy work clothes, try pouring a can of original Coca-Cola in the washer with your detergent and launder as usual. The combination of sugar and cola syrup works wonders!

Gum. The best way to deal with gum is to harden it first. Harden any item marred by chewing gum by placing it in a plastic bag in the freezer and leaving it overnight. Immediately upon removing the bag from the freezer, scrape off any gum that you can with a dull straight edge. If all the gum is removed, treat the fabric with an equal mixture of white vinegar and liquid dish soap. You may also try treating the area with lighter fluid, although you must do this outside and use extreme care, testing the fabric first.

Sometimes rubbing the area with egg white (*not* the yolk—no joke!) will remove the remaining residue.

If gum is still trapped, try working petroleum jelly into the fibers and scraping off the little balls that form. Be sure to follow the directions under **Grease** to remove the grease from the petroleum jelly.

Petroleum jelly will also soften old, dry gum. You want to work the petroleum jelly into the gum and then scrape off all that you can.

For those of you who ask, yes, peanut butter will work, too, but it is messier. My advice is to eat the peanut butter and use the petroleum jelly!

Carbona makes a Stain Devil for Chewing Gum Removal. It's a great little specialty spotter.

For dry-clean-only fabrics, you may freeze the fabric and scrape off what gum you can. Take it to your dry cleaner right away.

Hair dye. If you didn't listen to me when I told you to dye your hair naked in the backyard, then hair-dye spots may be a major problem for you. Here's what to do.

Clothing or fabrics stained with hair dye should be washed in warm water, to which you have added white vinegar and your normal detergent. Do this in a sink or container, adding about 2 tablespoons of detergent and 2 cups of white vinegar to a gallon of warm water. Let it soak for several hours.

If the stain still remains, try our favorite bleach, Brilliant Bleach. You can soak whites and colorfast fabrics for several days if necessary, without damage. Try to avoid the hair-dye problem if you can. I suggest using the same old towel when you do your hair.

Hand cream. Blot off all that you can and treat with Energine Cleaning Fluid, working from the back of the fabric. Once all of the stain is removed, launder as usual.

Ice cream. Yummy-yummy in the tummy—not so great on clothes! Sponge the garment as quickly as possible with cold water, club soda, or seltzer. If a stain still remains, treat it with cold water and unseasoned meat tenderizer. Let this soak on the fabric for about 30 minutes or so, and then flush with cold water to see if the offending spot is gone. Pretreat with Spot Shot Instant Carpet Stain Remover or Zout and launder as usual.

If a grease spot remains, treat with Energine Cleaning Fluid, working from the back of the fabric over a pad of paper towels to absorb the spot and the spotting solution.

Sometimes treating ice cream–stained fabric with a small amount of ammonia will also work. Then, of course, launder as usual.

Ink. How can one little pen cause so much grief? The first line of defense is rubbing alcohol. Sponge the ink mark or dip it into a glass of rubbing alcohol, letting it soak until the offending spot is removed. Don't be tricked into using hair spray. That may have worked in the past, but hair spray now contains a lot of oil, and that just spreads the stain.

Denatured alcohol—a much stronger version of rubbing alcohol—may be more effective. Test this first in an inconspicuous spot, as denatured alcohol may damage some fabrics.

You also can try using acetone. This too must be tested. (And remember, *never* use acetone on acetates.)

White nongel toothpaste rubbed firmly and vigorously into the stain may work. After this method, be sure to pretreat and launder as usual.

Often just soaking ink stains in milk will dissolve them.

Turpentine is effective on very challenging ink stains. Working over a pad of paper towels, tapping the spot on the back of the fabric using the back of a spoon or an old toothbrush. Don't rub. Work in undiluted dishwashing liquid prior to laundering, and wash in the hottest water possible for the fabric type. Dispose of all paper, etc., saturated with turpentine immediately—outside, please.

Some inks only respond to solvents, so you may need to use Energine Cleaning Fluid.

On leather, remove ballpoint ink by rubbing with cuticle remover or petroleum jelly. You may need to leave it on the stained area for several days to achieve success.

On vinyl, believe it or not, the best thing is for you to be so mad that you could spit! Saliva will remove ballpoint ink from vinyl—as long as you are quick. Apply generously and wipe with a soft cloth. For old stains, apply glycerin, let it soak for 30 minutes or so, and then attempt to wash the stain away with a wet, soft cloth rubbed over a bar of soap.

Ketchup. *See* **Tomato-based stains.**

Kool-Aid. Flush the spot as quickly as possible with club soda and then hold under forceful running water. If a stained area still remains, soak in Brilliant Bleach until the stain is removed. This may take hours or days, depending on the fabric and the stain. Soak only white or color-fast clothes in Brilliant Bleach.

For red, grape, fruit punch, and other red Kool-Aid flavors, treat with Wine Away Red Wine Stain Remover for instantaneous stain removal.

Lipstick. Lipstick is actually an oily dye stain. Water, heat, or wet spotters will only spread it, make the problem worse, and set the stain.

Rub in vegetable oil, WD-40 lubricant, or mineral oil, and let it sit on the spot for 15 to 30 minutes. Next, sponge the area with a little ammonia—sudsy or clear is fine.

Now, before you launder, work in undiluted liquid dish soap to be sure you have removed all of the oil.

Another method I have had real success with is GOJO Crème Waterless Hand Cleaner. Look for this at hardware stores and home centers. Work it into the lipstick, rubbing between your thumbs vigorously. Launder as usual. This method is great for those smears of lipstick on cloth table napkins.

In an emergency, try spraying the spot with a little hair spray. Let this sit for a few minutes, and then wipe gently with a damp cloth. Test this method in an inconspicuous spot first.

You will also find that Zout Stain Remover and Spot Shot Instant Carpet Stain Remover are generally effective on lipstick.

For really stubborn old stains, try moistening with denatured alcohol, then treat with undiluted liquid dish soap.

If you are getting dressed and you accidentally get lipstick on your clothes, try rubbing the stain with white bread. (Yes, it really has to be white!)

Makeup (oily foundation, powder, cream blush, cover creams). Sprinkle baking soda on the makeup smudge, then brush the area with an old wet toothbrush until the makeup is removed. White nongel toothpaste scrubbed in with a toothbrush is also effective.

Liquid dish soap or shampoo will generally remove makeup stains. Work the product into the stain vigorously between your thumbs.

For stubborn makeup stains, use nonoily makeup remover, pretreat, and launder as usual. (*See also* **Cosmetics**.)

Marker, washable. Rinse the stain from the fabric with cold water until no more color can be removed. Place the fabric on paper towels and saturate the back of the fabric with alcohol, using a cotton ball to blot the stain. Replace the paper towels with new ones as they absorb the color. Work in Fels-Naptha Laundry Soap until the spot is well-lathered, and wash in hot water with laundry detergent and fabric appropriate bleach. Rinse in warm water.

Marker, permanent. First of all, "permanent" usually means permanent. But before you give up and throw in the towel—or blouse, or pants, or whatever—here are some things to try.

Fill a glass with denatured alcohol (use a size appropriate to the stain) and dip the stained area into the alcohol, allowing it to soak. If it appears that the marker is being removed, continue the process.

If the stain appears stubborn, try scrubbing the marker spot with an old toothbrush, white nongel toothpaste, and some baking soda. Give it a really good scrubbing. Rinse. If the marker stain is almost gone, soak in a cup of warm water and two denture-cleaning tablets for whites, and Brilliant Bleach for colorfast clothes. This will require some time, but if the stain all comes out, it's worth it.

If the marker is still there, scrub with Lava soap prior to trying the denture-cleaning tablets or bleach.

Good luck. And look out for those big black permanent markers and Sharpies. They're great pens, but they're murder on clothes! I can't even tell you how many times I have accidentally written on my clothes during a book signing with a Sharpie in my hand!

Mayonnaise. *See* **Grease and oil**.

Meat juices. Once they are dry, meat juices are very tough to remove, so it's important to react quickly. Sponge the area immediately with cold water (not hot—it will set the stain) or with club soda. Next, apply un-seasoned meat tenderizer and cold water, working the mixture in well. Let it sit for 30 to 60 minutes. Pretreat and launder as usual, but be sure to use cool water.

On dry-clean-only fabrics, sponge with cold water and take to a pro-fessional cleaner.

Medicines. It would be impossible to list all the medicines on the market. But this section should give you an idea of what to look out for, as well as what to do for each family of medicine.

Alcohol. Medicines containing alcohol stain quickly. Treat these stains as you would spilled alcohol.

Iron. Iron or medicines containing iron products should be treated as rust.

Oily medicines. Oily medicines should be treated with a degreasing product. I have had great luck with Soapworks At Home All-Purpose Cleaner, used undiluted. Work it in well and then rinse.

You can also treat these stains as you would an oil or grease stain.

Syrups. Cough syrup or children's medicines can usually be removed with water. Soak the fabric with cool water as soon as possible. Running cold water full force through the fabric can be helpful, and you may also want to try working in Fels-Naptha or soaking the stain in Biz Nonchlo-rine Bleach or Brilliant Bleach. If the syrup is red, use Wine Away Red Wine Stain Remover. (See, I told you not to be fooled by its name! It is amazing on red stains!)

Mildew. Mildew is a fungus that grows and flourishes in warm, humid, dark conditions, such as the shower, the basement, and so forth. The best way to avoid mildew is to ensure that things are totally dry *be-fore* you put them away. Invisible spores can quickly grow to huge pro-portions, especially on natural materials such as cotton, wool, leather, paper, and wood.

Air needs to circulate to keep mildew from forming, so do not crowd clothes into closets.

Store clothing only after it has been cleaned and dried thoroughly.

If you are storing things such as leather purses, belts, shoes, even suitcases, clean them well, then sit them in the sun for an hour or so. Do not store things in plastic, as this caters to damp conditions.

If you smell a damp or musty smell coming from a closet, suspect mildew immediately and act quickly to dry it out. Even allowing a fan to blow in the closet overnight can make a huge difference by drying and circulating the air.

Okay—here's what to do if you already have mildew stains on fabrics. First, try working some Fels-Naptha Laundry Soap into the area and laundering. If stains remain and the fabric will tolerate chlorine bleach, soak it in 1 gallon of cold water to which you have added 2 to 3 tablespoons of chlorine bleach.

Moistening white or colorfast clothes with lemon juice, sprinkling them with salt, and laying the garment in the sun may also remove mildew. If in doubt, test this method first.

Leather presents a different challenge. Take the item outside and brush off all the powdery mildew that you can with a soft brush. Wipe the leather with equal parts of rubbing alcohol and water, or try massaging cuticle remover into the area. After 10 minutes, wipe vigorously with a soft cloth.

Wash leather with a complexion bar soap such as Dove or Caress and buff dry—do not rinse.

Remember that with mildew, the best defense is a good offense, so try to keep it from occurring.

Milk, cream, whipping cream, and half-and-half. Rinse fabric under a cold, forceful stream of water from the faucet. Treat with unseasoned meat tenderizer and cool water. Allow to soak for 30 minutes, then flush with cool water again. If greasy-looking marks remain, treat with Energine Cleaning Fluid, working from the back of the fabric over a heavy pad of paper towels. Launder as usual.

Treat washable fabrics stained from milk by flushing with cool water before working in detergent and a little ammonia. Wash in cool water and air-dry.

For dry-clean-only fabrics, take to a professional as soon as possible and identify the stain when you drop off the item.

Mud. The key word here is *dry*. Let mud dry. Never treat a wet mud stain, except for lifting off any solid pieces with a dull straight edge. Once mud has dried, take the vacuum cleaner and vacuum the area with the hose attachment. You'll achieve the greatest suction that way. This may be a two-person job. One to hold the fabric, one to hold the hose.

Rub the cut side of a potato over the mud stain and launder as usual.

For stubborn stains, sponge with equal portions of rubbing alcohol and cool water. For red mud stains, treat with a rust remover. (*See also* **Rust**.) Rubbing 20 Mule Team Borax into a dampened mud stain will often remove it.

Spraying with Spot Shot Instant Carpet Stain Remover prior to laundering is also helpful.

Mustard. The word makes me shiver! This is a terrible stain to attempt (notice I said *attempt*) to remove.

The turmeric in mustard is what gives mustard its distinctive bright yellow color—it's also what would make it a darn good dye!

Remove as much of the mustard as possible, using a dull, straight edge. Next, flex the fabric to break the grip of the embedded residue on the fabric fibers. Apply glycerin (in the hand cream section at the drugstore) and let it sit at least an hour. Pretreat and launder as usual.

If the fabric is white or colorfast, soak the stain in hydrogen peroxide for 30 minutes. Brilliant Bleach may remove the stain after a lengthy soaking.

For white clothes, dissolve a denture-cleaning tablet in ½ cup of cool water and allow the stained area to soak.

Things to avoid: Ammonia and heat. Both will set the stain, and you will never get it out.

Kind of makes you think that ketchup and relish are all you need on that hot dog, doesn't it!

Mystery stains. These are those spots and spills that you have no idea what they are or where they came from. The unknowns. Here's what to do.

- Blot with cool water (hot water sets stains).

- Blot with a sponge or cloth dampened with water and a teaspoon or so of white vinegar (not for cotton or linen).

- Blot with a sponge or cloth dampened with water and a teaspoon or so of clear ammonia (again, not for cotton or linen).

- Blot with rubbing alcohol diluted 50/50 with cool water.

- Sponge with a solution of Brilliant Bleach and water.

Nail polish. Okay, if you had polished your nails naked in the back-yard, you wouldn't be reading this, would you? Stretch the fabric over a glass bowl and make a little trampoline by securing the fabric with a rubber band. Drip acetone-based polish remover through the stain with a stainless steel spoon (not silver) and tap the stain with the edge of the spoon. Continue dripping the acetone through the fabric until the polish is removed. This requires time and patience. If you run out of either, walk away and come back later. Straight acetone, purchased at a hardware or beauty supply store, may work faster, but be sure to test an area first.

Do not use acetone on silk or acetates, and always test the acetone on an inconspicuous area prior to beginning.

If a color stain remains after the polish is removed, dilute hydrogen peroxide (50 percent peroxide, 50 percent water), apply to the stain, and set the fabric in the sun, keeping it moist with the peroxide solution. Do this only for white or colorfast clothes.

Nonwashable fabrics should be dry-cleaned.

Odors. Eliminate odors, don't use a perfumed cover-up. I like Odorz-out odor eliminator because it absorbs odors and removes them perma-nently—without leaving any telltale smells behind. It is nontoxic and safe for all surfaces, and it can be used wet or dry. It is also safe for the environment, and a little goes a long way. Keep some on hand. It's great for just about any odor you're likely to come across, such as smoke, mildew, mold, feces, urine, food, any kind of odor. Do not use a perfumed cover-up.

Oil (*see also* Grease and oil). Blot up all oil quickly. Avoid rubbing, or you will force the oil further into the fibers. Pretreat washable fabrics with your favorite spot remover, or use one recommended for oily stains in this book. Launder in the hottest possible water for the fabric.

Nonwashables should be dry-cleaned.

Ointment (A & D ointment, Desitin, zinc oxide). Anyone who has had a baby will be familiar with this problem stain. Use hot water and detergent, rubbing the fabric against itself to remove the oil. If the stain remains, treat as indicated in the section on **Grease and oil**.

For zinc oxide, soak the garment in white vinegar for 30 minutes after treating as above, then launder as usual.

Paint, latex. Treat this stain immediately for best results. It is important to remove paint *before* it dries, so keep the stain wet if you can't work on it right away.

Flush the paint from the fabric with a forceful stream of warm water. Next, treat the stain with a solution of liquid dish soap and water, or laundry detergent and water. Work it into the stained area, soaping and rinsing until the stain is removed. Do this as many times as necessary. If the fabric is colorfast, you can also work in some automatic dishwasher detergent and let it soak on the fabric for 5 to 10 minutes before laundering as usual.

You can also try a product aptly named OOPS! Just follow the directions on the can closely.

On fabrics such as cotton and polyester, try spraying the garment with oven cleaner and letting it sit about 15 to 30 minutes before flushing with plenty of water. Use *extreme* care with this method and use it at your own risk. Some fabrics cannot tolerate the oven cleaner, but if the garment is ruined by the paint, it is worth a try. Also use care where you spray the oven cleaner and what you set the fabric on afterward.

Paint, oil-based. Get busy and remove this spill ASAP. You're out of luck if it dries. If you must go to the store for products, keep the spill moist.

Check the paint can and use the thinner recommended by the manufacturer. Sometimes thinner for correction fluid will also work. Remember to test an area first with these two methods.

I fall back on turpentine when all else fails. Work the turpentine into the spill, and once the paint is removed, work in GOJO Crème Waterless Hand Cleaner. That will take out the oiliness from the turpentine. Remember to dispose of turpentine-soaked rags or paper towels outside, as soon as possible.

When working on a paint spill, work from the back of the fabric over a thick pad of paper towels. Tap the stained area with an old toothbrush or an old spoon as you work to force the paint out.

Now that you have removed the stain, saturate the area with detergent and work in vigorously. Cover the area with the hottest water you can use for the fabric, and let it soak overnight. Scrub again, between your thumbs, and launder as usual.

Pencil. Okay, how easy is this? Take a nice, clean, soft eraser, and gently rub the offending mark away! Just be sure the eraser is clean, or you will create a large stain. If the spot is stubborn, sponge with Energine Cleaning Fluid.

Perfume. Follow the directions for **Alcoholic beverages**. A few words to the wise: The best time to put perfume on is right before you put on your clothes, not after. And never spray perfume directly on your clothes. This will damage them. The combination of alcohol and oil is death to fabrics.

Perspiration stains. These stains really are the pits, so I've devoted a section in chapter 14 to their removal. (*See also* **Antiperspirants and deodorants.**)

Purple or bluish color on synthetic fibers. Sometimes synthetic fibers will develop a purple tinge after repeated laundering. Remove it with Rit Color Remover and launder as usual.

Rust. On white fabrics, saturate with lemon juice and sprinkle with salt, then lay in the sun. (No, not you—the fabric!) If the rust is stubborn, apply the lemon juice and salt, and pour water through the stain. Use boiling water if the fabric will tolerate it; otherwise use hot. Check the care label.

You can also cover the stained area with cream of tartar, then gather up the edges of the fabric and dip the spot in hot water. Let stand 5 to 10 minutes and then launder as usual.

There are good commercial rust removers on the market. Try Whink Rust Stain Remover, Magica, and Rust Magic. Be sure to read directions carefully when using commercial rust removers. Some cannot be used on colored fabric, so check carefully.

Sap, pine tar. *See* Tar.

Scorch marks. Sorry to say, but severe scorch marks cannot be removed.

Light scorch marks may be treated with a cloth dampened with 1 part 3 percent hydrogen peroxide and 3 parts of water. Lay the cloth over the scorch mark and press with a medium/hot iron. Do not iron off of the cloth, or you will scorch the fabric again. Make sure to try this method first in a small, inconspicuous space.

If the scorch is still visible, moisten the spot with the diluted peroxide and lay it in the sun.

Very light scorch marks may also be removed by wetting them with water and laying the garment in the sun.

If the scorch mark has appeared on white clothes, saturate the scorched area with lemon juice and lay it in the sun. Keep it moist with the lemon juice until the stain is removed.

For white cottons, sometimes boiling it in ½ cup of soap and 2 quarts of milk will remove the stain. Try this at your own risk. Some fabrics may not tolerate boiling.

For light scorches, you can also rub the fabric with the cut side of a white onion (not a red onion—it will stain), and then soak the fabric in cold water for several hours. Launder as usual.

Remember, scorching weakens fibers, so use care and always re-launder the item once the scorch mark has been removed.

Shoe polish. Work laundry detergent into the fabric immediately and rinse. For persistent stains, sponge with alcohol. Use undiluted alcohol on white clothes, and 1 part alcohol to 2 parts water on colored fabrics. Rinse again, or try using turpentine after first testing in an inconspic-uous spot.

Shoe polish has an oily base containing dye. Using the wrong things—such as water, heat, or wet spotters—will spread and set the stain. Work in vegetable oil or WD-40 lubricant and let it sit for 15 min-utes. Sponge on a little ammonia (not on silk, please), then work in undi-luted dishwashing liquid and launder as usual.

Energine Cleaning Fluid may also help to eliminate the final stained area.

If you have any discoloration remaining from the dye in the shoe polish, soak the fabric in Brilliant Bleach until the stain is removed.

If the shoe polish stain is old and heavy, you may need to treat it with petroleum jelly. Cover the polish and work in the petroleum jelly, let it soak for 30 to 60 minutes, and then scrape off all that you can of the polish and the petroleum jelly. Work in undiluted dishwashing liquid, and flush with a forceful stream of hot water. Pretreat and launder as usual.

Shoe polish, liquid. Blot up all that you can from the fabric. Do not rub—this will spread the stain. Do not apply water. Instead, saturate with alcohol—undiluted for whites, diluted as above for colors. Con-tinue to flush with alcohol, work in your favorite laundry detergent, then rub vigorously to remove all trace of the stain.

Silk spots. Spots on silk are hard to remove and must be handled with care.

Dry-cleaning solvent may spot-clean silk, but you're likely to be left with a ring on the fabric. Make sure to use the blow-dryer on the spot to avoid that telltale ring.

For unusual or heavy stains, take to a professional. Too much rubbing can remove the color from silk.

Silly Putty. First of all, let gravity do the work for you. Lay the fabric over a bowl and let the Silly Putty simply drop off. You'll only have to clean up what's left!

Scrape off the balance of Silly Putty with a dull edge such as an old credit card or knife back. Spray with WD-40 lubricant and let stand a few minutes. Scrape again, removing all the Silly Putty that you can. Continue to do this, changing from the dull straight edge to cotton balls. If any stain remains, saturate a cotton ball with rubbing alcohol, blot the stain, and rinse. Work in liquid dish soap and launder as usual in the hottest water you can for the fabric type.

If you don't have WD-40 lubricant, use petroleum jelly instead.

Soft drinks. *See* **Colas and soft drinks.**

Soot. Launder clothing in the hottest possible water for the fabric with your normal detergent, ½ cup of 20 Mule Team Borax, and ½ cup of Arm and Hammer Washing Soda.

Stickers. Heat white vinegar and apply it, undiluted, directly to the fabric. Allow the vinegar to soak until the sticker can be peeled back with ease.

Tar. Lift off as much solid matter as possible using a plastic (disposable) knife. Spread the stained area over a heavy pad of paper towels and apply glycerin to the fabric, tapping it with the back of an old toothbrush or plastic spoon. Change the paper towels as they absorb the tar. Finally, once you have removed all the tar you can, work in some turpentine or eucalyptus oil. Flush the stained area with alcohol, or work in undiluted liquid dish soap. Pretreat and launder as usual. Spot Shot Instant Carpet Stain Remover is a good spotter for this.

Tar, dried. Warm glycerin or olive oil and spread over the area, allowing it to soak until the tar is loosened. Then proceed as in **Tar.**

Nonwashables should be taken to the dry cleaner as soon as possible.

Tea. *See* **Coffee and tea.**

Tomato-based stains (ketchup, spaghetti sauce, tomato sauce, barbecue sauce). Flush these stains well with cool water as soon as possible. Make sure you apply water to the back of the fabric. Apply white vinegar and then flush again with a forceful stream of water.

Apply Wine Away Red Wine Stain Remover per package directions.

Urine. Fresh urine stains are fairly easy to remove. First rinse well, flushing with lots of cool water. Presoak using an enzyme powder or Biz All Fabric Bleach. Then launder as usual.

You may also soak urine-stained fabric in salt water, then rinse and launder as usual.

If the color of the fabric has changed due to the urine, sponge the area or spray with clear ammonia, then rinse and launder as usual.

Urine, old stains. Soak in clear hot water for an hour—the hotter the better. Add detergent and wash as usual, then rinse. Use the appropriate bleach for the fabric type, or Brilliant Bleach if you prefer. (*See also* **Odors.**)

Vomit. Shake off or scrape what you can over the toilet. Flush the fabric from the wrong side with cool water, using a forceful stream. Once you have removed solid matter and excess liquid, make a paste of liquid laundry soap and 20 Mule Team Borax and vigorously scrub the fabric. Rinse with salt water, then pretreat and launder as usual.

Quick treatment is important to avoid stains from foods and stomach acid. (*See also* **Odors.**)

Wine. Never serve red wine without having white wine nearby! And always tend to the stain *as soon as you can!*

For red wine spills, dilute the spot with white wine, then flush with cool water and apply salt.

If no white wine is available, sprinkle heavily with salt and flush with club soda or cool water.

Applying a paste of 20 Mule Team Borax and water usually works.

For red wine spills and other red stains, keep Wine Away Red Wine Stain Remover on hand. It is totally nontoxic, and works so fast on red wine and red stains that even I am still amazed. The directions are simple and easy. Blot up the spill, apply the Wine Away, and watch the red stain disappear. Blot with a wet cloth. You'll thank me many times for this one!

Yellow spots and stains. These stains are common on white clothes and linens. Denture-cleaning tablets will generally remove these stains. Fill a basin with water and add one or two tablets. Allow the tablets to dissolve, and then soak the fabric until the yellow is removed.

Royal Resource Guide

These products are truly fit for a Queen! Here's a list of the best cleaning products, what they do, and how to use them.

ACETONE. A great spotter, but be careful. It is exceedingly strong and can damage fibers. Look for this at hardware stores, home centers, and beauty supply stores.

ACT NATURAL CLOTHS. *See* Euronet USA.

ART GUM ERASER. You remember the little brownish tan rectangular eraser that you used in school, the one that crumbled as you erased? That's the one!

BAKING POWDER. If you bake, you already have baking powder in the cupboard. If not, look in the baking section near the baking soda. Baking powder and baking soda are *not* the same thing, so don't even go there!

BEESWAX. Usually found in drugstores, hardware stores, and natural product stores. If you don't see it, ask!

BITTER APPLE. This terrific product keeps pets from dining on your plants and so forth, saving you from more messes to clean up. It is not harmful to them, but it tastes terrible, so it discourages them entirely. Look for it at pet supply stores.

BIZ ACTIVATED NONCHLORINE BLEACH. A great all-purpose powdered bleach. Look for it in the laundry aisle at grocery stores and discount stores.

BORAX. Better known as 20 Mule Team Borax Laundry Additive. This can be found in the detergent aisle.

BRILLIANT BLEACH. *See* Soapworks.

BRUCE FLOOR CARE PRODUCTS. Look for these products at hardware stores, home centers, and wherever wood flooring is sold.

CALGON WATER SOFTENER. Look for it with the laundry additives at the grocery store.

CARBONA COLOR RUN REMOVER. Removes fugitive color from fabrics. Available in grocery and discount stores.

CARBONA STAIN DEVILS. A great series of spotters that target specific stains, such as gum, blood, milk, and so forth.

CHAMOIS CLOTH. Found in hardware stores and home centers.

CHARCOAL. This is the type made for fish tanks and is available at pet supply stores.

CLEAR AMMONIA. There are two types of ammonia, clear and sudsy (sometimes called "cloudy"). Clear ammonia doesn't contain soap. For that reason, it should be used where suggested in this book.

CLEAN-X CLEAN SHIELD SURFACE TREATMENT (FORMERLY INVISIBLE SHIELD). This is such a wonderful product—just the name gives me goose bumps! It turns all of those hard-to-clean surfaces in your home (the exterior of the washing machine and dryer, tub, shower, shower doors, sinks, counters, stovetops, windows, any surface that is not wood or painted) into nonstick surfaces that can be cleaned with water and a soft cloth. No more soap scum or hard-water deposits! It never builds up, so it won't make surfaces more slippery, and it's nontoxic, so you can use it on dishes and food surfaces, too! Call (800) 528-3149 for a supplier near you.

COLD CREAM. Choose plain old Ponds that your grandma used on her face, or the store brand.

CUTICLE REMOVER. This is the gel you apply to your cuticles to soften them. Let's be clear, it is cuticle remover, *not* nail polish remover, they are definitely not one and the same!

DENATURED ALCOHOL. This is an industrial alcohol reserved for heavy-duty cleaning. Don't use it near an open flame, and make sure to dispose of any rags that were used to apply it outside of your home. Launder or clean anything that you treat with it as soon as possible. Look for this in cans at hardware stores and home centers. Remember the Queen's rule: Always test in an inconspicuous place before treating a large area with this product.

DE-SOLV-IT CITRUS SOLUTION. Available in home centers or hardware stores, De-Solv-It Citrus-Solution has a multitude of uses both inside and out. Great for laundry.

ENERGINE CLEANING FLUID. A great spotter. Look for this at hardware stores, home centers, and even in some grocery stores (usually on the top shelf with the laundry additives).

EPSOM SALT. Usually used for medicinal purposes, but handy for laundry and other household uses, too. Look for this in the drugstore.

EURONET USA. Makers of the ACT Natural microfiber cloths and mops. They clean and disinfect without chemicals, using only water. They have been scientifically proven to kill germs and bacteria and even come with a warranty. They are easy to use, great for people with allergies, and can be cleaned and sanitized in the washer (this is particularly important with the mop). Use them in the kitchen or bathroom; to spot carpet; on windows, mirrors, or hard furniture; in the car; virtually anywhere you clean. I never travel without a cloth, and I keep one in my desk and briefcase to quickly clean up any of those little spills on clothes. Call (888) 638-3552 or visit the Web site www.euronetusa.com. They are a wonderful investment. My mop is almost 2 years old and is still doing the job.

FELS-NAPTHA HEAVY-DUTY LAUNDRY BAR SOAP. You'll find this wonderful laundry spotter and cleaner in the bar soap section of the grocery store. It's usually on the bottom shelf covered in dust because nobody knows what to use it for!

FINE DRYWALL SANDPAPER. This sandpaper looks like window screen. Make sure you buy a package marked "fine grade."

FINE STEEL WOOL. Look for the symbol "0000" and the word *fine*. And don't try soap-filled steel wool pads. They are not acceptable substitutes.

FRESH BREEZE LAUNDRY SOAP. *See* Soapworks.

GLYCERIN. Look for glycerin in drugstores in the hand cream section. Always purchase plain glycerin, *not* the type containing rosewater.

GOJO CRÈME WATERLESS HAND CLEANER. Not just a hand cleaner, GOJO is great for laundry, too. Look for it at home centers and hardware stores.

HYDROGEN PEROXIDE. Make sure to choose 3 percent—the type used for cuts, *not* the type used to bleach hair. (That's too strong and will remove color from fabric.)

LEMON OR ORANGE EXTRACT. These are found in the spice area of the grocery store where vanilla extract is sold.

LINSEED OIL. You'll find this at the hardware store, usually in the paint and staining section. It is combustible, so use care in disposing of rags or paper towels used to apply it. Keep it in the garage or basement away from open flame.

MEAT TENDERIZER. Great for spotting protein stains. Use the unseasoned variety, please, or you will have a whole new stain to deal with. Store brands work fine.

NAIL POLISH REMOVER. I caution you to use nonacetone polish remover first. It's much less aggressive than acetone polish remover.

NATURAL SPONGE. A natural sponge is the best sponge you will ever use. It has hundreds of natural "scrubbing fingers" that make any wall-washing job speed by. Look for these at home centers and hardware stores, and choose a nice size to fit your hand. Wash them in lukewarm water with gentle suds. You can put them in the washing machine if you avoid combining them with fabrics that have lint.

NATURE'S MIRACLE. An enzyme-based odor-removal product for urine-based pet accidents. Available at pet supply stores across the country.

NONGEL TOOTHPASTE. This is just a fancy name for old-fashioned plain white toothpaste. Gels just don't work, so don't even try.

ODORZOUT. A fabulous, dry, 100 percent natural deodorizer. It's nontoxic, so you can use it anyplace you have a smell or a stink. Also available in a pouch for shoes, laundry hampers, and so forth. Call (800) 88-STINK, or visit their Web site at www.88stink.com

OIL OF CLOVES. Widely available at health food stores, vitamin stores, and natural food stores.

OUTRIGHT PET ODOR ELIMINATOR. An enzyme odor-removal product for urine-based pet accidents. Available at pet supply stores across the country.

POWDERED ALUM. This old-fashioned product was once used in pickling. Look for it at drugstores, and if you can't find it, ask the pharmacist.

PREPARATION H. Sold in drugstores. An ointment intended for hemorrhoids.

PUREX LAUNDRY DETERGENT. Available wherever detergents are sold.

RED ERASE. Made by the same people who make Wine Away Red Wine Stain Remover, Red Erase is for red stains such as red soda, grape juice, grape jelly, and so forth. Look for it at Linens 'n Things, or call (888) WINE-AWAY for a store location near you.

RETAYNE. Used *before* you launder colored clothes for the first time, it will help retain color. Available wherever quilting supplies are sold.

ROTTENSTONE. Mild pumice, look for it at hardware stores and home centers.

RUST REMOVER. These are serious products, so follow the directions carefully. Look for products like Whink and Rust Magic at hardware stores and home centers.

SADDLE SOAP. You will find this in the hardware store or in the shoe polish section at most any store.

SHAVING CREAM. The cheaper brands work fine for spotting. Cream works better than gel.

SOAPWORKS. Manufacturer of wonderful nontoxic, user-friendly and earth-friendly cleaning, laundry, and personal care products. Try their At Home All-Purpose Cleaner and Fresh Breeze Laundry Powder, originally designed for allergy and asthma sufferers. Also try their Brilliant Bleach. Believe me, it *is* brilliant! Call (800) 699-9917 or visit their Web site at www.soapworks.com.

SOOT AND DIRT REMOVAL SPONGE. These big brick erasers are available at home centers and hardware stores, usually near the wallpaper supplies. They are used to clean walls, wallpaper, lampshades, and even soot. They also remove pet hair from upholstery. Clean them by washing in a pail of warm water and liquid dish soap, rinse well, and allow to dry before using again.

SPOT SHOT INSTANT CARPET STAIN REMOVER. My all-time favorite carpet spotter is a wonderful laundry spotter, too! Try Spot Shot Upholstery Stain Remover, too. Available most everywhere, or call (800) 848-4389.

SQUEEGEE. When buying a squeegee for washing windows, look for a good-quality one with a replaceable rubber blade. Always be sure that the rubber blade is soft and flexible for best results. Look for these at hardware stores, home centers, and janitorial supply companies. They come in different widths, so be sure to think about the size windows, etc., that you are going to use it for. A 12-inch blade is a good starting point.

SYNTHRAPOL. Great for removing fugitive color. Available wherever quilting supplies are sold.

TACK-TRAP. Bugs are drawn to the color of this sticky sheet. Sold in garden supply stores and some hardware stores.

TANG BREAKFAST DRINK. Yes, this is the product that the astronauts took to the moon! It is also a great cleaner. (Store brands work just as well.)

TRISODIUM PHOSPHATE (TSP). Cleaning professionals have used this product for years. It is wonderful for washing walls and garage floors and for any tough cleaning job. Look for it at hardware stores, home centers, and janitorial supply stores. Wear rubber gloves when using it.

TYPEWRITER ERASER. A thing of the past, but still available at office supply stores. Shaped like a pencil with a little brush where the pencil eraser would be, they can be sharpened like a pencil and will last for years.

UN-DU. Removes sticky residue from fabric and hard surfaces. Look for it at office supply stores, home centers, and hardware stores.

WASHING SODA. I like Arm and Hammer Washing Soda, which can be found in the detergent aisle at the grocery store along with other laundry additives. No, you cannot substitute baking soda; it's a different product!

WAX CRAYONS. Sold in hardware stores and home centers, they come in various wood colors for concealing scratches in wood surfaces. Don't be fooled by the color name; try to take along a sample of what you need to patch to get the best possible match.

WD-40 LUBRICANT. Fine spray oil for lubricating all kinds of things, WD-40 is wonderful for regenerating grease so that it can be removed from clothes. Look for this at hardware stores, home centers, and even grocery stores.

WHINK RUST STAIN REMOVER. This is a professional strength rust remover. When all else fails, this is the one to try. Remember it is a chemical, and you should follow the directions for use carefully. Use it on carpet, fabric, and porcelain. Look for it in grocery, discount, and hardware stores and home centers.

WHITING. Look for this at the hardware store, usually near the paint.

WIEMAN'S WAX AWAY. Removes candle wax from fabrics and hard surfaces. Look for it at grocery stores and discount stores.

WINDOW SCRUBBER. This looks like a squeegee wearing a coat. Look for it at janitorial supply stores and home centers.

WINE AWAY RED WINE STAIN REMOVER. This unbelievable product can remove red stains, such as red wine, red soda, cranberry juice, red food coloring, grape juice, from carpet and fabric. It is totally nontoxic and made from fruit and vegetable extracts. I just can't believe how well it works! Look for it at Linens 'n Things, where liquor is sold, or call (888) WINE-AWAY for a store location near you.

WITCH HAZEL. An astringent/toning product sold at drugstores.

ZOUT LAUNDRY STAIN REMOVER. A very versatile laundry prespotter, Zout is thicker than most laundry spotters, so you can target the spot. It really works! Buy it in grocery stores, discount stores, and so forth.

ZUD HEAVY-DUTY CLEANSER. This is a wonderful cleanser for really tough jobs. It works great on rust on hard surfaces, too. Find it at hardware stores, home centers, and grocery stores. Well worth keeping on hand.

Dealing with Household Damage

I honestly hope that you never have any reason to do any thing more than just glance through this section, but if you ever have a fire or flood in your home, remember that this information is here. I spent 15 years as the owner of a disaster-restoration company in Michigan, and I can tell you that in those first hours after a fire or flood, it's all you can do to remember your name. You'll need all the *accurate* information and support you can get! Here's what to do.

Turning Down the Heat on Fire Damage

The fire truck has just left, and there you stand amid what once was your home and is now a smelly, wet, black mess that you hardly recognize. You want to sit down and have a good cry, but there isn't any clean place to sit. What do you do now? Is everything ruined? This section will help you deal with the emotional turmoil, and give you sound information about what you, as the homeowner, need to do.

Just in Case

First, as soon as you are through reading this, put your homeowner's policy, along with your agent's name and phone number, in a fireproof box or bank safety deposit box. This enables you to easily find them and protects them from being destroyed in the fire. Make notes from these pages and put them with your insurance information.

Get on the Phone

After the fire is out, call your insurance agent or the 1-800 number that is often provided on your policy to report claims.

Call immediately. It may seem like the damage couldn't be worse, but it could. After a fire, there can be ongoing damage from acid soot residue. Fire produces two main pollutants—nitrous oxide (from burning wood, food, and so forth) and sulfur dioxide (from burning plastics and petroleum by-products, and so forth). When these pollutants combine with moisture and humidity, they form acid! Within hours, this can cause substantial and continuing damage.

Prompt attention from your local disaster-restoration firm will eliminate the problem and prevent further damage to valuables. Disaster-restoration companies are listed in your phone directory and are available 24 hours a day for emergencies. They will preserve, protect, and secure surfaces that may be subject to continuing damage, and will work with your insurance adjuster to estimate the damage.

What Is an Insurance Adjuster?

The insurance adjuster works for the insurance company. He is an expert in smoke damage, such as chimney fires, furnace backups, and actual fire damage. He will help you decide what can be saved and what can't. He will require a written estimate from a disaster-restoration company and any contractors or dry cleaners who will participate in the cleanup. Sometimes more than one estimate will be requested.

During this time, you will be receiving all kinds of comments and advice from friends, relatives, and even strangers. Ignore it! Your insurance adjuster is a professional and knows the best way to handle smoke damage. The adjuster may even be able to give you advice on a company that they have dealt with before if you are unsure whom to call.

Disaster-Restoration Companies

Disaster-restoration companies (i.e. cleaning companies) do two types of cleaning: structural and contents cleaning. Structural cleaning is wall-washing, carpet cleaning, cupboards—the things you can't remove from the house when you move. Contents cleaning is the upholstery, hard furniture, dishes, clothes, and so forth—things you take with you when you move. They will provide a complete estimate to the insurance company and a copy to you.

Once coverage is confirmed and appropriate authorizations are secured, the cleaning and repairs will take place as quickly as possible. This will include dry cleaning, laundry, and deodorization, also covered in this section.

Payment

After completion of all the cleaning and restoration, the insurance company will generally issue a check in your name and in the name of the firm that did the work. Once the work is satisfactory, you sign over the checks.

Deodorization

Deodorization is one of the most important parts of any smoke-damage cleanup. Everything smells—even your clothes.

First, the initial odor must be brought under control immediately to make the house habitable, if you are able to live in it during the restoration.

During any reconstruction, exposed interior wall sections will be deodorized, and any singed wood will be sealed to prevent odor. In serious fires, deodorization will take place after cleaning, too.

All clothing will have to be deodorized during laundry and dry cleaning, and in serious cases will be put in an ozone room that opens the oxygen molecules and releases odor.

Ozone machines are also used for deodorizing the home, resulting in a smell much like the air after a thunderstorm.

The best deodorization technique I have ever known is recreating the conditions causing the odor. In the case of smoke damage, a deodorant "smoke" is produced, which allows the deodorization process to penetrate in exactly the same manner the smoke odor did.

Additional odor control is done with duct sealing and deodorization.

All walls that are washed and painted should be sealed first with a special sealer to eliminate residue "bleed-through" from the oily smoke film. Then the walls are painted in the normal manner. This process is one that your disaster-restoration firm and adjuster will be familiar with.

With light smoke damage, many times the wall washing is necessary, but not painting. Deodorization is generally always advised.

What If You Don't Have Insurance?

The best advice I can give you is to carry insurance. If you live in an apartment or condominium, buy renter's insurance. If smoke damage occurs, you'll be glad you did.

But, if you don't have insurance, here's some helpful advice.

Go to a janitorial supply store and ask their advice on which cleaning chemicals to use. They can provide you with a professional-quality deodorant to wash clothes, linens, and hard surfaces. You will put this deodorant in the water that you clean with or wash clothes with.

Call a disaster-restoration firm and try to rent an ozone machine to deodorize the structure and your contents, bearing in mind that prolonged ozone use will yellow plastics.

Buy a soot- and dirt-removal sponge to clean walls. This is somewhat like a blackboard eraser that removes oily smoke film, so that when you begin to wash the walls the sooty film won't smear.

Rent a carpet-cleaning machine with an upholstery attachment to clean carpet and all upholstery that can be cleaned with water.

Wash hard furniture with oil soap and dry, then use furniture polish if you want a brighter shine.

Wash Everything

Wash everything thoroughly—this means walls, cupboards, collectibles, dishes, clothes, and so forth; otherwise the odor will remain.

Start in one room and do it completely except for carpet cleaning (you'll track during the cleaning process and spread soot on the carpet). Clean the carpet in all rooms last.

If you still have odor, do a final deodorization with an ozone machine, or if you can, hire a firm to come in and do it for you.

The Big Drip: Water-Damage Restoration

What a shock! When you left the house, everything was fine.

You come home and unlock the door; you walk in and hear the sound of running water. As you step in, water comes up to your ankles. Now you find water running across the carpet and floors, and lapping at the legs of furniture as the sofa and chairs try to soak it up. Here's what you need to do immediately.

Turn It Off

First, know where your water shut-off is and use it. Turn off the water and look for the source of the leak. **Be sure the electrical power source is off before you walk in standing water.** The leak could be from a toilet, the washing machine hoses, or a broken pipe.

How quickly you react will have an impact on what can be saved in your home.

Call the Professionals

Now that you have shut off the water and located the problem, call your insurance agent. Your agent will act quickly to help you, because by the time an adjuster receives the information, it is often too late to reverse some of the damage that has taken place.

Wet carpet and pad are restorable if they are taken care of as soon as possible after the damage has occurred.

A professional company that deals in water damage of all kinds can stop further damage from occurring and also save the carpet and pad.

To find a water-damage expert, look in the yellow pages under "water damage" or under "cleaning companies" or "disaster-restoration firms." Be sure to get a company that specializes in this problem.

Dry Out

First, the company will extract water from the pad and the carpet and treat both with an EPA-registered disinfectant. They will then install drying equipment, which consists of high-powered carpet blowers that are slipped between the carpet and the pad. They also will install dehumidification equipment to facilitate drying. They will advise you to keep your home's interior temperature at 70°F or warmer for ideal drying conditions. This drying equipment will also facilitate drying of upholstered furniture and walls as it dries the carpet.

Upholstered furniture will need to have water extracted from it and be treated with an EPA-registered disinfectant, too. Wood furniture will be wiped down and allowed to dry.

The water-damage restoration firm will check, usually every 24 hours, to see how the drying process is coming and to move equipment to continue the drying process.

What Is an Antimicrobial?

Many water-damage restoration firms have a wonderful antimicrobial product available that not only disinfects, but also inhibits the growth of mold, mildew, and bacterial spores. This is applied to the carpet after extraction takes place and has certainly saved many a carpet.

After all the carpet and contents of your home are dry, the upholstery and carpet will be cleaned and again treated with a disinfectant product or antimicrobial. Hard furniture will be washed and polished, and hard floors will be given a final cleaning. If your carpet or uphol-stery had a protective coating on it, this will be reapplied.

Walls will be washed as needed, and your home will be returned to normal once again.

Answers to Your Sea of Worries

Here are the concerns my clients expressed most often when I was in the disaster-restoration business.

The Pad Will Dissolve!

Not so! Most pads are made of nonwater-sensitive foam bonded with a dry solvent-soluble adhesive.

The Seams Will Separate!

Now, that is logical. Wet carpet naturally means shrinkage, right? Wrong! Nonwater-soluble adhesives are used on seams. Regardless of what happens, seams can be repaired.

The Carpet Shrank Off the Wall!

Only poorly installed carpet will come loose from the wall—and this is easily restretched.

The Carpet Will Fall Apart!

This is not likely. During the manufacturing process, carpet manufac-turers actually immerse carpet in water many times during the dyeing and rinsing process. Synthetic fibers, the primary backings, and latex adhesives are virtually unaffected by water for at least 48 hours.

Sewer Backups

If your water damage is due to a sewer backup, these restoration firms are trained to deal with it. Stay out of the water and waste. Let the trained experts deal with the water and bacterial problems; that's their job and they know what can be saved and what can't.

INDEX

Underscored page references indicate boxed text.

Carpet *(cont.)*
  stains *(cont.)*
    stain remover for, 17, 20, 145, 155
    watercolor paint, 155
  terms describing, 64
  urine changing color of, 160
  water damage affecting, 371
  water-damage restoration for, 370
Carpet-cleaning company, hiring,
    64–65
Car trips
  child safety tips for, 250–51
  cleaning car after, 254–55
  games and toys for, 252–54
  home preparation before, 247–48
  packing for, 248–49
Cashmere, 182–83
Casserole dish, 16
Cast-iron pan, 109
Cat litter spills, 272
Cat repellents in garden, 240
Ceiling fan
  dusting, 230
  energy conservation and, 58
Ceiling tile, water stains on, 84
Cement, 141–42
Ceramic tile floors, 75–76, 76
Chains, untangling, 322, 322
Chalk, 68, 156
Chamois, 138, 359
Champagne
  on carpet, 68
  on clothes, 323
  keeping fizz in, 323
  pink, 324
Chandeliers, 285–86
Chap Stick stains, 29, 171
Charcoal, 359
Chenille bedspreads, 211
Chicken pox, 261
Chiffon, 183
Chigger bites, 260
China, 19, 291–92, 293
China cabinet, 292
Chintz, 183
Chocolate stains, 333
  on carpet, 68–69
  on clothing, 322–23

Christmas
  cards, 306, 317
  cookies, 310
  involving children in preparations for,
    302
  lights, 304, 312, 312
  listing items for, 317
  ornaments, 313–14
  planning for, 300–301, 301
  protecting pets during, 304
  storing miscellaneous decorations for,
    315–17
  table, 305
  trees, 302–4, 313
  wrappings, 306–7, 314–15
  wreaths, 305, 316
Chrome, 19
  auto, 144, 255
  faucets, 96
  kitchen, 110
Cigarette
  ash, on carpet, 69
  odors, 247–48
Citrus peels as moth repellent, 283
Cleaning procedure
  assessing cleaning products for, 227–28
  decluttering, 226–27
  odor elimination, 228–29
  tactics for, 229–31
Cleaning style, personal, 4
Cleanser, homemade, 94, 103
Clean-X Clean Shield, 15, 104, 117, 241,
    359
Closets
  eliminating odors in, 229
  organizing, 275–77
Clothing
  beaded, 190–91
  bleach alternative for, 19
  buttons on, 205
  care labels on, 165–67, 277
  coats, 174
  deodorizing, after smoke damage, 367
  dresses, 174
  fabrics, 181–88
  flame-resistant, 38
  fur, 191–92
  hats, 202–3

Furniture
  dusting, 122–23
  lawn, 17, 131–33, 261, 285
  leather, 126–28
  marble, 128–30
  upholstered (*see* Upholstery)
  water-damage restoration for, 370
  wood, 120–22, 370
Furniture polish
  allergies and, 50
  homemade, 121
  old, removing, 121
  as shoe polish substitute, 200
  stains, 339
Furs, 191–92

G

Gabardine, 185
Games for car trips, 252–54
Garage floors, 77, 141–42
Garbage cans, repelling animals from, 240
Garden, animal control for, 240
Gardening
  general tips for, 236–37, 239
  natural fertilizers for, 237–38
  pest control for, 238–39
  tools, 241–42, 285
Garlands, Christmas, 316
Gift tags, 306, 317
Gift wrap, 306–7, 314–15
Glass
  doors, 292
  photo stuck to, 90
  picture frame, 90
  shelves, of medicine cabinet, 12
Gloves
  baseball, 258
  golf, 256–57
Glue
  on carpet, 69, 156
  in dryer, 171
  on fabric, 156
  removing various types of, 339–40
  super, removing, 129
Glycerin, 28, 361
GOJO Crème Waterless Hand Cleaner,
    28, 361

for cleaning
  cold medicine stains, 309
  golf clubs, 256
  grill, 134–35, 271
  lipstick stains, 217, 345
  massage oil stains, 324
  oil-based paint stains, 352
  work clothes, 194
Gold
  jewelry, 322
  in kitchen, 110
  marking clothing, 183
Golf balls, identifying, 257
Golf equipment, 256–57
Goo Gone, 329
Gophers, 240
Grass
  cutting, 239, 241
  stains, 340–41
    on carpet, 20, 70
    on clothing, 232
    natural cleaners for, 25, 28
    on shoes, 16, 232, 341
  watering, 239–41
Grasshoppers, 147
Grater, 109
Gravy stains, 296, 341
Grease stains, 341–42. *See also*
    Oil stains
  from barbecue, 134
  cleaners for, 25, 28, 29
  on kitchen cabinets, 106, 108
  on marble, 129–30
  on suede handbags, 202
  on wallpaper, 85
  on work clothes, 194, 195
Grills
  cleaning, 133–35, 271–72
  safety with, 271
Grout, 16, 75, 95
  cleaner, 95
Guacamole stains
  on carpet, 70–71
  on clothes, 317
Gum, 342–43
  on carpet, 71
  in dryer, 171
  in hair, 154
Gutters, 267–68

H

Hair
  care of, 243–44, <u>244</u>
  gum in, 154
  pet, removing, 161–62, 329
  Silly Putty in, 154
Hair coloring, removing, 288
Hair dye stains, 343
Hair spray
  allergies and, 50
  residue, 96
Half-and-half stains, 348–49
Halloween, 287–89
Handbags, 201–2
Hand care, 244–45
Hand cleaners, 19, 87, <u>239</u>
Hand cream
  homemade, 19, 244
  stains, 343
Handles
  door, 231, 308
Hand washing, 307
Hardware, protecting, during painting, 87
Hard-water marks, 92, 93
Hats, 202–3
Hat Saver, <u>203</u>
Heat conservation, 57–58
Heat scars on furniture, 120–21
Heel marks on floors, 17
Hems
  ironing, 177
  repairing, before washing, 169
Hide food for leather, 127, <u>128</u>
High chair, spills under, 153
Hinges, lubricating, 231
Hockey pucks, 259
Holidays. *See specific holidays*
Home dry-cleaning kits, 43–45, <u>44</u>
Homeowner's policy, storing, 366
Hoses, storing, 285
Houseplants. *See also* Plants
  for allergy sufferers, 55
  moldy soil in, <u>53</u>
  pets eating, 162
  shining leaves of, 151
Humidifier, 57, 309

Hydrogen peroxide, 361
  as bleaching agent, 35
  for laundry stains, 28

I

Ice cream
  preventing frosty film on, 260
  stains, 343
Indentations on carpet, 71
Ink Away, 26, 171, 233
Ink stains
  cleaners for, 26, 71
  on clothing, 233
  in dryer, 171
  on leather, 128
  on marble, 130
  on plastic toys and doll faces, 157
  on walls, 82–83
Insect bites, 260, 261
Insect control. *See* Pest control
Insurance
  fire damage and, 366, 367, 368
  water damage and, 369
Insurance adjuster, 366-67
Invisible stains, dry-cleaning, 179–80
Ironing
  ties, 204
  tips for, 176–79, <u>178</u>
Ironing board covers, 111, 177
Iron in medicines, 347
Irons, 110–11
Itching from mosquito bites, 260

J

Jade, 322
January chores, 311–18
Jeans, grass stains on, <u>232</u>, 340
Jewelry
  cleaning, 321–22
  marking clothing, <u>183</u>
Juice stains, 28
  fruit, 338
  meat, 346–47

R

Raccoons, 240
Radios, 112
Ramie, 186–87
Rattles, 153
Rayon
  cleaning, 187
  ironing, 178
Recipes
  Dad's Favorite Pumpkin Pie, 290
  Orange Blossom French Toast, 245
  Queen Mother's Christmas Cookies,
    The, 310
Red Erase, 309, 362
Red soda stains, 72
Red stains, 17, 27, 68, 216–17, 309,
    338, 339, 357
  product for (see Wine Away Red Wine
    Stain Remover)
Red wine stains, 17, 27, 29, 68, 72,
    216–17, 356–57, 364
Refrigerators, 104–5, 229
Retayne, 42, 362
Ribbons, storing, 315, 316
Ring-around-the-collar, 26, 29, 30,
    334
Rit Color Remover, 353
Road-salt stains, 13
Road trips. See Car trips
Roses
  black spot on, 18, 238
  cutting, 239
  pest control for, 147, 238
Rottenstone, 362
Rubber cement, removing, 339–40
Rugs, folding, 175
Rust, on
  baking pans, 108
  car bumpers, 256
  clothing, 18, 353
  concrete, 142–43
  countertops, 109
  dishwasher, 101
  garden tools, 241
  kitchen utensil, 109
  marble, 130
  sinks, 107
  steel wool pad, 108

Rust Magic, 353, 362
Rust removers, 28, 353, 362, 364

S

Saddle soap, 362
Salad bowls, wood, 109
Salsa on carpet, 72
Salt
  as cleaning essential, 228
  for laundry stains, 29
  stains
    on auto carpet, 145
    on boots, 297
    on leather, 128
    from road salt, 13
Sandpaper, fine drywall, 360
Sand stuck to body, 259
Satin, 187
Schedule for cleaning. See Annual
    cleaning checklist
School
  clothes for, 277–78
  organization tips for, 278–79
Scorch marks
  from ironing, 178–79, 353–54
  on lampshades, 215
Scraper for window washing, 138
Scratches on wood furniture, 122, 305
Screens, 140
Screws, painting, 87
Scrubber, window-washing, 138, 364
Scum, soap, 11, 93–94, 95
Seal of Approval, Queen of Clean's, 14, 30
Seams, ironing, 177
Seedlings, 236
Seersucker, 187
September chores, 274–82
Sequined clothing, 190–91
Sewer backups, water damage from, 371
Shampoo for laundry stains, 29
Shaving cream, 362
  for carpet stains, 69
  for laundry stains, 29
Sheepskin, 218
Sheets
  as beach blankets, 260
  fitted, folding, 175

Wood *(cont.)*
  marker on, 155
  paneling, 85
  pepper mills, <u>99</u>
  salad bowls, <u>109</u>
  tabletops, 289
Woodwork, 231
Wool, 188
Work clothes, 194–95
Wrapping paper, 306–7, 314–15
Wreaths, Christmas
  protecting door from, 305
  storing, 316
Wrinkles on clothes left in dryer, 170–71
Wristband
  paint-catching, 88
  for wall washing, 83

Y

Yellow spots and stains, 357

Z

Zinc oxide stains, 351
Zippers
  clothing, 204–5, 278
  tent, 264
Zout Laundry Stain Remover, 15, 27, <u>31</u>,
      364
  for cleaning
    chocolate stains, 323
    copier toner stains, 335
    driveway, 267
    furniture polish stains, 339
    grass stains, 340
    gravy stains, 296, 341
    guacamole stains, 317
    ice cream stains, 343
    lipstick stains, 345
    old stains, 283
    perfume stains, 324
ZUD Heavy-Duty Cleanser, 142–43,
      364

PARENTS OF TLC'S *19 Kids & Counting*

A LOVE THAT
MULTIPLIES

AN UP-CLOSE VIEW OF
HOW THEY MAKE IT WORK

MICHELLE &
JIM BOB DUGGAR

H HOWARD BOOKS
A DIVISION OF SIMON & SCHUSTER, INC.
New York · Nashville · London · Toronto · Sydney

During our growing up years Jim Bob and I both overlooked a lot of the sacrifices our parents made to provide for us emotionally, physically, and spiritually. We want to publicly acknowledge with a grateful heart all that they have poured into our lives. Their love, guidance, and many times sleepless nights have formed who we are today.

Thank you, Mom and Dad,
Ethel and Garrett Ruark,
Mary and J. L. Duggar

Howard Books
A Division of Simon & Schuster, Inc.
1230 Avenue of the Americas
New York, NY 10020

First Howard Books hardcover edition June 2011

HOWARD and colophon are trademarks of Simon & Schuster, Inc.

For information about special discounts for bulk purchases, please contact Simon & Schuster Special Sales at 1-866-506-1949 or business@simonandschuster.com.

The Simon & Schuster Speakers Bureau can bring authors to your live event. For more information or to book an event, contact the Simon & Schuster Speakers Bureau at 1-866-248-3049 or visit our website at www.simonspeakers.com.

Edited by Sue Ann Jones

Designed by Stephanie D. Walker—www.water2winedesign.com

Manufactured in the United States of America

10 9 8 7 6 5 4 3 2 1

Library of Congress Cataloging-in-Publication Data

Duggar, Michelle.
   A love that multiplies / Michelle and Jim Bob Duggar.
      p. cm.
   Includes bibliographical references.
      1. Duggar, Jim Bob—Family. 2. Duggar, Michelle—Family. 3. Families—United States. 4. Newborn infants—United States. 5. Family size—United States. 6. Child rearing—United States. 7. Christian life—United States. I. Duggar, Jim Bob. II. Title.
   HQ536.D864 2011
   277.3'082085—dc22

2010053829

ISBN 978-1-4391-8381-6
ISBN 978-1-4516-0616-4 (ebook)

Unless otherwise indicated Scripture quotations are taken from the King James Version of the Bible. Public domain. Scripture quotations marked AMP are taken from the Amplified® Bible, copyright © 1954, 1958, 1962, 1964, 1965, 1987 by The Lockman Foundation. Used by permission. (www.Lockman.org)

• Contents •

ACKNOWLEDGMENTS

We are ever grateful to the many people God has brought into our lives and who have encouraged us spiritually throughout our marriage. Pastor Cliff Palmer, Pastor Don Elmore, Pastor Clark Wilson, Dr. Ed Wheat, Dr. Bill Gothard, Dr. S. M. Davis, and Jim Sammons, thank you for your counsel and wisdom. We also appreciate the courage of Eileen O'Neil with TLC/Discovery channels and our producer, Sean Overbeeke, along with our film crew friends at Figure 8 Films in stepping out to share our family's life with viewers around the world.

Sue Ann Jones receives our enormous gratitude for her careful, thoughtful writing in helping us tell our story. As well, we owe many thanks to the publishing team at Howard Books/Simon & Schuster for their vision, including Philis Boultinghouse, Becky Nesbitt, Jessica Wong, and Jonathan Merkh. We are so thankful for our literary agent, Leslie Nunn Reed, who reached out to us five years ago, encouraging us to write, and has guided us through the whole process.

Especially, we want to thank our children for seeking God's will for your lives, working together, and being each other's best friends. You are a blessing from the Lord. We count it all joy to be your parents!

• Our Biggest Test Begins •

Friday, December 4, 2009

As another happy, pre-Christmas day began, the Duggar household was bustling with busyness.

Our seventeen children still living at home hopped out of their beds early to get ready for the arrival of a film crew coming to do a story about our supersized family. This one, from Australia, was coming to do a segment for a television newsmagazine there.

The children got dressed, brushed their teeth, combed their hair, and came downstairs for breakfast. The younger ones put on their notecard-sized chore packs, which list and remind them of their responsibilities and activities for the day. Besides household chores, each child would spend time on homeschool assignments and music practice for upcoming performances: a Christmas pageant sponsored by their music teachers, a harp recital at the mall, and then a piano and violin recital.

Ten of the older children were planning next week's mission trip to El Salvador with Jim Bob and thinking about what they had to pack and what gifts would be needed for the children they would see there.

The Australian TV production team arrived, and after we introduced our family and showed them around the house, they began videotaping the day's many activities. The children enjoyed meeting this crew and marveled at their beautiful Australian accents; the kids asked them as many questions about their country as they asked about our family.

As we went through the day, Michelle, twenty-four and a half weeks pregnant with baby number nineteen, started experiencing a lot of pain. Years before, she'd had a kidney stone that caused excruciating pain, similar to what she was experiencing now, so she thought maybe another stone was starting to pass. She slipped away to rest in the afternoon, but by that evening, when the production crew had left for the day, the pain had become unbearable.

Jim Bob called Michelle's doctor, who recommended that she come to the hospital for some tests. Grandma Duggar was staying with us at the time, and she stepped in to watch the kids while we were away. We told everyone we would be home in a few hours and headed out the door.

There was no indication that our happy lives were about to be turned upside down, that our relationship with each other would be challenged, or that our strong faith would be sorely tested.

We had no idea that within twenty-four hours our children would gather around their somber-faced daddy and hear him tell them the most frightening news imaginable: their mama's life and the life of the new baby were in grave danger.

"Pray hard," Jim Bob would tell them as tears welled up in his eyes. "Pray to God for Mama and for the baby; pray like you've never prayed before!"

PART 1

• Little Baby, Big Challenges •

Fear thou not; for I am with thee: be not dismayed;
for I am thy God: I will strengthen thee;
yea, I will help thee.

—Isaiah 41:10a

1

• Little Eyes Watching •

Lo, children are an heritage of the LORD:
and the fruit of the womb is his reward.
—Psalm 127:2

We believe that children are a blessing from God, and twenty-two years ago, in the fifth year of our marriage, we decided to let Him decide how big our family would be. By early 2009, He had given us eight daughters and ten sons—eighteen wonderful children—and an amazing life filled with enduring love, incredible joy, and fun-filled adventure. We were amazed at how God had entrusted us with so many blessings.

Sure, there were challenges along the way. We had endured some very stressful times in our marriage, when feeble income and over-whelming work and responsibilities had threatened to tear apart our dreams for our family. And we had suffered hard losses, including the death of Michelle's mother. But with faith and prayer we had survived all those difficult times, and as 2009 began, we felt confident that *nothing* could ever shake our relationship with God or with each other.

We never dreamed that by the time 2009 ended, we would find ourselves living in a whirlwind of fear, anxiety, and turmoil. Now, a year after the overwhelming challenge that turned our lives upside down, we're writing this book to share what we've learned from the experience and also to share how our faith in God and the Bible principles we live

by have sustained and guided us through a traumatic season of our lives, one that may not be over yet.

This is the story of how we survived the upheaval that swept through our family—and how we manage our family in everyday life. Because of the audience that watches our large family move through daily life on the TLC reality series *19 Kids and Counting*, we have had many people express interest in our faith, principles, and experiences. We hope this book answers some of the many questions we receive in hundreds of e-mails and letters every day from people telling us they watch our show or they've read our previous book, *The Duggars: 20 and Counting* (a number based on our then eighteen children and ourselves). We are very conservative Christians, and many of the writers introduce themselves by telling us how different they are from us: "I'm Jewish . . ." "I'm Muslim . . ." "I'm an atheist . . ." "I'm a flaming liberal . . ."

Sometimes they go on to say that they don't share any of our beliefs and they think our parenting practices are outdated, narrow-minded, misguided, ridiculous, and a host of other adjectives, some of them too harsh to print here.

And yet the majority of the letters—even from those whose beliefs are different from ours—also tell us that they like the end product of what we do and believe: a close-knit, love-filled family bustling with well-behaved, respectful, fun-loving, adventurous, and smart children who cherish their parents and siblings and show courtesy and kindness to those they meet.

One of the most frequent comments was that we'd never experienced "real life," with all its hardships, challenges, setbacks, and pain. The truth was, we'd been through plenty of hard experiences, but none as difficult as those we've experienced in the last two years. In this book we hope to communicate how the faith and principles that guided us through all the good times have kept us strong through the bad times too. Our hope is that through our story you'll find ideas for enriching your own family's life together, building love, joy, wisdom, and strength that will see you through good times and bad.

We're not parenting experts. We don't have all the answers; we're still learning every day. These are just the guidelines we follow, the practices that work for us. Since we're unable to respond to the hundreds of daily inquiries that come to us, we hope this book will provide answers and insights that will not only answer your questions about the Duggars but will also inspire you to look for ways to become the best possible parent and role model to your own children.

DIFFERENT NOW

As we write, our family's life seems to have returned to something like normal after experiencing events that turned our world upside down. But we are different people now than we were when 2009 began. We've experienced firsthand how quickly and cataclysmically everything can change, and now we value even more the beliefs and principles that sustained us through our ordeal—not only in matters of faith and of the heart but also of the home.

In the chapters to come we'll share how our parenting methods worked, failed, or evolved under duress. In reading about our experiences, perhaps you'll find ideas for developing your own household systems for managing things like schedules and organization. As you learn about our child-rearing practices, maybe you'll gain insights about how to shape your own children's hearts and minds lovingly and effectively.

Our primary goal in this book is to encourage you to recognize the God-given blessings in your own life and help you find ways to fill your family with everyday joy as well as lay a foundation of faith that will sustain you through difficult times. In short, we want to help you find ways to infuse your family with faith, fun, and hope for a bright future.

JIM BOB'S DAD MOVES IN

During our nearly twenty-seven years of marriage, God has given us constant joy through our big, expanding family; but to keep life inter-

esting, He's also sent plenty of challenges our way. For example, in our first book, we described how we coped with having five children under age five when we lived in a nine-hundred-square-foot home that was also the sales office for our used-car business.

Now we live in a seven-thousand-square-foot home, but we still live frugally, and we still encounter challenges, as well as joy, on a daily basis. We finished our first book in October 2008, when our joy about the marriage of our firstborn child, Josh, to the delightful Anna Keller was tempered by the sober awareness that my (Jim Bob's) dad, J. L. Duggar, had been diagnosed with a terminal illness, an advancing brain tumor.

When we built our home in northwest Arkansas (a nearly four-year family project completed in 2006), we intentionally included a handicap-accessible living area for family members who might need our assistance as they coped with health issues. Shortly after we moved into the house, that guest area had been put to good use by Michelle's dad when he lived with us following a terrible car crash with a drug-impaired driver. He stayed a year and then moved back home to Ohio to live with Michelle's siblings, leaving the guest area ready for the next time it was needed.

A few months later, my dad was diagnosed with a medullo-blastoma—a brain tumor. This stage of our lives began one day when Dad felt a little knot on the back of his head. He thought at first it was a bug bite, but when the "bite" got bigger instead of going away, he went to a dermatologist, who sent him to another specialist, who sent him to another specialist, until finally the tumor was identified. The doctor who diagnosed the problem told us he'd never seen anyone survive past about age fifty with that kind of tumor. Dad was seventy-one when he was diagnosed.

His doctors said the tumor had started in his brain and had eaten through his skull to protrude out the back of his head, causing the bump. One surgery was performed, but the surgeons said they couldn't remove the entire tumor without causing brain damage. Dad chose not to go through chemotherapy and radiation; he wanted to avoid the side

effects of those treatments so he could enjoy being with his family and especially his grandchildren during the remainder of his days here on earth.

For a while Dad's overall health held steady, but gradually his condition began deteriorating. We welcomed him and Mom into our guest room, and while Mom insisted on providing almost all of Dad's daily care and devotedly worked to preserve his dignity, our children loved having them there to play games, listen to stories, go on outings, and share meals with us.

Our kids love celebrating our family's special days together, including Grandma and Grandpa Duggar's forty-eighth wedding anniversary.

It was truly a joy to have my parents living with us, even though it was hard on all of us to see Dad's health steadily fail over the next eighteen months. Mom put him on a special diet that she credits with prolonging his life and keeping him active for much longer than anyone expected. In addition, a wonderful physician friend, Dr. Doty Murphy, came to our home frequently to manage the IV treatments that kept him from getting dehydrated.

Dad remained active, but nothing could stop the inevitable growth of the tumor. When it extended into the part of the brain controlling motor skills, the change seemed to happen overnight. One day Dad was at the park with Grandma and the kids. The next day he could no longer stand or feed himself.

COMPOUNDING PROBLEMS

By January 2009, Dad was unable to speak. But he remained an important part of our family; we visited his bedside often, and whenever

he felt up to it, we wheeled him out to the living room or to the dining table to join us for family time. The kids interacted with him whenever he felt like coming out. They would sit and carry on conversations with him, even though he couldn't respond, telling him about their music lessons or the new phonics sounds they were learning or some funny thing one of them had seen or done.

Then a major ice storm struck our area, possibly the worst in northwest Arkansas history. Many homes and vehicles were damaged or destroyed by falling trees. Without power, businesses couldn't open. Schools were closed. The governor declared our area a disaster area, and residents struggled to recover from an estimated seventy-seven million dollars' worth of damage.

Our yard turned into a giant ice rink (a wonderful thing, our middle six boys would tell you, when they were allowed to go out), and throughout the region ice-crusted power lines either fell on their own or were brought down by ice-coated trees falling on them. Huge limbs from the massive shade trees in our yard broke off and fell to the ground, littering our lawn with gigantic ice sculptures.

Roads were closed, and simply being outside was hazardous, with trees or limbs constantly falling and power lines dangling or already on the ground. But our devoted film crew, which for several months had been videotaping our family for the TLC reality series, called to say they were heading our way, determined to capture the Duggar family's reaction to the weather-induced woes and wonder.

That was a blessing for us because just as the power went out and trees started falling, Michelle realized we were running short of diapers. She called associate producer David Felter and asked if he could pick up some diapers on the way.

David, a single guy who'd never been anywhere near a discount store's baby department, gamely made the purchase and headed our way with producer Sean Overbeeke. They drove around a ROAD CLOSED sign only to end up in a ditch a little later. Passing firefighters pulled them

out and set them on their way again, and eventually they slid down our driveway, delivered the diapers, and started filming.

To our younger kids, having the power go out was a grand adventure. Our family almost never watches broadcast TV, so nobody missed that at all, and if you're a little boy with a bunch of younger brothers, what can be more fun than having to use the bathroom by flashlight? The kids were excused from doing most of their schoolwork because there was no power to run the computers, and they found creative ways of entertaining themselves, as always, whether it was Rollerblading through the living room or conducting circus acts such as balancing a stick horse on their noses.

On the other hand, to Michelle, the mother of a newborn (our eighteenth child, Jordyn Grace, had been born about a month earlier, on December 18, 2008) as well as the sixteen other children then living at home, having no electricity wasn't all that wonderful. Exciting, yes, just not the ideal.

And this wasn't just a short little power outage. No, power was out throughout our region, and at the Duggar home, for *nine* long days!

WATCHING DADDY'S RESPONSE

Thankfully, I (Michelle) am married to a creative and smart husband who's also a devoted father. He knew that lots of little eyes were watching how he would cope with the ice-storm disaster, and his optimism and good humor never waned throughout that long, difficult time. Jim Bob rarely gets rattled; he's always rock solid in his beliefs and in working toward the parenting goals we have set for ourselves. He looks at everything as an opportunity to teach our children something new. The ice storm was no exception.

We hold to the truths of the Bible, in which the apostle Paul wrote, "I have learned, in whatsoever state I am, therewith to be content" (Philippians 4:11). How could we teach our children those words and

then show frustration, fear, anger, or some other destructive emotion when an ice storm made our lives a little more complicated?

Seeing the vast amounts of damage to the trees in our yard, Jim Bob might have had a few moments when he felt completely overwhelmed, wondering, *How am I going to get this huge mess cleaned up? What if the power stays off for several days? How can I get my family through this calamity?* But those little eyes watching him never saw him hesitate. Instead they saw him thank God that everyone was safe, fed, and relatively warm, and then ask Him for strength and wisdom to meet the challenge. And through it all, the smile on his face and the love sparkling in his eyes never faded.

However, one thing *did* change. There have been very few times when Jim Bob has done *anything* without one or two kids in tow, especially work outside, but on that first icy morning he told everyone to stay put while he cautiously stepped out onto the frozen yard to assess the damage. What he saw was breathtaking. Everywhere he looked, the ground was covered with frozen trees, limbs, and power lines creating a massive, impenetrable thicket of ice.

Normally, our home would at least have had radiant floor heat, thanks to the nine thousand feet of Vanguard PEX pipe embedded under the floor tile that was connected to our outdoor wood-burning furnace, but a few days earlier, a part on that system had malfunctioned and we were still waiting for its replacement when the ice storm struck. With no electricity to power the forced-air fans on either the wood-fueled or natural-gas furnaces, our house was quickly growing cold. That situation would have been stressful enough under ordinary conditions, but we had a sick, bedridden grandfather and a newborn baby to think of, in addition to the twenty-one other family members living in our house (ourselves and Grandma Duggar plus our sixteen other living-at-home children, in addition to Josh and Anna, who fled their frozen home in town to seek refuge with us).

We were all looking to Jim Bob to figure out how we would survive this trial, knowing that he was relying on the One who had all the an-

swers. Thus we moved through the icy day with a sense of adventure rather than fear.

Later that first morning Jim Bob made another trip outside, carefully maneuvering over the ice to the storage shed in our backyard. He retrieved a small generator and fired it up on the front porch to operate the furnace fans, which brought a little relief from the steadily increasing cold. But he quickly realized we would need more fuel to keep the generator running—it had to be refilled about every ninety minutes—so he asked Josh and our next-oldest son, John-David, to try to get to town to buy gasoline. They were gone several hours, not only because they had to drive so slowly on the ice, even in a four-wheel-drive truck, but also because so few service stations were open. Power was out everywhere, which meant that only stations with generators could operate their pumps. It took them a long time to find one that was open.

While they were gone, we looked out the windows and watched in amazement as frozen limbs fell minute by minute and splintered trees covered our property—and stared at the utility pole leaning precari-

The weight of the ice caused dozens of trees to fall on our property.

ously in our backyard, the broken line coming out of the box dangling ominously in midair. Then, while some of the children watched, a huge tree fell on the storage shed where the generator had been stored, totally crushing it.

When he saw the destroyed building he'd just entered a short while earlier, Jim Bob's mood momentarily changed. He sat the children down at our long dining table and earnestly explained how dangerous their outside world had suddenly become. No one, he said, was to step foot outside until he gave the okay—and that might be several days

away. "Just like that tree that fell squashed the shed, a tree or limb could fall and squash *you*. I love y'all, and I don't want anyone to get hurt, so *no one* goes outside until I say so," he said, his eyes focusing on each child in turn and waiting for an acknowledgment.

One day passed and then another. We normally do eight to eleven loads of laundry a day, and by day three, with none of our four washers and four dryers running, the mountain of dirty clothes in our laundry room threatened to equal the mountain of ice-covered debris outside our house.

Then Jim Bob had a brilliant idea. He carefully walked, slid, and skidded his way over the ice field to the shop building several hundred yards away where we park our bus. Ever so slowly, he navigated the giant vehicle up and down the hills in our driveway and cautiously pulled it up next to our frozen-over house. He turned on the bus's generator and plugged in some electrical cords, and in what seemed like a wonderful miracle, we were able to power one washer, one dryer, two furnace fans, and several strings of low-wattage LED Christmas lights to provide some nighttime illumination. Our home filled with a web of electric cords snaking along the floors and stairs.

It still wasn't easy to catch up with the forty loads of laundry that had accumulated and then keep up with the ever-growing pile of dirty clothes, but by running the single washer and dryer constantly we made progress, slowly but surely.

The outdoor temperatures were so cold we simply lifted the garage door on our home's massive pantry (the space that would be an ordinary garage in other homes is a pantry in ours) so that the food in our three large chest freezers stayed frozen. Fortunately we still had water, and our cooktops and ovens run on gas, so we could still cook.

"Isn't this something?" Jim Bob asked the children one night as we all settled under the glow of the Christmas lights strung around our eighteen-foot-long dining table. "Even though we don't have power, we can still enjoy a healthy, hot meal, and we're all together and safe. We have so much to be thankful for!"

A PERFECT TIME FOR COMPANY

We thanked God for His blessings and His protection during the ice storm, and we asked Him to keep us strong and hold us close during the difficulties we knew were coming: not just during the complications from the ice storm but also Grandpa Duggar's declining health. Dr. Murphy faithfully continued to come to our home to check on Grandpa and set up his IVs, despite the icy conditions. On one of those cold, hard days, he warned us that Grandpa was failing fast and might have less than a month left to live.

About that same time we worriedly noticed that Grandpa wasn't the only one having health problems. Our six-week-old baby, Jordyn Grace, had what first seemed like nothing more than a runny nose for a day; we assumed she'd been infected with the same minor cold symptoms that had passed through the rest of the children a few days earlier. But when you're just a month old, a minor cold can progress into a serious respiratory problem in the blink of an eye, and that's what

On the second day of a major ice storm, our baby, Jordyn, had to be hospitalized due to a respiratory problem. In this photo, Jordyn is about one year old.

happened to Jordyn. On the second day of the ice storm, her minor symptoms suddenly evolved into a struggle to breathe. A woman who's mothered eighteen children recognizes when one of her little ones is in distress, and that evening, I (Michelle) knew it was time to head for the emergency room.

When doctors at the hospital in Springdale said Jordyn needed to be admitted for observation and respiratory treatments we couldn't provide at home, especially since we had only limited power provided by the generators, we both stayed with her. Jordyn was struggling to breathe, and we

didn't feel comfortable having just one of us stay with her; with two of us there, one could attend to Jordyn while the other slept or grabbed a bite to eat. We often rely on "tag-team" parenting when things get too difficult for one parent to handle alone.

So we called home and made arrangements with the older children and with Grandma Duggar, who quickly offered to step into the supervisory role (no wonder our children long ago nicknamed her Super Grandma!). While her main focus would be tending to Grandpa Duggar's needs, she would be there to support our older children as they kept the household running.

A few days later, while driving through the winter wonderland to return home after Jordyn was discharged, one of our older kids called with a brilliant idea. Since many of the roads were impassable and we were holed up in a giant igloo with limited power and a horde of little kids who couldn't play outside, they suggested that we invite our friends Gil and Kelly Bates and their seventeen children to come visit from Tennessee!

We quickly agreed. And no, we hadn't completely lost our minds. You see, the Bateses are another huge family who share our conservative Christian beliefs and parenting philosophies, and they're among our very closest friends.

Best of all, they own a tree-trimming service!

Gil had told Jim Bob recently that the middle of winter is typically the slowest time for their business. "Come to northwest Arkansas," Jim Bob now told Gil on the phone. "With all the ice-storm damage, there's enough business here to keep you busy for weeks!"

They took us up on our offer and arrived a few days later, when the roads had cleared, and we were delighted to see them. Our boys moved out of their large, dormitory-style room into our bus, parked outside, giving the Bateses a big room and bathrooms of their own. Our youngest children were deliriously happy to have some of their favorite friends to play with; all the older girls gathered comfortably in the kitchen to chat, cook, and bake, and the Bates and Duggar older

boys went to work under Gil's direction cleaning up the tree debris from our yard and at several other homes and businesses in our area as well.

John-David and Josh had already used a rented backhoe to clear away some of the debris from our driveway, but Gil and his teenagers taught our older boys and Jim Bob a lot about how to safely trim standing trees. The rest of us watched in awe as they fearlessly climbed the tallest trees, tethered to a safety line, cutting and clearing damaged limbs as they moved about the treetops as easily as monkeys.

Now, before we knew it, our yard was cleaned up, the dangerous tree limbs removed. The still-frozen hill in front of our house was perfect for sledding. Jim Bob retrieved a pile of old signs left over from his unsuccessful run for the U.S. Senate a few years earlier, and the children quickly transformed them into slick toboggans that skidded down the icy hill at lightning speed.

Northwest Arkansas was still trapped in an ice locker, but at the Duggar home there was, as always, plenty of fun to be found.

Big News at the Birthday Party

The power was still out and the Bateses were still with us when Grandpa Duggar's seventy-third birthday rolled around on February 3. Grandpa felt well enough to be lifted out of his bed and onto one of our rolling office chairs for an appearance in the living room. Jana had baked his favorite banana cake and the kids had decorated the table with happy birthday banners and streamers.

There was lots of laughter but also lots of tears. We all knew this would be Grandpa's last birthday, and although we were at peace, knowing he would happily spend the rest of eternity in heaven with Jesus, we also knew how much we would miss him as part of our daily lives here on earth. By then the tumor had taken away his ability to speak, smile, walk, stand, or move his arms, but we sensed his happiness to be among us, surrounded by the family he loved. With him seated at the

GRANDPA DUGGAR'S FAVORITE BANANA CAKE

1 box yellow cake mix (plus
   ingredients specified on box)
2 boxes vanilla pudding mix (plus
   milk specified on box)
5 bananas

Prepare yellow cake as directed and
bake. In a bowl, prepare pudding as
directed on box. Pour pudding over
cake. Slice bananas and lay slices on
top of cake. Refrigerate until cold,
about 1 hour. Serve and enjoy!

DUGGAR SIZE IT!

Use 1 industrial-size cake pan (or two
9 x 13 pans)

2 boxes yellow cake mix (plus
   ingredients specified on box)
4 boxes vanilla pudding (plus milk
   specified on box)
8 bananas

head of the table as my mom fed him his birthday cake and ice cream, we were sadly aware that he was living his final days. And our children were watching it happen—and watching the way we responded to that sad, slow decline toward death.

Grandpa's last birthday was another momentous occasion for our family. The TLC film crew lined us all up in birth order—the Bateses and their sixteen children (Kelly was pregnant with their seventeenth), and the Duggars with our eighteen children plus daughter-in-law Anna.

The camera slowly panned over one set of smiling faces and then the other, and just when we thought the shot was completed, Josh cleared his throat and said, "Everybody, Anna and I have an announcement . . ."

Josh and Anna surprised everyone when they announced they were expecting our first "grand-Duggar."

2

• More Babies on the Way •

God blessed them, and God said unto them,
Be fruitful, and multiply.
—Genesis 1:28

Mackynzie Renee Duggar, our first grandchild, was born October 8, 2009. What a joyful event that was for all of us! If you believe, as the Bible says, that children are a blessing from God, then having a big family *and* a grandchild is simply over the top.

Amazingly, a couple of months before we celebrated Mackynzie's birth in October, we celebrated some exciting news of our own. In August 2009, when baby Jordyn was just six months old, Michelle asked me (Jim Bob), "Honey, could I talk to you about something?" She led me into our bathroom and shared a wonderful surprise. "You're a father again," she told me. An early-pregnancy test showed a positive reading. We were expecting another baby!

You probably won't believe *this*, but I could hardly believe *that*. It just wasn't on my radar for possibilities at the time. I knew that having another baby was completely possible—God had proven that again and again. But the timing was really surprising.

Jordyn had been born December 18, 2008. We choose to follow some Old Testament directives about when intimate relations between a husband and wife should resume after childbirth. After the birth of a male baby, couples were told to abstain for forty days, and after

the birth of a female baby, eighty days— almost three months (see Leviticus 12:2–5; 15:19). As Christians we aren't bound by Old Testament law, but we've found that some of the practices laid down all those years ago for our biblical ancestors still have merit today. This is

A family portrait with our first grandchild, Mackynzie Renee Duggar, born to Josh and Anna on October 8, 2009.

simply one of the practices we choose to follow. So our intimate relationship hadn't resumed until March 2009.

In August, Michelle was still breast-feeding Jordyn, which works as a natural means of birth control for some mothers, but not for Michelle. Now she'd gotten pregnant again, and we were delighted to know that another baby would be joining us in March 2010, when Jordyn was fifteen months old, which is a fairly short time between Duggar births (normally Michelle can get pregnant again around nine months after the previous birth; this time she was pregnant again after only five months).

I try to be a good listener and confidante, but I do have one serious weakness: I'm totally unable to keep good news a secret for long. So even though we planned to wait a little while before telling the rest of our children that a new brother or sister was on the way, I spilled the beans much earlier than I had intended.

It happened that very afternoon. We had just bought a giant roll of black plastic sheeting, twelve feet by one hundred feet, to put under the concrete slab we were going to pour for a basketball court in our backyard. It was a hot, muggy day in northwest Arkansas, and all around me were sweaty little kids looking for a fun way to cool off.

One of the parenting ideas we try to practice is to keep our children

on their toes, never knowing when some fun, new adventure is about to unfold for them. That day I looked at the black plastic, looked at the kids, and said, "I've got an idea."

"What is it, Daddy?"

"What are we gonna do? Are we going somewhere?"

"Are we going to the park? Should we get everyone on the bus?"

"Are we gonna have an ice cream party?" (I assume this question came from the messiest Duggar when he saw me looking at the big rolls of plastic sheeting.)

I love building my children's anticipation and enthusiasm. I smiled at them and said, "I've got a surprise."

"Daddy's making a surprise! Hey, everybody!" The first scouts tore off toward the house to raise the alarm.

I pulled out my cell phone and called John-David, who was working nearby at one of our rental properties. I asked him to bring the backhoe to the house.

The Duggar kids were beside themselves with curiosity and excitement as John-David used the backhoe to help create Dad's big surprise.

"Daddy told John-David to bring the backhoe!"

"What are we gonna do, Daddy?"

"Why do you need the backhoe?"

The tribe watched in wonder as I directed John-David where to dig. He scooped out a shallow hole at the foot of our sloping front lawn. Then we unrolled the black plastic all the way down the front-yard hill, brought out the garden hose, and greased up the plastic with Dawn dishwashing liquid and water. Voilà! A poor-man's water slide and swimming pool.

The kids rushed inside to put on their swim clothes—modest swimwear that covers everything from shoulders to knees. In a matter of

FAVORITE DUGGAR FAMILY SNACKS

Some favorite snacks at the Duggar home are: dill pickles (everyone's favorite!); canned green beans spread on a plate and spritzed with vinegar; black olives (which make great fingertip decor before they're eaten); frozen-and-thawed or canned peas or corn eaten as finger food (they especially enjoy eating them frozen, without thawing, in the hot summertime!); as well as carrot and celery sticks, apple wedges, and banana slices (with peanut butter), orange slices, lemons, and limes. (Yes, lemons and limes! It's not uncommon for someone to spend his or her own money at the grocery store to buy them. The only condition is that as soon as the kids eat them they have to go brush their teeth to remove the fruit's acid.)

We also freeze blueberries, strawberries, seedless grapes, and banana slices (to name a few) to create yummy frozen treats. We buy large bags of mixed frozen fruit as a special treat.

Since we've had at least one toddler in the house now going on twenty years, we have daily snack times that are two hours before the scheduled lunch and dinner meals, and then another snack time at 8:00 p.m. before bath, Bible time, and bedtime.

moments, everyone was slipping and sliding and having a great time, and I was right there in the middle of them, slipping, sliding, and shrieking with joy just like they were.

Carrying fresh-from-a-nap Jordyn on her hip, Michelle came outside to watch the children having the time of their lives. I quietly asked Michelle if this might be a good time to spring the news to the kids about the new baby we were expecting. She smiled and nodded, so we gathered up all the kids and told them we had a surprise to share. When we broke the news, the children gasped, flashed wide smiles, clapped their hands, and cheered, understanding the amazing blessing we'd been given.

PREPARING FOR A NEW GENERATION

It was fun for me (Michelle) to be pregnant at the same time as our daughter-in-law, Anna. Jim Bob and I, along with Josh and Anna, even went to a couple of doctor's appointments together. Jim Bob told the receptionist, "My wife's having a baby—and my baby's having a baby."

Since their marriage, Josh and

Anna had been living in a small home they rent in nearby Fayetteville, about eight miles away from us, and they work together at Josh's car lot, where they sell pre-owned cars to support themselves. Once Josh left our home, the heart ties between us remained strong, but the apron strings were cut. We had done our best to prepare him for adulthood and family responsibilities, and as soon as he and Anna said, "I do," they were financially on their own.

From the beginning, however, they were already a step ahead of where we were when we started out. After we were married in 1984 we lived in a mortgaged, nineteen-thousand-dollar fixer-upper home and sold used cars out of the front yard, in addition to Jim Bob's job at a grocery store. Then we moved to an even smaller home on a busy street where we could have a real used-car lot out front.

For a while I ran the car lot during the day, relaying customers' questions by phone to Jim Bob at the grocery store or, later, on the wrecker after he had left the grocery store and started a towing service.

Josh and Anna were following a similar path with a couple of important differences. For one, they are committed to living debt-free, a concept that we didn't adopt until a few years into our marriage. And they've kept their home and business separate, rather than turning their front yard into a car lot (something that newer zoning codes don't allow anyway).

But they've chosen, on their own, to adopt one idea that both Anna's and Josh's parents followed. They're letting God decide how many children they'll have in their family; they even included that promise in their wedding vows.

Two months after they were married, Josh and Anna joined Jim Bob and several of our children on a December mission trip to El Salvador. While the rest of the family members came home healthy, Josh and Anna managed to contract mononucleosis while they were there. Despite that setback, by early February, when we gathered during the ice storm to celebrate Grandpa Duggar's birthday, they were far enough along to confirm Anna's pregnancy.

Josh not only got to break the news to the rest of the family, the day before he had the privilege of letting Anna know she was pregnant! She had already gone through several early-pregnancy-test kits only to be disappointed by negative results. She couldn't bear to go through the suspense and possible disappointment again. So she asked Josh to look at the test stick first and tell her what it said. She left it in a cup in the bathroom for him and then busied herself in the kitchen.

As the film crew's cameras rolled, Josh checked the test and then settled down beside Anna on the couch. "I have some news for you, babe," he told her gently. "You've joined the mommy team!"

PREPARING FOR PARENTHOOD

One of the joys of owning a car lot is getting to drive all sorts of fun vehicles. In all our family's history, we've never owned a *new* car, but we've had lots of interesting ones. When Anna's mom and sisters flew from Florida for the baby shower our girls and I hosted for her, Josh picked them up at the airport in a limo he'd recently traded for!

Jim Bob has taught our children that the secret to successful buying and selling is to always buy big items, like used cars and equipment, for a bargain price so that later the purchases can be resold for a price that lets the next buyer get a good deal while you make a fair profit. He tells them, "You make your money when you *buy* something!"

Following that guideline, Josh uses his astute business sense (we'll tell you more about that later in the book) to buy all sorts of vehicles for his pre-owned car lot, things he knows he can resell. He follows other advice Jim Bob teaches the family: "Always negotiate to buy items at a price you could instantly get back if you decide to wholesale it."

As a result, at various times Josh has owned, through the car lot, everything from Jaguars and high-end SUVs to Hondas and Toyotas. His lot can hold cars he's bought at auctions or from new-car stores that they got as trade-ins, as well as older clunkers that individuals have traded to Josh when buying newer vehicles.

Unfortunately, when they were on their way to their first prenatal appointment with Anna's obstetrician, they were driving one of the latter—a pickup truck that broke down on the highway!

Josh had traded for the truck the day before. He drove it home that night, and it had run fine. The next morning he'd had a little trouble starting it, but once it got going it seemed to be all right. But then, on their way to the doctor's office, the pickup started lurching and hesitating until finally Josh steered the sputtering vehicle into a parking lot on the side of the highway, where it coughed another time or two and finally died.

A short while later, they finally arrived at the doctor's office—riding in John-David's tow truck!

Josh is blessed to have a wife who's unflappably patient and understanding. She's shown those qualities repeatedly in the two-plus years they've been married. And as we write, she is pregnant again with our second grandchild.

EARLY ARRIVAL

Josh jokes that he's chronically late for almost everything, but his firstborn daughter may be the one who'll break that mold. One morning more than a week before the baby's due date, Anna woke up in labor.

When Josh called with the news that baby Mackynzie was on her way, we were with the rest of the family attending one of our favorite yearly family events: the Advanced Training Institute Homeschool Conference at the ALERT Academy in Big Sandy, Texas. Jim Bob excitedly passed on the news to me, and I immediately started repacking my suitcase. No doubt Anna would have preferred to have her own mother and one or more of her own sisters to be with her as she gave birth to her and Josh's first child, but in their absence I was delighted to be able to assist—assuming I could get there in time!

We talked it over with Josh and Anna, and with our older daugh-

ters, and it was decided
that Jill would fly home
with me. Within an
hour or so of Josh's call,
we were in the car, and
Jim Bob was driving us
to the nearest airport.
As our plane landed in
northwest Arkansas, I
called Josh to see how
Anna was progressing.

*Michelle and our daughter-in-law, Anna, had fun
being pregnant at the same time.*

"You need to hurry!" Josh told us.

They had decided to do a home birth, and Jill and I walked through
the door just as Anna started to push. She was so calm and focused,
breathing through the contractions and coping bravely with the pain.
Josh was excited but as steady as a rock. Watching him (which you can
do on the TV series videos), it's hard to believe he's a first-time dad,
joyfully catching his baby girl as she made her entrance into the world.

Mackynzie Renee Duggar was here! What an amazing moment
that was in so many wonderful ways. We'd just become grandparents,
incredibly blessed by God to watch the creation of another generation.

Meanwhile, in the Texas campground where the rest of the family
was attending the homeschool conference, Jim Bob hurriedly packed
up all the gear, loaded all the children, and headed home. He couldn't
wait to see his first grandchild, and he glowed when a friend said,
"Congratulations, Grandpa!"

It was a wonderful milestone in our lives. And in a few more
months, Lord willing, we'd be going through childbirth again ourselves,
welcoming the nineteenth child into the Duggar family.

3

• A Surprising Test Begins •

~

*Likewise the Spirit also helpeth our infirmities: . . . the Spirit itself maketh
intercession for us with groanings which cannot be uttered.*
—Romans 8:26

Our roller-coaster year rolled along. January's ice storm and
Grandpa Duggar's death in mid-February had gotten 2009 off
to a rocky start, but Michelle's positive pregnancy test in August and
Mackynzie's birth in October lifted our spirits and filled our hearts
with joy. In our big, active family, it seems there's a major or minor crisis
about every thirty minutes, but most of 2009's crises seemed to get resolved according to our most frequent advice: wait a minute; it'll pass.

Then came Thanksgiving, when we welcomed family members
from near and far to join us. The house was full of loved ones sharing
happy sounds, delicious aromas, and a rich sense of thankfulness and
contentedness.

And with Thanksgiving came . . . a stomach virus. Or was it the flu?
Something was sweeping through the family, infecting one child after
another. Fearful that we were all coming down with the H1N1 virus—
swine flu—which was causing such concern around the country at that
time, we took the first couple of young patients to the doctor. Tests
showed it wasn't swine flu but some other kind of virus.

The illness progressed through the whole family, knocking each one
of us out of commission for about three days each. When I (Michelle)

BROCCOLI CHEESE SOUP

An easy way to feed a crowd on a cold winter day.

7 pounds frozen broccoli
2 pounds Velveeta processed cheese
1 quart whipping cream
Enough water to cover and cook broccoli
1 cup cornstarch mixed with cold water
   to thicken after soup is hot

In a large soup pot, cook broccoli first. Add Velveeta and whipping cream. Heat on low until cheese is melted, stirring constantly. Slowly stir in cornstarch blended with cold water to thicken. Serves a crowd!

looked at five-year-old Jackson's throat and saw white spots, I nearly panicked. "We've got strep!" I told Jim Bob.

Back to the doctor we went, taking not only Jackson but also eleven-month-old Jordyn, who was showing symptoms of sore throat and fever. Again the tests came back negative for what we feared most. The doctor said the problem was the Coxsackie virus rather than streptococcus. The potential complications weren't as severe, but many of the symptoms were the same.

By the time the virus had run its course through the Duggar household, fifteen of the seventeen children living at home had been sick, as well as Jim Bob and me. We were wiped out! A friend asked how we were holding up, and I told her, "I don't know whether to say our nights are long or short. We're not getting a lot of sleep at our house!"

I didn't keep track of how many boxes of tissues and Popsicles we went through, but it had to be dozens. The last patient recovered just as everything was gearing up for Christmas—and a host of other activities.

The biggest thing on our calendar was an up-

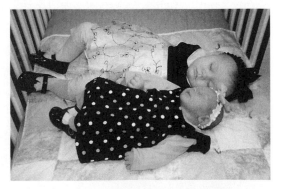

Our daughter Jordyn (top) loved having her new niece, Mackynzie, come to our house for "napovers."

coming Christian mission trip that would take ten of our older children and me (Jim Bob) to El Salvador. We'd made similar trips to that area of El Salvador in the past, but this year a hurricane, along with its aftermath of mud slides and rock slides, had destroyed thousands of the crude shacks occupied by families in the poor villages we would be visiting. We were going to help rebuild homes; plus, with our friend Todd Hertzberg and his family, we had committed to bringing wrapped gifts in our checked luggage for the 250 children who had already been invited to a Christmas party at one of the other poor communities.

A few days before we were scheduled to leave, I gathered a half dozen of the middle Duggar children who would be going on the trip and headed to a local discount store to meet the Hertzbergs and do some shopping. It was a joy to see our children diligently searching for special gifts for the El Salvadoran children, piling several shopping carts high. Following our assigned list, they picked out, for example, eighteen gifts

All our children sing and play musical instruments. Here (from left to right), Joy-Anna, Jedidiah, Jason, Jinger, Jeremiah, and Josiah are ready for a Christmas recital.

for ten-year-old boys and twelve gifts for nine-year-old girls. Then we went to the Samaritan Thrift Store and picked up hundreds of clothing items that were being donated. The children stuffed the clothes in big, military-style duffle bags to take to El Salvador.

The children also were preparing for musical Christmas recitals and programs, we were meeting with out-of-town editors about starting this book, and the Australian film crew was scheduled to spend the first weekend in December with us, shooting video to broadcast in early 2010 on the

popular TV newsmagazine *Sunday Night*. There were still homeschool lessons to be taught, more than twenty people to feed (film crews and other visitors in our home at mealtime are always invited to join us), and lots of tender hearts and minds needing attention.

We managed to slip out on the evening of December 3 for a double-date dinner with some friends, heading to one of our favorite casual restaurants that serves the most delicious sweet-potato fries. Oh, they were good!

And a few hours later, oh, how I (Michelle) regretted eating them! I had indigestion. The kidney stones that have bothered me on and off for years often flare up when I get dehydrated, and when back pain joined my indigestion, I assumed that's what was happening. Tossing and turning and walking the floor throughout the night, I knew that eating those greasy sweet-potato fries had been a mistake.

A LONG, HARD ABSENCE BEGINS

That Friday morning, December 4, we had to get up earlier than usual because the Australian team was scheduled to arrive in time for break-fast at eight thirty. They showed up as planned. We all gathered around the long dining table, pleased to get acquainted with these new friends who'd come so far to meet us. Afterward we gave the crew a tour of the house, settled in for some quick interviews, and then went about our normal day (if any day is ever normal in the Duggar household!) while they did their filming.

I (Michelle) had hoped that as

I had to give up some of the food I enjoy, like fried chicken and mashed potatoes, when my kidney stones and gallstones flared up.

time went by the indigestion and kidney-stone discomfort would ease, but instead it worsened. I'm constantly aware that my mood and disposition set the tone for our home, so my goal is always to maintain a pleasant, optimistic demeanor, knowing that all those little eyes are watching me. But the back pain seemed to increase steadily, coming in waves; whenever it intensified, I slipped away to our bedroom to curl up on the bed. Then I tried lying back on my recliner, seeking a position that would ease my misery. Meanwhile, Jim Bob and the older children covered for me, leading the family through its daily schedule and helping the film crew with whatever it needed.

By that evening the pain exceeded what I was able to bear. After Jim Bob talked to the doctor on the phone and explained my symptoms, she recommended we come to Mercy Hospital in Rogers. We quickly headed out.

I could never have imagined that it would be nearly two weeks before I would see our family again—or that seven months would pass before I was home again.

PRAYING FOR PEACE

At the hospital tests revealed a gallstone the size of a marble—and possibly those suspected kidney stones as well.

Jim Bob spent the night with me in the hospital, leaving Super Grandma and our older children in charge of the family. The next morning, I was resting as comfortably as possible, and we were encouraged by the doctors telling us that, even if I needed surgery to eliminate the gallstone, there were precedents of that being done during pregnancy without serious consequences. We prayed continually and hoped for the best.

As the day passed, my pain increased despite the antibiotics prescribed to treat the gallstone. I began experiencing nausea and my blood pressure was rising. Then another scary complication occurred: I started having contractions.

I was terrified as I realized what was happening. My due date was still more than three and a half months away. Only twenty-four and a half weeks into my pregnancy was way too early for this child to be born. The thoughts that went through my mind were tormenting: *Is my baby going to die? Am I going to die?* My fear caused my blood pressure to soar, which also increased the contractions.

I asked God for peace. I wanted to do everything I could to keep my baby safe, and that meant I had to stay calm.

Meanwhile, my doctors were becoming increasingly concerned. They knew if I continued to have contractions, everything would get worse. Tests were showing protein in my urine and elevated blood pressure—conditions that could indicate preeclampsia, a serious, and possibly fatal, complication of pregnancy.

They were doing everything they could to stop, or at least delay, my labor. But they also gave me two injections of steroids designed to improve the baby's lungs in case a premature birth did occur. The injec-

I'm blessed to have so many wonderful daughters to help and encourage me. From left to right: Jinger holding Jennifer, Michelle, Jessa, Joy-Anna (front), Jana, and Jill holding Johannah. Not shown: Jordyn and Josie and daughter-in-law, Anna.

tions created an optimal delivery "window" for a premature birth. To have the best impact on the baby's lungs, the steroids need to be in the mother's system at least forty-eight hours before delivery, and they are usually effective for seven days.

We kept praying and thinking that if only my blood pressure would stabilize, maybe the baby could be born much closer to the expected due date, March 18.

Jill and Jinger came to the hospital to help. They fed me ice chips and did whatever they could think of to make me comfortable. I know it was hard for the girls to see their mother in such distress, praying aloud and asking God, "Please protect our baby. Please let the baby survive, Lord." But if they felt fearful they didn't let it show. They prayed with me. We all knew that anxiety could make my blood pressure rise even more, so they also prayed that I would find peace in the midst of this life storm.

The day passed slowly, and my situation didn't improve. That evening the doctors told Jim Bob, "Michelle needs to be at a hospital with a neonatal intensive care unit, in case we can't get the contractions stopped and the baby has to be delivered early."

They said they were going to call an air-evac service but needed to know where we wanted to go. Our choices were Springfield, Missouri, or Little Rock, Arkansas, both about two hundred miles away. Because we were more familiar with Little Rock, that's the option we chose.

It all felt like a bad dream, a situation that was slipping out of control. We kept praying, "Oh God, please have mercy on us. Please stop Michelle's pain. Please stabilize her blood pressure. Please let our baby live!"

About an hour later, an Angel One Flight helicopter, sent from the University of Arkansas Medical Sciences (UAMS) Hospital in Little Rock, landed on Mercy's helipad.

FLYING UNDER THE STARS

Jim Bob asked to ride in the helicopter with me, but of course that's not allowed; there isn't enough room. As the helicopter was being dispatched from Little Rock to Rogers, he hurried back home to break the news to the children and pack a suitcase. He called ahead and asked our oldest daughter, Jana, to go with him. He knew he had at least a three-hour drive to Little Rock, and he wanted to try to get there before I arrived in the helicopter.

The air ambulance arrived at Mercy Hospital, and it took about thirty minutes to transfer all the monitors and other equipment and get me loaded and stabilized. Jim Bob had left to get a head start on the helicopter, but Jill had stayed behind at the hospital to see me off. Jessa had picked up Jinger earlier, and John-David had come to drive Jill home.

It broke my heart to think of my two precious children, Jill and John-David, standing alone in the parking lot, watching their mother fly away in that helicopter. I knew it had to be an almost overwhelming sight for them, especially for Jill, who'd been with me throughout the day and knew how terribly sick I was and how close we were to losing the baby.

As soon as the helicopter roared off into the night sky, they headed home. By the time they got there, Jim Bob and Jana were almost two hours into their drive to Little Rock. They'd left after he gathered our children and Grandma Duggar around him and urgently asked them to pray.

"This is really serious," he had said, wiping away his own tears as he looked into each loved one's worried face. "There's a chance our baby might not make it. There's a chance we could lose the baby—and Mama too."

Not wanting to frighten his family but at the same time preparing them in case the unthinkable happened, Jim Bob looked at those dear ones gathered around him and urged them to pray hard, begging for

God's mercy on Mama and the baby. Then he hugged each one, and he and Jana headed out the door and into the night.

The helicopter flew under a spectacular canopy of stars in a beautiful evening, crisp, cold, and clear. Whenever I opened my eyes, I looked up into the confident faces of the respiratory therapist, Buck, and flight nurse, Cindy.

"Have you ever ridden in a helicopter before?" one of them asked me.

"As a matter of fact . . . just last week," I told them. Our film crew had chartered one for some aerial shots of our property, and they had invited all of us to take a ride. I didn't even bother telling Buck and Cindy that I'm terribly prone to motion sickness. As ill as I was, it didn't seem possible that things could get worse.

Then I saw the tiny incubator tucked into a cramped space in the aircraft and knew I was wrong.

IT'S A GIRL!

Back at the house, the children, plus Grandma Duggar, Josh and Anna, and baby Mackynzie, gathered under the colorful Christmas decorations strung along the banister and upstairs catwalk and spent the rest of the evening in prayer. Later Jill told us that the youngest kids asked again and again what was happening. Why is Mama sick? Why did she have to fly in the helicopter? Why did Daddy and Jana have to leave? Why, why, why?

"We were scattered all over the living room, some sitting on the chairs and couches, some on our knees, everyone praying," Jill said.

During Jim Bob and Jana's drive to Little Rock they alternated between praying together and calling friends, asking them to pray too.

I (Jim Bob) was driving over the Arkansas River coming into Little Rock when I happened to look up and see a helicopter fly right over the highway in front of us. "Jana, there goes Mama's helicopter," I said.

I pushed the accelerator a little harder as we watched the chopper descend out of sight in the direction of UAMS Hospital. We arrived

there just a few minutes after Michelle was wheeled into her room. The staff member who greeted us didn't ask our names. "Hello, Mr. Duggar," she said. "You're looking for your wife, right?"

We teach our children the biblical directives to "pray without ceasing" and "in everything give thanks" (1 Thessalonians 5:17–18). The first thing Michelle, Jana, and I did when we were able to be together again was to pray, thanking God for the dedicated and skillful people who'd brought us safely to that point and asking His mercy on us and our unborn child in the days ahead.

Some of the first tests performed were ultrasounds to assess Michelle's gallbladder. With a smile, one of the technicians provided us with a little additional information. The next morning, Sunday, December 6, I called the family back home and told Jill, "Round up everyone tonight at six, and we'll send you all a message on the computer."

Sitting together on Michelle's hospital bed, we recorded a short piece of video and e-mailed it back to the family. Our goal was to reassure our children and also to share a wonderful little tidbit of news.

At 6:00 p.m., the older kids set up one of the laptop computers on the kitchen counter, and everyone gathered around it. Then they downloaded our video message and were delighted to hear about their next sibling . . .

"It's a girl!" we told them.

"A girl!" they all exclaimed together, cheering long and loud.

EL SALVADOR

By Monday, Michelle seemed to be improving slightly; antibiotics seemed to be reducing the inflammation in her gallbladder. She was feeling a little better—although she was still prone to frequent blood-pressure spikes that zapped every ounce of her strength and gave her a splitting headache.

With Michelle's health somewhat stabilized, the next issue to be addressed was the mission trip to El Salvador. Ten of our oldest children

and I had nonrefundable airline tickets to fly there the next morning from Northwest Arkansas Regional Airport in Fayetteville.

No question about it, I wasn't leaving Michelle. But what about the kids? The trip meant a lot to them. It had been a highlight in the lives of those who had already been to El Salvador; most of them had been two times before. Serving the impoverished people we met there had made an unforgettable impact on them and reinforced the ministry mind-set we wanted them to have. And in addition to the "ordinary" work they planned to do assisting with clothing and food distribution, the children had been asked to help with cleanup operations following a tragic hurricane that had struck the region the month before, causing, among other damage, a devastating rock slide that had destroyed everything in its miles-long path.

We heard story after story describing residents there who'd lost everything. Here was a chance to make a difficult situation better for a group of devastated people. Back at our house in Springdale, twenty huge duffle bags were already packed with donated clothes and brand-new Christmas gifts for more than two hundred children.

If our group of fifteen didn't go—ten Duggar children (from the oldest set of twins, then age nineteen, through the youngest set of twins, then age ten), plus our cousin Amy and her friend Zach, and our friends Mandy, Heidi, and Amara Query—the children who'd already been invited to the little church's Christmas party wouldn't have a Christmas at all. And that was one of our group's top priorities in making the trip: spreading the true meaning of Christmas, sharing the Gospel, and demonstrating a Christlike servant's heart by doing the difficult work that needed to be done.

There were also security issues to consider. We knew this was a part of the world where gang activity, robberies, and other situations could change conditions from safe to dangerous in a matter of seconds. Almost every store or restaurant of any size has at least one guard standing at the entrance with a shotgun. But some of our kids and I had been to El Salvador three times with the same group leaders who

had organized and would be supervising this next mission; I trusted them to watch over our children this time.

Michelle and I talked it over—and, of course, prayed about it, asking for God's guidance.

It was a hard decision for all of us; we were hesitant to let them go, and we knew the kids were nervous about being so far away from their mother when she was seriously ill. Yet we all perceived that it was God's will that they should go, and we truly believe the safest place to be is in the center of God's will. Gradually, as we made our decision, a peace covered us.

The next morning at ten o'clock, twins Jana and John-David, Jill, Jessa, Jinger, Joseph, Josiah, Joy-Anna, and twins Jedediah and Jeremiah, plus their cousin and friends, boarded a plane at Northwest Arkansas Airport and headed to El Salvador.

A FAMILY SCATTERED

That day and the next, my (Michelle's) vital signs showed some improvement, although I still felt miserable most of the time. Whenever my blood pressure spiked, I endured terrible headaches. When the doctors learned of my family history of aneurysms, they immediately ordered an MRI, a normally painless procedure that turned out to be an agonizing ordeal for me.

The twenty-minute test in the small, tubelike chamber required that I lie perfectly still—despite the turbulent gymnastics of the baby inside me. The baby did *not* like the loud, pounding sound of the MRI as it created the image the doctors needed to see. She kicked, squirmed, and jumped inside me, responding to the noise as I tried to hold myself perfectly still while twisted slightly onto my left side, a position that would ensure that she continued to get plenty of oxygen.

It was all I could do to keep from crying my urgent prayers aloud as the pain in my head and back intensified and tears rolled off my cheeks while the thunderous test continued: *Please, God! Help me get through*

this without moving. Please, God! Protect our baby's little ears. Please, God! Keep her heart rate strong and my blood pressure steady. Please, God! Hold us both in Your hands.

When the test was over and I was wheeled back to my hospital room, I cried and cried and cried, both from relief that the difficult procedure was over, and because my head was pounding—and also, I think, because the whole situation just seemed to momentarily smother me. I was sad to be so far away from my children—the little ones back home, missing their mama, and the older ones fifteen hundred miles away in another country. I didn't know what the future held, didn't even know if I would survive this ordeal. For a few moments, the situation seemed overwhelming. But in order to cry I had to draw in big gulps of air, and the deep breaths sent sharp pains shooting up my back.

"I'm at the end of myself," I sobbed to Jim Bob. "I feel so miserable, and I hurt so bad, and I can't even cry without hurting more."

Holding my hand, Jim Bob cried for me.

OPTIMISM BEFORE THE CRASH

What a gift it was when the doctors came later to say the MRI revealed no signs of aneurysms. *Thank You, God!*

For a while that Tuesday and Wednesday, my vital signs showed a slight improvement, and when we talked to the kids in El Salvador Wednesday night, I was glad we could tell them that I was doing better. It felt good to hear the relief in their voices—and it warmed our hearts to hear their excitement, and their emotions, as they described the work they were doing and the people they were meeting.

We were also relieved to hear that the governor of the province where the mission work was being done had sent a seven-man military escort to protect the group's comings and goings. God had provided greater security than we could have ever imagined.

Ten-year-old Jed, making his second trip to El Salvador, cried a little bit when he talked to me, but not because he was homesick. "Mama,

this is so special," he said, his voice breaking. "We got to go and help the children at an orphanage, and we helped dig mud out of some families' homes, and we helped rebuild some houses. I want to come back next year. I think God might be calling me to be a missionary someday, Mama."

I told him, "Jed, you're a missionary right now, wherever you are. You're serving God right now as you help those children and families."

What a special moment that was for this mama and her boy, hundreds of miles apart but connected heart to heart.

We hung up from the phone call Wednesday feeling very glad we'd let our children go.

The 2009 mission trip to El Salvador was the second for twins Jedidiah and Jeremiah.

The improvement in my symptoms gave us hope that I might be on the road to recovery and that I could carry the baby full term, even though we knew my condition was still precarious.

Then, on Thursday, December 10, the world seemed to crash in upon us.

Suddenly I felt flushed and consumed by heat. My head seemed ready to explode. I knew my blood pressure was soaring, even before the nurse checked it. During the previous week I'd had rounds of illness when pain, nausea, and despair seemed to conspire to make me miserable, but those previous episodes seemed mild compared with what was happening now.

I truly thought I could be dying.

Medical personnel bustled around me, responding to what had obviously become full-blown preeclampsia. The darkness seemed to be closing in around me. And yet, somehow, it was a shock to both Jim

Bob and me when the doctor came in and said, "We have to take the baby—now, within the next thirty minutes."

It was too soon! Too early for our baby, then at just twenty-five weeks, four days gestation. But I was at the point where my out-of-control blood pressure made a stroke or seizure, or even death, a strong possibility. The only cure for preeclampsia is to deliver the baby.

The doctor's statement made it clear that we had no choice. Still, we asked for a moment alone to pray.

"Father, if this is not Your will for us, please show us," we prayed. "Give us a sign by having Michelle's blood pressure come down. Please, God, make Your will clear to us."

The nurse came in and checked my blood pressure again. Instead of going down, it had skyrocketed.

The nurse's name was Lisa, and as she stood at my bedside, looking over the monitors, I read concern in her face. I grabbed her arm. "Am I going to die?" I asked her.

"No, honey. You're not going to die. We're going to take good care of you and your baby."

Jim Bob had stepped into the hall to talk with the doctor, and when he came back into the room, I saw the same look of concern on his face and tears filling his eyes.

And then the transport team arrived and wheeled me away.

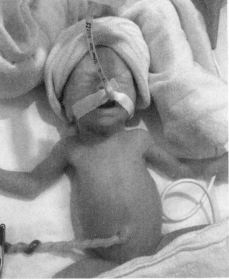

Josie Brooklyn Duggar weighed just twenty-two ounces when she was born three and a half months premature.

4

• Praying Without Ceasing •

~

As thou knowest not what is the way of the spirit,
nor how the bones do grow in the womb of her that is with child:
even so thou knowest not the works of God who maketh all.
—Ecclesiastes 11:5

Josie Brooklyn Duggar was born at 6:27 p.m. on Thursday, December 10, 2009, at UAMS Hospital in Little Rock—two hundred miles from home, three and a half months ahead of her due date. She was twelve inches long and weighed twenty-two ounces. Her head was the size of a billiard ball; she could have worn her daddy's wedding band on her thigh.

She came out kicking and flailing her arms—a good sign, doctors said. Jim Bob managed to record Josie's birth on a tiny video camera, and when the neonatal team whisked her away to the neonatal intensive care unit (NICU), he followed, filming the first few minutes of her life.

Meanwhile, immediately after Josie was born, the neonatal team intubated her, started IVs, enclosed her in an incubator, and then wheeled her by my bed in the recovery room on their way to the NICU.

Because of the spinal block I'd been given for the C-section, I couldn't sit up—or even lift my head. But they positioned her near enough that I could roll my head slightly to the side and see my precious girl.

She looked like a perfectly formed baby, but she was so tiny and

fragile it took my breath away. Our precious gift from God had a soft, downy cap of dark blonde hair, and her skin was so transparent it seemed that every vein and artery was visible. Tubes and wires protruded from her little body as she lay twitching in her tiny bed.

One of the nurses guided my hand through a port on the Plexiglas incubator. I touched her tiny left hand with my finger as tears rolled onto my pillowcase. It would be three days before I was able to touch her again, very briefly, and six long weeks before I could hold her.

A NEW LIFE JOURNEY BEGINS

While Michelle was still in the recovery room, I (Jim Bob) called our family back home. I had called them after Michelle was taken into surgery, urging them to pray for Michelle and baby Josie. Grandma Duggar, Josh and Anna, the Querys, and many other family members and friends had been waiting on pins and needles to hear from us again.

"You have a new baby sister!" I told the family, including our seven youngest children, listening back home on the speakerphone. "The delivery went well, and Josie looks perfect. They're doing tests to see how she's doing. We think Mama's going to be okay. Just keep praying."

I had sent them pictures from my cell phone, and they were amazed to see how small Josie was.

"When's Mama coming home?" I heard a little voice ask.

It was a question I didn't know how to answer. "I don't know when

When doctors told us Josie would be born within thirty minutes, I hurriedly donned the disposable scrubs the hospital gave me and took a quick swallow of soda for my supper.

Mama's coming home, but we'll be together soon," I said. "We'll work it out somehow."

At the time, I had no idea how that would happen, but keeping our children near us was one of the guiding principles that governed our lives. It's why we chose to homeschool, why I had found a career that would let me work from home so that I could spend more time with Michelle and our children throughout the day. There were exceptions, of course, like the older children's current trip to El Salvador; but my goal was to keep us as close together as possible. Standing in the hospital hallway between the rooms where my wife was still battling a serious condition and my infant daughter was fighting for her life, knowing we had long, hard challenges ahead of us, I couldn't imagine how God would bring that about. I simply trusted that He would.

The news spread quickly. After several attempts, I finally connected with Jill in El Salvador around ten o'clock. Back home in northwest Arkansas, family and friends called other friends, and in a couple of hours the word had gone out on Twitter. The next morning, TLC posted an announcement on its website, and in a few hours, more than three thousand messages of encouragement and well wishes poured in.

About the same time, our *People* magazine contact, Alicia Dennis, was experiencing a health crisis within her own family. We called Alicia, not to tell her our own news but to offer her our prayers and support. We connected with her at a Texas children's hospital where her four-year-old daughter was taken after seizures due to a virus affecting her brain.

Alicia and I (Michelle) cried together as we talked, mom to mom, both in the hospital with our children, fearful about what our little ones were facing.

Alicia posted a brief note about us on People.com, and within another day or so we felt the love and support of thousands more people around the world. Of course some of the messages were filled with criticism and condemnation, but that was nothing new for us,

HONEY-BAKED OATMEAL

3 cups rolled oats
2 teaspoons baking powder
¾ teaspoon salt
1½ teaspoons cinnamon
2 eggs, beaten
½ cup butter, melted
½ cup honey
1 cup milk

Combine dry ingredients in a 1½-quart bowl. Combine liquid ingredients in a separate container. Add liquids to dry ingredients. Stir until evenly combined. Spread in a greased 8-inch baking dish or pie pan. Cover with foil. Bake at 375 degrees for 35–45 minutes. Stir. Bake uncovered 10–15 minutes more. This recipe can be assembled and kept, covered, overnight in the refrigerator before baking.

and they were far outweighed by messages of love, hope, prayers, and encouragement.

Other prayers came from strangers closer to home. One afternoon when I (Jim Bob) arrived at the hospital, a man waiting in the portico came striding toward me as soon as he saw me. "Mr. Duggar!" he said.

He told me he was the music minister at a Little Rock church where we have mutual friends. "I woke up this morning at seven o'clock, and God just seemed to put on my heart that I should come to the hospital and pray for you and your family and your baby. I just now got here and was praying about how to find you, and you walked in," he said.

I smiled and said thanks.

He told me a story about a time during his younger years when he hadn't instantly obeyed God's promptings, and terrible consequences had resulted. "So now, when I feel God telling me to do something, I do it," he said. "This morning I felt Him telling me to come here and pray for you—and here I am."

I thanked him again for coming—and led him upstairs to the NICU, where we joined in earnest prayer for Josie.

STRUNG OUT BY DISTANCE

For the first five or six days of Josie's life, the medical team's focus was simply on keeping her alive. Two ultrasounds showed no brain bleeds, a common problem for preemies. Her lungs were working, and her vital

*Josie was not allowed to be held
for her first forty days of life.*

signs were good. *Thank You, God!*

Michelle's condition didn't improve as quickly as we'd hoped, but every indication was that she *would* recover and regain her strength. The doctor told us that although the cure for preeclampsia is to deliver the baby, the condition is like a freight train that takes awhile to stop once it gets going.

One of the hardest things for both of us was being away from the rest of our family. We are both accustomed to being surrounded by children all the time; now we felt like our hearts were being stretched from one place to another, and from one continent to another.

We were concerned not only about Josie but also about little Jordyn, our baby back home in Springdale whose first birthday would be December 18, just a week and a day after Josie was born. Grandma Duggar, Josh and Anna, and our friend Debbie Query and her son, Peter, were doing a wonderful job caring for the seven youngest Duggars, but by Saturday, two days after Josie's birth, Jordyn had come down with a cough and other symptoms of a cold or sinus infection that was causing them some concern.

Still in the hospital because of my blood pressure, I (Michelle) kept in touch with the home base throughout that day, constantly asking about Jordyn. Since she'd had respiratory problems during the ice storm that required hospitalization, I wanted to make sure we stayed on top of the situation. I certainly didn't want my two youngest babies in hospitals that were a three-hour drive apart!

That evening, I asked Josh and Anna to take her to the pediatric after-hours clinic, where the doctor found that her right ear was in-

fected and her lungs sounded a little crackly, which could be a sign of pneumonia. Josh called to let me know he had picked up some prescriptions and they were on their way home with Jordyn. I called the nurse at the after-hours clinic for more details—and thank goodness I did!

"Oh, no!" I said when the nurse told me what had been prescribed. "She's extremely allergic to amoxicillin!"

Several more phone calls were made, and Josh returned to the pharmacy to pick up a different prescription. I whispered a prayer of thankfulness that we'd dodged what could have been a second calamitous situation.

Two days later, on December 14, my heart got another boost when we got a call late in the afternoon from our older children, who had made it home safely from El Salvador. Now at least my family was secure within the same state. Twenty-four hours later, they were on their way to Little Rock along with Grandma Duggar, cousin Amy, and the Querys.

On December 15, 2009, the day after half of our family had returned from El Salvador, everyone drove to Little Rock to see their new baby sister, Josie Brooklyn Duggar.

I hadn't been released yet from UAMS, but the kind folks there understood how important it was for me to see all my children again—and for them to see Josie. After each child went through a quick health screening, the staff led our family to Josie's NICU room to see their minuscule sister in her incubator. Josie, still on a ventilator, was connected to what seemed like a dozen cords and tubes, and some of the older girls cried, seeing the tiny baby who seemed dwarfed by all the

medical apparatus humming and beeping over her, keeping her alive. Her skin was still transparent, and she truly looked pitiful.

Jim Bob wheeled me in a wheelchair to another hospital room where the staff had gathered my family. Even though I would be released later that evening, we agreed it was a good idea to greet the children in a "controlled setting" so the younger ones wouldn't mob me or injure my sutured abdomen. Nothing worked better to raise my spirits than the gentle embraces of all those little (and big!) arms.

That evening I was released from the hospital, and our whole family (except Josie) gathered in a nearby hotel. It was wonderful to be together again.

Our family's favorite time together, without question, is nightly Bible time, when we gather at bedtime, usually in our pajamas, to listen to Daddy read a Bible passage and then discuss it with the children. It's also a time when we talk about our day—and maybe share what's planned for tomorrow.

Sharing Bible time in that hotel room was the best thing that had happened to us since Josie was born. How it blessed us all to be together again! We told our children all of the miracles surrounding Josie's birth, and they shared with us the wonderful adventures they'd had in El Salvador. We also loved hearing Jim Bob's voice reading the Bible to us, and everyone enjoyed talking together and asking God again to bless our family and give us strength for whatever lay ahead.

The Querys had to leave early the next morning to keep commitments back home, and they took Jessa with them so she could keep her appointment with an orthodontist. She would be our third child in braces!

The rest of the family returned home later that day, leaving Jim Bob and me alone in the hotel. Wiping away tears as I watched John-David drive our family bus away, I turned my focus back to the job at hand: helping Josie survive.

I'd been pumping breast milk since Josie's birth, but it wasn't given to her until her sixth day of life. The hospital's lab stored the breast

milk until it was needed. On the same day she started receiving the breast milk through a feeding tube, she was taken off the ventilator and began breathing "room air" on her own.

Shortly after that, Josie cried a raspy little whimper, and we heard her voice for the first time.

What happy milestones those were! We rejoiced that our tiny little preemie seemed to be overcoming every challenge, and although we knew she still had a long way to go, we thanked God for giving her another day of life.

Then we learned the reality of what Josie's neonatologist would repeatedly stress to us: never trust a preemie.

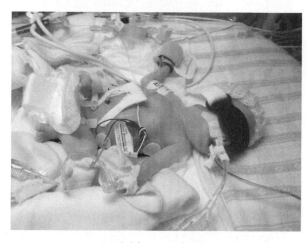

Josie's life was so fragile.

5

Miracles and Milestones

Be of good courage, and he shall strengthen your heart,
all ye that hope in the LORD.
—Psalm 31:24

Just as we were celebrating how well Josie was doing—breathing on her own and receiving her first few drops of breast milk through a feeding tube—we received an urgent phone call at 7:00 a.m. from one of Josie's UAMS doctors. He said a routine X-ray showed "free air" in her abdomen, which meant her intestines were leaking. He said she would probably need emergency surgery and since UAMS wasn't equipped for surgery on a "micro-preemie" like Josie, she was being transferred immediately to Arkansas Children's Hospital a couple of miles away.

We rushed to ACH, where a volunteer escorted us through the maze of long hallways and elevators to the NICU. When Josie's little incubator was rolled into the room, we were shocked to see the difference in her. She was back on the ventilator, and her abdomen, extended and tight, looked like a big, inflated balloon. Because of her obvious distress and the risk of infection, all feedings had been stopped.

Dr. Robert Arrington, known as Doc A, said they hadn't determined what had caused the perforation in Josie's bowel, but it was pretty common in preemies during the first seven to ten days of life.

Showing us the X-ray, Doc A explained the possible causes and their corresponding treatments.

We expected him to say Josie would be undergoing immediate surgery but, as we would quickly learn, Doc A thinks outside the box. Before they risked doing major abdominal surgery on tiny Josie, he wanted to insert a drain tube in her side to release as much trapped air as possible and then administer antibiotics. Maybe, he said, the perforation would heal on its own.

The situation reminded us of a sermon by the late Ron Dunn we'd heard years earlier. Pastor Dunn said most people think that one of these days they will get their "ducks in a row" and then only good things will happen to them. But the truth is, "Good and bad run on parallel tracks, and they arrive about the same time." As we were experiencing, on the same day something really good happens, something bad can happen too. But God promised in Romans 8:28, "All things work together for good to them that love God." We can trust Him to make even the bad things in our lives work for good. That's why we thank God for *everything*, even the challenges He allows to come our way.

A Prayer Answered

It was quickly becoming obvious that we might be at Children's for several weeks—possibly several months. We talked about how we were going to be able to take care of Josie in the Little Rock hospital and also stay close to the rest of our children, especially during the holidays. Christmas was the next week.

We prayerfully decided that we needed to move our whole family to Little Rock during Josie's hospital stay. So we needed a house, but how could we quickly find one with five bedrooms, the minimum size Michelle said we would need? How were we going to make it all work?

The morning after we had that conversation, we were at Josie's bedside in Children's when my (Jim Bob's) cell phone rang. I stepped out in the hallway to answer the call and was surprised to hear from Dr. Paul

Wendel, our friend who had directed Michelle's care back at UAMS. He said a friend of his had just called him, asking about us.

"She heard about Josie, Jim Bob," he said. "She lives near the hospital, and she and her family are leaving town for ten days over the holidays. She wants me to ask if you would like to stay in their house while they're away. She said she woke up early this morning feeling the Lord had laid it on her heart."

My own heart pounded in my chest, remembering my conversation with Michelle a few hours earlier.

Before I could say anything, Dr. Wendel continued with his message. "It's a nice house, Jim Bob, in a nice neighborhood," he said. "And it's big. It has five bedrooms."

Thank You, God!

I returned to Josie's room, knelt down in front of Michelle's chair, and said, "Do you want to hear some good news?"

Hearing about Dr. Wendel's call, Michelle melted into my arms, and we both cried.

The peace that came over us was indescribable. As we faced the toughest situation of our lives, God was telling us through someone we didn't even know, "I love you, and I'm going to take care of you. Trust Me!"

What an incredible gift, and what an amazing answer to prayer. Isn't God good?

We were blown away by the unknown woman's kind offer, but we were a little reluctant to borrow someone's house. I kept thinking, *Does she really understand that we have* seventeen children *living at home?*

About thirty minutes later, I stepped back into the hallway and was greeted by a friendly, smiling woman who said, "Hi, I'm Anne. I've brought you my house key and my alarm code. Here's the address."

Seeing the shocked look on my face, her smile widened. "The Lord laid this on my heart. You can move in Monday if you want. We'll be back after New Year's."

She told me that a few years earlier God had gotten her through

a battle with cancer and also that one of her three children had been hospitalized for ten days. "I know how hard it is to go back and forth to the hospital when you live close, let alone when you live so far away. God bless you all," she said.

We were stunned by Anne's generosity and blessed by her thoughtfulness. We spent a couple more nights in the hotel we'd been staying in since Michelle's discharge; then, on Monday, we drove to the house to meet Anne's husband, Randy, and get a tour of the home.

It was breathtaking—the kind of home you see in home-decorating magazines. And it was beautifully decorated for Christmas, complete with a Christmas tree and all the things we would never have had time to bring together.

We were a little nervous about turning the kids loose in such an exquisite place, and Michelle gulped when she saw the *white* carpeting, picturing one of our little ones "redecorating" the beautiful canvas with finger-painted ketchup and peanut butter.

It was a wonderful gift, and when we told Anne about the very specific prayer we had prayed the night before she had called, we could tell that she was as blessed by the whole story as we were.

After we'd moved in for the holidays, some of Anne and Randy's friends brought us a delicious chicken-and-dumplings meal. He told us he'd known Anne for years. "A lot of us, when God puts something on our heart asking us to do something, we just think about it and don't do it," he said. "Anne isn't like that. When God tells her to do something, she does it."

Because Anne had a heart tuned to God's heart, our family would be able to spend Christmas together in a beautiful, comfortable home away from home. What a gracious blessing!

CHRISTMAS COUNTDOWN

Monday, December 21, was a good day for many reasons. Not only were Jim Bob and I (Michelle) moving into our "gift house," it was

also our daughter Jinger's sixteenth birthday. It was a good day for Josie too—a "good day" being defined as one in which there were only minor issues and no major crises. In fact, Dr. Arrington told us the perforation in Josie's bowel had healed on its own, just as he had said—and we had prayed—might happen. Again we thanked God for His mercy.

We planned to celebrate Jinger and Jordyn's birthdays when the family arrived in Little Rock on December 23, a day we call "Christmas Adam" (because it's the day before Christmas Eve and God created Adam *before* Eve).

We both counted down the hours, so very eager to see all our chil-

Our fourth-oldest daughter, Jinger, loves to cook and has fun coming up with creative recipes!

dren again. While I visited Josie during the morning, Jim Bob rushed out to a discount store for a whirlwind round of Christmas shopping. We try to keep our family's focus on Christmas being Jesus' birthday rather than letting it be a holiday focused on commercialism, but we still enjoy giving gifts, recognizing Jesus as the greatest gift the world has ever known. Our children draw names for a low-cost family gift exchange, and Jim Bob and I give each child gifts as well. That's how Jim Bob ended up at the discount store on "Christmas Adam," buying just about every Nerf gun the store had, plus a shopping cart full of other fun surprises.

The evening before, the children had participated in a Christmas music pageant at the Jones Center in Springdale. It saddened us to be unable to attend, and we admired and ached for the older children, who stayed up most of the night after the music pageant, packing

up all the necessities for themselves and their siblings—seventeen people in all.

They came to Little Rock in two big vans, traveling through heavy rain the whole way. The windshield wipers went out on the van driven by poor Jana, already sleep deprived and exhausted. She said she stopped and Rain-Xed the windshield and basically tailgated the other van, which Grandma Duggar and Jill took turns driving through the rain.

We were ecstatic when they all arrived in Little Rock, so glad to have our arms full of children again. As the little ones came pouring through the door, the house erupted into a symphony of voices happily greeting us and telling exciting stories about things that had happened during the long, two-hundred-mile trip. Shoes had gotten lost and found and lost again, and songs had been sung, and games had been played—oh, my!

How wonderful to have our family together again. But then, shortly after everything had been carried inside and the younger kids had discovered the house's appealing playroom, Jana turned pale and started vomiting. Wiping her face with a cool cloth, I (Michelle) hoped it was simply a matter of stress and exhaustion that would be cured by resting. But then Justin started throwing up too, and I knew we were heading into another round of stomach virus, something Jim Bob and I could *not* carry into the NICU!

Sure enough, the bug ran its course through the whole family over the holidays, and there were days when Jim Bob and I couldn't

APPLE DUMPLINGS

2–3 cans crescent dinner rolls

2–3 apples, cored and cut into 8 slices per apple (Granny Smith or Fuji apples are best)

Butter or margarine

1½ cups granulated sugar

1 teaspoon cinnamon

1 12-ounce can Mountain Dew or Sprite

Spread out triangular dinner-roll dough. Put 2–3 apple slices in each one and then roll from the large end to the small end. Place dumplings in a 9 × 13-inch casserole dish.

In a small saucepan melt the butter. Stir in the sugar and cinnamon. Pour butter mixture over apple-filled rolls. Pour the can of Mountain Dew or Sprite over the rolls. Bake 45 minutes at 350 degrees or until golden brown.

visit Josie. The hospital didn't allow visits from children under age eighteen during flu season, but as things worked out, one or more of the older girls were healthy whenever Jim Bob or I was sick, so someone was always available to visit Josie each day. Whoever was there took daily pictures and videos to share with the little ones back home.

Christmas Eve arrived, and the house bustled with activity, but not all of it was holiday-related. I (Jim Bob) had been searching the newspaper for a large home to rent on a month-to-month basis. I found one that might have worked, except it

*The Cornish House—
just five minutes from the hospital.*

had a beautiful small lake right at the back door. Even though it was winter and the kids would be inside most of the time, I felt it would be too dangerous for the little ones.

Then, a few days later, I was in a Little Rock business office and mentioned to a woman working there that we were looking for a large house to rent. She called a Realtor friend, Jon Underhill, who made some calls and then contacted me and offered us, for a reasonable rent, a large historic home that was close to the hospital.

Grandma Duggar, John-David, Jinger, and I piled into a van to check out the house. It felt so good to be doing things again with a carful of loved ones!

The *five-bedroom* Cornish House had 8,150 square feet—more than our Springdale home!—and a fenced yard. It wasn't perfect (for example, despite having four bathrooms there was only *one* shower), but the rent was reasonable. It was empty, so we could move in right away, and it was about a five-minute drive from the hospital.

As always, we prayed about it before signing the rental agreement.

By that evening we had agreed it would be a good temporary home for the Duggar family in Little Rock. Knowing our family could be together again for the long haul made Christmas an even merrier time for all of us.

And there was something else that made us laugh that day: the plaque in front of the Cornish House describing the home's history. It said the house had been built in 1919 by a banker and his wife who had six children. Despite their own large family, the wife, Hilda Cornish, "was prominent in social and political issues of the day," the plaque says. "She was a leader in advocating birth control." We later learned she had been one of the founders of Planned Parenthood in Arkansas.

Life is full of ironies, isn't it? A historic house built by one of the biggest advocates of birth control was about to be occupied, many years later, by one of America's biggest families with a personal conviction *against* birth control!

Again and again during that time of trials and triumphs, we were amazed at how God worked all things for good. After Christmas, Grandma Duggar, Jessa, and Jana returned to our home in northwest Arkansas and filled a small box truck with several mattresses, Jill's harp, ironing boards, irons, laundry baskets, clothes, and what seemed like a million more necessities, and hauled it all to Little Rock, where we unloaded it in the Cornish House.

On Craigslist.com we found additional items needed for our second household. When Jessa and I took our box truck to inspect a used refrigerator, washer, dryer, couch and love seat, the seller told us he had recently changed girlfriends and his

We moved what seemed like a million necessities, including Jill's harp, to the Cornish House in Little Rock.

new girlfriend didn't want to use the old girlfriend's stuff. The items were in excellent condition, and the price was right, so they were soon installed in the Cornish House.

By December 30, we were able to move out of Anne and Randy's house directly into the house that would be our home for . . . well, we didn't know how long we'd be there. But we were comforted to know we could all be together.

We were relieved to see that the Duggar damage inflicted on Anne and Randy's beautiful home was minor: one broken bar stool and a slightly dented lamp. We gave the house a good cleaning and offered to pay for the damaged items, but Anne and Randy wouldn't hear of it. "We're in the furniture business," Randy said. "It's not a big deal."

CONCERN AND CELEBRATION

It would be impossible to recount here all the joyful ups and terrifying downs we endured with Josie's health during the seven-plus months we were in Little Rock with her. There were many days when her health was so fragile it seemed unlikely she would survive. Then Dr. Arrington and his medical team would try something new or something different, and by God's grace we would get through that difficulty and move on to the next challenge.

As the days rolled along, our faith and our steady belief that God was in control were both enhanced. Josie's health remained precarious, but amazing, everyday things happened in our family life that made us realize God was using our situation to show us His mighty power and His will for us. We believed He could instantly heal Josie of all her health issues, but instead He was showing us that He had a bigger plan for her life . . . and ours.

The news about Josie's premature birth and related health problems had spread quickly. Each time we were interviewed, whether it was by the *Today Show* team or *People* magazine or some other national media

outlet, we had a new opportunity to publicly thank others for their prayers and to share our belief that each child is a blessing from God.

We certainly learned a lot about preemies through our long experience, and our daily schedule constantly changed to adapt to Josie's situation. When she was first born, we longed to hold and caress her but learned that preemies cannot tolerate any more than absolutely essential touching during their early days. Josie was due March 18 but was born December 10, so the natural progression would have been for her to still be inside Michelle for more than three more months. During those three additional months in the womb she would have developed the outer layer of skin that would have been very receptive to touching when she arrived on her due date. But without that layer, touching could induce distress, causing her heart rate to soar and her oxygen level to drop drastically.

So at first, while she was receiving nourishment through a feeding tube, she remained in an enclosed, temperature- and humidity-controlled Isolette with only the doctors or nurses touching her through flexible ports whenever essential attention was needed. For us, visiting her meant standing at her bedside, usually with our hands simply resting on top of the Isolette as we talked to her, prayed for her, or sang to her. As many times as she must have heard her mama sing "The Blessing Song," we expect her to burst forth singing it herself as soon as she learns how to talk! Sometimes we were allowed to put our clean hands through the ports and simply let them hover over her, without touching, but that was as close as we got for the first forty days—with a few exceptions.

I (Michelle) had gotten to touch her left hand with one finger as she was being wheeled from the delivery room to the NICU. Three days later, while we were still at UAMS, Jim Bob rolled me into Josie's NICU room in a wheelchair late one night. It was probably about the third time I'd seen her; I hadn't been able to visit the NICU more than that because I was still recovering from the C-section incision and because my blood pressure remained high and a constant headache all but incapacitated me.

But that night I managed to stand up and rest my hands on the incubator, praying over Josie and talking to her. In the early days of their lives, micro-preemies have one-on-one nurse staffing, and the nurse that night, so kind and thoughtful (as all of them were!), said, "Would you like to touch her?"

I was amazed; the "no-stimuli" order had been thoroughly explained to us. "Oh!" I exclaimed. "I can touch her?"

She said, "I'll let you. But you have to do it exactly as I tell you."

She said I couldn't stroke her. "Just lay your hand on her real lightly."

Josie was scrunched up in the fetal position, and I gently cupped one hand around her little diapered bottom and her feet and the other over her head. It was the sweetest moment, and I was grateful that the monitors showed that her heart rate did not go up and her oxygen level stayed level. Another blessing! Afterward I cried softly as I laid my hands on top of Josie's Isolette again and thanked God for her precious little life!

My own recovery was slower than we hoped. It took several weeks for my blood pressure to return to normal and I could stop taking the medication prescribed to control it. Likewise, Josie continued to have problems that refused to be resolved. We were very fortunate that she didn't have many of the vision, hearing, lung, brain, and heart problems that are common to preemies, but she continually suffered with constipation and other digestive issues that bloated her little tummy and caused obvious and serious distress. Almost all babies, especially preemies, suffer bouts of reflux, but Josie's symptoms went far beyond that problem.

Still, each problem in the digestive area that caused us concern seemed to come with progress somewhere else that gave us reason to celebrate.

FEEDING-TIME FEARS

At first, visiting Josie meant simply standing by her bedside and talking with Dr. Arrington and her nurses. As time passed, we were able

to touch her more frequently, but all her care was done by the nurses. Initially she was fed through a feeding tube inserted directly into her intestines, bypassing her stomach. Then the tube was redirected to her stomach to see if it could function as it should.

Although the constipation, bloating, and similar issues continued to be a problem—and although most of the time we sensed that Josie simply didn't feel good—for the most part, she steadily gained weight. So her digestive system *was* working; it just wasn't working the way it should.

Gradually, Josie's third layer of skin developed, and her overall condition improved to the point that we got to hold her regularly. What a thrill it was the first time I (Michelle) got to hold her, skin to skin! Another fountain of tears flowed down my cheeks; I was so happy to get to do what I'd almost always gotten to do immediately after giving birth.

Then, more joy came when Doc A said one of Josie's scheduled tube feedings could be replaced by a bottle feeding. She would be given the same breast milk mixed with fortifiers that was being supplied through the feeding tube every three hours or so around the clock. We knew that was a big step toward the longed-for day when I could hold Josie in my arms and breast-feed her as I'd done with all our other children.

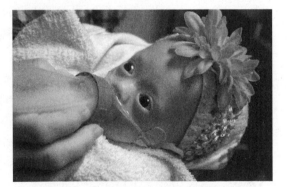

We rejoiced when Josie was well enough to be bottle-fed.

But we quickly learned that bottle-feeding a preemie is no simple matter! The nurses handled that job while an occupational therapist began training me exactly how it had to be done—a process that went against some of my strongest mothering instincts.

Josie was too small and weak to cough effectively when even a drop of liquid ended up in her bronchial tubes, let alone if she choked on a

big gulp of breast milk. During feedings she had to be held in the exact position necessary to keep the milk from going directly into the back of her throat, and the angle of the bottle had to be adjusted so that, at first, when she clamped down on the nipple and started hungrily sucking, she didn't get more than she could easily handle.

So instead of cradling her on her back in the crook of my left arm and holding the bottle with my right hand, as I might do when bottle-feeding a normal baby, Josie needed to lie out in front of me, turned perpendicular to my body so that I could ease her onto her side rather than her back. That would put the milk in her mouth rather than sending it immediately into her throat.

When you think about it, the occupational therapist said, the natural position for a baby to breast-feed isn't on her back but on her side, turned toward her mother's breast. But when most of us bottle-feed a baby, we end up holding the baby on its back and offering the bottle at whatever angle seems to work. Normal babies are usually able to cope with that position—although side lying would be easier for them, too, when they're being bottle-fed.

She taught me to bottle-feed Josie by positioning her perpendicular to my body on a "mom pillow," my left hand supporting her head and her neck. My right hand held the bottle, with my ring finger under her chin to help her keep it in the right position for nursing.

Another concern was Josie's epiglottis, the little flap at the back of the throat that normally seals off the bronchial tubes whenever we swallow. The tube that had been in Josie's throat for several weeks after she was born kept the epiglottis from doing its job—and also from developing as it should. Even after a preemie's feeding tube is removed, the epiglottis may fail to work; it just hasn't become strong enough to do its job. And the hard fact is, it may never get to that point.

Because of that problem, preemies need to lie on an incline—their heads elevated when they're being held or on a mattress-like wedge in their beds—so that the head is not lower than the feet.

Although it was a bit nerve-racking to remember all these instruc-

tions, the positioning of the baby wasn't hard to understand. The thing that *was* difficult for me, because it was such a contrast to what moms normally do, was holding the bottle at a lower angle so that when Josie first started sucking, *she got air instead of milk!*

When Cathy, the occupational therapist, showed me that position the first time, I blurted out, "Oh, that's going to cause her to have so much gas on her stomach!"

Cathy answered, "Yes, but that's okay because it's better for her to have gas on her tummy and be able to take food by mouth than to have to be fed through a tube."

So I started each bottle-feeding by watching carefully to make sure nothing was in the nipple, no milk at all, just air. When Josie would latch on to the nipple at the very beginning she was usually very anxious to eat, so if the nipple was full of milk she would suck too hard and get too much milk at once, a situation that could easily choke her.

She had to learn to pace herself, and she also had to learn the complicated process (for a preemie, at least) of sucking, swallowing, and breathing sequentially, not all at once. And I had to learn the pacing process as well, first giving her an empty nipple and then introducing a little bit of milk at a time until she'd developed her rhythm.

I saw how important the pacing could be when Doc A said I could try a session of "non-nutritive" breast-feeding to help Josie learn to adapt to nursing. I couldn't do all her feedings that way because when you're breast-feeding an infant, you can't regulate the flow of milk the baby's getting as I was learning to do through the pacing of the bottle-feedings. Also, the ACH lab had tested my breast milk and found it to contain twenty calories per ounce, but Josie would do best if she could get more calories than that. So throughout the day I delivered my pumped breast milk to the hospital lab, and they added the fortifiers that brought it up to twenty-six calories. That way, as Dr. Arrington said, we would "put a little meat on her bones" faster.

To begin the nonnutritive breast-feeding, I followed the nurses' directions and spent a long time in the hospital's "pumping room," empty-

ing my supply of milk. Then I took little Josie in my arms and, wearing a nipple shield that mimicked what she was used to, I let her see what breast-feeding was all about.

She latched on immediately—what a smart little girl! But then, my body automatically "let down" in response to her sucking. And despite the time I'd spent in the pumping room, I still had enough milk to give Josie a huge mouthful!

She choked, and her mama panicked!

She didn't have the strength to cough, but she squirmed, struggled, gagged, and grimaced. Her heart rate dropped, and her oxygen level fell. Alarms went off on her monitors, and I was alarmed too!

However, with her trained eyes, the nurse on duty could see that, except for coughing, Josie was doing everything she was supposed to do to recover; she just needed a little help. The nurse provided a little suction and then listened to her lungs.

"It sounds like she still has just a bit in one lung, but it should be fine," she said. "It's natural for babies to get a drop or two of breast milk in their lungs once in a while, and since breast milk contains natural antibodies it usually doesn't cause a bacterial infection."

Once again I sent up a flare-prayer of gratitude, so thankful that Josie hadn't choked during a bottle-feeding when she would have gotten not only breast milk but the fortifiers in it that could have caused an infection.

There was another important requirement that added to the stress of feeding Josie: the bottle provided only part of the nourishment she needed in each feeding. The fifteen milliliters Doc A ordered for her to be fed by bottle had to be given successfully in fifteen minutes, because it would be immediately followed by the remainder of the feeding, given through the feeding tube. That way she got adequate round-the-clock nourishment with the fewest calories burned.

Feeding Josie was a wonderful experience—and also a stressful one. I rejoiced at getting to hold her in my arms, lift her onto my shoulder to burp her, and then cuddle her for a moment or two when we were finished. But it was also frightening. Thinking that I could cause her to

have major problems if I made a mistake in how I held her, or in how I held the bottle, feeding time was a high-pressure situation for me. Usually by the time I diapered her and put her back in the Isolette, I was sweating and exhausted—but thankful that with each feeding we were one step closer to taking Josie home.

RIDING THE ROLLER COASTER

During the six long months Josie was a patient at Children's we learned firsthand what the doctors meant when they told us that the first few months of a preemie's life is a roller coaster of highs and lows. "You'll have days when everything's fine, and then something will happen and she'll go from stable to critical in the blink of an eye," one of them said. "That's just the way it is with a preemie."

In the faces of the other families we met on the elevator or elsewhere in the hospital, we saw the weariness that came from riding that emotional roller coaster. At first, we asked how other families' babies were doing, and many would say, "Oh, our daughter is doing great; the doctor said we might get to go home next week!"

But then we met parents who told us, "Our son isn't doing well. Now they're telling us there's nothing else they can do, and he has less than twenty-four hours to live."

After that, we were almost afraid to ask, but often we could tell by their faces whether their child was doing great—or not so great. The talented medical personnel at children's hospitals all around the world save thousands of babies every day. These hospitals are places where miracles seem to happen on a regular basis. But some babies simply don't make it. Three babies in Josie's six-infant micro-preemie "pod" in the NICU died during our stay there. We grieved with those parents—because we knew that almost any day could also be Josie's last.

6

• Difficult Priorities •

The LORD is my light and my salvation; whom shall I fear?
The LORD is the strength of my life; of whom shall I be afraid?
—Psalm 27:1

At first Josie got just one bottle feeding a day, but gradually, over the next few weeks, she progressed to having more and more bottle feedings that supplemented the every-three-hour tube feedings. Then she was weaned off the tube feedings one by one until she was fed totally by bottle. My (Michelle's) goal was to be there for every feeding possible, and when she progressed to being totally bottle fed, each feeding took from thirty to sixty minutes because it had to be done so carefully. In between feedings I spent time in the lactation room, pumping breast milk to hand off to the lab and also to store in our freezer back at the house so that when Josie came home, we would have plenty on hand.

During the last two months or so of Josie's hospital stay, I was spending most of my awake time at the hospital; I tried to get there for Josie's 9 a.m. feeding and often stayed to do the 11 p.m. feeding at night. My life revolved around Josie's schedule.

Jim Bob and our older girls managed the rest of our family back at the Little Rock house, and for most of them life went on as usual. Jim Bob was constantly finding new adventures for the kids to enjoy. Of course, he made many daily visits to the hospital. The older girls

also came to help, but for the longest time I didn't trust Josie's feedings to anyone other than the nurses. Gradually, as they increased in volume, they also increased in time between feedings, following Doc A's orders, so I could slip back to the house for short visits during the day. I was thankful we lived so close to the hospital, but overall, it was a heartbreaking situation for me. Inevitably whenever I left the house during the day to go back to the hospital, a little one cried, seeing me go. I longed for the day our whole family could be together again under one roof.

Those were difficult days, exhausting physically and emotionally. Many nights I would leave the hospital after midnight to slip into our dark, still house. I would quietly climb the stairs to our bedroom, with each step asking God for strength to take the next one. All around me, my family slept peacefully, and I was grateful to know they were near and that they were being loved and cared for by Jim Bob and the older children while I was away. I was also thankful for dear friends, old and new, who stepped forward to help. They prepared and delivered meals, and shared fellowship, words of encouragement, and prayers for our family.

My being at the hospital most of the day, away from those precious little hearts and minds, was not ideal. But we agreed that my priority at that stage had to be Josie. So when daylight came, I would enjoy a little time with my family and then head off to the hospital again for Josie's morning feeding.

It was a thrill for us when Josie grew strong enough that we could hold her outside of the Isolette.

Many friends asked how I could maintain such a schedule, and I could only credit God's goodness and grace. My answer was always to cite 2 Corinthians 12:9, the scripture I had claimed long ago as my life verse: "My grace is sufficient for thee: for my strength is made perfect in weakness. Most gladly therefore will I rather glory in my infirmities, that the power of Christ may rest upon me."

Many times I seemed to get through the day not just hour by hour but minute by minute, constantly thanking God for the wonderful gift He had given us in our family and in our newest baby, and asking Him to hold us up when weakness threatened to pull us down in the face of otherwise overwhelming challenges.

ONE STEP FORWARD, TWO STEPS BACK

After all those long days and nights in the hospital, and all those trips back and forth to the hospital, April 6, 2010, was an extremely happy day for the Duggars. It was the day Josie, weighing a whopping four and a half pounds, left the hospital for home, nearly four months after her December 10 birthday. Watching us drive away with her, Dr. Arrington told a *People* magazine writer, "This is the first time Josie has seen sunlight."

The kids had decorated the Little Rock house to welcome Josie into her family, and we'd made careful preparations in our upstairs bedroom to create a special space for all the monitors and equipment that came with her, including a small oxygen tank. While Josie was well enough to come home, her health was still precarious. She continued to have digestive issues. We also knew that eventually, when she reached a certain weight, she would return to Children's for hernia-repair surgery; but for now, she was strong enough to go home, and we were thrilled to make that happen.

As we drove up to the Cornish House, an enthusiastic beehive of children came swarming out the door and down the driveway, eager to greet the little sister that many of them hadn't seen since the day shortly

LAYERED SALAD

Another great recipe from Michelle's sister, Pam Peters. (Big sisters can have such great influence on our lives!) This salad is not only delicious; it's also pretty.

First layer:
½ head lettuce, shredded
6 boiled eggs, chopped
½ pound cooked bacon, crumbled (we use turkey bacon)
Second layer:
½ head lettuce, shredded
1 (15-ounce) can peas, drained
1 small onion, chopped
Third layer:
2 cups real* mayonnaise
1 (16-ounce) container (2 cups) sour cream
2 cups shredded cheddar cheese

Spread layers in a 9 x 13 pan; top with the cheddar cheese. Chill in fridge at least 2 hours.

* Be sure to use real mayonnaise or you'll miss out on the amazing flavor!

after her birth, when they'd been allowed to walk by her incubator.

Everyone was given a chance to say hello before we took Josie upstairs, where Mama, Daddy, and Josie would be bunking in the same bedroom. We attached the monitors and oxygen and closed the bedroom door. Michelle would be staying with Josie at all times. We agreed that I (Jim Bob) and/or one or two of the older girls would always be home with her and Josie as well in case an emergency arose.

We expected to keep Josie in the Cornish House another two to three weeks, staying close to the hospital in case problems developed. Then, finally and joyfully, we would move out of our Little Rock house and take her home to Springdale.

As soon as Josie's nursery area was set up in our bedroom and she was sleeping peacefully after her first at-home bottle feeding, I had to load up nine of the middle kids and drive back to Springdale. The children were scheduled to complete some testing there with our homeschool group, and I was getting reports from Grandma Duggar and others that the grass was growing like crazy and other maintenance and repairs were needed. John-David and Joseph had spent quite a bit of time tending to things back in Springdale while we were in Little Rock, but there was simply more to do than they could keep up with.

Sometimes cleaning and decorating (or undecorating) our Tontitown house requires using the scissor lift to reach the highest cobwebs or to hang or retrieve the highest decorations.

So I left Michelle and Josie at the Cornish house with Jill, Jessa, and Jinger. Then Jana and I, along with the "middle" Duggar kids, headed back home to Springdale feeling confident that we had come through a fiery test and that soon we'd be making this same trip with all of our family together, heading home for good.

I was wrong.

EMERGENCY AT 2:00 A.M.

Josie made it through the first day and night in fairly good shape, but I (Michelle) could tell that as time passed she was suffering increasing discomfort. It was the constipation problem flaring up again. With each passing hour, Josie's tummy seemed to become more distended and tight, and although she would sometimes cry with hunger, she just didn't seem interested in her bottle.

When Jill and I got up for her 2 a.m. feeding, she was fussy but refused the bottle. I knew immediately that something was terribly wrong. I was watching the monitors when her heart rate slowed and her oxygen dropped low enough to make the alarms go off. And her temperature was falling. I hurriedly pressed her to me, skin to skin, and covered both of us with blankets, trying to warm her up, but her breathing was slow and shallow, and she was in obvious distress.

I honestly thought we might lose her. "Jill, call 911!" I said.

Jill's voice trembled as she relayed to the dispatcher the vital signs and other information I was giving her, and within moments, it seemed, the ambulance and paramedics were in front of our house. The gate across

the driveway had to be unlocked—a complication of city living—and I carried Josie outside and climbed with her into the back of the ambulance.

A few minutes later we were back at our home away from home, Arkansas Children's Hospital. And there we would stay for nearly two more months.

AMAZING ANSWER TO AN AGONIZING MYSTERY

"Never trust a preemie," Dr. Arrington had told us, and that advice proved valid again and again during Josie's first six months. Back in the hospital, Josie was a miserable little girl for a while, and she had a frightened, worried mama. Finally, the latest round of constipation was resolved, but chronic digestive issues continued.

During the next six weeks, a wide array of tests were performed to determine why Josie's digestive system was working so poorly. Normally you can't keep a baby from pooping on her own. But Josie had to have regular enemas and rectal stimulation to have bowel movements.

As the tests continued, we held our breath, praying for a good outcome. Possibilities included cystic fibrosis and something called Hirschsprung's disease, a congenital condition that causes blockages in the lower intestine and requires surgical treatment. We thanked God, weak with relief, when both test results were negative. But still her problems persisted, and the team continued down the list of possibilities, working from most likely to least likely, trying to find what was making Josie so miserable. Her tummy was obviously hurting; she seemed to be constantly bloated despite having enemas every six hours, and she just wasn't thriving like a six-month-old baby should.

We knew, because the medical team had told us, that Josie's stomach and one part of her intestine were not "tacked down" as they should be, and those body parts had a tendency to shift around abnormally. Certainly that situation could cause problems but rarely as severe as those occurring in Josie.

The tests continued. When Josie was checked for allergies, all tests came back negative.

Finally, when all the obvious culprits had been ruled out—when the medical team had gone down the list, from the most likely to least likely possible causes of Josie's problems—the doctors decided to take Josie off breast milk temporarily and put her on a lactose-free predigested protein formula, a product called Pregestimil.

Overnight, Josie became a different baby.

Soon her belly shrank back to normal size, she smiled and gurgled and cooed, and she even produced a couple of dirty diapers on her own without the help of an enema.

All these months I had been vigorously expressing milk day and night, knowing that breast milk is the very best thing any newborn can have. The medical team was doing everything under the sun to enable Josie to take increasingly larger feedings so she could grow and thrive. All that time we earnestly worked our hearts out to feed her "mommy's milk," not realizing that the dairy products that were coming through my milk were causing her intestines to stay inflamed.

Finally—*finally!*—we all realized that Josie Duggar had a rare condition for someone her age: lactose intolerance—one of a handful of babies born each year who is unable to digest lactose in milk.

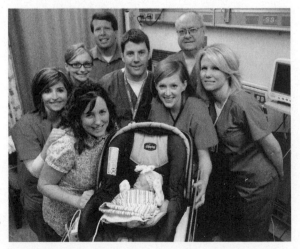

We are so grateful to Dr. Arrington and all of the other health-care professionals who worked to keep Josie alive!

PART 2

• Shaping Hearts and Minds •

But seek ye first the kingdom of God,
and his righteousness;
and all these things shall be added unto you.

—Matthew 6:33

7

• Living Under the Microscope •

Let your light so shine before men,
that they may see your good works,
and glorify your Father which is in heaven.
—Matthew 5:16

Josie was again released from the hospital June 3, 2010; her second homecoming was a much quieter event than her first. In fact, Michelle and her longtime friend Cindy Pascoe brought Josie home to an empty Little Rock house.

It was a good thing the rest of the family was on a trip when Josie was released—because several of them had chicken pox!

Jim Bob had taken everyone, including Josh, Anna, and Mackynzie, on a big trip out east. Their first stop was one of the annual home-school-related events we enjoy, the Nashville conference sponsored by the Advanced Training Institute (ATI).

During one of our family's trips out east, the children got to perform at Pigeon Forge.

Our big forty-five-foot-long bus (bought used a few years ago from a Port Huron, Michigan, hockey team) was just pulling into the Nashville conference's campground June 1 when five-year-old Johannah asked Jill to scratch her itchy back. Jill lifted Johannah's shirt to see what the itch was all about and said, "Uh-oh."

PERFECT TIMING

I (Michelle) was in the NICU with Josie and Dr. Arrington, preparing for Josie's planned release a couple of days later, when Jill's photo of Johannah's back came in to my cell phone. I showed Dr. A the photo and said, "Guess what this is!"

His eyes widened when he recognized what he was seeing. "Where are they?" he asked.

"Well, they're not here in Little Rock," I answered.

"That's good!" he said. "It's crucial that Josie *not* be exposed!"

Josie and I settled into the quiet Cornish House to be close to the hospital and also to wait out the chicken pox episode. The rest of the family continued their trip out east. By the time the bus arrived back home in Springdale two weeks later, eleven more Duggars, all of the youngest ones, had broken out.

The older children had already had the infection years earlier. Two weeks after baby Jinger was born in December 1993, when we had five other children all under the age of five—Josh, John-David, Jana, Jill, and Jessa—they all came down with chicken pox. In the years since then, the rest of them had not gotten it.

We were glad the infection swept the family when it did. It was better that everyone got it all at once rather than two now, three a week later, and on and on until the thing had run its course. That situation could have delayed Josie's arrival back home in Springdale a month or more. Although it was really hard for Jim Bob, Grandma Duggar, and the older children to cope with twelve young "patients" at once, espe-

cially while Mama was far away and unable to help, it all worked out in the end to be perfect timing.

Some other family events and commitments kept us scattered for another week or so after the chicken pox cleared up. But on June 21, 2010—just after Josie's six-month birthday—*all* the Duggars were together again in our Springdale house for the first time since our ordeal began on December 4, 2009.

What a wonderful day that was!

A FOUNDATION OF FAITH

The health-related challenges we've recently endured—my life-and-death struggle with preeclampsia, plus an agonizing gallbladder attack

> ### WHAT'S IN *YOUR* KITCHEN?
>
> Whatever you buy or have in your home to eat is what will be consumed! So be careful what you bring home. We try to have veggies and fruits for snacking. Little ones whose tummies are the size of their fists need to graze throughout the day. At times they will eat more than others, like during growth spurts. Our goal is to encourage eating veggies and fruits, low-fat proteins, and whole grains. Steamed instead of boiled and baked instead of fried.
>
> The mealtime rule is you have to try one bite, and then if possible another bite. When dishing out their portions, we remember the size of their tummies! One or two tablespoons is a start, and if they take a bite of each thing on their plate, then they may ask for seconds of their favorite dish.

leading to surgery in late summer 2010; our premature baby's fight for survival; the family chicken-pox epidemic—drew us closer to God and each other more than ever before. We fervently love God and are grateful to Him for getting us through these experiences. If it had been left up to us, we wouldn't have chosen some of the trials we've been through. But looking back, we can see how God worked "all things" for our good.

I (Michelle) certainly wouldn't have chosen to experience the agony and pain of preeclampsia, but on this side of the situation, I see how my own suffering helped me understand more personally the tremendous suffering Jesus went through when he died an agonizing death through crucifixion. He chose to endure that terrible death not as punishment

for His own sin—He had none—but as punishment for *our* otherwise unforgivable mistakes.

And we could see how Josie's premature birth and health problems—again, things no one would have chosen—had worked for good, not only in making us rely more determinedly on our faith to bring our family through a fiery test but also in helping us become more compassionate and understanding, in a more personal way, of the problems other families are enduring.

For example, soon after Josie was born, a Christian friend in New Jersey, Hudson, called to remind us how God had worked his family's difficulty for good when one of their nine biological children, Nathaniel, was born with spina bifida.

Their experience, which began in the NICU and continued down through the years, opened their eyes to what it's like to grow up with a disability. Then they realized that, as hard as it is to have a disability in America, it's even worse in other parts of the world. After they learned how to take care of Nathaniel, Hudson and his wife, Patti, thought, *Maybe God allowed us to learn all these new skills so we could adopt other children with spina bifida.*

The younger children, including two-year-old Jennifer, loved creating artwork to show Mama while she was away from them tending to Josie.

To date, God has blessed their family with a total of twenty-one children, including twelve adopted from the United States, Ethiopia, Guatemala, and China. Many of their adopted children have special needs.

During his call after Josie was born, Hudson shared some inspiring words that had helped his family when Nathaniel was born. "God's will is what we would choose if we knew all the facts," he said. His family's

decision has led to exhausting work, desperate prayers, financial challenges—and a more rewarding and fulfilled life than they ever dreamed possible.

When Josie was born prematurely, we could have thought God made a mistake. We could have become fearful, bitter, or angry. Instead we deliberately *chose* to allow that life storm to draw us closer to God, trusting His promise to bring good out of every situation.

Wisdom is looking at life from God's perspective. We know that God doesn't make mistakes. He created Josie, He loves her even more than we do, and He knows what He's doing. These facts are affirmed for us when we consider that little Josie has had a big impact on a lot of hearts and lives. We have had literally thousands of letters and e-mails from people all over the world who've said they are praying for Josie.

One even wrote to say,

Michelle, Jim Bob, and family,
I have been watching your show the past few months and have really enjoyed getting to know your family. I am not a religious person at all and I do not attend any church. But I wanted you to know, when I saw tiny Josie be born so early, I got down on my knees in front of my TV and prayed for her.

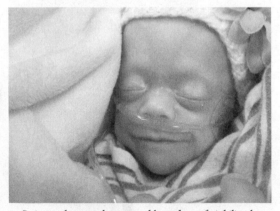

Josie was born at the outward boundary of viability, but her sweet personality was evident right from the beginning; she was obviously a little girl who loved to smile.

Josie was born at about the age of viability. If she had been much younger, she probably would not have made it. We were able to watch the end of her second trimester and her whole third trimester *outside* the womb. Our prayer is that the world will see

that each baby, even the tiniest ones like Josie, are precious creations of God.

WHY NINETEEN CHILDREN?

Our faith is an essential part of our family's life; it's the foundation— the *why*—of everything we do. It's why we have a huge family. We spelled out the details in our first book, *The Duggars: 20 and Counting!* But here's the short version:

When we got married on July 21, 1984, we decided to plan our family size ourselves. We thought that eventually we might want one to three children. Michelle took birth control pills for three years before we decided we were ready to become parents. After our first child, Josh, was born in March 1988, we again used oral contraceptives, thinking we would decide the spacing of our children ourselves.

Despite being on the pill, Michelle got pregnant—and then suffered a miscarriage (we found out later that sometimes the pill will allow conception but then might cause a miscarriage).[1] We were devastated.

At that point we read in Scripture that children are a blessing from the Lord and a gift from Him. We asked God to forgive us for taking matters into our own hands and to give us a love for children like His love for them. We committed to letting Him decide how many children we would have and when they would be born. We stopped using birth control, not knowing after the miscarriage whether Michelle would be able to get pregnant again or if she could carry another child to term. God

After Michelle suffered a miscarriage in the late 1980s, we were blessed with twins: John-David and Jana, who turned twenty-one this year.

answered that question a couple of months later when she became pregnant—with twins!

Jana and John-David were born in January 1990, and a new baby Duggar has arrived, on average, about every eighteen months since then (our second set of twins, Jedediah and Jeremiah, were born in December 1998).

We had thought that having our first child, Joshua, was a big life change. When Jana and John-David were born, life *really* got exciting. Then came Jill, Jessa, Jinger, and Joseph. By that time we wondered if we could handle any more children. The seven we had were a great blessing, but our hands were full. We were way outnumbered!

Strangers would come up to us, see all the kids, and say, "Don't you know what causes this?" Friends and family members thought we were crazy to spend our lives having and taking care of all of those children. Maybe they thought they could save us from ourselves by making comments. We don't get upset or react to negative comments because we had that same mind-set ourselves before God changed our hearts about the value of children.

Admittedly, we often felt overwhelmed, but we had given this area of our life to God, and in faith we kept going. We are so thankful we didn't stop, because then we had Josiah and Joy-Anna. Then, after the birth of our tenth and eleventh children, twins Jedidiah and Jeremiah, some of the very people who had been so critical started complimenting and encouraging us as though we were having our first child. We didn't know if they gave up and decided they just weren't going to be able to change our minds, or if they finally understood that we consider each child a blessing from God and saw that our older children were turning out okay!

We dedicated ourselves to training our children to love God and serve others. Now, as we look into the precious faces of our children, we often think about how different our lives would have been if we didn't have each one of them. We are thankful for each child, and each one is grateful to be here.

STEPPING OUT IN FAITH

We happily welcomed each addition into our family and made changes in our lives that made it possible for us to support them and live debt free while also operating a home-based real estate business. That process is also explained in our first book, and we're still living and enjoying that family-focused lifestyle today.

As our family grew, so did our faith. As time passed, we would see again and again how God worked every setback into a blessing. Disappointments and challenges continue to happen in our lives, but we stopped asking God *Why?* several years ago, when one of the most vivid examples of Romans 8:28 unfolded for us.

In 1997, a totally unexpected, almost ridiculous idea occurred to me (Jim Bob): I felt God put on my heart the idea that I should run for a seat in the Arkansas legislature. It was a ridiculous idea because no one in my family had ever had any political aspirations or connections, and I was terrified by public speaking. Michelle was as surprised as I was when I told her about the idea.

Here's how it came about: We had a child who underwent minor corrective surgery at Arkansas Children's Hospital (our introduction to ACH several years before Josie's arrival). The day before a follow-up appointment in Little Rock, I heard on a Christian radio station that some Christians in the Arkansas legislature were planning a rally the next day to try to ban partial-birth abortion in our state. Michelle and I decided we would swing by the rally after the doctor's appointment.

More than two thousand people showed up in front of the capitol, begging the senators and representatives to pass this ban. Instead, they voted it down. I didn't hear any audible voices or see any lightning bolts from heaven that day, but I felt God speaking to my heart, telling me to run for state representative. My only credentials were that I could vote the right way on life-and-death issues, and I could probably encourage others to vote the right way.

By the time my campaign actually began, we had nine children and

Michelle became pregnant with twins. We worked hard, bringing our conservative Republican message to the voters and knocking on doors all over our area, almost always with a child or two accompanying us.

God confirmed His direction to me, and beginning in January 1999 I served two, two-year terms in the legislature. This experience took me completely out of my comfort zone, but repeatedly we saw God's leading as several important bills were passed and a lot of bad legislation was stopped. It was an honor to serve the people in our community by representing them at the capital.

During my (Jim Bob's) 2002 campaign for the US Senate,
we dressed all the children in red and traveled around the state in our motor home.

Then, just as God had put it in my heart to run for state representative, one Saturday morning He impressed on me to run for the US Senate. I have learned when God speaks to me with His still, small voice and impresses on my heart to do something, it's very important to obey first and understand why later.

I was running against an incumbent and had no party support, but

we believed it was what God wanted me to do. Again the whole family campaigned together during the primary. We rode in parades, knocked on doors, and with many friends volunteering we had campaign rallies and barbecues all over the state.

We had just sold a piece of property, and Michelle and I felt led to spend $110,000 of it on the race, even though that was a drop in the bucket compared with the $2 million my opponent spent. By then we had thirteen children, and when Election Day rolled around, we took the whole family with us to vote, showing our kids the heart of what it means to live in a democracy. Trying to get all the kids in and out of the cramped voting area, we were barely aware of an AP photographer at the polling place who took our picture that day.

I received 22 percent of the votes and lost the primary, but we had peace. We had worked hard and been diligent in doing what God had asked us to do. We didn't understand *why* He'd asked this of us and then let us lose, but we knew we didn't have to understand. We had put our lives in His hands and we trusted His plan.

That night, we sat down as a family and talked about what had happened. We thanked God for all the miracles we had seen, all the special people we had met, and even for the outcome of the race, knowing it was His will. Then we prayed, "God, we're ready for our next assignment!"

WHY WE DON'T ASK *WHY?*

The fact is, sometimes God asks us to do something we don't want to do. We try to teach our children this concept about life's choices from the time they are young. When we ask them to do something, they always have a choice. They can choose to obey and do what is right. Or they can choose not to obey and face the consequences.

As adults, we have the same choice when we feel God directing us. We can trust that God knows what is best and do what He's ask-

ing us to do. Or we can choose what *we* want to do—and face the consequences.

God will never ask us to do something that violates the principles found in His Word. But He will stretch our faith, and He will bring situations into our lives that test our relationship with Him. Following His guidance, I had run for the Senate—and lost. But soon we saw how obeying Him had led us to that position where we could share our faith from a much bigger platform—bigger, in fact, than we could ever have imagined.

The photograph taken on Election Day as we were walking into the polling place with our big family around us appeared the next day in *The New York Times* with a caption identifying me as the Arkansas father of thirteen who had run for US Senate and lost.

We didn't even know the picture had been published—we don't normally read *The New York Times*. A few days later, a New York–based freelance writer called, saying she'd seen the photo and wondered if we'd be willing to let her write our story for a national magazine.

We talked about it, prayed about it, sought counsel about it, and agreed. The story ran in *Parents* magazine, where it was noticed by Eileen O'Neill, CEO of the Discovery Health Channel. She asked Bill Hayes, with Advanced Medical Productions, a film-production company, to contact us. She wanted to know if we would be willing to do a documentary about our family to be broadcast on the Discovery Health Channel.

Because our family almost never watches broadcast TV, and we don't have cable, we'd never heard of Discovery Health. Again we prayed and sought counsel about this request, and we came to believe the documentary could be an opportunity to share with the world that children are a blessing from God. We agreed to the project as long as they agreed that our faith would not be edited out. Our faith is the core of our lives, we said. If you leave that out, you're not telling the whole story.

They agreed. When the documentary aired in 2004, it had the most viewers of any show the network had broadcast up to that point.

A few documentaries later, the channel's parent company asked us to do a weekly reality series (another thing we'd never heard of). That's the show that now airs regularly on TLC, attracting an average of one to one and a half million viewers on TLC each week.

Given the experience we've had, is there any doubt why we believe so fervently that God works *all* things for good? As we have obeyed and trusted Him, the Christian life has become an exciting adventure for us. Instead of focusing on the difficulties that sometimes happen and wondering *why* they've happened, we try to maintain a positive focus and a curious attitude, watching eagerly for the miraculous way God is going to use each temporary setback to do something wonderful.

Scott Enlow and Sean Overbeeke film a promo shoot for TLC.

8

Opportunities to Reach Out to Others

The fruit of the righteous is a tree of life,
and he that winneth souls is wise.
—Proverbs 11:30

Last year we were visiting the Bates family, our friends in Tennessee, and I (Michelle) had loaded several of the kids in our Suburban to pick up some take-out snacks from a fast food restaurant. I pulled up to the drive-through speaker and read off the items we wanted. The order taker repeated the list back to me and then asked, "Will that be all, Mrs. Duggar?"

I thought surely I'd misunderstood her, but when I pulled ahead to the pickup window I found a little crowd of curious faces peering out at us. "I *told* you it was her!" one of the uniformed girls squealed to her coworkers.

I was dumbfounded! It's one thing to be recognized when we go out in Springdale, but to have my *voice* recognized at a drive-through a thousand miles from home? Amazing! (Of course it could also have been the umpteen sandwiches I was ordering.)

YOU LOOK FAMILIAR

Our family's TV series, *19 Kids and Counting!* is now broadcast on the Learning Channel (TLC), and sometimes a series of our shows will

be replayed over and over for several hours a day. That has landed our family in a new phase of life as far as public recognition.

It used to be that whenever we went out in public with our children, people would say things like, "You've sure got a lot of children. Are you a school group or something?"

In the next phase, which came after the initial documentaries about our family had aired on television, people would think they'd seen us somewhere before but just couldn't quite remember where. Maybe they would say, "Do you work at Dr. So-and-So's office, by chance? Or have I seen you at the post office?"

Now, it seems just about anywhere we go, people come up and speak to us, and usually they know our names. Some can recite all of our children's names in order. Many people say they know us so well they feel like part of our family. Several have said they take notes as they watch our show, gleaning ideas to apply to their own families.

It doesn't matter if it's at a fast food drive-through in Tennessee, driving down the interstate in Florida, stopped at a traffic light in Ohio, or standing on the sidewalk in New York City (where we were

In 2009, Gil and Kelly Bates and their seventeen children visited us during the Arkansas ice storm; then we traveled to Tennessee to help build an addition on their house.

astonished when a police van swooped over to the curb and an officer popped out and asked, "Hey, are you that big family from Arkansas?").

Sometimes people recognize us when there are just a couple of us. One day last year I (Michelle) made a quick trip to the grocery store and invited then-four-year-old Jackson to come along. Pushing the cart down one of the aisles we were stopped by a woman who said, "Oh! It's Michelle Duggar. I watch y'all on TV—and who's this? Why, it's Jackson. Hi, Jackson. How are you?"

We chatted a moment before the woman moved on down the aisle. Jackson, sitting in the seat of the grocery cart, leaned into me and whispered, "Mama, how did she know my name?"

Members of the film crew for our TV series, 19 Kids and Counting, *have become like family to us.*

I told him, "Honey, she sees you every week in her living room. She watches our family on television, and she feels like she knows us."

We think of these encounters as ministry opportunities—chances to show God's love. Even if we're on a quick shopping trip to the store, we try to take time to visit with those who approach us and encourage them spiritually if possible. Many people have helped *us* along life's way; we're happy to pass on that encouragement. That's what it's all about, encouraging one another and building each other up.

SETTING LIMITS

Even though we love meeting others, we now have to limit our family's interaction with drop-by guests so we don't disrupt our family schedule too much. We've had viewers drop by our house as early as seven in

the morning, wanting to meet us. Others have come as late as 10 p.m. wanting to stop in and say hi.

Setting limits has also become necessary because of some rather bizarre situations that have happened. One occurred a few years ago when we received an e-mail from a young lady who lived out of state. She wrote that she loved watching our show and wanted to meet our family. We thought maybe we could encourage her walk with the Lord, so we told her she could come visit us on July 4. She arrived in the morning, and we introduced her to our family, showed her around the house, and took her with us to the Springdale Fourth of July Rodeo parade. Then we returned to the house, where we visited until that evening; we took some pictures together and said good-bye.

A few weeks later we received an e-mail from a viewer who asked, "Did you know your daughter Jinger's diary is for sale on eBay for a hundred thousand dollars?"

I checked the site and asked Jinger, "Are you missing your diary?"

She felt sure it was in her dresser drawer, but when she looked, it was gone. When I showed her the eBay picture, she was shocked to realize someone had stolen it out of her drawer.

Who would have done such a thing?

The eBay listing showed that the diary was being sold from the same town where our recent guest lived. I contacted the young lady and confronted her about stealing Jinger's diary. I told her we still cared about her, and that we forgave her. But I also said that what she had done was wrong and that we would take further steps if the diary wasn't immediately returned.

She admitting stealing it. Then, maybe to ease her conscience, she said she didn't read the diary and that it was the first thing she had ever stolen. We received it back overnight.

The experience provided good lessons to teach the children: first, that we can't trust everybody, and second, that we need to forgive others even before they ask.

TRUTH, DISTORTIONS, AND BELIEFS

One evening I (Jim Bob) invited Michelle to go out on a date. We left the oldest children in charge, and twenty minutes after we'd left, one of them called and said a woman had rung our doorbell, saying she was a writer and wanted to ask a few questions. One of the little ones had answered the door and allowed her to step into the house.

Then she said, "You don't mind if I take a few photos, do you?" as she snapped pictures left and right.

Our oldest daughter, Jana, politely spoke with her and told the woman she would have to talk to her dad. She gave her my cell phone number, and the woman gave Jana her number. By the time the kids called me, the "writer" had already left.

I immediately called the woman. It took several tries to make contact, but I finally reached her. She said she was a reporter for *Star* magazine, and she was in town to do a story about our family.

I told her firmly that I did not appreciate her coming into our house as a reporter without an appointment when Michelle and I weren't there and that she did not have permission to take pictures inside our home.

She said, "We'll see about that." She said she would be in town several days to interview people, including some of our former high school classmates.

Sure enough, the next week one of the top *Star* stories was headlined, "The Great Cover-Up! Exclusive Duggar Family Pictures and Interview." The woman had gone around town talking to people we had gone to high school with as well as others who know us. Then she sensationalized the story. She also

Because of security issues, we've had to install a fence and gate in front of our Tontitown home.

took excerpts from our first book, including a story describing Michelle's teenage years, before she was a Christian, when she would wear a bikini to mow the grass at her family's house. Then, the article said, after Michelle got saved, she started dressing modestly. *That* was "The Great Cover-Up!"

After this incident, we installed a gate at our driveway entrance.

Another tabloid, the *National Enquirer*, also did a Duggar story, but at least that reporter didn't just show up at the door unannounced. She called to tell us the *Enquirer* was doing a story about our family—with or without our input. We decided to talk with her and spent about an hour on the phone with her. The next week we were surprised when the *National Enquirer* printed an excellent article. Maybe our family's story is so unusual just as it is, the *Enquirer* didn't feel the need to change anything!

We find it amusing how many reporters copy and paste information they find about us that someone else has copied and pasted without checking the facts. For instance, even though Wikipedia and some Internet blogs report that we are part of a QuiverFull movement, we are not. We are simply Bible-believing Christians who desire to follow God's Word and apply it to our lives. God says children are a gift and a blessing, and we believe it.

We believe God made women and men with unique qualities, strengths, and weaknesses. Men are not superior to women. As a matter of fact, we believe women are the most special of all of God's creations, and men should treat them like queens. We teach our sons to open doors for ladies and, when possible, to lend a hand when they see a woman carrying something heavy. We teach them to treat women with respect, just as they want others to treat their mom or sisters respectfully.

Sometimes our beliefs get distorted so it seems we're against a lot of things. For example, we're not *against* women getting college degrees, starting their own businesses, or having good-paying jobs. The Proverbs 31 passage in the Bible describes the virtuous woman as one

whose number-one priority was to provide excellent care for her family physically and spiritually; she made products that she retailed and she bought real estate on the side. We appreciate the women who serve in wonderful and vital ways. We're grateful for the women doctors and nurses who have helped deliver and care for our children. We are thankful for the conservative women who have served in public office.

Likewise, we're not *against* TV. We simply choose something else for our family. Yes, it *is* kind of ironic that we have a weekly TV show but don't watch broadcast television ourselves. We do turn it on and pull out the rabbit-ears antenna when there's a presidential speech or some other good, history-making event we want our children to see.

This attitude began before we were married, when a doctor friend, Ed Wheat, challenged us not to have a TV our first year of marriage. He sold us on the benefits of concentrating on each other without the TV's distraction. That first year of our marriage in our little nine-hundred-square-foot, fixer-upper house was wonderful; we were living on love.

I (Michelle) fell in love with Jim Bob in part because of his fun-loving sense of humor.

Then, after we fulfilled our pledge, someone gave us a television, and in 1985 we excitedly got cable service. But soon we realized we were both addicted to it, even though we were shocked to see how bad the broadcasting content had gotten in a single year! Gradually we realized that as we sat there staring at whatever show happened to be on, our communication dropped off.

After three weeks, we decided as a couple that television was detrimental to our marriage. We shut off the cable service and got rid of the TV. Looking back, we consider that decision one of the best things we've

done for our family—not only because there is so much portrayed on TV we're not comfortable with, but also because it robs us of our most precious resource: *time.*

Now we occasionally gather everyone to watch a rough-edit version of our show on our computer. Or we might watch a live broadcast of the show with my brave sister and brother-in-law, Deanna and Terry, who welcome the whole Duggar clan into their home. But usually by the time the segment is over, the youngest ones have fallen asleep or wandered off to play. It's just not all that interesting to them to see their family relive an ordinary day.

To our children, the best thing about having a television series is "playing" with the film-crew guys, Sean, Scott, Jim, Frank, Bill, and John, who have become like family members to all of us. The little kids love it when they get to carry one of the cameras or ride on sound technician Jim Goodwin's shoulders while he follows someone around with the microphone boom. They especially love getting to record the "teasers" to be used before commercial breaks: "Coming up next on *19 Kids and Counting.*"

The older children have a better grasp of what's going on, and they understand that we consider the show a family ministry. Josh and Anna welcomed the crew to film their engagement and wedding in 2008 because they wanted to encourage other young people to wait for the one God has for them. The cameras were rolling when they had their first kiss, which was also part of the wedding ceremony.

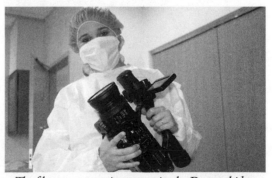

The film crew sometimes recruits the Duggar kids as part of the videography team. Here, Jessa prepares to shoot footage of Jordyn's C-section delivery.

INTERNATIONAL INTERVIEWS

We get broadcast and print inquiries from international reporters who want to know how a couple could raise nineteen kids in today's world. We forward most of the inquiries to our publicist, Shannon Martin, at the Discovery Channel (parent company of TLC) for consideration. Then we prayerfully consider her recommendations, believing that God has opened up this short window of time in our lives when we can share God's love and Bible principles on a wider scale than we could without the media attention.

Not all the things we agree to do are news- or documentary-style stories. One Japanese broadcaster sent several people to our home to film for five full days for a twenty-minute segment on a popular Japanese TV game show! Contestants watched various film clips that depicted a mysterious problem in the Duggar household; then they had to guess what the problem was. As the clips continued, they told the story of our family but also continued to report the problem we were dealing with.

And what was the problem? We sometimes run out of hot water!

We enjoy meeting these international teams, and for the most part, we've been pleased with how they report our family's lifestyle and our beliefs. One positive outcome of Josie's premature birth being announced internationally was the flood of heartwarming prayers and encouragement that poured in from around the world. Hundreds of parents wrote and e-mailed to share their own experiences as NICU veterans. We especially loved the messages that told us about preemies who had overcome severe problems and were now rambunctious toddlers or rugged football players or busy college students.

Those letters inspired a mental picture for me (Jim Bob), a future hope and dream I shared with *People* magazine: Josie, as a future bride being escorted down the aisle on the arm of her daddy, who tells her she's a beautiful miracle. We continue to pray that Daddy's dream someday comes true, and we know that many others share that hope.

SHARING WITH THE MULTITUDES

Matthew 9:36 says Jesus saw the multitudes and had compassion on them. He looked beyond others' outward appearance and social status to discern the hearts and spiritual needs of those around Him. He guided His spiritual truths around their mental roadblocks and taught principles through stories and analogies. Through His three and a half years of public ministry, He impacted the world.

We want to follow Jesus' model for ministry. He went around meeting others' physical and spiritual needs. He washed His own disciples' feet and fed the poor. At the end, He gave His sinless life as the sacrifice to pay for the things *we* have done wrong. He offers an abundant life to those who seek Him and eternal life to those who ask. Jesus is the ultimate example of the servant-leader spirit, and that's the spirit we desire for each one in our family. We train our children to look around and see others' physical and spiritual needs and be motivated by love to reach into their lives.

That's why we want our programs and interviews to be not about us but about helping other families and individuals. We hope to show them how to develop a relationship with Jesus and find true meaning in life. Just as others have encouraged us over the years, we pray that our shows help strengthen other marriages and relationships between parents and their children.

We have another hope, as well. From the beginning, when we did the first media interview with a local TV station long ago, we've said that the challenges of being in the spotlight would be worth it if someday we hear that one girl who was considering an abortion heard us say that children are a blessing from God—and decided to keep her baby.

How blessed we've been, over the years, to receive letters and e-mails telling us that prayer was answered. Here's an example:

I want to personally thank your entire family for the inspiration they have given me. I grew up actively practicing my Christian

faith, but somewhere in the transition to adulthood I lost my way. I found a man and we "dated" for about four years, and then I found out I was pregnant and I was scared. On the night before my scheduled abortion I was flipping through the TV stations looking for something to watch, and came across 17 Kids and Counting!, *and somewhere through the course of the show it came to me—if you can handle seventeen children, I can surely do it with just one.*

I now have the most precious gift from God. I never imagined how wonderful children could really be until I had one. I ended up marrying that boyfriend a couple of months before I gave birth, and we are still married today. I have found my way back to the Lord, and although my husband has not, I pray each and every day that God will give me the strength, patience, and perseverance to lead him to God.

All marriages are tough, but I feel as though this dynamic definitely creates new challenges for both of us. It was through Josh and Anna's website that I learned about the movie Fireproof *and the "Love Dare." I am not quite finished with the dares, but I hope that upon my completion my husband and I will have fireproofed our marriage and journeyed closer to God together and can live much happier lives.*

I know that you, Jim Bob and Michelle, agreed to do the show hoping to inspire others and to share your faith. I hope that your show never gets canceled and that you never want to stop taping. I cannot imagine what all you have done for people when I look at how God has used you to work in my life. You have protected my unborn child, brought me back to the Lord, and helped in repairing my unstable marriage. Once again, I thank you. Never forget that you are tools for God to use and you are allowing him to use you very well!

THE POWER OF AN ENTHUSIASTIC GREETING

One of the first things we try to teach our children when we're out in public or having guests in our home is the power of an enthusiastic greeting. We tell them that genuinely expressing Christ's love to each person you meet through a joyful countenance and caring words opens the door to share further with him or her about our faith.

If we're successful in these lessons, then those people who stop us in the grocery store or on the sidewalk somewhere are greeted by a host of bright, friendly smiles. We tell our family that people want to know you care about them, and a child's bright, sincere smile can be a powerful encouragement to anyone. It can lift weary spirits and warm broken hearts. That's the first step in how we teach our children to serve others and begin developing a ministry mind-set. The Bible says it's "more blessed to give than to receive" (Acts 20:35), and we emphasize that lesson to our children by reminding them always to give others a smile.

We teach them to overcome shyness by constantly reminding them of another foundation of our faith: Jesus' instruction to treat others the way you would want to be treated (Matthew 7:12). To us, it's not cute when our little ones turn away when someone speaks to them, or hide their faces in Mama's skirt, or stare back, wide-eyed and wordless; we believe that behavior is disrespectful of the other person. In contrast, eye contact shows respect; it tells the other person, *You're important; you're special.*

THE BLESSING OF HOSPITALITY

One of the character qualities we teach our children is hospitality: "cheerfully sharing food, shelter, and spiritual refreshment with those whom God brings into our lives." It's related to fellowship: "the oneness of spirit enjoyed by those on the same side of a struggle."

There's something special about sharing fellowship and food with those you love. Some of my (Michelle's) fondest childhood memories are of the wonderful aromas wafting from our family's kitchen and then gathering with family and friends to enjoy rich fellowship around the table.

Our prayer is that you too will enjoy many memory-making recipes with your loved ones—perhaps some of the recipes we share here!

Turning away means the child fails to acknowledge the other person, and it also nurtures in the child a self-centered focus, something we want each one to learn to overcome as he or she matures. "How would you feel," we ask, "if you smiled and said hello to someone and that person turned away or refused to answer you? Is that how you want to be treated?"

It is vital to us as Christians that we express God's love to everyone we meet. So we practice introductions and shaking hands. We role-play ways to return a friendly person's greeting, beginning with a smile and a hello. And then we head out to the store—or to New York City—and get some real-life practice.

Yes, we also teach our children about the possible dangers awaiting them and we teach the talkative ones (five-year-old Jackson comes to mind) to be friendly with everyone, but if anyone talks about bad things or says, "Don't tell your mom or dad," you instantly go tell!

Like other parents, we've established guidelines to keep our family safe. We stress that when we're out in public, they're never to go *anywhere* alone. When we're away from home, we use our system of buddy groups, partnering our young adult children with younger ones and going out two by two to keep everyone accounted for.

HAVE A SERVANT'S HEART

Our faith teaches us to follow Jesus' words and example, and one of His strongest examples was putting others first by serving and helping. He said whoever wants to be great must be the servant of all. We try to teach that principle to our children on a daily, and sometimes an hourly, basis. In our family these training moments come quite often.

For example, our family's rule is that older kids get first pick of seats in our van, both because we want the younger ones to learn respect for the older ones and also because it's much harder for the bigger ones to climb over seats or squeeze through narrow openings to get to the back.

Like all rules, this one occasionally gets challenged. In fact, while I (Jim Bob) was writing this chapter, I heard a report about two of our boys who had ridden with Mama to drop off some items at our nearby thrift store. When the older one got out to unload the items, the younger one climbed into his brother's seat. (Yes, we have car-seat disputes in our family too!) When the big brother returned and asked his brother to move over so he could have his seat back, the younger one said it was now *his* seat.

We all are born selfish, wanting the best for ourselves. Of course the younger one should have graciously moved over, but what would Jesus have done had He been the older brother? When we sat both boys down and talked to them, they realized they both had been self-centered, and they both apologized, following another lesson we've taught them—that apologies need to be made quickly with a humble spirit: "I was wrong for being selfish and not moving over. Will you please forgive me?"

Modesty Matters

Another part of our life in the public eye that's linked to our faith is the way we dress. Actually, we prayed about this area of our lives and established standards long before the world showed up on our doorstep.

The styles we choose for ourselves aren't specified in the Bible, but the Bible does encourage modesty. In Exodus 28, which includes God's instructions for making garments to be worn by Aaron's sons, verse 42 describes "linen breeches to cover their nakedness; from the loins even unto the thighs they shall reach." And Isaiah 47:2–3 mentions the thigh as being "nakedness." From these passages we drew an understanding that God defined an exposed thigh as nakedness, and we agreed that in our family we would wear clothing that covers the thighs. That usually means the boys wear pants or sometimes long shorts that are at least knee-length.

The girls have a personal conviction about wearing dresses based on Deuteronomy 22:5: "The woman shall not wear that which pertaineth unto a man, neither shall a man put on a woman's garment." Our girls choose skirts and dresses that are about midcalf when they are standing so their knees will be covered when they're sitting.

We believe that a man's physical drives are excited by what he sees, and it is *defrauding* for a woman to wear clothing that accents her body,

Modesty is important! Our goal is to dress to draw attention to our countenance.

instead of bringing attention to her countenance. *Defrauding* means "stirring up sensual desires that cannot be righteously fulfilled." We know that certain desires are a normal part of adolescence and adulthood, but as much as possible, we want to help our children to learn to have self-control over those desires. And we don't want to defraud others. The Bible tells us not to be a "stumbling block" (Romans 14:13). So we choose to dress modestly.

That includes when we're swimming. The girls order swimwear from www.wholesomewear.com, and the boys usually wear a surf suit. These swim garments cover all the body parts we don't want to expose but still allow us to enjoy swimming—or playing on Daddy's hillbilly waterslide.

We're realists. We know the world is full of sensual images at every turn. So while we try to avoid those images whenever practical, we also teach our children self-control, morality, and common sense. If we meet a scantily clad person while we're out in public, you might hear one of us softly say, "Nike!" That's our code word to our boys that it's probably best to drop their eyes to the sidewalk for a few steps.

We're not rigid about our dress code, but we do teach principles of modesty to our children, and as they grow older they make their own choices. Our older girls buy most of the clothes for our whole family now. Like many teenage girls, they enjoy shopping and love finding bargains. (You probably already know that most of our purchases come from thrift stores and consignment shops because frugality, something we'll talk about in a later chapter, is a very important part of the Duggar family life.)

We don't dress one way at home and another when we're out in public or in front of the cameras. Our faith and modesty are part of our everyday life, not just an image we put on for others.

One afternoon, while we were living in Little Rock, we went on a tour of the USS Razorback *submarine.*

9

• Developing a Servant Heart •

The Son of man came not to be ministered unto,
but to minister.
—Matthew 20:28

Our goal is to teach our children to have a ministry mind-set, always looking for ways to serve others.

This gift of serving doesn't have to be a major production. We sometimes get e-mails from viewers who've seen our family on TV serving a meal at a soup kitchen or helping rebuild a home in El Salvador or doing some other seemingly elaborate ministry project. Often these parents say they want to develop a ministry mind-set in their children too, but then they add something like, "I'm a mom with young children, and we're barely making ends meet. What can I do to help my children learn how to have a servant's heart?"

I (Michelle) have a special place in my heart for those exhausted mothers with young children. Been there, done that! And I'm still doing it! A few years ago I was a mom raising five children under five, and even fewer years ago I was a mom tending ten children under age ten! I know what it's like to have a tight budget, limited time, and quickly evaporating energy.

Here are some of the ideas I share with these fellow moms.

If there's enough money in your budget, perhaps you and your children can bake some bread and mix up some fresh honey butter or make

a batch of cookies or muffins for someone who needs a little encouragement. Take your gift to an elderly neighbor, another tired mom with sick children down the street, or to the fire station or police department in your town.

Your visits don't have to be long; in fact, it's probably best if they're short—thirty minutes or less. You may not have time to do anything but hand over the cookies and offer a cheery message: "We were just thinking of you today, and we made this for you. We hope you enjoy it. God bless you!" Know that even these brief encounters and little gifts can be a blessing to others. Most important, your children will learn to invest in the lives of others.

When we take cookies to our local firefighters, they graciously pose for a picture with the kids.

Another way to include the little ones is to have your toddlers draw (or scribble) a simple picture as a gift for the person and then add your own note or Scripture verse to their artwork. It can also be a gift to someone just to have the children sing a little song (along with you) or quote a Scripture verse to share encouragement.

MINGLING GENERATIONS

We love singing and playing instruments as a family at our local nursing homes. Sometimes our piano teacher even schedules her piano recitals at a nursing home. The students learn to play in front of others and get to encourage and show love to the seniors at the same time. It also helps the piano students relax, knowing some members of the nursing home crowd probably won't notice if they make mistakes. These performances help them focus not on themselves but on others, playing "as

unto the Lord," as the Bible would say. The elderly people also love to sit and talk with the kids after listening to them play.

Nurturing a love of ministering to others also builds up the love within your own family. On the way to our visit, we coach our kids, saying, "This person could be your grandma or grandpa, or this could even be you someday. How would you want somebody to treat you if you couldn't walk or talk or if your legs hurt? Wouldn't it be nice if someone came and told you a funny little story or sang a song for you? Or you could ask them about when they were little—what things were like back then. Ask them if they have ever served in the military or ask what kind of work they've done over the years."

We tell them, "You're blessing people with your smiles, and you give them a smile of their own. You watch and see: when you smile, they're probably going to smile back."

It's so cute to see these little guys start out feeling timid and afraid, obviously thinking, *I don't know these people.* But then, even though they're afraid, they start singing and smiling—and suddenly someone claps or says, "That was nice!" Then we can see the understanding dawn on those little faces: *I've blessed that person!*

We talk about it again on the way home. One might say, "Did you see that lady? She had tears in her eyes, she was so happy."

Sure, some of the little ones might also say, "Mama, why was that one lady talking out loud while we were singing?" or, "Why was that man in the wheelchair making those strange noises?"

I (Michelle) explain, "You know how baby Jordyn or baby Jennifer chatters and talk-talk-talks sometime while you all are doing your schoolwork? It's the same thing. Sometimes when people get older they kind of become like babies again in their minds. They just chatter away. It doesn't mean they aren't having fun; they're probably really enjoying it. I think they really liked having you visit."

We believe these little visits teach our children to come out of themselves and not be shy and learn how to have a friendly conversation

with others. This is an important part of growing up, to be thoughtful, respectful, caring adults.

Of course, it's true that not everyone is able to carry on a full-blown conversation. But we find that it's totally possible for elderly people and toddlers to communicate beautifully, even though they don't hear or understand each other completely. I tell our little ones, "Did you see how that lady clapped her hands when you sang the 'Blessing Song'? Did you see how that man smiled when you gave him your picture?"

The children learn, *I may not be able to do much, but I can sing and make someone smile. Even though I'm tiny, I can give something. I'm blessing someone else—and I feel blessed myself.*

Nursing homes are usually quite receptive to visits like these, except during flu season, when little ones can carry in some uninvited germs. It's always best to call and ask the activities director when the best time for a visit would be.

If you're new in your community or don't know any elderly or lonely neighbors who would appreciate a visit, ask for ideas at your church. Pay attention to prayer requests and think of ways you might encourage someone who's going through a rough time.

You may not know this side of heaven the impact you have had on others.

These visits also provide another benefit. Through our family's outreach activities and field trips, the children learn how to interact not only with those their own age but also with people of all ages—another bounce-back blessing.

TANGIBLE THANK-YOUS

Another simple and inexpensive way to help children develop a ministry mind-set and a servant's heart is to show them ways to demonstrate an attitude of gratitude. Sometimes as a homeschool writing project, and other times just out of the blue, we ask our children to write notes of thanks or appreciation to someone outside the family who has done

something good. It might be a thank-you to someone at the nursing home who told them a story, or it could be addressed to firefighters and police officers in our area who serve our community with such dedication and courage.

A thank-you note creates something the recipients can hold in their hands and read again and again. And writing the note helps the kids practice not only speaking but communicating through writing.

Years ago our oldest child, Joshua, wrote a letter to Fayetteville mayor Fred Hanna expressing gratefulness to him for his stands on several issues and thanking him for making a difference in our community. A few days later Josh received a handwritten letter from the mayor saying how much Josh's letter had meant to him. Mayor Hanna said he had shown the letter to several others and had displayed it in his office. He said many times people will write or e-mail to complain about something, but few take the time to say thank you.

We like sharing little unexpected acts of kindness—like surprising our TV series producer, Sean Overbeeke, with a cake and candles on his birthday.

It doesn't take much to make a difference for good in someone's situation. Once you and your children start looking, you're sure to find plenty of ministry opportunities all around you. If your experience is anything like ours, you'll soon find yourself blessed beyond measure as you and your family work together to bless others.

TAKING A STAND

We not only want to help and encourage others one on one, we also want our children to see us standing up for those who can't speak for themselves—and joining us in that stand when it's appropriate. That's

CORN DIP

Many of our favorite recipes originate from my (Michelle's) home state of Ohio. My sister Pam Peters, the eldest of seven in my family, has shared many recipes with us, including Corn Dip, an appetizer or snack that fits right in with any tortilla-chip-dipping party!

(And if you need a corn-related activity for your party, try Cornhole, a great game that we highly recommend for family fun. You can make your own Cornhole boards and bags as a fun family project. Find patterns at www.cornhole-game.org.)

Soften in microwave:
¾ stick of butter (6 tablespoons)
8 ounces cream cheese

Mix together butter and cream cheese, and then stir in:
16 ounces frozen shoe peg white corn, cooked (Green Giant is a good brand to use.)
1 teaspoon to 1 tablespoon jalapeños, chopped or pureed (We go the mild route and puree ours so we can't see them.)

Serve with corn tortilla chips. Very unique, yummy flavor!

why we've taken our children to right-to-life rallies on the steps of the Arkansas capitol building.

To support children's homes, homeless shelters, and pregnancy counseling centers, we've also participated in fund-raisers such as banquets, service projects, and walking or running events. We usually opt for *walking* the 1K portion, although Jim Bob and some of our kids picked up enough speed to take the top places in one of those events.

Last summer we took the family all the way from Arkansas to Michigan to present some Duggar-family musical performances at an outdoor tent revival. We also visited Michelle's family in Ohio, and we accepted an invitation to speak at a church in Canton. During our program the church took up an offering to benefit the Ohio Children's Home.

That kind of speaking engagement is a relatively new thing for us. We're still not comfortable as public speakers, but again we want our children to see us overcoming our natural fears to reach out and encourage others, stressing our belief that children are a gift from God and sharing some of the ideas that have worked for us in our big family. We try to make it clear that we don't claim to be experts and that we're still learning ourselves.

Michelle usually introduces her message by saying she's much more accustomed to sharing one-on-one (or one-on-nineteen) than with a large audience. We may not be polished speakers, but our hope is that a message from our heart will reach another heart and make a difference in someone's life.

Michelle has always had a learning spirit, and over the years she has read many child-training books and learned from other families who are raising godly children. She is quick to glean ideas that we then discuss, considering whether those ideas would be effective for our family and planning how we might implement them.

Speaking Up for Our Community

Sometimes serving others means taking a stand that's not popular with everyone. Shortly after Josie was born and Michelle had been discharged from the hospital, a friend, Arkansas state representative John Woods, called and said, "I thought you would want to know about a meeting this afternoon of the state's Alcoholic Beverage Control Board."

He said the board, known as ABC, would be considering whether to allow alcohol to be sold in a Springdale convenience store, something that has been prohibited for years. In our town, prepackaged alcoholic beverages can be sold only in dedicated liquor stores. Now the board would decide if that rule would continue.

We knew that if one convenience store was allowed to sell alcohol, soon all would be. We believed that decision would change the character of our town, and we were adamantly opposed to it. Plus, this convenience store was close to a junior high school.

Springdale has been named one of the top places to raise a family, and we've been blessed to have grown up here and raised our family here. We know many people drink, and that is their choice, but this discussion was about the children in our community being exposed to alcohol at every turn.

I (Jim Bob) asked Michelle if she felt up to attending the board meeting. The truth was, she probably didn't feel like it, but we both agreed it was important. We knew that those who stood to profit from a yes vote would be there, so we told our friend we would go.

The hearing was being held across the street from Arkansas Children's Hospital, just down the street from UAMS, and we arrived at the 1:30 p.m. start time—and then sat through two and a half hours of other discussion before the Springdale permit was finally brought up for consideration. This application had already been vetoed by the director of the board, but the determined folks representing the convenience store had appealed for a vote of the entire board.

We decided Michelle would be the one to speak, and when her turn came, she spoke from her heart as a mother. I was so proud of her and had tears welling up in my eyes. She spoke for eighteen minutes, explaining why she didn't think a yes vote by the board would be good for our community. It would give minors greater access to alcohol, she said, and she predicted it would change the civic landscape of Springdale.

Attorneys representing the convenience store asked her if she was against cigarettes, and she could enthusiastically say yes. She told the board that her mother, who died in 1990 at age sixty-four, had smoked most of her life, and Michelle had seen the health consequences she suffered. And then she pointed out an important difference between alcohol and cigarettes.

"We all know cigarettes are bad for us, but people don't go home, smoke a pack of cigarettes, and then beat their wife and kids," she said.

The fact was, we had owned a convenience store ourselves at

Michelle and her mother, Ethel Ruark.

one time, and because of our beliefs chose not to sell cigarettes, even though the decision dropped our profits considerably. The principles that governed our decision were, first, that a good name is better than riches and, second, that we did not want to profit from another person's loss—in this case, the loss of health due to smoking.

Michelle told the ABC board she didn't believe much good comes from alcohol. "People who want it know where to get it," she said. "Don't put it out there in front of our children at the convenience stores they ride their bikes to for candy bars and snacks. I don't want that for our community."

Michelle wasn't the only one who spoke against the permit; there were four or five others, including a state representative, a pastor, and some parents who were raising their family near that convenience store.

At the end of the meeting, we were gratified that the board ended up denying the permit but shocked to see a television news report that night saying something like, "Michelle Duggar stages ABC protest hours after getting out of the hospital following the premature birth of her nineteenth child."

Oh, well, I (Michelle) thought. *That's not the way it really was, but the Lord knows the truth, and that's what's important.*

COPING WITH CRITICISM

Anytime you stand up for what you believe is right, you open yourself to criticism. That's just the way the world operates. We've certainly received our share of it.

They might say, "When I first heard on the news that you had your nineteenth child, I thought you were crazy; but then I watched your show and I love the happiness I see in your family."

Some viewers can't stand our convictions or how we do things, but they admit to being fascinated. They might say, "I don't even know why I watch your show. You've gone completely overboard on your conservative beliefs, and the way you dress is old-fashioned. I really have

nothing in common with you at all." And then maybe they'll add, "By the way, I love your kids. They're awesome!"

The vast majority of the one hundred to two hundred e-mails we get through our website every day are positive—or at least ambivalent. But inevitably each day there also will be one or two that say things like, "You people are disgusting. You ought to have yourselves neutered."

That line may have been inspired by news reports surrounding a billboard campaign that was proposed by PETA—People for the Ethical Treatment of Animals. The group was ready to pay an outdoor billboard company to put up signs around the area saying, "Doggies Multiply Faster than the Duggars!"

When the billboard company contacted us about using our name on the billboards, we thanked them for doing what was right, seeking our permission, but we said a definite "No!"

Like everyone else, we don't enjoy being ridiculed. But we recognize that everyone has a right to his or her opinion. Long ago, when we felt God calling us to get involved in politics, we got on our knees and gave our reputation to God. We knew He wanted us to stand for truth and we knew that would not be well received from everyone.

We learned to obey what God puts in our heart to do, and we don't worry about what others think. When I (Jim Bob) was running for state representative the first time, we had nine children. That made us different from a lot of families, and some folks simply don't like people who are different.

As we went around town handing out campaign cards, we could see that some people were shocked by our family picture on the front and information about what we stood for on the back. Some had never seen such a big family, and they were repulsed by the whole idea. At one house, a woman opened the door, and I introduced myself. She said, "I know who you are, and I'm not going to vote for you until you get a vasectomy!" Then she slammed the door in my face.

On the other hand, most people have been very nice. Several have

told us that their grandparents had ten-plus children, and they share their fond memories of getting together with their cousins.

When Michelle got pregnant with twins in the middle of the campaign, it was a surprise for us, but I think it stunned most people in town. Everyone seemed to develop an opinion about us pretty quickly (people either loved us or thought we were crazy), but amazingly, when the election results came in, we had won 56 percent of the vote compared with the opponent's 44 percent.

When we're targeted for criticism or condescension, we remember Jesus' words in the Sermon on the Mount. He said we should feel blessed when people "say all manner of evil against you falsely, for my sake" and that we should "bless them that curse you, do good to them that hate you, and pray for them which despitefully use you" (Matthew 5:11, 44).

The value of Jesus' instructions has been proven to us repeatedly. For example, a few years ago, a columnist in San Francisco wrote a short but vile piece about us. It was one of the most well-read articles about us up to that time. It created a lot of controversy in the area where it appeared, and many people wrote to the publication either defending us or criticizing the writer for excessive harshness.

We did not react or respond at all. Actually, the media blitz caused by the article was funny to us. Because it mentioned www.duggarfamily .com, it became the number-one referral link to our website during that month.

Another negative article appeared when I (Jim Bob) was running for the state legislature. Because I didn't have a Republican opponent, I didn't think I had to file a pre-primary report. I was wrong, and by the time I realized my error the deadline had passed, and I filed my report late. As a result, the agency that oversees such things, the Arkansas Ethics Commission, fined me fifty dollars for the late filing. (Later the law was changed to exempt primary candidates from filing if they're running unopposed.) Our local newspaper ran a front-page news story

about another candidate and me, sensationally reporting, THOUSANDS
IN ETHICS FINES.

The article was critical of me and, to my mind, at least, totally un-
fair; my first reaction was to call the reporter and set him straight. But
then those words from the Sermon on the Mount floated through
my mind, Jesus' instructions to bless our enemies. So I didn't call the
reporter, and whenever I came in contact with him, which happened
pretty frequently because he covered politics, I made a point of being
nice to him and showing respect for him.

After I won the legislative seat in the general election, I maintained
my conservative philosophy as I began my work in Little Rock. I agreed
to interviews whenever the reporter called, and I showed him kindness.
Gradually, the articles he wrote about me or quoting me became more
favorable and balanced. But even when his old attitude reappeared
from time to time, I maintained my pleasant demeanor toward him.
By following that biblical directive, over time my "enemy" became my
friend. The reporter actually sent me a Christmas card a couple of years
later, and he signed his name under the words, "your friend."

Our children have heard these stories again and again as examples of
how important it is to have the right response to criticism or injustice.
Anger and ugliness never accomplish the best outcome, but kindness can
work wonders, and forgiveness is a cornerstone of the Christian faith.
I show our kids how these modern-day Duggar experiences prove the
truth of something Joseph, an Old Testament hero, said to his brothers long, long ago after they had sold him into slavery: "Ye thought evil
against me; but God meant it unto good" (Genesis 50:20).

I teach our children that because we live in the public eye and under
the microscope, we're going to incur criticism—justified or not. "We
can learn from our critics," I tell them, "either because what they're saying is true—or because of the way we respond when it isn't."

When we follow God's guidelines, we can trust Him to make something good out of the hard thing that's happened to us. Sometimes
criticism becomes acclaim.

10

• Making Faith Fun •

O come, let us sing unto the LORD:
let us make a joyful noise to the rock of our salvation.
—Psalm 95:1

If you ask our children what their favorite part of being a Duggar is, a lot of them would probably tell you it's Bible time. It's when we wind down together at the end of the day, talk as a family, and share a Bible reading.

Because we call it *Bible* time, you might think this is a serious, "churchy" family tradition where fun is hard to find. Not at all. We've worked to create this as a delightful close of the day for our children. At Bible time, we gather comfortably in our pajamas in the boys' room, the boys on their beds and the rest of us sprawling over the floor, to hear stories, from the Bible and from each other, and do fun family things—like decide names for the next baby! We might also talk about what each person has accomplished that day or maybe tell a funny story about something someone saw. Usually we thank whoever helped fix our meals that day or helped out with the laundry. Then we may sing a song together as a family or pray about a request.

I (Jim Bob) love to sit in the midst of my children and tell them, "Tomorrow, I've got something really special planned." Sometimes I tell them what's in store, and sometimes I keep them guessing. Every night, I try to make Bible time new and exciting—or at least interesting enough to keep everybody awake.

We also read the Bible. The Old Testament book of Proverbs has thirty-one chapters, and it's full of wise and practical verses, so sometimes during Bible time we read the proverb that corresponds with the day of the month. On October 1, for instance, we might read Proverbs chapter 1. Other times we spend a month or so reading a book in the Bible verse by verse. Sometimes I just open the Bible and read wherever it opens. It's amazing the insights we've found "by accident."

Sometimes I take a little one's special request to read an exciting story, like the one about Daniel in the lions' den.

I like to keep everyone guessing and make them eager to know what's going to happen next, so I read right up

I (Jim Bob) like to keep our kids guessing what fun activity I'll have for them next. Who knows? They might even get to ride a camel, like Justin (left) and Joseph did when we went to a wildlife park.

to the most exciting part—Daniel is thrown in with the lions and the king says, in effect, "Let your God save you now!"

Then I close the Bible and say, "Well, that's all for now. Good night, everybody."

Inevitably there are loud groans and protests: "Daddy, you have to tell us what happens next!"

But my answer is usually, "You'll have to wait until tomorrow night to find out what happens—unless you want to read it yourself."

BRINGING BIBLICAL LESSONS TO LIFE

Most nights, I try to think of life illustrations as I read to help the children understand how Scripture applies to everyday life. Michelle and I also tell stories about ourselves to reinforce the biblical lessons.

For example, I tell them about my family's financial struggles during my boyhood and how those experiences motivated me to become the best dad I could to them. One of their favorite stories is about the time there was no food in our house except a jar of rice my mom had displayed as decoration. That morning, Mom cooked that rice for my sister Deanna and me. One way or another, I say, the Lord made sure we had *something* to eat.

Or I may tell them how, when I was in junior high, our family got behind on our house payments and the bank foreclosed. My parents lost thousands of dollars in equity, and we didn't know what we were going to do. We ended up moving into a rental house that was out in the country but close to a new highway the state had just built. The landlord wanted to sell the house to us, and my mom prayed that she and Dad could buy it, but they just didn't have enough money, and someone else bought it.

A year later, my parents' finances changed and Mom's prayer was answered, and they ended up buying the rental house from the new owner. Then they heard that a developer wanted to put in a large hotel and convention center in our area. Dad

JILL'S MINESTRONE

Our daughter Jill loves to cook, and soup is one of her specialties. It's amazing to see how she (and all our girls) can throw together ingredients from whatever we have on hand to make a gourmet meal. Improvising with different ingredients is easy to do with soup recipes.

6 cups water
3 tablespoons chicken base
1 cup onion, diced into ½-inch pieces
½ teaspoon (1 clove) garlic, minced
1¼ cups (2 whole) carrots cut into
    ½-inch slices
1½ cups (1 squash) zucchini cut into
    ¼-inch half-circle slices
1 (14-ounce) can diced tomatoes
1 (15-ounce) can kidney beans, rinsed
½ cup (2 ounces) uncooked macaroni
½ teaspoon salt
½ teaspoon oregano, dried
5 ounces frozen spinach, broken apart

Heat water in saucepan. Add chicken base and whisk to dissolve. Add onion and garlic to broth. Bring to a boil. Reduce heat to low and simmer 10 minutes. Add carrots, zucchini, tomatoes, kidney beans, macaroni, and salt. Bring to a boil again, and then reduce heat and simmer 20 minutes. Add oregano and spinach and bring to a boil. Remove from heat. Let stand 10–15 minutes before serving.

went to Springfield, Missouri, to talk with the developer, and he and Mom ended up putting together the real estate deal for the project. As real estate brokers, they sold the developer many acres of land between the rental house and the new highway. Then they wisely used their commission to purchase two additional properties next door, which became income-producing commercial properties.

I tell my children, if Grandma and Grandpa had not suffered that foreclosure, they would not have had the opportunity to complete that large real estate transaction, which was a great financial blessing for them. God does bring good out of bad!

I tell them that my childhood family went through some awfully hard times,

Jim Bob's mother, Mary Duggar (shown here with our daughter Jana), always encouraged her children to trust the Lord, no matter what challenges they faced.

but through them all, their grandma repeatedly told my sister, Deanna, and me, "Praise the Lord in all things! We can trust the Lord. He will get us through this!" And she was right. We never slept on the street and we never went hungry. Praise God!

These stories teach our children a lot about trusting God during tough times. They can understand how, with each setback, I grew more determined to become a good provider for my own family in the future so that they won't face the worries and hardships I experienced.

Everyone loves a good story with a happy ending. I'm not at the end yet, but I'm certainly happy. When I sit down at Bible time with my big, joyful family around me, I see again how God used the hard stuff of my childhood to instill faith in me. My faith truly grew from watching my mom's faith during the tough times.

Another story I tell our children is how beneficial Bible time has been to *me*. I wasn't a strong student when I was in school. When it came time to take a test, others might finish in five minutes and they would get an A. In contrast, I might sit through the whole class period and barely have time to finish, struggling to think of the answers, and I would get a C. I was also afraid to get up in front of my class to do book reports or give other presentations. For one thing, I wasn't that great of a reader.

Looking back over our twenty-plus years of Bible time, I can see that it's really helped me become a better reader and a leader. Now I'm able to read something and explain it to my children in a way I really struggled to do in school. I'm better at articulating the lessons I want to share with them. So it's been a great benefit to all of us.

It's so easy to get busy with life's responsibilities and think you don't have thirty minutes to an hour to do Bible time every evening, but if that is your situation, I would encourage you to rethink your priorities. As I look back through the years, I agree with my children: Bible time has been some of the best moments we have had together.

Duggars on Parade

We try to make our faith not only meaningful but also fun for our family, so we're always looking for new and different ways to share and celebrate the Gospel message. A couple of years ago, we decided to enter a living nativity as a float in our town's annual Christmas parade.

The kids had done living nativities at our home in earlier years. For a decade the big church next door to our Johnson Road house put on a "living Christmas tree" musical performance with about two thousand people attending each night for four nights. The Duggar kids loved dressing up in robes and headdresses and arranging themselves in a live manger scene in our front yard just as the big church's performance was ending. They considered it a gift to give the passersby a little something extra to enjoy as they were waiting in traffic while heading home.

Our nativity may not have looked as "professional" as the church's, but the kids always had a blast standing in front of a spotlight portraying a Middle Eastern husband and wife along with angels, shepherds, and others dressed in animal costumes. Joshua used his preaching skills to narrate the Christmas story right out of the King James Version of the Bible.

The kids doing a living nativity scene at the Johnson Road house.

The year we decided to participate in the Christmas parade, we decorated our forty-five-foot-long bus with hundreds of Christmas lights powered by the bus's generator. Behind the bus we pulled a sixteen-foot trailer that was also outlined with lights and outfitted with the manger scene to become our parade float. The cast included Mary and Joseph, portrayed by Josh and Anna, plus other Duggar children and friends portraying angels, shepherds, and wise men; a doll played the role of baby Jesus. We asked our friends at Wilderness Drive-Thru Safari to supply some live animals to add authenticity, and they showed up with a miniature donkey, a baby goat, a monkey, and a camel. Perfect!

We connected the trailer to the bus (after overcoming the problem of a towing-hitch ball on the back of the bus being a different size than the hitch on the front of the trailer) and loaded the cast of characters onto the float. By the time we'd added the crowd of extras who would walk alongside the float handing out candy, plus the camel-and-donkey caravan behind it, we could have been a whole parade, all by ourselves!

I (Jim Bob) had planned to ride the camel, regally bringing up the rear as one of the wise men who brought gifts to the baby Jesus, but the

beast growled at me when it was time to mount up, so I opted instead to be a pedestrian wise man. The growling camel didn't bother our son Joseph, so with our safari friends' help, he confidently climbed into the riding seat and bobbed calmly down the street, waving to the crowd. We had so much fun.

I (Michelle), eight months pregnant at the time, rode inside the bus with the littlest Duggars, watching the faces of the bystanders as they spotted the different elements of the float. Riding inside, safe and warm, and thinking about the Christmas scene we were depicting, I had a powerfully poignant appreciation for the Virgin Mary, Jesus' mother, who had ridden to Bethlehem on a donkey when she was nine months pregnant. What a brave and strong young woman she was.

NOAH AND THE DUGGARS

Starting at young ages, our children take piano and violin lessons so they can learn to express themselves through music. Jackson, five, and Johannah, four, already enjoy beginner piano lessons.

Music is a big part of our family's lifestyle. If you come to our home almost any time of the day or evening, you'll probably hear someone practicing the piano, violin, harp, or some other instrument. And much of the time the kids aren't just practicing, they're playing for enjoyment. This is true especially for the older girls, who play simply for the joy of playing—but also as a way to relieve stress or anxiety. Which means we heard a lot of beautiful music last year in the days before Jana and Jill had their wisdom teeth surgically removed!

Most of the music our children play is classical or Christian hymns. We teach them that their music, both instrumental and vocal, is another way they can praise God and share their love for Him. We do lots of recitals and musical programs in our area—and elsewhere too.

One of our most memorable appearances was in Branson, Missouri, less than a two-hour drive from our home in northwest Arkansas. Branson is an entertainment mecca, home of dozens of live music shows, the *Shepherd of the Hills* outdoor drama, and the Silver Dollar City amusement park, among other things. One of our favorites is the spectacular stage play *Noah, the Musical*.

During Bible time one night, I (Jim Bob) asked the children, "Did you know Noah and his family lived in a time when everyone else in the world turned away from following God?" We read the story of how Noah followed God's instructions to build an ark—in the middle of the desert—to prepare for a prophesied flood that would wipe out everything on earth except the family members and animals Noah gathered into the ark.

I pointed out to the kids how Noah's story shows the contrast between a devoutly believing family, unified in their love for God, and the people around them who did not share their faith—and even ridiculed them for following what God told Noah to do.

Then came the exciting news: "Tomorrow morning we're going to wake up at about seven o'clock. We're going to get on the bus and go to Branson and see the play *Noah, the Musical*," I said. "And who knows? Some of you might even get to be *in* the play!"

Of course, some of the little ones had no idea what a *play* was. All they knew was that another Duggar family adventure lay ahead.

When we arrived at Sight and Sound Theatre in Branson, we were warmly greeted by the show's director, who surprised us by saying *all* of us could be in the play that evening if we wanted to!

First, we all got fitted for our costumes, similar to the robes and headdresses we had worn in our living nativity during the Christmas parade. Then we settled down to watch the matinee so we would have

a better idea of what we were expected to do. Later that evening, we got outfitted with our final costumes and makeup, plus a beard for me (I would probably be as old as Noah before I could grow a decent one on my own!). I looked so different with all that hair sprouting from my face that two-year-old Jennifer refused to have anything to do with me (besides bearded daddies, she's also afraid of horses and sports team mascots—a very serious little girl).

Then we waited backstage and moved out on cue, following the person in front of us as some of us played the parts of Noah's family members working on the ark. We all were so grateful to get to participate in this incredible experience of retelling Noah's story onstage.

We have welcomed selected film crews from around the world into our home. This crew came from Japan.

LAUGHTER AND JOY

Another way we keep our faith fun is that we live life with joy. These stories exemplify how the joy of our faith overflows into the everyday. There's a lot of laughter in the Duggar house, and that's the way we like it. We have a good time together. One thing that made us laugh recently was a DVD we received in the mail from a foreign film crew that visited us earlier to tape a segment about our family. The DVD was the finished program about the Duggars that would be broadcast in another country.

We popped the DVD in a computer and laughed uncontrollably as we heard ourselves speaking fluent Korean. The producers had dubbed the Duggar voices so we magically became multilingual. Few things make us laugh harder than seeing and hearing Mama, Daddy, or one of the kids suddenly speaking a language we don't know!

PLAYING, PREACHING, AND PRANKS

Another thing that makes us laugh is watching movies together, but not the Hollywood kind. Our kids love watching old home videos of themselves or their siblings in their early years. To them, the *real* Duggar reality series is just as entertaining as the one on television.

They especially love the old movies of Josh playing church. He was probably eleven or twelve at the time, and Jim Bob was running for the legislature. Josh has always been an outgoing leader who can talk to anybody about anything. In the old home movie, he has gathered up a flock of his younger siblings on the bunk beds, and he's delivering an impassioned message combining the Gospel message and political commentary. "They that be with us are more than they that be against us!" he shouts as part of his loud, earnest speech. His words are accompanied by dramatic hand gestures, wild facial expressions, and a domineering stage presence that had his little congregation falling over with laughter.

Our children love to play—and they also like to play good-natured pranks on each other and sometimes our houseguests. You may have seen the episode on our TV series when a young professional photographer was sent to our house by *People* magazine for a Duggar-family portrait after the birth of our eighteenth child, Jordyn-Grace Makiya.

The young man was concentrating on arranging us perfectly, getting the lighting just right, and then pulling off the near impossible job of getting all twenty-one of us (including Josh's wife, Anna) looking at the camera at the same time. During a brief break while he swapped out some of his equipment, Josiah, one of our biggest pranksters, walked up to the photographer carrying the newborn baby wrapped in a blanket.

"Would you like to take her picture?" he asked innocently, extending the bundle toward the photographer—just in time to trip over a light-stand cord (or pretend to). As he stumbled, he dropped the baby on the hard tile floor right at the photographer's feet, nearly causing the

poor guy to faint! But it wasn't really the baby; it was one of the little girls' life-sized baby dolls.

It took the photographer a moment to recover, and when he did he took some great pictures. But we're guessing if *People* wants him to photograph the Duggar family again, he's gonna want more money!

With ten boys in our family, there are always good-natured pranks and jokes going on. Josiah is one of the most clever pranksters. (He's also a talented musician.)

The Duggar kids do like to play pranks, especially the boys. When Josh and Anna came hurrying out of the reception hall following their wedding, planning to make a fast getaway in Josh's car, they found it not only decorated with shoe polish but also completely encased in a thick shroud of plastic wrap that was almost impossible to get off. (You know how hard it is to find the end of the roll once it's stuck down—and no one in the crowd seemed to have a pocketknife.)

Maybe that's why, when they finally made it to Myrtle Beach, Josh told the film crew he and Anna had to keep their honeymoon location a secret "because there are lots of pranksters in my family."

WHO *IS* THAT CHILD?

We also have friends who enjoy playing little pranks on us. One of them is Mike Huckabee, former Arkansas governor and now Fox News talk show host. He invited us to bring our family to New York City and appear on his show a couple of years ago. As our segment on the live show began, he brought the two of us onto the set and explained that he thought it would be fun to give us a little test.

GOLDEN WHOLE WHEAT BREAD

Jinger (and our fellas too!) enjoys making delicious homemade whole wheat bread with our Bosch mixer. In a matter of two hours we have a wonderful hot, healthy meal on the serving line. We bought some industrial mini-loaf pans at a used-restaurant-supply store that can make eighteen small loaves—like the kind you get at a fancy restaurant. Hot, fresh home-made bread served with hearty soup (like Jill's Minestrone, page 117), a big green salad, and fresh or frozen fruit for dessert—now that makes for a delicious meal!

3 cups warm water (110–115 degrees)
6 tablespoons oil
2 tablespoons honey
1½ tablespoons active dry yeast
8 cups (2⅔ pounds) whole wheat flour (hard white wheat flour is our preference)
2¼ teaspoons salt

Combine water, oil, honey, and yeast in a 4–5-quart mixer bowl with a dough hook. Use wire whisk to dissolve yeast. Let sit until foamy, 5–10 minutes.

Combine flour and salt and add to liquid mixture while mixer is running. Mix until almost all ingredients are fully incorporated. Increase to medium speed and mix for 7–8 minutes or until gluten is developed (a small piece of dough can be stretched paper-thin without tearing). (Note: Dough should pull away from the bowl halfway through the kneading time. If it doesn't, add more flour, 1 tablespoon at a time.) Cover with plastic or a clean dish towel and let dough rise in a warm place for one hour. Divide for desired use (see suggestions below). Cover and let dough rest for 20 minutes. Shape, let rise, and bake accordingly.

VARIATIONS
—Replace ¾ cup whole wheat flour with all-purpose flour.
—Substitute hard white wheat flour with hard red.
—Raisin Bread: Add 1 cup raisins and 2¼ teaspoons cinnamon (¼ cup chopped nuts, optional) to dough along with flour.

SHAPING THE BREAD
For loaf bread......................... 6 balls (1½ pounds).........8½ × 4½ loaf pans
For rolls .... 8 balls (12 per ball)..........6 rows of 4 rolls on cookie sheets
For 12-inch pizza crusts........ 11 balls (13 ounces).........12-inch pizza pans

LOAF BREAD
Press each ball out flat into a ½-inch-thick rectangle. Roll up tightly, pressing dough into roll with each turn. Pinch the ends together. Place dough, seam side down, in greased pan. Let rise for 1½ hours or until doubled in size. Bake at 350 degrees for 30–35 minutes or

GOLDEN WHOLE WHEAT BREAD (CONTINUED)

until lightly browned on bottom and sides (200-degree internal temperature). Remove from pans and cool on wire rack.

ROLLS

Roll each ball into a 12½-inch log. Cut into twelve 1-inch slices. Roll each piece into a smooth ball. Place on greased cookie sheets, six rows of four (sides can be touching). Let rise for 1½ hours or until doubled in size. Bake at 350 degrees for 15 minutes or until lightly browned on bottom.

PIZZA CRUSTS

Roll out dough on lightly oiled surface. Place on greased pizza pan. Prick in center and along crust's inside edge to prevent bubbling. Let rise until desired thickness is reached, 15–30 minutes. Par-bake at 375 degrees for 6–7 minutes or until starting to brown.

Probably thinking of how some of us parents, especially when we're concentrating on something else, want to call the nearest child to come help us with whatever we're doing but end up going through the names of every *other* child first, and sometimes the dog and cat as well, before we can finally get the right name to come out, Governor Huckabee asked our children to come out one by one, or with an older child carrying a younger one, to see if we could instantly name each one.

Well, the pressure was on! We confidently named each Duggar child as he or she stepped onto the set. And then Jessa came out carrying . . . well, instead of instantly naming the infant she was carrying, we were instantly confused. Who *was* that child?

It turned out she wasn't ours! The governor had "borrowed" a baby from a staff member for Jessa to carry out to us. Everyone had a good laugh.

NAILING IT DOWN

I (Jim Bob) was born on a Sunday in 1965, and the next Sunday I was in church. When I was seven, I went to my mom after a revival service

at Calvary Baptist Church in Fayetteville and told her I wanted to become a Christian. She took me to talk with the pastor, who explained the simple Gospel message.

At the end of our talk, the preacher asked if he could lead me in a prayer, and I agreed. At the end of the prayer, he looked up and said, "How do you feel?"

I told him I didn't feel any different. Then he led me in a second prayer, asking again for God to forgive me, take control of my life, and take me to heaven when I die. Then he said, "Now how do you feel?"

I was embarrassed that I didn't feel anything, so I said I thought I might feel different this time. Well, that was my first lie, and it came right after getting saved! *Now* I understand that salvation is not a feeling; it is a relationship with God.

Years later, in my early teen years, I started having doubts about my salvation. Then I heard a man teach that sometimes those who commit their life to God at an early age have doubt that they understood what they were doing during that childhood experience. He said, in effect, "Don't let your doubt keep you from being sure of your salvation. Don't worry if you did everything way back then with the proper procedures. Nail it down *right now.*"

So I prayed, asking God to forgive me, and committed my life to him—and I haven't had a doubt since!

Michelle became a Christian at fifteen after a friend told her about how we can be forgiven for everything we have done wrong. Although her beliefs didn't come as early as mine did, they've been just as strong as mine. We are two people who love the Lord, and we want to give our family the same strong foundation of faith that we value so dearly. We all want to live for Jesus, to thank Him for what He has done for us.

WORSHIPING TOGETHER

We took our children to church from their earliest days of infancy. Our roots are in the Baptist church, and we still feel a close connection to

that denomination. But as our family grew and reached Sunday school age, we did not want to find ourselves scattering in different directions when we arrived at the church door as each one headed off to his or her Sunday school class, which is usually determined by age. We wanted to stick together as a family during church worship and Bible study time.

Our pastor at Temple Baptist Church, Don Elmore, taught a class called the Oasis that was intended for senior citizens. We asked him if we could come as a family to the class, and he said sure. It worked out great. Our kids loved being among friends who reminded them of their grandparents, and the older members of the class seemed to enjoy having a group of well-behaved youngsters in their midst. When the class had social gatherings and activities, we all joined in.

Pastor Elmore is an excellent teacher who has a gift for telling stories and presenting lessons so they are memorable and appealing to everyone, no matter what age. We would all listen to his colorful lessons and then talk about them on the ride home or later during that week. It was rewarding for all of us.

Some teachers think they have to talk to children on a juvenile level in order for them to understand biblical concepts, but we've decided that's not always the case. Children are smart and eager to learn, especially when surrounded by older siblings and parents who love them and want the best for their lives.

It's why we homeschool the way we do—with all the children gathered around our long table for some of the lessons, hearing the same instruction before working on related assignments that are geared for their ages and abilities.

The youngest ones may not understand the ideas the moment they hear them, but we believe the information goes into their brains and accumulates like a big pile of snow. The snowdrift gets bigger and bigger and bigger as the children hear new information, especially when it's presented appealingly. Then, gradually, as these children mature, the ideas they have heard start melting and soaking into their hearts and minds, and they begin comprehending.

The Bible says God's Word won't return void (see Isaiah 55:11), and we strongly believe we see that principle played out as we read to them during Bible time and discuss what the stories and passages mean. We see how these lessons, presented repeatedly and interestingly, make a difference in their lives when they see them applied and watch how they work in real life.

An example of this occurred when we watched a video of a gifted pastor preaching about being a giver or a taker. He gave funny examples from current-day life, describing the zany things people say and do that identify them as givers or takers. Then he linked those examples to scriptural passages, including one from the story of Daniel.

Hearing that, our son Jed's eyes grew as big as saucers. "That's exactly what Daddy was talking about last night in Bible time!" he said.

Another snowflake lands with the others. . . .

As time went on and our family grew, we almost outnumbered the senior citizens in our Sunday school class! Around that time, we met Clark and Denise Wilson, who had moved from Mississippi to northwest Arkansas to do church planting. They started a little Baptist church that was meeting in an office trailer. We decided to join them.

Their focus was on encouraging families to worship together—the

We got to know Clark and Denise Wilson and their family when we started attending a church they planted in Springdale. Later, Clark helped us build our 7,000-square-foot house.

way *we* loved to worship. Several other likeminded families joined that church fellowship, and through the messages and teaching, we grew into a close-knit group, all desiring to train our families to impact the world for Christ. Some got involved in politics, ran and got elected,

while others developed family music outreaches. We all have a heart for widows and the fatherless, knowing that God says caring for and serving them is true religion and ministry.

Our church services included each family's prayer requests and praise reports to share what God had done in our lives that week. It was truly a time of revival in our hearts, and we saw God open many doors. We loved worshiping together as families—although, as you can imagine, with so many small children from infants on up, there was quite a bit of noise. The preacher would press on through the dull roar of children wiggling and babies crying.

We eventually outgrew the office trailer and started taking turns meeting in the different families' homes where there was more space. The Sunday morning services then expanded to include a fellowship dinner afterward; we call it a pot-faith dinner—because we don't believe in *luck*. Everyone brought food to share, and the families stayed for several hours after church and had a great time of fellowship together. The girls would talk or play games while the boys usually played football in the yard. The adults would visit while keeping an eye on the children.

After a few years, Pastor Wilson and his family moved back to Mississippi to be near their family and assist his mother, who was ill. At that point the men in the church took turns sharing each week, or we would watch excellent teaching videos by gifted preachers like Pastor S. M. Davis and then discuss how we could apply the lessons to our lives. We were like iron sharpening iron.

We have been fellowshiping and worshiping together in this family-integrated church setting since 1999, and it has worked well for our family.

Our experience confirms that a church is not a building or a list of rules or traditions. It is a group of believers getting together to have fellowship, Bible study, worshiping God together, and challenging each other to fulfill Christ's commands.

FRIENDLY CHAPEL

One night shortly after Josie's birth, I (Jim Bob) was going from Michelle's UAMS hospital room to Josie's NICU pod and noticed a man in the labor-and-delivery waiting room leading his family in prayer. I thought to myself, *That is a godly man!*

Later, as I was walking back to Michelle's room, the man and his granddaughter stopped me and asked if I was the father of the family with nineteen children. The granddaughter said she loved watching our show, and the man introduced himself as Paul Holderfield and told me one of his daughters was in labor.

We continued visiting, and he told me a fascinating story. He said his dad, Paul Holderfield Sr., had grown up near Little Rock during a time of tense racial prejudice. Paul Sr. was a Golden Gloves champion boxer in his younger days; then he became a fireman. He was a tough guy who developed a serious alcohol addiction, probably following in his own father's footsteps. Even though his widowed mother prayed for him daily, he didn't want anything to do with God.

One day in 1957, he and several other white firemen were standing out in front of the fire station when a black man who had been his neighbor years before came walking down the street. The neighbor had given him rides several times to boxing matches.

Paul Sr. tried to turn away so the man wouldn't recognize him, but as he got closer he came straight up to him, stuck out his hand, and said, "Mr. Paul." With all of his white friends watching, Paul just stuck his hands in his back pockets and pretended not even to have seen the man's hand. He was concerned about what his fellow firemen would think of him if they found out he was friends with a black man.

Totally rejected, the man walked away.

Afterward Paul felt horrible, consumed with guilt. Years later, God used that shameful situation for good. Paul's godly mother, who had continued praying for her son through the years, became very ill, and her declining condition had a strong impact on Paul Sr. When she

seemed at death's door, Paul told God if He would allow his mom to live until Sunday, he would give Him his heart.

When that happened, Paul got alone and cried, asking God to forgive him for the awful things he had done. He asked Jesus to take control of his life. He told his wife and his three kids they were going to start going to church, and he threw away his alcohol and cigars and instantly stopped his filthy language. God made him a new person!

He had never forgotten the shameful incident when he had refused to shake his black friend's hand. Now he resolved to make amends for his former bigotry by reaching out to some of the poor African-American boys at the North Little Rock Boys Club. He invited some of them to attend his church, but the church did not receive them well. He couldn't believe the discrimination shown by people claiming to be Christians.

Paul got permission from the Boys Club to start a regular Bible study there, and through that effort, several boys turned their lives around. One of them, a boy named Nate, went on to become a firefighter himself; he was the first African-American fire captain in North Little Rock.

Eventually Paul Sr. had a vision to build a church in the North Little Rock community that once had the highest crime rate in the whole state of Arkansas. The church Paul started reached out to those who needed help the most; it became a church where people of all races and colors could worship God together. Under his leadership, the church started a soup kitchen to feed the poor and homeless and opened a thrift store to provide clothing and basic necessities.

Paul's little church flourished and is known today as the Friendly Chapel Church of the Nazarene in North Little Rock. The man I met in the UAMS hallway was Paul's son, Paul Holderfield Jr. He told me that twelve years earlier, after his father's death, he had gone from driving a bread route to becoming the pastor of the church his dad had started forty years ago.

Today about five hundred people attend services in Friendly Chapel

each Sunday, he said. About two-thirds of the congregation are black, and the rest are a mix of other nationalities and races. Some are homeless, some come from middle-class families, and some are professionals and business executives. It is a diverse and ministry-minded congregation.

The church's soup kitchen serves meals to one hundred to as many as five hundred homeless and poor people each weekday. In its thrift store, nothing costs more than two dollars. It also operates a temporary shelter for those needing vocational or spiritual assistance.

Nate, the boy who was inspired by Paul Sr. to become a firefighter, has led the music at Friendly Chapel for more than thirty years.

As Paul Holderfield Jr. was telling me (Jim Bob) about his dad and their church, I thought it might be a place where our family could worship while we were living in Little Rock. It sounded like a church where we could be a part of the mighty work the Lord was doing in that community.

I grew up attending a large conservative Baptist church in Springdale that was almost totally Caucasian. With the explosive growth of several large corporations since my growing-up years, the mix of nationalities and races in northwest Arkansas has changed. Despite the multicultural makeup of our community now, Michelle and I and our children had never attended a church reflecting that diversity. To be honest, we just hadn't thought about it.

In Little Rock, the more we learned about Friendly Chapel, the more we wanted our family to share its true heart for doing God's work. It is one of the most ministry-minded congregations we've ever known, reaching out to the poor, providing basic needs for people who don't have clean clothes or a place to sleep and who have nothing to give in return for the kindness shown them. Friendly Chapel's Christians love the poor like Jesus loves them. We were amazed to see how the church's focus on selfless service impacted that whole community.

We attended Friendly Chapel regularly during our six months in Little Rock, and we made lifelong friends there. The girls got to spend

a day in the soup kitchen and were able to help a little with the thrift store.

In June 2010, when all the Duggars back home in Springdale had recovered from the chicken pox and it was safe for Josie to join her family, our Friendly Chapel family and some other friends helped us move out of the Cornish house. Many of them were the same friends who had brought our huge family meals during our difficult time in Little Rock and helped us in countless other ways. What a gift their friendship has been to us as they joined us in making our faith not only meaningful and fun but also taught us how to meet the needs of others practically.

Here is a poem that Paul Holderfield Sr. adapted for the church's ministry:

SOAP, SOUP, AND SALVATION

Soap, soup, and salvation may cause you to smile
But this combination is really worthwhile.
These three great essentials in everyday life
Were always put into practice by Brother Paul and his
  wife. . . .

When one is filthy without and hungry within
They're in no condition to repent of their sins.
But soap in the shower and soup in the bowl
Put them in a condition to think of their soul.

Soap, soup, and salvation—when these you apply—
Gets them fit to live and ready to die.
Down at the Friendly Chapel, this wonderful three,
Soap, soup, and salvation, are all three free.

Original poet unknown; adapted by Paul Holderfield Sr.

PART 3

Big Hope for Our Children's Future

Be ye doers of the word,
and not hearers only.

—James 1:22

11

• Homeschool, Duggar Style •

And these words, which I command thee this day, shall be in thine heart:
And thou shalt teach them diligently unto thy children.
—Deuteronomy 6:6–7

We have homeschooled our children because we want to spend time with them and train them to become mature Christians who love God. We want to instill in them qualities of Christlike character, and we hope to shape them into responsible leaders who can make a positive impact on their families and the world around them.

And as we're working toward those goals, we want to make homeschool fun and fascinating too.

We shared our homeschool routine in *The Duggars: 20 and Counting!* so we won't repeat the overall structure here. Instead we'll share a closer look at how we teach some of the lessons and subjects we consider priorities.

One of the advantages of homeschooling is that we can incorporate our faith into the curriculum. When I (Michelle) first began my role as a homeschool teacher almost eighteen years ago, I

During one long-distance field trip, we took our homeschoolers to Petersburg, Kentucky, to meet Ken Ham and tour the incredible Creation Museum, which he founded there.

felt the Lord impressing upon me the importance of getting His Word into my children's hearts and minds. Not just teaching them to *know* His Word but to hunger and thirst for it as an essential part of their lives.

SALT THE OATS!

But how could I do that? Everyone knows the old adage that says you can lead a horse to water but you can't make it drink. How could I make my children *thirst* for God's Word? The answer came in a message I heard somewhere that said simply, Salt the oats! Show your children how interesting God's Word can be. Once they get a taste of that "saltiness," they'll thirst for more.

To bring out that saltiness, as we're seated together around the table during our family homeschool time, we memorize passages of Scripture that are especially meaningful to us. And we create hand motions to do together that help us seal the memorized passage in place.

In the past we've memorized passages depending on what was happening in our family. For example, we learned Matthew 18 when the children seemed to be going through a stage of bickering and I wanted them to learn the biblical model of conflict resolution. I didn't want them to argue.

We learned that passage, and when one of them would come to me, tattling, I would say, "There's an answer for this in Matthew 18, remember? What do you do?" (We'll go into a little more depth about how we teach our children to use Matthew 18 in a later chapter.)

Other passages we've memorized include Romans 6, which talks about overcoming sin by God's grace, and Psalm 1, which expresses who we should spend time with and what we should be busy learning if we want to be a man or woman seeking God.

Last year, after Josie was discharged from the hospital, I spent three weeks with her alone in the Little Rock house waiting for the kids back home in Springdale to get over the chicken pox. During that time I committed myself to memorizing another favorite passage, Matthew 5, which includes Jesus' Sermon on the Mount, so that I could teach

it to our family as soon as homeschool lessons resumed. I don't always memorize the passage ahead of time, but because of my solitary schedule during chicken pox season, I was able to do so. The more of the chapter I committed to memory, the more eager I became to share Jesus' profound teaching with my children. I longed to get those words embedded in their little hearts and minds, hoping they will meditate on them and incorporate them into their daily lives.

THE DUGGAR METHOD OF MEMORIZATION

Come to our home as we begin memorizing Matthew 5, and here's what you might hear:

"'And seeing the multitudes, he went up into a mountain.'

"Now say it with me: 'And seeing the multitudes, he went up into a mountain.'

"Again: 'And seeing the multitudes . . .'"

We'll say the first verse over and over again. Then I'll say, "Okay, what motions do you think we should put with that verse?" Suggestions will be made, and we'll agree on motions to accompany the verse. Maybe we will put our hand to our eyes for "seeing the multitudes," and perhaps we'll put the fingertips of both hands together in a pointy shape while we say, "He went up into a mountain."

Verse by verse we'll memorize the chapter and add the motions. Sometimes we get through two or three verses a day. Each day we start over at the beginning of the chapter, reviewing what we've already memorized, complete with motions, and then we memorize the next few verses.

We're all sitting at the table together facing each other, which makes it much easier to help each other. Each sibling sees someone else make the motion and is helped to remember what to say. (Everyone likes to watch Jeremiah, because he never seems to forget anything.)

The motions work with the mouth, the eyes, and the memory—a multisensory experience that helps us all learn faster and remember longer.

In the afternoon we do wisdom book lessons around the dining room table.

We always review the entire passage we've learned from the beginning and then add the new verses. The day we completed memorizing Matthew 18, we repeated the whole thing, plus the last few verses up to verse 32! What a wonderful feeling of accomplishment that was for all of us.

We talk about each verse as we're memorizing it, and I explain what it means. Some of the younger ones might not understand what the concepts are behind the words we're memorizing, but gradually, as we review our memorized texts and discuss them, it begins to make sense and sink in.

We occasionally quote together the passages we have memorized to keep them current in our hearts and minds. Also, we encourage our children to quote the scripture they have memorized and think about each verse as they are falling asleep at night. We've learned that by meditating on God's Word this way and by thinking pure thoughts, we shift our focus off the busyness of that day and prepare for the next one.

MEMORY LANE

During the part of our homeschool day called Memory Lane we review the Bible passages we've memorized, as well as other memorized lessons such as the operational definitions of character qualities (from the Advanced Training Institute; see the Resources section). It's just about everybody's favorite part of the school day—because that's when I

hand out treats as rewards! It may just be a single Skittle or one M&M, but it's a reward and everyone who can recite a memorized tidbit—a character-quality definition or a memorized verse—gets one.

Sometimes we'll recite "popcorn style," which means I call a name and that child pops up and quotes something we've memorized—anything he or she wants from our Memory Lane folder. For instance, I'll say, "Jedidiah! It's your turn." And he'll pop up and quote a quick portion of Romans 6. I'll hand him a Skittle or an M&M and say, "Johannah, you're next!" And Johannah will pop up and quote the definition of self-control: "Instant [she claps her hands, our motion for the word *instant*] obedience to the initial prompting of God's spirit" (or as much of the definition as she can remember; she's only four).

Another way we do Memory Lane is to recite together the operational definitions of three or four of the character qualities we've learned over the past months. We also memorize—and then recite during Memory Lane—quotes by famous Christian leaders and founding fathers.

Often my older children, those who've already graduated, will join us for Memory Lane, in part because it's fun and also to help coach some of the younger ones.

Usually Memory Lane is something we do in the afternoon, around naptime. When my children were all really young, I *had* to take a break and put everyone down for a nap—sometimes Mama took one too! Now that our family has spread out over a wider age range, from preschool to high school, Memory Lane is something we do while one or two of the youngest children nap in a playpen next to the dining table where we do our schoolwork.

But, seeing how much fun we're having, the little ones often fight those heavy eyelids as long as they possibly can. They want to be part of the fun. So, many times, I'll let the little ones sit at the table with us for the first few minutes of Memory Lane, watching, absorbing—and learning.

Recently little Jordyn, who then was about eighteen months old, sat buckled in her little high chair at the table as we started quoting

Matthew 18 during a Memory Lane review. She started mimicking our motions—learning just from watching. And when we finished, she held out her little hand for a Skittle too, of course. Then we had a popcorn round, and Jordyn got to go first. She wasn't really quoting anything, but following Mama's lead, she echoed the first five words of the first verse—and got a wild round of applause from her brothers and sisters, as well as another Skittle.

We continued on with the popcorn round, and Jordyn quickly fell asleep with her head resting on the table. We shifted her into the playpen beside my chair, and she snoozed away. What a wonderful way to fall asleep (except that we didn't get to brush her teeth)—surrounded by your loved ones as they quote Bible verses and wise definitions.

Before a visit to George Washington's home in Mount Vernon, Virginia, our children learned about our first president during homeschool.

LINKING CHARACTER QUALITIES TO WISDOM

Another big part of our homeschool curriculum is learning to identify bad character and replace it with Christlike character. Knowing precise definitions of character qualities gives us the basis for building and praising the character of God in others. We memorize and study them,

and then look for them in other areas such as science, math, medicine, or law, which we study in the Wisdom Booklets from the Advanced Training Institute (see the Resources section). We also look for the positive character qualities in one another.

For example, maybe our character quality for the month is *kindness*, defined as "seeing needs in the lives of others as opportunities to demonstrate my love for Christ." We want to incorporate these qualities into our lives constantly, but while we're focusing on a specific one, we pay extra attention to it: for example, noticing when someone shows special kindness to his or her siblings.

That child might make a little thank-you card, noting that he or she saw someone showing kindness to someone else. Maybe the card says, "I saw Josiah show kindness when he helped Jedidiah carry out a heavy bag of trash without being asked." It wasn't really the second brother's job, but he saw someone who needed help, so he helped him. Maybe that night at dinner or Bible time we might ask if anyone wants to share a praise report. Someone might say something like, "I saw Jinger cleaning the kitchen and dining room without even being asked!" Then we all clap for her.

We're teaching them to notice, and praise the good character qualities of Jesus as they see them demonstrated in others' lives.

We also encourage our children to do kindness in secret, as well as when it's noticeable; that's another biblical concept. Jesus said when we do kindness in secret, "thy Father which seeth in secret himself shall reward thee openly" (Matthew 6:4).

Then, as we continue our Wisdom Booklet work, we might look for kindness as we study science, history, law, or medicine. You would be amazed at the insights and correlations we find. For example, in science and history the Wisdom Booklets might introduce the story of George Washington Carver and the amazing research he did, focusing on the peanut, and the discoveries he made. We learn that he was an incredibly humble man and showed kindness to many people. He turned down the wealth of the world to continue working in his little

laboratory at the college where he felt God calling him to work. He called it "God's little laboratory."

Then we look at a map to understand more about George Washington Carver, and we find—what do you know!—his birthplace is less than a hundred miles from us at George Washington Carver National Monument in Diamond, Missouri. Everybody on the bus! (It usually doesn't happen quite that fast, but we do love making things at least *seem* spontaneous sometimes. And we do love family field trips.)

The Wisdom Booklets offer innumerable ways for homeschoolers to focus on different parts of a subject at increasingly advanced levels. They suggest such a wide variety of projects you could never exhaust all the choices provided. And we firmly believe that curiosity is the best way to learn. Arousing curiosity is another way we "salt the oats."

INDEPENDENT STUDY

Our homeschool assignments, music practice, and chores keep the kids busy throughout the day. We do Wisdom Booklets and memorization together, usually in the afternoons. In the morning, after everyone's up, dressed, and fed, and when morning chores are completed, those in grades three and up typically settle in for self-paced work on the computers. For about three years now we've used the Switched on Schoolhouse (SOS) software from Alpha Omega Publications (see Resources section); it works very well, describing each subject in text, pictures, diagrams, and video tutors.

Working at his or her own pace, the student has three opportunities to answer the questions or problems presented. Each answer is graded, and after three tries, the answer is revealed. If the student misses too many questions on the quiz at the end of each section, it is reassigned to him or her. Right now our older daughter Jessa is in charge of checking all the computer grades and watching for those who are having trouble with something. And of course all the children know they can come and ask us questions anytime they don't understand something. Youngsters

in third grade and younger complete their assignments in Accelerated Christian Education (ACE) workbooks while seated at the dining table with Mama or in the schoolroom with Mama or one of the older girls.

Starting around age five we use Typing Tutor software to teach the children computer-typing skills. Piano, violin, and harp lessons also help them develop hand-eye-brain coordination while also giving them a beautiful means of expressing themselves.

WHEN AND HOW?

We homeschool year-round but take breaks from the computer work when we're traveling. We enjoy practicing Memory Lane while we're riding on the bus. When we moved temporarily to Little Rock after Josie's birth, we took the computers, and the older girls and Jim Bob made sure schoolwork continued as usual—or as close to "usual" as we could manage.

Other homeschool parents sometimes ask how our schedule changes after the birth of a new baby. I answer that it depends on the delivery. Usually after two weeks I'm able to get back into a somewhat normal schedule, even though I don't do any heavy lifting. During those early weeks I also might take a nap while the youngest ones are napping. Jim Bob or one of my older girls is always so sweet to help hold down the fort if I need a nap. They make sure the children finish their schoolwork and music and complete their checklists.

Usually my newborn babies just sleep and eat, so most of our days continue pretty much as usual, except that we have a precious little new addition snoozing or gurgling through our homeschool days with us. I usually have the baby in a bouncy seat and move him or her wherever I'm working. While nursing the baby, two great items I recommend are the My Brest Friend nursing pillow and a good nursing cover or cape. These aids let me nurse the baby discreetly while simultaneously leading Memory Lane exercises, teaching things like ABCs or phonics flashcards, helping younger ones with their reading, or leading multiplication drills.

These are the methods and ideas we use in our homeschool now (or at least we were using them when we wrote this book), but we're always open to new ideas, software, and other materials.

The resources we've found at www.titus2.com also have helped us tremendously in getting our lives more organized.

PAN-FRIED BEAN-AND-CHEESE QUESADILLAS

8 cups cooked pinto beans
3 tablespoons taco seasoning
2–3 cups cooked rice (optional)
2 cups shredded cheddar cheese
Olive oil
30 tortillas
Optional toppings: lettuce, tomatoes, sour cream, salsa, taco sauce

Mash or blend beans. Add taco seasoning and stir in rice and cheese. Heat a tablespoon of olive oil in a frying pan. Place one open-face tortilla with mixture spread on half of it in pan. Cook till golden brown on bottom. Fold top over. Add whatever toppings you like, and it's ready to eat. Makes 30 quesadillas.

READING ABOUT THE DUGGARS

We've enjoyed presenting several musical programs at both public and Christian schools, and we've also participated in reading events and other programs we've been invited to help with.

Sometimes these appearances lead to some insightful conversations later around our dining table, and sometimes things happen that make us laugh. Last year, when we (Jim Bob and Michelle, not the whole family) were invited to be interviewed by a public relations class at the nearby University of Arkansas, I (Jim Bob) dropped off Michelle at the front of the classroom building so she could hurry on ahead, and then I parked the car (we were running on Duggar time, as usual). We wanted to give the students in the class a copy of our first book as a little gift, so when Jim Bob came into the building, he was carrying an armload of them.

Another student riding the same elevator glanced at Jim Bob, noticing the stack of books he was carrying, and said, "I tell you what, I'm glad I'm not in a class that has to read about the Duggars."

Jim Bob smiled and said, "Yeah, that'd be awful."

12

•Vocations, Goals, and Roles •

Whatsoever ye do, do all to the glory of God.
—1 Corinthians 10:31

Wₑ pray daily for our children, that God would protect them and that they won't be led into temptation, and we are excited to see what God is going to do through them. Our goals for them are that:

1. They keep a close relationship with God.

2. They learn to listen to God's still, small voice and follow His plan for their lives.

3. When they make mistakes they humbly confess those things to God and to whomever they have wronged and maintain a clear conscience.

4. They would look for ways to serve others and express gratefulness for what others have done for them.

If we meet our goals and teach our children those things, they will be a success in life.

As they get older, we encourage our children to pursue the direction they feel God leading them to a future occupation, whether it is being a missionary to Asia or ministering to others as a nurse or starting

their own businesses. There is no safer place than being in the center of God's will.

In our travels through the years, I (Jim Bob) have heard many young people say they would love to be in full-time Christian work. I respond that God does call some to devote themselves totally to full-time church and mission work, but even the apostle Paul, who wrote several books of the New Testament, also had a "secular" career to support himself. He was a part-time tent maker while he was busy sharing the Gospel with others every day.

We teach our children that they can have a great impact working side by side with others in the workplace, interacting with them daily. Once others know you are a Christian, we say, they're going to watch your every move to see if you act like one. With God's help, you can point them to the One who has the answers for life's challenges—not by preaching to them every chance you get, but by living out your faith and waiting for God to create a time that will open an opportunity to share your faith. A good question to ask non-Christians in order to direct a conversation to a spiritual level is, "How would you like to be forgiven for everything you have ever done wrong?" Most people are interested in having God's redemption plan explained to them.

We talk frequently with our young-adult children about the importance of pursuing training for a job that they would enjoy and that would allow them to support themselves and their future families. Recently we shared the story of a woman we met who said when she'd had the choice of going to architecture school or majoring in accounting, she had chosen accounting because she could graduate quicker. Once she got her degree and got a good-paying job, however, she realized she hated accounting. She ended up quitting the career she had trained for and now wishes she would have pursued something she enjoys. She even pays someone else to do her taxes for her, she said, because she can't stand doing them herself!

Spending time with those who work in the field the young people are interested in can help them decide if it's the right career for them

*Josh and Anna enjoy
running their own
business selling
pre-owned vehicles.*

before they spend thousands of dollars and years of their lives preparing for that line of work. We suggest as they're considering a specific career that they ask themselves, Is this a job that I would enjoy doing for years to come? Is travel going to be involved? Will it take me away from my future family, or will I have to relocate to do this job? Will the job require me to work nights, weekends, or holidays? Will it require me to do anything that would violate my convictions or conscience? How much will this job pay? Do I want to get advanced training now while I'm young to get better pay throughout my career? Is there a creative business I could start that would provide a sufficient income while allowing me to serve others (either trying my own idea or adapting someone else's successful business model)?

There are many questions to consider. If you make the wrong decision, we tell our kids, you could waste years of your life. If you make a wise decision, you could reap many benefits.

When I was getting out of high school in 1983, I thought I wanted to go to a computer school in Little Rock and learn how to work on computers. I figured before long everyone would have one, and they would have to be repaired from time to time.

The Bible says, "A man's heart deviseth his way: but the Lord directeth his steps" (Proverbs 16:9). I planned to get computer training in Little Rock, but the Lord directed my steps to Michelle, and I fell in love with her. She had one more year of high school, and I wasn't about

to leave her to go to Little Rock. So I kept my high school job, working at a grocery store and praying about what to do.

One day a thought came to me, *What do most people spend their money on?* The answer was food, houses, cars, insurance ... My parents were third-generation Realtors, so I already knew how that business worked. I signed up for a real estate class and got a real estate license. Since then I have ended up making more money working part-time—buying, selling, and renting real estate—than all of the other work I've done combined. It's been a career that has let me work from home and spend most of each day with my family.

After Michelle and I got married, we both got life insurance licenses. We made a little money with that, but selling insurance was primarily a great learning experience for us. Next we opened a small used-car lot; then we added a towing service, and this combination of businesses became our primary income through the years until the rental properties started making a big enough return for us to live on.

During the early years of our marriage, Jim Bob worked such long, hard hours in our car-sales and towing businesses that he was often exhausted during the few hours he was home.

Our first book details our trials during our "last and least" business experience: a convenience store that I did not pray about before purchasing. I overrode Michelle's cautions, and as a result we endured two and a half years of headaches and hard work that generated less than minimum wage. Now we know what we're talking about when we urge our children to pray about each decision; get wise, godly counsel; and compare everything they do to God's Word and His principles of finances. We know from experience the severe consequences that can occur when those principles aren't followed.

We were six years into marriage before our Sunday school teacher showed us the Jim Sammons Financial Freedom Seminar (www.iblp .org), which literally changed our whole view of finances and family principles. We encourage others to go through the seminar, follow its biblical principles, and watch how God uses its teachings to strengthen their marriages and show them a clear life direction. I tell others the twenty-session seminar will be worth a thousand dollars for every hour they watch if they will apply the principles it teaches. I urge them not to make any major financial decision without watching it.

DREAMS FOR OUR DAUGHTERS

As our older twins, John-David and Jana, were talking one day about John-David's work with our community's Tontitown Area Volunteer Fire Department, Jana listened carefully as John-David described the various tests and challenges involved with the training. He's served with the department for about a year and a half, and he's had some interesting experiences.

"I might like to join the fire department too," Jana said.

Now twenty-one years old, Jana is one of our family's biggest daredevils. She's nearly fearless—except maybe when it comes to public speaking. Like the rest of the family, her twin brother admires her

John-David started Duggar Towing. He stays busy towing cars and fixing vehicles.

tremendously. A couple of years ago when Josh, Jana, and Jim Bob went skydiving, John-David wanted nothing to do with it—except for saying he would love to be a pilot so he could fly the plane. While Jana's personality may be as a risk taker who dares to do

anything, John-David has always loved to *drive* anything, from back-hoes and tow trucks to our forty-five-foot-long bus. He's mechanical and can fix about anything that breaks.

Our next-oldest daughter, Jill, has expressed interest in becoming a nurse, even though she has a fear of pain and needles. It's amazing where encouragement can come from when you have a dream. Jill was encouraged last year when she overheard a nurse at the hospital describing the start of her own career. The nurse said, "When I started nurses' training, I freaked out every time anyone came near me with a needle. Thankfully, you do get over it!"

While spending a lot of time at the hospital with Josie last year, Jill was able to see the joys of nursing, and she could talk with nurses who answered questions and provided encouragement. Both Jana and Jill have attended several births and have taken some doula childbirth-assistant training.

With this background in mind, it probably won't surprise you to read that when John-David decided to take a first-responder course last year to supplement his firefighter training, Jana and Jill decided to join the volunteer fire department and take the course too. They knew they could probably apply what they learned in the course to help their family as well as helping others in our community and those they encounter in their mission work.

During the training, each firefighter, wearing full gear,

We're so grateful for our oldest children at home: Jana, Jill, and John-David completed first-responder training with our local volunteer fire department.

had to crawl through a dark structure with a fifty-pound air tank on his or her back. The girls completed the task, although they came home completely exhausted afterward. "They're trying to kill me!" Jana joked.

Becoming volunteer firefighters and first responders has been a real learning experience for the girls, one that has stretched their capabilities. Now, with their first-responder training completed and their firefighter training continuing, Jana and Jill are responding with John-David to car crashes and assisting at medical calls. Just yesterday they worked a major brushfire in our area.

It has been a joy to see our older children expand their knowledge and experience and find ways to make a difference with their lives. We're eager to see how the Lord leads them during the next few years.

Our older girls, including Jessa, Jinger, and Joy-Anna, our "older daughter in training," have also developed many other skills. They know how to cook and bake for an army! If they chose to, they could develop a catering-style baking or meal-preparation service. They also are capable of teaching music lessons and working as paid musical performers, especially with the harp, violin, and piano. They have already had jobs providing background or featured music at weddings and other events. They can design and sew clothes for themselves and others. They can cut, perm, and style hair and might want to become licensed to provide those services to others.

We are totally supportive of our daughters deciding to become firefighters—or just about anything else they feel the Lord is leading them to do. Our goal is to provide all of our children with a solid scholastic education so they're prepared to pursue whatever additional training or education they feel led to do. Ideally, all of our children will have the skills and knowledge necessary to support themselves as adults.

Proverbs 31:10–31 says the virtuous woman is not a lazy person who sits around the house eating bonbons but a wise woman who is diligent in everything she puts her hand to. The virtuous woman not only manages her household well but also is very savvy at making business decisions and buying and reselling merchandise.

Early in our marriage we decided that if I (Michelle) worked, we would not become dependent on the money I earned. We both agreed that when we started having children, I needed to be home with them.

I had real estate and insurance licenses and I did substitute teaching at our local public schools. Jim Bob and I also worked together in our different businesses before Josh was born. Any income I earned went into savings or was used for extras.

I've kept my real estate license for more than twenty years now, and I still help Jim Bob in our commercial real estate business, visiting prospective properties with him and helping him evaluate their potential.

We are helping our daughters prepare for life. Once they're married and having babies, though, we hope they will make their families their number-one priority and will stay home to nurture their children. (Note: We personally know some single moms whom we highly respect, who have sacrificed financially by choosing a job that allows them to spend more time with their children. It hasn't been easy, but these women have raised godly children.)

BUTTERSCOTCH BROWNIES

One of Mama's favorites when made with Sucanat, a whole-cane sugar that can be used in place of either brown or white sugar.

1 cup brown sugar, or Sucanat (If using Sucanat, add 2 teaspoons water.)
¼ cup vegetable oil (or 3 tablespoons olive oil)
1 egg
1 teaspoon vanilla
¾ cup flour
1 teaspoon baking powder
½ teaspoon salt
½ cup nuts, chopped (optional)

Mix together the first four ingredients. Then add remaining ingredients and mix well. Spread into a greased 8 × 8-inch baking dish. Bake at 350 degrees for approximately 20 minutes. Do not overbake. Enjoy!

PREPARING OUR SONS FOR FAMILY AND COMMUNITY LEADERSHIP

We have raised our sons a little differently from our daughters. We provide more financial support for our maturing daughters than we do our sons. For example, we have provided our older daughters with cars when they get old enough to drive.

Our sons have to work to earn the money to buy their own cars. We want them to feel the pressure of needing to support themselves financially so that someday they'll be ready to support their families. (And, of course, given our frugality principles, none of the Duggars has ever owned a *new* car.)

Josh and John-David already own their own businesses: Josh and Anna have a pre-owned auto sales lot, and John-David owns a towing business. The two brothers work together, and they are often assisted by their younger brothers, especially Joseph and Josiah, who are watching and learning as they help clean, repair, and mark the cars offered for sale.

Our boys (and our girls as well) learned a lot of carpentry and construction skills while we were building our house. Every child eight and older had his or her own used cordless drill! The older boys have continued to develop those skills since our house was completed. In fact, as we were starting this book, John-David and Joseph were in Tennessee helping our friends the Bates family complete a remodeling project.

We enjoy watching our children consider all the possibilities for their future.

WHAT ABOUT COLLEGE?

As we were completing this book, several of our older children were beginning the process of earning a college degree through CollegePlus! This program lets students earn a bachelor's degree in a fraction of the time and for much less money than enrolling in a traditional brick-and-mortar college.

Students learn and study from home and then transfer a large bulk of their credit to an accredited college to complete their degree in the major of their choice. For example, our girls who want to pursue degrees to become registered nurses can complete their prerequisites online and then attend the local community college or the nearby University of Arkansas while living at home.

The beauty of a program like CollegePlus! is that the family does not have to be fragmented for the sake of college. Another advantage is that it lets our children earn a degree without being exposed to teaching that is opposed to a conservative Christian worldview. CollegePlus! fits our values and allows our children to keep moving forward in the special ministry God has entrusted us with. The program helps students understand and fulfill the unique calling and purpose God has placed on their life.

Through CollegePlus!, high school students can be dually enrolled in college and high school courses so that, through College Level Examination Program (CLEP) testing, they can graduate early from both.

I (Jim Bob) recently heard an alarming statistic that cited government figures indicating student-loan debt has surpassed consumer credit-card debt in the United States. Years ago we learned about the pitfalls of debt, so when it came to college for our children, using student loans was not a part of the equation. Recently a family friend from Ohio completed the CollegePlus! program and graduated from college with a bachelor's degree in business in two years; he graduated 100 percent debt-free.

CollegePlus! is helping students in all fifty states earn degrees that cost more than 70 percent less yet hold the exact same form of accreditation.

You can learn more about CollegePlus! by going to www.college plus.org/duggars.

PREPARING OUR KIDS TO DO GOD'S WORK

We heard someone say that the sign of good parenting is not what you do for your children but what you teach them to do for themselves. We are devoting our lives to giving our children a spiritual, practical, and academic education that prepares them to do God's work in their future homes and in the world.

It's fun to hear our children talk about what they want to be in the future, especially the youngest and middle children. Right now, for

instance, five-year-old Jackson says he wants to be a policeman so he can "shoot guns and help people." James wants to fly military jets with the Blue Angels. Jeremiah wants to be an artist while his twin brother, Jedidiah, dreams of being a missionary. Four-year-old Johannah says she wants to "play outside and eat yogurt."

Our son James wants to fly military jets with the Navy's Blue Angels when he grows up.

Eating yogurt is a good thing to do, both now and in the future. But like all parents, we want our children to know how to do much more than eat. We want them to know how to feed their own children someday. The more skills and knowledge we can help them acquire while they're growing up, the more capable they'll be someday of supporting their own families—and then teaching their own children to support themselves.

We love seeing the spark in a little one's eyes when he or she learns a new letter of the alphabet. We were thrilled to hear the excitement in Joseph's voice when he came home from the Bateses' Tennessee remodeling project and said, "I put all the siding on the south wall by myself." Our hearts are blessed when a child calls home from a poor village in El Salvador or a Christian outreach program in Indonesia and says, "I feel God telling me this is what He wants me to do with my life."

JOSH, THE ENTREPRENEUR

Our goal is to encourage and teach our children in a godly, love-filled, and fun way. When you bring them alongside you and mentor them to learn the same skills you possess, they're likely to feel inspired to

accomplish remarkable things. We saw that happen in our oldest child, Josh.

He spent his first few years growing up in the house that served as both our home and the office for our used-car business. When Jim Bob expanded into a towing service, we got Josh a little pair of coveralls, and he often rode along with Dad to pick up disabled or impounded cars. Jim Bob taught him the names of the streets as they were driving around town, and before long little Josh had become our own little human GPS.

We talked to our kids a lot about the benefits of having their own businesses when they grew up, but Josh didn't wait. When he was about seven years old, he started his own business: selling rocks on our front porch. With his enthusiastic brother John-David assisting him, he collected some choice specimens from our back yard, cleaned them off, and lined them up on the porch railing with a sign proclaiming, ROCKS FOR SALE!

When Michelle's sister, the boys' Aunt Freda, became their first customer, the boys were thrilled. She carefully selected five rocks for ten cents each and asked the boys to calculate how much she owed. When the purchase was complete, she told them, "I'm buying these rocks, but I'd appreciate it if you would keep them here for me. You can store them in your backyard, and I'll go look at them whenever I'm here."

The boys didn't quite understand why she didn't want to take her new rocks home with her but happily agreed to her request.

Sales fell off after that, but Josh was already on to something bigger. By that time we had accumulated several bicycles that we had bought used for the kids at different stages. They were always breaking down, so I was always fixing them—usually with Josh, John-David, and their sisters sitting in the little garage beside me, watching and handing me tools, and eventually using the tools themselves, especially Josh and John-David.

Josh saved up a little money and bought a broken bike at a yard sale. He fixed it with John-David's help and then parked it in the front

yard with a FOR SALE sign hanging from the handlebars. J & J (Josh & John-David) Bike Sales bought, repaired, and sold many bikes that year. Some days we would have as many as three bicycles parked in our front yard for sale at one time. As the business expanded Josh learned how to do more complicated repairs, sometimes necessitating a trip to the local bike store for parts.

We knew we were probably spending more money on gasoline driving Josh back and forth to the shop than he would make when he sold the bike, but the lessons he was learning were far more valuable.

I (Jim Bob) heard Josh tell someone recently, "My dad always had us boys under the hood of a car." It's true; I loved fixing things, especially tinkering with cars, and it was just natural that I would pass that knowledge on to my children. When you own a used-car business, you spend a lot of time working on cars, so almost every day our kids had an opportunity to stand beside a car or crawl under a car with Dad and talk about why something wasn't working and what needed to be done to make it run.

Josh's entrepreneurial creativity got a boost from something I had heard about the previous year. Another dad had offered his children a hundred dollars if they would give up drinking soda pop for one full year. I thought that was a creative idea that would probably pay for itself by saving dental expenses. Josh eagerly signed up for the "program," and by February 2000, he had completed the challenge and was ready to collect.

I told him, "Okay, you've earned your money, and I'm ready to give it to you. Or . . ." I paused like the best television game-show host, ". . . instead of that hundred dollars, I'll give you a car."

I showed him the 1974 260 Datsun-Z I'd ended up with on some kind of trade a year or so earlier. The car didn't run, but that hardly mattered; Josh was only twelve. It was probably worth about five hundred dollars, primarily for parts. I thought it would be a good project car for Josh to tinker with. I told him, "This deal is only good *today*. Take it or leave it."

He took the deal, and for the next year or so, he, my dad, and I worked together on the car frequently while Josh continued his used-bike business. A year later, when he'd built up some savings with his bike sales, he was browsing through the classified ads (a skill Grandpa Duggar and I taught him) and saw a 1984 Mazda pickup advertised for two hundred dollars. He asked me about it, and I said, "Let's go look at it."

*Before he was even old enough to drive, Josh (right), with the help of his dad,
and John-David (left) restored a 1984 pickup he bought for $150.*

On the way, I coached him a little on how to negotiate the price if he decided to buy it. He ended up buying it for $150, and we hauled it home on a trailer (it was another vehicle that wouldn't run). We worked on it and finally got it running, and Josh ended up driving it for two or three years after he got his learner's permit at age fourteen and then his license.

Soon he would be buying, repairing, and selling old cars the same way he had sold bikes. He had grown up riding around town in his family's cars with shoe-polish FOR SALE signs painted on the windows. Before long, he was driving his own SALE cars. But first he expanded into a sideline business: selling singing fish.

BIGMOUTH BILLY BASS

You surely remember those ridiculous head-bobbing, tail-flapping plastic fish so popular a few years ago. Each one was mounted on a wall plaque and embedded with a motion sensor so that when you walked by it, the fish, Bigmouth Billy Bass, would sing, "Take me to the river. Drop me in the water." (We would just like to add, if you *don't* remember those silly gag-gift items, count yourself fortunate. For a while they seemed to be everywhere, especially for the Duggars, as you'll soon see.)

One day Josh was in a big-box store with Michelle and, having the inherent Duggar radar for bargains, he found a clerk marking down a big stack of Bigmouth Billys in the clearance section; the new price was one dollar each after starting out at an original twenty dollars. Josh's entrepreneurial thoughts started spinning. He called me (Jim Bob) on Michelle's cell phone to discuss his idea.

I've taught our children that, in the world of buying and selling, you make your money when you buy an item at a good price rather than when you sell it. When we purchase something intending to resell it later, we always want to buy it under wholesale so that we can resell it at a bargain price later and still make a profit.

That day Josh called me, excited about the prospects of this new business venture. "I think I can sell them for at least five dollars each," he said.

He had saved up another $120 from his bike business, and that day he spent everything he had on his new investment, buying all but five of the store's Bigmouth Billys. John-David was along, and he chipped in five bucks to buy the remainder.

For quite a while after that, it seemed that "Take me to the river. Drop me in the water" was *always* playing somewhere in our home. The boys lined up ten of the singing and flapping Bigmouths, and the rest of the kids delighted in walking down the row of them and setting them off, one by one, until "Take me to the river" was ringing in everyone's ears.

Incredibly, Josh sold more than thirty-five of the singing fish for ten dollars each. Then he and Grandpa Duggar took a load of them to the local flea market, where he sold twenty more at five dollars each.

He still had eighty left. One day Grandpa took him to a convenience store, where he made a pitch too good for the chain's district manager to refuse. "Look, I've got these great items that retailed for twenty dollars, and you can buy them for three dollars each."

Josh made a nice profit off his Billy Bigmouth sales (although he may have inflicted some mental anguish on his family members, who had to listen to "Take me to the river" almost constantly for more than a month). His success in sales continued as he expanded into buying and selling cars from home, which eventually led to his opening the car lot.

Learning by Doing

John-David's story is similar to Josh's, except that John-David's interests lean more toward repairing and driving vehicles. As soon as he got his driver's license, he was driving our family's large bus around the country, and he now operates the towing business as well as occasionally helping Josh with the car lot. Anytime we need something fixed, we call on John-David.

It's so rewarding for us as parents to see our children using the skills we've helped them learn. We love being the ones who help prepare them for the future, and we can hardly wait to see what that future holds for them.

13

Daily Training, Tips, and Practicalities

Train up a child in the way he should go:
and when he is old, he will not depart from it.
—Proverbs 22:6

Each day is different in the Duggar home. There's almost always a planned schedule, but as I (Michelle) always say, there's the plan . . . and then there's reality. Our home is usually abuzz with what I call serene chaos. You have to be flexible to have a family of nineteen children!

We're often asked how we train our children and keep our family running smoothly through ordinary days. But the truth is, we don't really know what an *ordinary* day is, and things rarely run smoothly according to plan at our house. Most days do pass happily, busily, and, if all goes well, productively. If those are your parenting goals rather than perfectionism, we hope the ideas, tips, and principles we share here will be helpful to you. As always, we don't claim to be experts in parenting, but we're happy to share what we've learned along the way.

KITCHEN HELPERS

Children learn by doing, and they love helping their parents and older siblings *do* just about everything. That's how we've taught our children practical skills ranging from tire changing to cooking. We almost never

do anything alone; we've almost always got at least one and often more of our children alongside us. And we try hard to make working together fun.

Having a huge family means spending a lot of time in the kitchen. I (Michelle) certainly couldn't spend much time in there alone, not with a tribe of creative youngsters scattered around the rest of the house getting into mischief! So I taught the children to work with me.

Then, as now, when there are cans to be opened or potatoes to be scrubbed or bread slices to be spread out for sandwiches, our little guys are right there with me. Actually, they're usually in there with the older girls, who spent so much time in the kitchen learning to cook that now, they enjoy doing almost *all* of the cooking for our family, as well as most of the kitchen instruction for the little ones.

I have been amazed at what they have the younger kids doing—and the little ones love to be in the middle of everything, knowing they're helping. They love to put on their aprons and wash the lids of the cans before they're opened or scrub those potatoes. (Important tip: Spread a couple of towels on the counter beneath a plastic, flat-bottomed tub with a little water in it. *Don't* give them access to the faucet, and especially not the sprayer!)

The older girls have even found ways for the younger kids to do "dangerous" jobs (which are oh-so-exciting). Standing beside an older sister, the younger ones are sometimes given a small pair of kitchen shears and allowed to cut things like green onions or celery for a recipe. I never would have thought of doing that ten years ago, but it's such a joy now to see the children enjoying working together. The young ones feel needed and an important part of whatever is going on.

Of course there *are* times when, instead of helping, they need to sit at the kitchen counter watching and chatting with the big sisters as they work.

In our family everyone works together to keep our home running. Even the toddlers have little jobs to do (usually with a lot of coach-

Older children help, encourage, and mentor their younger siblings—or sometimes their younger niece, as Joy-Anna enjoys doing with our granddaughter, Mackynzie.

ing), such as putting their dirty clothes in the laundry bin. In our first book we described how we've grouped different ages of children, older with younger, into buddy teams that look out for each other, with the older ones making sure everyone's accounted for whenever we're traveling. Throughout the day the older ones help their younger team members with daily tasks such as toothbrushing, hair combing, music practice, and helping them pick out their clothes for the next day.

Everyone who's old enough has a "jurisdiction" he or she is responsible for—an area of the house to be cleaned or a chore to be done.

MENTORING AND EXPECTATIONS

Working alongside our children is a means of mentoring them. We show them how something's done. Then we watch them do the job, sometimes repeatedly, until we're satisfied they know how to do it safely and effectively. Then we turn them loose to do it on their own (maybe while secretly watching from around the corner or through the window the first few times). That's the way I (Jim Bob) taught our children how to do simple construction jobs when we were building our house (after our carpenter friend Clark Wilson taught me).

It's also how I've taught them to check the oil, fix a flat tire, and restock our big pantry after a trip to the market (a system based on what I learned during my years of working in a grocery store as a teenager and early in our marriage).

Yes, there are times when Michelle cringes as she watches one of

them take off on the lawn mower for the first time, but so far we've all survived those first-time experiences.

We told you earlier how Josh and John-David picked up on a host of life and career skills by spending lots of time under the hood of the car with their daddy. We've continued that same principle with the rest of our children, of almost always having at least one of them beside us whenever we're working.

Mentoring a child isn't the fastest way to get a job done. It's almost always easier to do it ourselves, but that doesn't provide the valuable teaching we want our children to experience. It comes back to that perfectionist mind-set. Parents need to realize that it's almost always more important for the child to learn something than it is for that task to be completed perfectly. It's a little hard for some parents to get past that attitude, but if all your child does is watch *you* do something, he or she is probably not going to learn how to do it successfully.

On the other hand, when children know their parents have high expectations of them as well as confidence that they can do what is expected of them, they can accomplish amazing things. Confidence is contagious! Knowing that their parents believe in them, children look forward to learning new things and conquering new challenges. Children love pleasing their parents.

An example of that occurred about five years ago, when Josh had just turned seventeen. We headed out in our older-model motor home on a month-long vacation to California. We made it almost twenty miles and then realized the twenty-foot-long camper trailer we were pulling behind the motor home was just too heavy to tow.

We called my (Jim Bob's) parents, and they brought over our fifteen-passenger van. We connected the camper trailer to the van and put Josh in the driver's seat. Following the motor home, he drove the van and pulled the trailer all the way to California, up and down the Golden State, and then all the way home to Arkansas. Quite an accomplishment for a seventeen-year-old! A lot of parents wouldn't allow their teenage son to drive a fifteen-passenger van pulling a twenty-foot trailer

We take our job as parents seriously—but that doesn't mean we can't be silly sometimes too, as we were with the Chicken Blessing Lady at a visit to Dollywood in Tennessee.

to California and back. But we had thoroughly taught Josh the responsibilities of being a careful driver, we expected him to take his job seriously, and we had confidence that he would succeed—which he did.

Another example is the commercial sewer-auguring machine we bought several years ago at a pawnshop. It seemed like once a month we had to rent an auger to clean out a drain at one of our rental buildings or we had to hire someone to do it for us. We negotiated with the pawnbroker and bought our own auger for a good price, and within a few months it paid for itself. I taught our older boys how to use the machine, sometimes lifting the auger up on a roof and running the snake down a roof vent, and other times running the snake through the main drainpipe after pulling an overflowing toilet.

It can be very nasty work with "stuff" splattering around, but we typically save a hundred dollars or more, and usually the clean-out job takes only thirty to sixty minutes. Now the older boys who have worked beside me are teaching the younger boys to help with this job.

CHORE CHECKING

We don't stress over a messy house. That's quickly obvious to all who visit us. I tell friends, "If you're coming to see *us*, come anytime. If you're coming to see the *house*, please give us two weeks' notice." Someone gave us a little sign that says, MY HOUSE WAS CLEAN LAST WEEK. SORRY YOU MISSED IT. Jana commented recently that we need two of those signs so we can put one by the front door and one by the side door.

We have no hope of having a perfectly clean house 24/7. But we do expect our children to work hard and do their best at their chores and the jobs we ask them to do. We try not to ask them to do something and then forget about it. When we give them a job, we expect them to check in with us when they're finished—or keep working until we see that they've completed the job satisfactorily.

Recently six of our older children were away at recitals or practices for recitals, and I (Michelle) gave our three youngest boys some jobs our bigger kids usually do. The boys had only rarely been asked to sweep the tile floor in our living room and our two kitchens (the one we call the "pretty" kitchen and the industrial kitchen where the serious cooking is done). I described what I wanted them to do and showed them some of the dirt or crumbs that needed to be cleaned up. Then I told them where to empty the dustpans and reminded them to call me for an inspection before they put away their brooms.

Each boy was assigned an area, and James drew the job of sweeping the industrial kitchen. The girls and I had done a lot of baking that day, and that floor was especially dirty, littered with flour and crumbs.

Although I knew James *wanted* to do a good job, I also knew he's a boy who is very easily distracted. When I didn't hear the sound of sweeping in the industrial kitchen, I called, "James, where are you?"

Sure enough, he had swept something interesting out from under one of the counters and paused momentarily to go get a brother or sister to admire his "find." Along the way, he stopped to see what Justin had swept up in the living room, and then he heard the sounds of another sibling doing something interesting in the playroom. After that, all thoughts of sweeping the kitchen evaporated.

I sent him back to his task, and in a few moments he came out with a big smile. "All done, Mama. Come and look," he said.

I stepped through the swinging door and smiled at him, standing there so sweetly with his broom. But as I looked around . . .

"Oops! I forgot to sweep that side," James said, scurrying over with the broom.

I left, and a little later, he called me to inspect his work again. The same thing happened. I didn't have to say anything. His eyes followed mine as I looked over the floor, and before I said a word, he spotted the areas he had missed. It was after many inspections that we finally agreed the floor was swept clean. *Then* he got a hug, thanks, and lots of praise for sticking with a difficult job.

We expect our children to do their best when we give them a job, and we check their work, both to make sure they're learning to do the job right and also so we can acknowledge and praise them for helping.

OBEDIENCE AND SELF-CONTROL

It's normal for everyone, especially children, to get distracted occasionally. But the older a child gets, the more we expect him or her to have the self-control to stay focused for longer periods. James was nine that evening he swept the industrial kitchen for the first time. It was a big job, and he is a high-energy boy. He's the one who is constantly losing his chore pack, losing his workbook, or losing whatever the thing was that he had in his hand just a second ago—and then losing track of what he was looking for when he sets out to find whatever he lost!

Still, he's learning that we expect him to work harder and focus more intently, and we're seeing steady improvement.

We start teaching our children

GROUND TURKEY SEASONING MIX

We use ground turkey instead of hamburger; it's cheaper and lower in fat. We add this seasoning mix and then use the ground turkey in recipes that call for ground beef. Delicious and healthy.

2 tablespoons nutmeg
2 tablespoons thyme leaves
2 tablespoons garlic powder
2 tablespoons sage

Put ingredients in a tightly covered container and shake until well blended. Label with these instructions:
½ teaspoon per 1 pound ground turkey seasoning mix
2 tablespoons ketchup
1 tablespoon soy sauce

In a skillet brown the turkey with the seasoning mix, ketchup, and soy sauce. Drain and serve, or use in other recipes calling for ground meat.

self-control at a very early age—often as early as eighteen months, when we start blanket training. It's a wonderful idea another mother shared with us years ago that trains little guys to entertain themselves and stay put for up to an hour or so. Usually this training begins with a blanket on the floor, but once the concept is understood it can be adapted to other places. For the Duggars, it means toddlers learn to sit quietly on a chair, entertaining themselves or listening to their siblings during family homeschool time. Or it might mean sitting at the kitchen counter watching Mama or the big girls cook dinner.

We described details of how to blanket train your children in our first book. In the time since that book has been published, we've heard from hundreds of parents who say it has not only helped bring peace and harmony to their busy homes, it's also taught their children to have self-control and self-discipline, to entertain themselves, and to be pleasant in almost any setting.

The important thing about blanket training is making it a *fun* experience for the child. While they're learning to stay in one spot and play quietly with a favorite toy reserved specifically for blanket time, it's crucial that they be praised for the good work they're doing. When our toddlers are sitting quietly at the table during school time, I (Michelle) often point out their accomplishment to their older siblings: "Look at Jennifer! Look how quietly she's playing with her toy while we do school. She's practicing such good self-control and obedience. Thank you, Jennifer."

And Jennifer beams as the praise falls upon her.

Once children gain self-control through blanket training, then activities such as attending church, eating out in restaurants, and visiting with guests become pure pleasure. They might be sitting on someone's lap, sitting in a high chair at the restaurant, or playing quietly beside Mama on the couch while she visits with guests; a blanket isn't necessary for blanket training!

This isn't to say we expect our children to sit silently like statues all the time. All of our children have been wigglers from time to time, and

we Duggars do love to talk and ask questions. But gradually, over time, the child learns to sit relatively still and maintain self-discipline while either listening to what's going on around him or her or quietly playing with that special toy or reading a favorite book.

Remember that the concept of blanket training hinges on the child learning that it is fun. That might include not only a special toy or book but also a little song to help the child "play" self-control. Four-year-old Johannah's favorite song right now describes a child who's sitting quietly when—oh no!—a wiggle worm comes crawling across her shoe! The silly song suggests that the child will "squash the wiggle worm" when she "feels the urge to squirm."

We also teach self-control as a part of potty-training. I remind the little potty-trainees that the operational definition of self-control is "*instant* [I clap my hands] obedience to the initial prompting of God's spirit."

In the same way, I tell them, they need to respond *instantly* (clapping my hands again) to that initial prompting of their little bodies telling them they need to head for the bathroom.

Even though they might not understand the big words at first, I say it so many times, always with the hand-clapping and other motions, that they soon catch on. I tell them, "My prayer is that when you're learning to instantly obey Mommy and Daddy that you'll also learn to instantly obey God when you feel His prompting in your spirit."

The wonderful thing is seeing the joy that comes over their little faces when they are successful at self-control.

We believe the joy that comes from succeeding at self-control leads to an understanding of the real meaning of obedience, which is defined on our character-qualities chart as "Freedom to be creative under the protection of divinely appointed authority." We don't force our children to sit still by making angry threats. Granted, there is a place for correction and reproof but never in an angry, condescending way. We want to lovingly teach our kids to sit still by praising and rewarding them for

choosing to practice self-control; that makes for lots less correction all the way around.

TRAINING AND FORGIVENESS

We praise our children's character in front of the family, a practice that multiplies the praise. But if a child has done something wrong, we talk to him or her privately, if possible. We don't believe humiliation is a beneficial part of the training process. Once we talk to wrongdoers privately and establish what consequences are necessary to learn this lesson, we have them go back and apologize to the one they wronged or the one who witnessed the situation. This step of humbling ourselves before others is a life lesson all of us must learn as part of having healthy relationships.

As parents, we've learned that if we are consistent in training our children during their toddler and preschool years, they will have learned basic self-control by the time they're school age. There are exceptions, but our experience has shown us the importance of being consistent. We've also learned that a lot of times it is the parent who is being trained to be consistent!

I (Michelle) am far from perfect. Like our children, I don't always have the behavior I know I should have as a godly mother. But my goal is to discipline consistently, correct lovingly, and then assure the child that everything is forgiven so he or she doesn't have to carry around guilt for that disobedience.

I urge parents not to use "rejection for correction"; don't use words or actions that put your children down, thinking that will train them to obey you. If we as parents respond wrongly by raising our voices, yelling, or exploding in anger, we train our children to act the same way; that reaction builds a wall between us, and it pushes the child away. Instead, humble yourself and ask forgiveness if you have responded the wrong way in correcting your kids, and tell them that by God's grace you are working to become the parent He wants you to be.

When I deal with our children with a loving response, even though they have misbehaved, I'm strengthening my relationship with them while also strengthening their relationship with God, whose Word lays out the concepts of self-control, discipline, correction, and forgiveness.

Here's an example of how it plays out for the Duggars: Let's say one of the little guys is disobeying and I'm busy fixing breakfast and don't deal with that disobedience right when it occurs. Ten or fifteen minutes later, that boy will probably do something else he knows he shouldn't. Then, a little later, he'll try to get by with something else, and by that time I'm irritated and find myself snipping and snapping, not just at the culprit but also at the ones who aren't misbehaving.

Finally I realize what's happening, and I take that child aside. When I'm correcting our children, I get down on their level and say, "Look in Mommy's eyes." When the boy has done that, I tell him, "You know what? God never intended for Mommy to feel this way toward you. It's my fault we got to this point because I didn't do what I should have done earlier. Remember earlier when I was cooking eggs and you did such-and-such and you knew you shouldn't have done that? Remember right after that, you did that other thing, and then a little later you did yet another thing? I should have stopped and corrected you right then! Because I didn't, I built up frustration and wasn't talking sweet. I'm sorry for getting frustrated and angry with you; I should have taken care of the first situation when it happened. Will you please forgive me for that?"

When they do, I ask, "What did you do that was wrong?" (appealing to their mind and conscience).

The little boy in our example might have a long list to confess if Mommy hasn't been consistent in her child training! Or, if it's a single incident, one of the little girls might say, "I hit my brother on the head and ran off with the toy—but I had it first!"

I ask, "Would you want someone to treat you that way?" (appealing to the child's heart).

"Noooo," the culprit replies.

"What should you have done?"

"Well, I should have . . . asked him to . . . please give my toy back?"

Sometimes I need to help them with the proper response to "What should you have done?" This is a teaching / training moment. It's so important for children to know not only that they did something wrong, but also how to make it right. We want them to learn how to handle themselves when they're in a similar situation in the future; we want them to know how to use the right approach to ask for something and to take turns.

Next I may ask, "Now what do you need to tell Mommy?"

Then I hear this sweet voice say, "Mommy, I was wrong for . . . Will you please forgive me?"

Next I decide on the appropriate consequences. If two children were arguing or fighting over a toy, for instance, often I'll say that neither of them gets to play with the toy for a few hours, or sometimes for the rest of that day. Then the little one is probably sent to find the toy-theft, head-bonked victim to offer an apology—and not just a quick, "Sorry." Duggar-style apologies include looking the wronged person in the eye and giving a description of the wrongful deed: "I was wrong for being selfish and for taking your toy and hitting you on the head. Will you please forgive me?"

Because all the children have been in the apologizer's shoes at one time or another, it's very common then for the "victim" to hug and encourage the brother or sister, accepting the apology; if they don't hug on their own, we ask them to do so. A few seconds later they're playing happily together again.

After everything is resolved and the apologies are made, there are lots of hugs and kisses with Mommy so they know no matter what they do, I still love them. At that point, the situation has been dealt with, and our relationship is restored. In contrast, if you don't come to the point of making things right with each other, then those offenses can build a wall and cause many future relationship problems.

Yes, this rather elaborate process can be tiring when it's required again and again, but the more the children are consistently trained in

the right response, the more natural it will become for them to do right in the midst of those weak or selfish moments, especially when they know without a doubt there *will* be a consequence for their wrong behavior. I believe that many times children don't respond right (outside of selfish and willful disobedience) because we as parents haven't lovingly trained, explained, modeled, corrected, or expected it from them.

In Part 4 of this book, I'll share more about how I strive to correct my children with patience and a soft voice.

CONFLICT RESOLUTION

With eighteen children living in our home, occasional bickering, tattling, and arguments are inevitable. But we've learned to resolve or even prevent a lot of those problems by following and teaching our kids the biblical method of conflict resolution.

Everyone probably knows an adult who's been estranged from his or her family for years because of some major or minor dispute that happened long ago—sometimes so long ago that the people involved no longer remember exactly how the estrangement started. We never want that to happen to any of our loved ones, especially our children. So it's important to us that they grow up knowing how to settle disputes in a way that nurtures their relationships with their siblings.

We stress to our children that their responses to any situation have consequences, either positive or negative. The Bible offers strong guidance on how we should communicate with each other and how we should respond when something is said or done that has the potential to upset us. The psalmist wrote, "Let the words of my mouth . . . be acceptable in thy sight, O Lord" (19:14). Our goal is always to speak to each other in a way that is pleasing to God. We're not perfect, so we don't always meet that goal. But we try to use our own and our children's lapses as teachable moments.

One of those moments happened recently when several of the children went into the woods near our home to play in their clubhouse.

Nine-year-old Jason rode his bike, and the rest of them walked. After they'd played there awhile, eleven-year-old Jeremiah hopped on Jason's bike and took off toward the house. Understandably, Jason wasn't very happy about his brother stealing his bike. He tore off after Jeremiah, yelling at the top of his lungs as he chased him all the way back to the house.

Before long, both boys were standing in front of me (Jim Bob), on the verge of tears. Jason said Jeremiah had taken his bike without permission. Jeremiah said, "Daddy, all of a sudden I realized I needed to go to the bathroom really bad." He insisted that as he jumped on the bike, he told Jason, "I have to borrow your bike. I'll be right back."

But Jason didn't hear Jeremiah. All he knew was that Jeremiah had taken his bike. Once I got both sides of the story, I asked the boys what needed to happen next. They looked at each other, realizing they'd both reacted wrongly so both of them needed to apologize. Jeremiah apologized for not communicating clearly and loudly enough to Jason about why he needed to borrow the bike. Jason apologized for reacting so harshly.

The incident taught the boys how important good, clear communication is, and how much damage a harsh reaction can cause. If that relatively minor in-

An argument between Jeremiah (shown here) and Jason over a borrowed bicycle created an opportunity for learning about apologies and forgiveness.

cident hadn't been resolved quickly, they could have stayed mad at each other all day (or longer), urging their siblings to align with them on one side of the argument or another. Instead, the two apologies cleared the air and wiped the slate clean.

Incidents like this one also give us opportunities, either at the time they occur or later during Bible time, to talk to our children about biblical principles of love, forgiveness, and conflict resolution. For instance, in the case of the borrowed bicycle, we talked later about Jesus' example of forgiving others even before they ask for forgiveness. Jesus said we are to forgive others for their mistakes just as God forgives us for ours.

We also remind our children that Jesus said we need to do something good for the person who has been mean to us, which is usually just the opposite of what we naturally want to do! But, we tell them, as you invest in your adversary's life, any bitterness you have toward him or her is removed.

ATTITUDE CHECKS

We try to stay vigilant about monitoring the mood and tone of communication going on in our home. If I (Michelle) hear one of the kids say something harsh or hurtful to a brother or sister, I try to quickly pull that child aside and say, "It's not like you to say something like that. Are you okay? Is there something on your heart that you need to talk with me about?"

Sometimes it seems half the family, especially that middle group of kids, can backslide into whining, arguing, and bickering, and it may continue awhile before we realize it's happening.

Some of that happened recently, with bad attitudes flashing back and forth and different kids saying things like, "You did so-and-so," and the other one answering, "I did not!" Somebody had apparently done something wrong or hadn't given a brother or sister a turn, or one had moved something that another sibling had meant to come back for later. Nitpicky things. One of them would come to me and report the situation, and I would say, "Go tell them I said to . . ."

Then someone else would come along and complain about someone else, and I would send another message back to the culprit. The bickering and tattling seemed to go on and on and on, and finally, it occurred

to me: *Michelle, what are you doing? These aren't the little ones who don't know how to fix arguments. These are kids you have trained for years to handle this kind of fussing peacefully among themselves. They know this is unacceptable. As the mom, you shouldn't be using your own energy handling a problem they know how to fix.*

By the time our children are eight to ten years old or older, they know they're not supposed to tattle about petty little issues to Mama or Daddy. When it's a three- and four-year-old, we'll take the time and spend the energy dealing with it, teaching and training them to resolve their own minor disagreements. But the bigger kids supposedly grew out of that stage long ago. They *know* how biblical conflict resolution works.

That day, we'd just gotten home from a long trip somewhere, and we were out of our normal routine. The house was in an upheaval because we were unpacking the bus, and a lot of the middle children were getting cranky and starting to nitpick at each other. Then came the tattling and complaining.

So here's what I had to do. I called the middle group of children together, the ones who were doing the arguing and not responding right to one another. Realistically, I could see that the situation was arising from our momentarily upside-down day as we tried to get back into our routine. But that didn't excuse their response. I knew I needed to help them get back on target.

I told them, "You know how to resolve disputes. I have trained you from the time you were little. I know it's crazy right now. I know our schedules aren't flowing right now as they should be. We're trying to finish unpacking. But I'm *not* going to allow you to revert back to those negative attitudes of arguing, complaining, and tattling on each other. The little ones are watching you to see how you handle feeling frustrated when things aren't going the way you want. So now, you tell me how you're supposed to handle the problem."

I replayed one of the incidents: somebody wasn't holding the dustpan as she was supposed to do to help the one who was sweeping the playroom. What *should* have happened? I asked.

"I should have talked politely to my sister and encouraged her to hold the dustpan like she was supposed to do before I came to Mama," the instigator said.

"That's right," I answered.

They know this because they've memorized Matthew 18 and it provides a biblical guideline for handling disagreements. It tells us when there's a disagreement, you go to your brother (or your sister) *alone*, and try to lovingly encourage him or her to do what's right. In kind, levelheaded words, point out the transgression with the goal of restoring your relationship. In other words, the victim is to ask the offender to do what is right, as God teaches us, and to turn his or her heart toward God. Matthew 18:15 says when that happens, "If he listens to you, you have won back your brother" (AMP).

That's how God says we work at conflict resolution. "If he'll hear you, you've gained your brother or sister," I tell our children. "If your brother or sister won't hear you, *then* you get someone to go with you—that's Mama or Daddy. One of us will come in at that point," I say.

"But if you come to me first with a grumbling, complaining attitude, tattling on your sibling—*That person is irritating me and I want to get him or her in trouble, so I'm gonna tell Mama*—and you haven't done step number one and tried to encourage your sibling to turn his or her heart toward God and do what is right, then *you're* not doing what is right and *you* will receive correction too."

We remind our children that they love one another. "And when you love someone, your heart's attitude is not that you want to get him or her in trouble; it's that you love that person so much, you don't want him or her to act wrongly. So first go to your brother or sister and try to work out your differences calmly and in a sweet voice. If that doesn't work, *then* come and get Mama or Daddy."

In a family this size we can't be dealing with multiple petty little disagreements all the time. After I (Michelle) had this talk with the middle kids, they knew that if they had a disagreement with one another they needed first to try to work it out agreeably themselves. They also

knew that if one of them came to me before that crucial first step was done, then both children were likely to be corrected—one for doing the wrong thing to begin with, the other for failing to try to resolve the issue peacefully before tattling.

After the talk that day, there was no more bickering. That middle group of children had been reminded that there would be praise and rewards for them as they show maturity and responsibility, but on the swing side of that, there would be consequences for those who knew the right thing to do but didn't do it.

By now, our children know that a peaceful, harmonious home is much better than one filled with acrimony and bitterness. Sometimes all it takes is a reminder that we are a family who loves one another and we enjoy being together and working together. They're learning that yes, they may end up being assigned to a job they don't really like and they got a tough job the last time chores were handed out. But when they do their job as though they're doing it for God (which they are!), without a complaining or murmuring spirit, they learn to feel the joy that comes as they accomplish difficult tasks.

They're also learning that it's much more fun to work as a team than alone. But being part of a team means they have to resolve petty differences quickly and kindly before the situation escalates and gets both of them in trouble.

To understand the importance of peaceful conflict resolution, children have to learn that their responses bring consequences: praise and rewards for the right response and temporarily unpleasant consequences for the wrong response. Teaching this lesson takes patience and consistency, and we admit to falling short occasionally on both counts. But we know that one of our God-given responsibilities is to train our children how to deal with struggles and challenges. When we succeed in doing that, we see the immediate payoff in a calmer, more pleasant home when we follow the biblical principle of conflict resolution.

SING A HAPPY SONG

During one of those "mommy moments" when I was tempted to let myself feel exhausted and overwhelmed by the job of being a good, consistent parent to all my children, I determinedly pushed myself in another direction. Instead of feeling discouraged, I reminded myself of the importance of speaking life and encouragement to my children and myself.

At that moment, a little song formed in my mind, a heartfelt offering of praise and worship that pulled my heart toward God and away from the pressures and challenges of being a busy parent to our many children. Thus the "Duggar Happy Family Song" was born:

> *We are a family, a happy, happy family.*
> *We serve each other every day.*
> *We are a family, a happy, happy family;*
> *We're building character God's way.*
> *God designed the family;*
> *He's given us His principles to follow faithfully.*
> *If we do as He commands,*
> *Our family will honor God and stand!*

Our children enjoy singing and playing together.

14

• Life Is a Classroom •

Those things, which ye have both learned, and received, and heard,
and seen in me, do: and the God of peace shall be with you.
—Philippians 4:9

Some of our young-adult children have already graduated, but we tell them they will never be finished learning. As a homeschooling family, we believe that life is a classroom and that a child's education continues 24/7 year-round.

For example, ever since we built our house, the boys and I (Jim Bob) are always examining how things are built and appreciating the creativity of different designs. One year we went through the Chesapeake Bay Bridge and Tunnel, and as we were driving, I was asking the kids how such a huge underwater tunnel could be built. Discussing the possibilities, we came up with a lot of clever speculations. Then we stopped at the visitors' center and found a book that described the amazing way they built it. (I don't want to ruin the surprise, so you and your family will have to look it up for yourselves.)

We encourage our children to be on the lookout for interesting puzzles and discoveries throughout each day. Sharing what they find with their family creates excitement and curiosity—and great learning opportunities. (That may be why little James got so excited about whatever it was he found under the counter that evening when he was assigned the job of sweeping the industrial kitchen. He just had to go

share the thrilling news . . . and thus, the sweeping was temporarily forgotten.)

When you have this kind of mind-set, school is much more appealing, and work can be fun. Plus, having a basic understanding of how things are made and how the parts work together helps you learn how to maintain things that are in your care. This kind of curiosity and understanding is how John-David has acquired such excellent mechanical ability.

WORKING TOGETHER

While we were living in Little Rock after Josie's birth, I brought a bunch of the children back to the Springdale house for a few days to take care of some appointments, and also because we had some jobs to do. For one thing, it was late March and the Christmas decorations were still up! We had left in such a rush after Josie was born that we hadn't taken time to put them away.

I wanted everything to be nice and clean when Michelle and the baby finally came home (which turned out to be nearly four months away), so I marshaled the troops and declared a cleaning day. I told them, "Let's get the house cleaned up so it looks nice for Mama and Josie when they get to come home, and then we'll do something fun."

At the time, I had no idea what that fun thing would be, but the kids know I enjoy coming up with creative new things for us to do together, so they hustled to get their assigned areas cleaned. When I carried a load of Christmas garland to the garage, I happened to see an old disc swing we had taken down when we moved from our house on Johnson Road. *Hmmmmm!*

I mentioned my idea to John-David, and he went to the shop and made it happen. He got out the old, used bucket truck we had traded for several years ago, and used it to tie the disc-swing rope high up in a tree in the front yard.

It wasn't long before the Duggar army had finished the cleanup

and everyone was lined up outside, waiting a turn on the grand new disc swing. And it wasn't just any ol' swing. It had about a forty-foot arc that swung out over the hillside, so riders could *really* swing high. Looking at the video shot by the TLC film crew later, I knew it was a

good thing Michelle hadn't been home to watch her children flying through the air!

The disc swing is just an example of how we make working together fun—either while we're working or in knowing there will be some kind of reward when we're finished, even if that reward is just the satisfaction of knowing we did a good job.

Of course, there *are* some challenges in kids having an attitude of discovery and an eagerness to share. Someone always has an exciting story to tell Mama and Daddy about something that happened or something that was lost or found or

We try to teach our kids by example to work hard—and then play hard too. A handful of our brave kids followed Jim Bob's bungee-jumping lead.

eaten or spilled or broken or stuck in someone's hair or found in the freezer beside the Popsicles. It takes a lot of patience and also some finesse to listen to these stories while also trying to get out the door to go to a doctor's appointment or round up all the other kids to come to the dining table or get everyone on the bus so we can go on a field trip.

Molding children into enthusiastic workers requires that we, as parents, not only make the work fun whenever possible but also that we make the children feel appreciated for what they're contributing to our family effort. We also learned long ago that there's no place for a perfectionist attitude in the Duggar domain!

When I (Michelle) was a new mom, I thought I had to keep my house in order constantly or else I just wasn't a good wife and mother. Nowadays, if I can walk through the hallway without tripping over something, I say the house is clean enough, even though there may be dust everywhere I look. I had to grow into that attitude, but my life is so much easier now that I have.

We don't fuss at our family continually about keeping the house clean, but there are chores that have to be done every day, and we're training the children that everyone needs to help. Yes, it takes extra time and work to train a seven- or eight-year-old to do a job correctly, and the truth is that he or she isn't going to do it perfectly. On the other hand, we've learned that once a clever seven- or eight-year-old figures out to do a cleaning job with that little child-sized broom and dustpan, he or she can whiz around and get into places we could never dream of getting to with our adult-sized broom.

Even the little guys like having a "jurisdiction" so that they scurry around, doing their part when our family goes into quick-clean mode. Everyone pitches in, and it feels oh-so-good to look around and see what we've accomplished. We can mess the house up in a hurry, but we can also clean it up in a hurry! That cleaned-up state might last only five minutes, but it's wonderful while it lasts!

We shower our workers with lots of encouragement, praise, and motivation—maybe including the promise of doing something fun together, like go to the park when the work is done. Or maybe each one gets a piece of candy, or perhaps just a hug and a big "Thank you. You are such a big help to me!" Other times, maybe we'll pay someone five dollars for cleaning out the van or one dollar for being the one who finds a lost item. They don't get a reward for helping every time, because a reward is a *gift*, not something that is *due*. We teach them that sometimes the reward is simply the satisfaction of knowing they did their job well.

Sometimes people ask if we give our children set allowances, and the answer is no. In general, our children earn money when they work

for it. We believe that, if we gave our children what they want without helping them learn to earn it, we would stifle their drive to work. The result could be self-centered, lazy young people.

LEARNING TO SERVE OTHERS

Of all the things we want to teach our children, the two most important are (1) to love God and (2) to love others. We work hard to instill in our children a ministry mind-set and a heart for others, and we try to give them lots of opportunities to put that mind-set into action. Otherwise, it's like teaching the children about fishing but never *going* fishing. In contrast, when they "put feet to their dreams," when they go out and actually minister to others, it opens up a wonderful world of servanthood to them. They develop a desire for helping others and meeting others' needs.

The work our children, including Jill, did in El Salvador included cleaning up the debris created by a terrible hurricane-induced mud slide that had buried several villages.

We want to expose our children to a variety of ministry settings to help them realize that opportunities to serve others are everywhere. They've used their hands directly to help restore homes and villages after a hurricane-induced mud slide in El Salvador, and they used their voices to answer phones for a call-in radio telethon for Arkansas Children's Hospital. They've helped prepare and serve food for the homeless, and they've played in musical-recital fund-raisers for a variety of charitable causes. They've helped widows and disabled

residents of our area with home repairs and yard work, and they've played with children in homeless shelters.

Striving to have a ministry mind-set while believing that all of life is a classroom means we're always looking for ways to help our children gain knowledge and develop skills that will help them serve others.

DUGGARS ON A MISSION

Earlier we mentioned the mission trips several of us have made to various parts of the world. That work has been tremendously rewarding, and has caused some of our children to consider becoming missionaries when they grow up.

The trips happened due to our friendship with Mike Schadt, who had been a missionary to Italy. When he got back to the States several years ago, he volunteered at a Florida college to provide free, noncurriculum classes to teach international students how to speak and read English. Because the classes were voluntary, he decided to use the Bible as the class's "textbook," so while he was teaching English to these international students, he was also exposing them to God's Word.

One of Mike's first students was Alex Lara, a Salvadorian man who had "won" a year-long trip to America to receive health training he could use back in his own country. He enrolled in Mike's English class and not only learned to speak English but also ended up developing a relationship with Christ because of Mike's kindness and his sharing the Bible. When Alex was preparing to return to El Salvador, Mike said to him casually, as so many of us do, "If you ever need anything, let me know."

A few weeks later, when Alex was back in El Salvador, he contacted Mike and asked if he might come down and help his people. Mike gathered up some friends and made the trip. What he saw inspired him to set up SOS Ministries, which has organized informal groups of Christian friends who have traveled to El Salvador dozens of times since then to provide service and ministry to the needy people there.

An attorney friend of ours, Todd Hertzberg, is one of the part-

time SOS missionaries who invited me (Jim Bob) to come along on a trip to El Salvador about five years ago. Josh and I went with a Christmastime group that took food to families in one particularly impoverished area where the people lived in shacks and shanties with no running water and, at the time, no electricity. Todd and his family and the SOS group also hosted a Christmas party for the children of the area, complete with gifts for the two-hundred-plus youngsters who attended.

By that time, Mike's little ministry had constructed a community church building that also serves as lodging for the mission groups when they're there, with volunteers sleeping on mattresses on the floor. Most bring their own pillows and bedding, and they know, going in, they'll be taking cold showers and surviving on the bare necessities. Our group bought beans, rice, cooking oil, and other staples at local stores and distributed the food to several poor families.

What Josh and I saw and did on that trip changed us; it strengthened our desire to serve in that area of need. I realized that this kind of experience is worth every penny it costs us because we're doing much more than investing our financial resources in the people we're serving; we're also investing in the lives of our children as we let them see the tremendous rewards of serving others not only with their money but also with their lives.

We returned to El Salvador the next two Christmases, taking Josh, Jana, John-David, and Jill the second year, 2007, and a Duggar group of twelve in 2008 (myself plus ten of our older children as well as Anna, who by then was married to Josh).

Having heard their siblings' stories about the families they'd met in El Salvador, especially their comments about how much the children there loved to play soccer, the Duggar kids who got to go on the trip in 2008 prepared by emptying their piggy banks and family accounts to buy soccer balls. They pooled their money and bought all the balls they could afford and then packed them, deflated, in a large duffle bag along with a small air pump.

The work we did there continued to open our eyes and touch our hearts. The poverty is so deep, the standards of living so low. One afternoon as we crossed the river we saw a woman and a little girl—we assumed it was a grandmother and granddaughter—washing their clothes and their dishes. Others were drawing drinking water out of the same stream that the village sewage empties into. Realizing how these people are living made us not only more aware of the tremendous needs of those we'd come to serve but also humbled us as we thought of how easy life is for us in America, with hot running water, washing machines, dishwashers, and flush toilets.

A similar realization occurred as some of our kids helped restore an area in El Salvador in December 2009 where a huge mud slide had devastated a village. The slide had occurred without warning in the middle of the night, rumbling through the village and destroying dozens of homes before many residents had time to flee. They met one family who had lost a young mother-to-be. The rest of the family members that lived nearby had managed to escape, but the young woman, eight and a half months pregnant, couldn't get out before the house was crushed. Her family never saw her again.

Helping one resident of the village dig through the rubble of his demolished house, our kids were stunned to see how excited he was when they brought him a broken plate and a bent fork. They were the only things he was able to salvage from his former home.

Once again our group helped host a big Christmas party for the children of that area. We also delivered food to an orphanage there and enjoyed meeting the children, even though their stories are heartbreaking. Some of them had lived in the orphanage all their lives; others had ended up there due to parental abuse and neglect, or parental death.

Those children in the orphanages profoundly impacted the Duggar kids. The adolescent girls' stories were especially devastating. They cried, telling some of our children that they knew they had reached the age, usually twelve or so, when there was no hope of being adopted into a loving family, a legal process that in El Salvador can take four to six

years. When they reached the age of eighteen their only choices would be to stay at the orphanage and become a nun or leave, a decision that would probably mean they would be homeless and would have to survive on their own.

TAKING A CHANCE

December 2009 was when I (Jim Bob) stayed back in Little Rock with Michelle during Josie's birth and a Duggar group of fifteen made the Christmastime trip to El Salvador (the ten oldest Duggar kids plus my niece Amy and her friend as well as our friends Mandy, Amara, and Heidi Query).

Todd Hertzberg and his four children wanted to make the annual Christmas party even merrier for the two hundred children expected to attend. By that point, Alex had sent Todd a list of the names and ages of all the children in the village. Todd decided to attempt something a little risky: they would gift-wrap all the Christmas gifts they were taking to the children and put each child's name on his or her gifts.

It was risky because security agencies advise travelers not to bring gift-wrapped items on airplanes, warning that they may have to be opened for inspection. The Duggar kids knew that was a possibility, but with the hope of making Christmas extra special for the children, they decided to take the chance that they could make it through security with the personalized, gift-wrapped packages.

Lots of Christmas shopping occurred before the 2009 trip as the Hertzbergs and Duggars worked to accumulate enough gifts for two hundred children. During the next couple of days, as the children waited anxiously to see if Michelle's health would improve enough for them to be able to make the trip, they spent many hours working with other members of the group wrapping all the gifts, labeling them with each child's name, and attaching a personalized note that Todd Hertzberg had written in Spanish to explain the true meaning of Christmas.

In earlier years, gifts for the children's Christmas party had been hurriedly dropped into gift bags after the group arrived in El Salvador. But in 2009, Todd shared his wish that each child's gifts could be *wrapped*, making them extra special. Most of them had probably never received a wrapped Christmas gift, he said. Todd wanted them to have the joy of tearing the paper off a present. The truth was, most of the children probably had never received *any* Christmas gifts before Todd and his family started the annual Christmas party.

So all the gifts were wrapped, and the last thing each gift wrapper did was write his or her own name on the gift tag, wishing the child a blessed Christmas, adding yet another little token of personalization.

Our older children were very excited to learn on Monday before their scheduled Tuesday departure that they would still be going on the trip.

Their flight from Arkansas to Houston took off more than an hour late, but John-David had asked the gate agent at the Northwest Arkansas Regional Airport to call ahead and beg the Houston crew to hold their connecting flight for the Duggars' party of fifteen. When they landed in Houston, the airline had electric carts waiting to whisk them off to the international-departures terminal, a great relief for all of them. But still they wondered, *Will our luggage make the connection? And even if it does, will we be able to get those gifts through customs in El Salvador?*

Their flight landed in San Salvador about 11 p.m., and they were both astonished and relieved that eventually all thirty pieces of their checked luggage showed up on the baggage belt. But they still had to get through customs, and they all knew that in previous years, some of their luggage had been opened and inspected. If that happened now, they wondered, would the customs inspectors insist on unwrapping all the gifts?

As they entered the customs area, a uniformed airport employee greeted them in perfect English. Amazingly, he had been there the year before when the Duggar party had landed, and he remembered them. He told some of the group he had learned to speak English by watching American television. He helped them collect their luggage and head toward the customs line, explaining that as each incoming passenger

goes through the turnstile, he or she was to press a large lighted button. The automated system selects those whose luggage will be inspected; if the light turns green, the passenger is admitted without further delay. If the light turns red, he or she is routed to the inspection area.

Given all the prayers that had been going up ever since the Duggar group left Arkansas, is it any wonder that the inspection button was broken on the night they landed in San Salvador?

Of course, customs officials could still order their bags to be opened. The Duggar kids credit their free-spirited cousin Amy with helping them through that situation. She was at the head of the group, and when she stepped up to the stern-faced custom official's podium, he asked her if she spoke Spanish.

Amy smiled her charming smile, shrugged in her good-natured way, and said apologetically, "Taco, burrito, enchilada?"

The official stared at her a long moment. Then he broke into a huge smile and waved them all through. Not a single bag was opened, and every gift remained wrapped!

El Salvador has been an extraordinary learning experience for our children, and now they're eager to take their servants' hearts to other places. As we were finishing this book, our oldest twins were returning from a month-long mission trip to Singapore, Malaysia, and Indonesia.

Michelle and I both have said that missions are among the greatest life experiences for our children. It is truly more blessed to give than to receive.

THE DUGGAR PACKING SYSTEM

We've learned a lot from our mission trips and other travels, and a lot of that knowledge pertains to packing! It's quite an undertaking to plan a trip for as many as twenty-one Duggars (our nineteen children and ourselves; we're glad that when Grandma Duggar, Josh, Anna, and Mackynzie come along, they do their own packing!).

So many people have asked us for travel tips that we decided to

include some of our favorites in this chapter. First, a few comments about our family's clothing preferences. We've already described our emphasis on modesty and our girls' decision to wear skirts that come below the knee and non-sleeveless tops with high necklines. Our boys usually wear long pants (although sometimes it seems they're growing so fast that long pants become high-water pants overnight!).

As our daughters Jessa and Jinger have gotten older, they have used their fashion sense to revolutionize our wardrobe. They have started their own Duggars' Modern-Modest clothing line. Given their creative ideas and enthusiasm, we expect it soon will be sweeping the country!

During their shopping trips, they have found many combinations of newer style clothing that are very cute and also modest.

They also gave the boys new hairstyles, and they're trying to get Dad to change his as well. So far they haven't been able to convince him to give up his hairspray and to start using forming crème!

Jim Bob and I plan out the trip, but when it comes to actually packing for the trip, we leave that up to the Duggar family travel experts: Jessa and Jinger, our organizational specialists. They have developed some efficient systems of planning and packing.

The system they use varies with how long our trip will be, how we're traveling, and what we'll be doing. But no matter what system they use, packing usually begins in our living room, which is just a few steps away from our laundry room and family clothes closet. (See our first book, *The Duggars: 20 and Counting!* for an explanation of how we came to use a family clothes closet and how it works.)

The girls designate a spot in the living room for every person they're packing for; since Jim Bob and I pack for ourselves, as do Grandma Duggar, John-David, and the other older girls, that usually leaves eight boys (Joseph through Jackson) and five girls (Joy-Anna through Josie) to pack for.

Once the spots are designated, they talk about how many days we'll be away and what clothes will be needed. Generally we wear the same clothes everywhere we go, whether it's a casual or dressy occasion; we

just try to dress in a way that's comfortable enough for fun times but also looks nice enough for public appearances. The exception is when we're heading to a function where the guys need to wear their suits. (We buy most of our clothing at thrift stores, but the guys' suits were purchased new for Josh and Anna's wedding in 2008. They were a gift from Anna's parents, who got a wonderful bargain from a friend who owns a clothing business.)

If the children will be giving a musical performance somewhere, Jinger and Jessa will probably make note of it so that everyone can color coordinate that day.

When flying, we are typically gone for three to five days. The girls will stack and roll one day's pants for all eight boys in one plastic store bag (the kind you get at grocery and discount stores, and one day's shirts in another. These bags are given labels such as "Joseph thru Jackson pants/Tuesday." They do the same thing for the girls, selecting tops and skirts or dresses, as well as matching hair bows. Then the plastic bags are loaded into suitcases. Packed this way, all boys' clothes fit into two large suitcases, and the girls' into one. (We tie matching, bright-colored ribbons on all of our suitcases so they're easy to spot on the baggage carousel.)

When we get to the hotel, all we have to do on Tuesday is open one shirt and one pants bag, and all the boys have their clothes for that day. We usually have five rooms (preferably with two sets adjoining), and the girls deliver the next day's clothes to each room before bedtime, including a bag of underwear and a bag of socks for the boys. Everyone knows to leave dirty clothes in the corner of the bathroom. At the end of the stay all the dirty laundry is collected in white plastic garbage bags, which are tied and thrown into suitcases to be washed when we get back home.

When we're traveling by air, the last thing the girls do once everything is packed in suitcases is weigh them. We don't want to have to pay for any overweight bags! So they bring out the bathroom scale and check each bag. A typical Duggar road trip requires ten suitcases weighing a total of four hundred to five hundred pounds!

For road trips, the girls sort the clothing differently. For instance, they will use the racks in the bus cargo compartment for hanging dresses and shirts, and each boy will have his own bag for pants. We pick out the day's clothes from the compartment the night before.

The girls pack a pair of play shoes and a pair of dress shoes for each boy. Our girls like having a variety of shoes. Jessa and Jinger may take twenty pairs of shoes for the four youngest girls; their shoes need to match those cute little dresses! When we're gone more than a week or so, we plan on doing laundry every three or four days.

As you can imagine, it takes a while to get everything packed; sometimes the Duggar luggage holds as many as a hundred shirts, another hundred pairs of pants, plus more than fifty pairs of shoes! For longer trips, the girls start packing a week before we leave, which means our living room may be covered with stacks of clothes for several days. But their clever systems always work well for us.

A VERY IMPORTANT TRAVEL ITEM

A few years ago we learned about another important thing we need to take when we travel, besides a few hundred pounds of clothes, shoes, diapers, and other stuff. The lesson came when we were traveling out west and Jim Bob signed us up for a family airplane tour over the Grand Canyon.

Our flight was scheduled for early afternoon, and we had just enjoyed a big lunch at McDonald's with burgers, fries, and shakes. Then we boarded the small plane for the breathtakingly scenic experience. That day the air was choppy, and we were the last flight allowed because of all the turbulence. We bounced up and down the whole time, and most of us ended up carrying our lunches off the plane in motion-sickness bags! So now we try always to remember to bring along some motion-sickness "Sea-Bands" to wear on our wrists—with throw-up bags as backups!

PART 4

• Big Hearts, Full of Love •

Thou shalt love the Lord thy God with all thy heart,
and with all thy soul, and with all thy mind.
This is the first and great commandment.
And the second is like unto it,
Thou shalt love thy neighbour as thyself.

—Matthew 22:37–39

15

Protecting and Cherishing Our Relationships

And so faith, hope, love abide . . . ,
these three; but the greatest of these is love.
—1 Corinthians 13:13 AMP

Our goal is to base everything we say and do on God's kind of love. That kind of attitude comes easily when everything's rosy, but trials can test almost anyone's faith. We've experienced that kind of trial ourselves in the last few years as we've endured some stresses and challenges, including major and minor crises.

When Michelle's mother died in 1991, we experienced for the first time the grief that comes from losing a beloved member of the immediate family. Our oldest child, Josh, was only three years old when she died; the twins were toddlers, and Jill was just a baby. Today, none of them remember that difficult experience at all.

When my (Jim Bob's) dad got a malignant-brain-tumor diagnosis, we were relieved when Mom and Dad agreed to move in with us so we could help with Dad's care. We prayed for healing, knowing that God, who made each one of us, can heal us supernaturally if He chooses. Or He could give the doctors treatments to use to promote Dad's healing.

Except for our temporary moves to Little Rock when I was in the legislature, we had lived in the same area of northwest Arkansas as my parents throughout our marriage, and our children grew up feeling very close to Grandma and Grandpa Duggar. The kids were delighted

to have their grandparents move in with us at the beginning of 2008, and because Grandpa was still able to function normally for months, the children got to spend a lot of special time building memories with him. It probably didn't really sink in until the last few months of his illness that he was, in fact, dying.

My mom devoted herself completely to taking care of his personal needs, protecting his privacy and his dignity, and asking (or allowing) us to help only when it was absolutely necessary. By February 3, 2009, when we celebrated his birthday with the Bates family after the ice storm, he was unable to stand or speak, but he knew it was his birthday and obviously loved being the center of the two big families' attention. He beamed when Josh announced that Anna was pregnant and a new generation of Duggars was on its way.

A HARD BLESSING

We grieved, knowing Dad's death was imminent, and we couldn't help but think how it would happen and how it would impact our children. After all, we were determined to honor his wish to die at home rather than in the hospital, and our home, at that time, was full of more than thirty children, our own plus the Bateses'.

All we could do was shower Dad with all the love we felt for him and ask God to prepare us and the children for what lay ahead. Then God, in His great mercy, made that hard event as easy as it could have been.

The Bateses were still staying with us the week after Dad's birthday. The ice storm had caused such devastating damage in our area, there was plenty of work for talented tree trimmers like Gil and his sons. They are our dear friends, and we loved having them there. On the morning of February 9, however, our house was almost empty—rare for the Duggars. Gil and his boys were working, and Kelly had taken the rest of the Bates family to visit a nursing home. All of our children except baby Jordyn, Jennifer, Jessa, and John-David had left for their violin group lessons.

Normally at that time of day our house would be bustling with activity and noise as the children practiced piano, harp, or violin or talked about their school assignments. That morning, when our home was empty and unusually quiet, Grandma's voice suddenly echoed over the intercom: "Jim Bob, come here!"

I rushed for the stairs, but John-David was already ahead of me, responding as instinctively as I did. Michelle followed as soon as she'd finished diapering the baby.

"He's gone," Mom said simply, looking up from Dad's body as we stepped through the door to their room.

Several days earlier, we had made arrangements for how we would handle Dad's death at home. There was no need to call an ambulance; instead our dear friend Dr. Murphy came to make the pronouncement and summon the coroner. Then the funeral home staffers removed Dad's body. While our hearts ached to know Dad would no longer be with us, we were comforted to know that, as Christians, we would all be together in heaven someday.

On that difficult morning, we were so thankful all this happened while the children were away. Still, they had to be told, and when they returned from group lessons late that afternoon, we gathered them in the girls' upstairs bedroom, where I gently shared the news that Grandpa Duggar had passed away.

All of the older ones took it as well as possible; we had tried to prepare them ahead of time, telling them Grandpa was very ill and would probably be going to heaven soon. It would be sad for us when he died, we had told them, but the Bible tells us we don't have to grieve like those who have no hope of eternal life. We believe Jesus' promise that we will see Grandpa again in heaven; Grandpa had asked God to forgive him of his sins and had given his life to Him. We are grateful to God for all the wonderful, fun times we had together.

"We're all going to die one of these days unless the world ends and Jesus comes back and takes us straight to heaven with Him," I (Jim Bob) had told them. "It's hard to lose someone we love. We'll be

sad because we'll miss Grandpa; that's normal. But we have to be happy for *him* because at the very moment he dies, his spirit will be in a better place where there are no more brain tumors, no sickness at all. And someday we *will* see him again."

Despite all those preparatory talks, the news was especially difficult for our younger children to grasp. "Grandpa's down in his bedroom," said Jackson, who was four at the time.

"No, Jackson, he's not," I answered. "I'm sorry. He's not there."

"I just know he's there," Jackson said, and he wouldn't believe otherwise until he had gone downstairs to look for himself.

A couple of days later, before the visitation at the funeral home, I gathered the family again to prepare them for this new and difficult experience.

"When we get there, you're going to see Grandpa's body, lying in the casket," I said. "But remember, that's just his shell. His spirit is already in heaven with Jesus, and he's happy and healthy again. There's sadness for us, but Grandpa's not sad."

For the same reason that Josh and Anna had allowed the TV crew to film their wedding four months earlier, we invited the crew to film Dad's funeral. Both events showed the importance of our family's foundation of faith as we commemorated two emotional milestones, one joyful, one sad.

As parents, we wish we could spare our children every hard and hurtful event in their lives, but we know that's not realistic or even preferable. It's important for youngsters to grow up overcoming occasional difficulties so they learn they are capable of doing so. We know it was hard for our oldest boys, Josh, John-David, and Joseph, to serve as three of their grandpa's pallbearers. It was hard for *us* to see them in that role; but at the same time we felt proud of our sons for carrying out that job with dignity and love.

The memorial service wasn't totally sad, however. Several friends shared colorful stories about Dad's fun-loving personality, laughing about his pranks and jokes. The funeral director even joined in; he

printed this picture of a ketchup bottle on the back of the service leaflet.

J.L. loved ketchup. And just like ketchup, he made everything just a little bit better, too!

Even though the service included lots of laughter, when it was my turn to speak, I told the gathering that Dad probably wouldn't have liked it. "He hated funerals," I said. "In fact, he probably wouldn't be here today if he didn't have to be."

TALKING ABOUT FEELINGS

We talked a lot about Grandpa in the weeks following his death, and some of those memories continued to produce occasional tears. I managed to maintain my composure most of the time, but I would cry when I remembered many of the special times with Dad, and sometimes I let our kids see my tears. I wanted them to know it was okay to be sad.

My dad's death was our children's first real experience with that type of grief. I wanted our kids to understand that God gave us an amazing array of feelings, and it's natural to have them. The shortest verse in the Bible, John 11:35, is "Jesus wept," which describes Jesus' response when His close friend Lazarus died. If Jesus expressed His emotions by crying, then we know it's important for us also to express our emotions during the loss of a loved one.

PUMMELED BY LIFE STORMS

Josie's premature birth and the subsequent challenges we faced as we tried to take care of her and also meet the needs of the rest of our big family was an ordeal we could never have anticipated or prepared for. It was a time when we sometimes felt as though we were lost in a maze of questions—about decisions we had already made and decisions we were having to make in emergency situations.

We prayed constantly for our little micro-preemie Josie, for our marriage, and for our family. We prayed that Josie would survive if it was God's will, and that the rest of us, by God's grace, would be able to survive our lives being turned upside down.

Our relationship with each other was strained as we struggled to cope with our need to protect and nurture our large family, and also help our sick little baby to survive. Jim Bob and I (Michelle) are accustomed to spending a lot of our time together and with our family. That closeness means we maintain a comfortable connection; we generally know what the other one is doing. But from December until July, our time together was limited. I spent many long days and nights at the hospital with Josie while Jim Bob went back and forth between the hospital and the Little Rock house, checking on our family there, or back and forth between Little Rock and Springdale, managing home and business concerns. Jim Bob and I spoke often by phone, but it wasn't the same as face-to-face communication and companionship.

Then, as one period of anguish seemed to be lifting and Josie was finally recovering, we suffered another heartbreaking loss. Shortly after Josie was discharged from the hospital the first time—and then rushed back to the NICU by ambulance less than forty-eight hours later—I received a call from my sister Pam in Ohio. She said that our father, eighty-four-year-old Garrett Ruark, had fallen and broken his hip.

Daddy's health had been fragile for the past few years after incurring serious injuries in a head-on car crash with a driver who was strung out on methamphetamines. We had just finished building our current

home when the crash occurred, and we gladly moved Daddy into our first-floor guest room.

He lived with us several months. As with Grandpa and Grandma Duggar, our children loved having a grandparent nearby to talk, read, and play games with. Eventually my siblings invited Daddy to live with them in Ohio, his home turf, so he moved up there.

When Daddy fell and broke his hip I longed to rush to his bedside, but I was busy day and night helping Josie, and we knew he was in good hands. At that time, Josie's lactose intolerance had not been diagnosed, and I was still pumping milk every three hours during the day and about every six hours at night. When I wasn't in the "pumping room" at the hospital, I was in the NICU feeding Josie her bottle, talking to her doctors and nurses, or providing nonmedical care for her that I, as her mother, wanted to do.

Daddy's condition deteriorated into pneumonia, and with each worsening report I felt more anguish, torn between wanting to be with my father and my baby. By then Josie had been discharged from the hospital for the second time, and she and I were staying in the Little Rock house to be near the hospital in case problems arose.

Jim Bob and the rest of the family had left nearly three weeks earlier on the whirlwind trip out east to the homeschool conference. Their trip also included a stop at the home of the Bates family near Knoxville and a day spent in Albany, Georgia, where the children appeared as extras in a Christian movie, *Courageous*, being filmed by Sherwood Pictures, the ministry of Sherwood Baptist Church that has also produced the popular Christian movies *Flywheel*, *Facing the Giants*, and *Fireproof*.

Now they were back home in Springdale, where twelve of the kids were recovering from chicken pox.

The day Daddy died I was alone with Josie in the Little Rock house. The old, three-story mansion we rented had never seemed emptier than it did that day.

Josie had to be fed the Pregestimil formula every three hours. While she was still in the NICU, I did most of the daytime feedings but usu-

ally came home to sleep at night and let the nurses take care of her feeding until morning. After her discharge, she and I moved to the Little Rock house, where I was solely responsible for all of her care and feedings.

It was a joy to have Josie home from the hospital and thriving at last. Still, solo parenting a preemie on only three hours' sleep at a time was a challenge. When the call came about Daddy, my tears flowed in a torrent of grief and exhaustion. I poured out my heart to God, thanking Him for my daddy's life, asking Him to comfort my siblings and their families, and also asking Him to help me get through my sorrow and hold up physically for the sad and stressful days ahead.

Back in Springdale, Jim Bob loaded the family back on the bus and set out for Ohio.

I called a Little Rock friend who's also a NICU nurse at ACH; she and her husband graciously agreed to spend the night in the Little Rock house with Josie while I rushed to Ohio to attend Daddy's funeral. Arriving there, my sorrow over losing my dad was eased by being surrounded again by Jim Bob and our children. It had been nearly ten days since I'd seen them, when they had briefly stopped by the Cornish house on their way back to northwest Arkansas from their trip out east. They had stood outside on the porch, looking through the glass window, to say hello to me. It had been such a strongly poi-

gnant moment. I had longed to hold each one of them in my arms but couldn't because I couldn't risk exposing Josie to chicken pox.

The day after Daddy's funeral, I would leave my family again to fly back to Josie in Little Rock. In the little time we had

I was alone with Josie in the Little Rock house when my daddy died in Ohio. The old three-story mansion had never seemed emptier than it did that day.

together, Jim Bob and I talked to our children about this additional hard loss for our family, reminding them what death meant for Christians from both an earthly and an eternal perspective. Our family sang two songs as part of the funeral service. We spent a little time with family and friends. Then I headed for the airport, and Jim Bob and our children loaded back onto the bus for the long drive home.

FINALLY HOME

The next week, Jim Bob and some of the older boys, with strong help from our Friendly Chapel friends and other friends from the Little Rock area, brought a box truck and vans to move Josie and me from the Cornish house back home to Springdale. How wonderful it was to return to that house full of children after nearly seven months away! Not all of the kids were there, however; Jana and John-David were on their month-long mission trip to Singapore, Indonesia, and Malaysia.

In another week or so, Josie and I were alone again in a big, empty house, and Jim Bob and the rest of the kids were on the road again, traveling to Camden, Michigan, to keep a commitment we'd made months earlier. John-David and Jana, returning from their overseas mission trip, met the rest of the family in Camden. The children performed vocal music as part of a weeklong tent meeting called the "How to Be Successful" conference, organized by our friend, Camden mayor Harold Walker, with former Michigan State Trooper Tom Harmon preaching. There was a great turnout, with six to eight hundred people attending each night, which is more than the population of the whole town. Hearts were touched, and lives were changed.

After the revival, the family drove to O'Hare International Airport in Chicago, where Jim Bob got on a plane to San Antonio to meet me for the Vision Forum Baby Conference, another speaking commitment we had made the previous year. Jill flew home to Springdale to

take care of Josie for the two nights I would be away. Our little pree-mie by then had progressed to the point of being almost like a normal baby, except for her lactose intolerance, and with Grandma Duggar's help, the very experienced Jill managed just fine.

Finally, on July 10, 2010, for the first time since December 15, 2009, all twenty-four of us—Jim Bob and me, our nineteen children plus daughter-in-law Anna, granddaughter Mackynzie, and Grandma Duggar—were together in one place, safe and happy.

Thank You, God!

SURVIVAL STORY

In a little over two years, our family lost two beloved grandfathers, gained three precious babies—granddaughter Mackynzie and our own Jordyn and Josie—and survived the upheaval of the anxious after-math of Josie's premature birth.

There were times during those two years when we felt happy, times we felt sad, and times we felt scat-tered both mentally and physically. While our love for each other and for our family never waned—not one iota!—our hearts still bear the emotional scars from those mo-ments when fear, exhaustion, and confusion seemed to muddle our thinking, steal our focus, and make us concerned about the future.

As we finish the writing of this book, we rejoice that Josie is thriving and our family is again together at

TORTILLA SOUP GRANDIOSO

4 (15.5-ounce) cans diced tomatoes
2 cans tomato sauce
4–5 cans beans (a variety of black, pinto, garbanzo, etc.)
3 large chicken breasts, cooked and cubed
4 cups frozen corn
¾ bunch fresh cilantro, chopped*
1 lime, juiced
Grated cheddar cheese, sour cream, and tortilla chips for toppings

In a large pot heat the tomatoes, sauce, beans, chicken, and corn. Simmer. After removing from heat, add lime juice and cilantro. Serve with grated cheddar cheese, sour cream, and tortilla chips!

* The fresh cilantro and lime juice add the special flavor to this soup!

home in Tontitown, healed and whole. We will be forever thankful that God brought us through our time of fiery testing. When we lost our footing, we found Him again through repeated prayer and by encouraging each other. We also felt the power of prayers being offered on our behalf by friends, known and unknown, around the world. If you are one of those friends, thank you!

16

• Michelle's Heart for Children and Moms •

*She looketh well to the ways of her household,
and eateth not the bread of idleness.*
—Proverbs 31:27

As I (Michelle) was walking in to Arkansas Children's Hospital one day, I noticed a young woman sitting outside on one of the benches. She seemed distraught, and I felt God prompting me to offer her a word of encouragement.

I stopped by the bench and asked her if I could sit down. She smiled and scooted over to make room for me. I said, "Hi, I'm Michelle. Are you doing all right today?"

She said her name was Sarah, and then she sighed. Her baby was in the NICU, just like Josie was. In fact, he had been born on March 19, one day after Josie's original due date. But like Josie, Samuel came way too early, at only twenty-four weeks gestation, near the limits of a premature baby's chance of survival. Samuel had suffered a bowel perforation, as Josie had. And now his life seemed ever so perilous.

My heart ached for Sarah. It is such a hard thing to see anyone suffer but especially a tiny, precious baby. So much of what this family was experiencing, we had just walked through ourselves with Josie. We talked some more. She was such a good listener, and we connected sincerely, from one mom's heart to another.

I asked, "Sarah, could I pray with you?"

When she said yes, we bowed our heads and linked our hearts as we prayed for little Samuel and little Josie.

What a blessing Sarah was to me that day! As a result of feeling led to be an encouragement to her, I came away from the encounter uplifted as well. That's what God means when He tells us, in his Word, to encourage one another and build each other up.

Sarah was one of dozens of parents we met at ACH who were facing extraordinary difficulties. Some of them lived far away but, like us, had a baby who had been born with problems and needed the expert care of the big hospital's NICU. Some could only be with their baby on weekends because they had to hang on to their jobs back home in order to have insurance. Some simply couldn't afford to make the long trip from some far-off corner of the state and stay in a hotel while they were there.

MOMS CONNECTING HEART-TO-HEART

I believe there's an intangible tie that binds mothers' hearts together, especially during times of stress and struggles. Whenever I see another mom out in public, perhaps herding a bunch of children through a grocery store or trying to get them to sit still in church, I always try to speak a word of encouragement to her—or at least offer her a bright smile. I remember so well what it was like when I would take five little ones under age five to the grocery store by myself!

Oh, what a special joy—and a serious challenge—that was! Sometimes

What could be more fun for Johannah and Jackson than dressing up like a cowgirl and cowboy and riding stickhorses?

my cart was overflowing with children and groceries! By the time I got to the checkout line I was usually frazzled and worn out.

But it seems that so often when I get to the end of my rope, God sends someone my way with the perfect bit of encouragement. It might be another shopper who compliments the kids on their manners or their good behavior (if we happen to be having a good-manner-and-good-behavior day). Or it could be someone who asks, "Are all of those children *yours?*" and then, after I say yes, replies, "What a beautiful family!"

Some grocery-store rules that we have implemented over the years have really helped our children know what is expected of them when we are shopping. When the children go into a store they are to:

+ Whisper quietly.

+ Sit still inside the cart or hold onto the side of the cart as we walk.

+ Not touch or pick up anything without permission or unless they've been asked to do so. (If it's candy or cookies and they're shopping with Dad, they may not have time to ask before he already has them in the cart!)

+ It's fine to make suggestions, but don't nag or we *won't* get the item.

+ Be good helpers, and you may get to go again next time.

In My Weakness, His Strength

It *is* exhausting being a mom, whether you have one child or nineteen. Long ago I realized I simply couldn't do it on my own. One night—actually, in the middle of the night, when I was still up, folding laundry—feelings of weariness flooded over me. That was back in the time when we had seven kids, and doing laundry by myself was a round-the-clock job. So, whenever I was up feeding a baby during the night, I was also doing laundry. I knew if I didn't stay caught up, we wouldn't have clean underwear for the potty-trainers the next day.

That night I stood in that laundry room crying. *Lord, You must have the wrong person here!* I silently prayed. *I simply can't do this. I'm not capable; I feel so overwhelmed and inadequate. I'm so grateful for these precious gifts You've given me, but, Father, I need Your help!*

My cry was like that of a helpless baby: the only way that baby's going to be helped is if a loving parent comes to meet its need.

That night I felt God saying to my heart in a soft, clear voice, *Michelle, it's easy to praise Me when things are going great—when the house is neat, the dishes are clean, the laundry's done, and your children are healthy and behaving themselves—but are you willing to praise Me right now, when it's not easy?*

Immediately to my mind came these words from Scripture: "Offer the sacrifice of praise to God continually" (Hebrews 13:15).

I said, "Father, I love You, and I'm going to praise You even when I don't feel like it. With You, I am capable; without You, I am nothing. I desperately need You." Then, through my tears, I softly began to sing, "The joy of the Lord is my strength. The joy of the Lord is my strength."

As I sang, a release came over my heart as if a burden had been lifted. I finished the laundry around 2 a.m. and went to bed.

Shortly after the laundry-room experience, my little ones were taking piano lessons at the home of an older woman we call Nana. I was sitting there drifting off to sleep while listening to their lessons when Nana asked me, "Are you okay, Michelle?"

I answered, "Yes, I'm fine. I was just up late last night doing laundry."

Nana's face seemed to light up. "Laundry? Do you need help doing laundry? I *love* to do laundry!"

The idea had never occurred to me. *Have someone help with our laundry?* Amazed, I told Nana, "Well, sure, I could use some help."

The next Saturday, Nana came to our house and said, "Just have the kids carry all the dirty laundry to the laundry room, and I'll do it." Later that day, when she was all finished, I was so touched by the gift she had given me, I cried again!

Nana said, "It's a joy for me. I love doing laundry."

God sent His angel Nana to our home twice a week for many years. What a powerful lesson it was for me to remember that God's strength is "made perfect" in my weakness—and to realize I didn't have to understand *how* He would help me; I just had to cry out in humility and believe He *would*. My job was, and is, to keep praising the Lord, even when I don't feel like it.

As an encouragement to other women, I like to share this beautiful poem by Roy Lessin. (He has also authored one of my favorite books, *How to Be the Parents of Happy and Obedient Children*.) This poem is good to keep displayed before our eyes.

CONTINUE ON

A woman fretted over the usefulness of her life.
She feared she was wasting her potential being a devoted wife and mother.
She wondered if the time and energy she invested in her husband
*   and children would make a difference.*
At times she got discouraged because so much of what she did
*   seemed to go unnoticed and unappreciated.*
"Is it worth it?" she often wondered. "Is there something better that I could
*   be doing with my time?"*
It was during one of these moments of questioning that she heard
*   the still, small voice of her Heavenly Father speak to her heart.*
"You are a wife and mother because that is what I have called you to be.
Much of what you do is hidden from the public eye, but I notice.
Most of what you give is done without remuneration.
But I am your reward.
Your husband cannot be the man I have called him to be
*   without your support.*
Your influence upon him is greater than you think
*   and more powerful than you will ever know.*
I bless him through your service and honor him through your love.
Your children are precious to me.
Even more precious than they are to you.

I have entrusted them to your care to raise for Me.

What you invest in them is an offering to Me.

You may never be in the public spotlight, but your obedience shines as a
*   bright light before Me.*

Continue on. Remember you are my servant.

Do all to please me.

THE POWER OF PRAISE

Jim Bob and I both are flexible, fairly self-motivated people who set goals and try to accomplish as much as we can every day. We try to motivate our children to do well, but neither of us is a perfectionist; we don't insist that everything has to be done our way or it's not good enough. We're saddened when we hear parents wrongly using rejecting words or put-downs for correction or in a misguided attempt to motivate their children to do better or do what the parents want them to do.

Others withhold praise until their children have reached a certain high standard of accomplishment; too many children in this kind of setting grow up feeling as though they never measure up. It's easy in that situation to develop low self-worth.

Our friend Pastor Don Elmore says when expectations are high and reality is low, in between the two is frustration. As parents we

We generally serve fruits and vegetables as snacks. But occasionally, Jason (left), James, and Justin find that a hot donut is a treat worth smiling for.

want to lovingly motivate our children to do their best, but at the same time we need to give our expectations to God. We need to praise our children for whatever they accomplish, as if we didn't expect them to

accomplish anything. The more we share words of affirmation in a spirit of love, the more they will want to please us, and ultimately the Lord. Then, inevitably, they will accomplish what we desire for them.

I have the following poem framed and in view where I can see it each day. It's another token of encouragement I share with young mothers when the opportunity arises. May we keep our perspective on what is most important as we nurture our little ones.

LOVE

If I live in a house of spotless beauty with everything in its place,
   but have not love—I am a housekeeper, not a homemaker.
If I have time for waxing, polishing, and decorative achievements,
   but have not love—my children learn of cleanliness, not godliness.
Love leaves the dust in search of a child's laugh.
Love smiles at the tiny fingerprints on a newly cleaned window.
Love wipes away the tears before it wipes up the spilled milk.
Love picks up the child before it picks up the toys.
Love is present through trials.
Love reprimands, reproves, and is responsive.
As a mother there is much I must teach my child,
   but the greatest of all is . . . LOVE.

ANGER RESOLUTION

I want our home to be a safe place where our children feel love and acceptance. I want it to be a fun place, not a house where parental anger suddenly erupts, where they have to be on pins and needles, always worrying they are making a mistake. Anger is a destructive force. Even if we take our children to church every time the doors are open, anger in us or in our home can destroy everything we are trying to teach our children. It can build a wall between them and us.

One day a few years ago, I learned an important lesson about anger and harsh words when I felt like I was at my wits' end. That day God

seemed to touch my heart gently and speak calm words into my mind as I was on the verge of losing my temper. (After the laundry-room experience, I'd learned to watch for God's powerful presence in my life in the most ordinary settings and situations.)

That particular lesson was about having the proper response to my anger by speaking to my children with a soft, gentle voice. It happened because of a can of pineapple.

We probably had eleven children under the age of eleven when the incident happened. During homeschool, we were studying what the Wisdom Booklets teach on the subject of anger, how everyone feels angry sometimes and how destructive those feelings can be if they're not managed appropriately.

The lesson about anger included several Bible passages that explain the proper way to respond to anger. I began reading the passages to my children, and when I got to Proverbs 15:1, the words stood out to me and my eyes filled with tears. It says, "A soft answer turneth away wrath: but grievous words stir up anger."

Strongly impacted by that verse, I visualized several times I'd said harsh words to my children or responded quickly and abruptly, without thinking. In our faith we say we are "convicted" of something when God brings an important lesson into our minds, convincing us of its truth. That day, standing there in front of my children, I was convicted of the different times I had mishandled the anger I had felt toward them. Wiping away tears, I told them, "I am so sorry for the angry words I have spoken to you. Will you please forgive Mommy?"

They all said they would.

I silently prayed to the Lord: *Father, I don't want my children to re-member me as a mama who was constantly fussing at them and raising my voice at them. I want them to remember me as a joyful and happy mama who loves being with them. God, please help me in those difficult moments to have the right response to the anger I feel welling up inside me.*

We went on with the lesson, and the more we studied the proper

response to anger, the more I resolved in my heart to follow the biblical guidance.

Then God, in His wisdom, gave me an opportunity to put what I was learning into action.

A little while later, I was in the kitchen preparing a snack while mentally repeating my new anger-response plan: *A soft answer turns away wrath; but grievous words stir up strife. I'm not going to bicker, not going to nag, not going to ask the kids ten times to do something. I'm going to lovingly say it once, and if they don't obey, then I'll quickly correct them in love, encourage them in a soft voice to do what's right, and then move on. I'm going to use a soft, low voice, no matter what. If they don't listen, I'll follow through with correction, but even then, I'll stay calm and speak softly.*

I had opened a big can of pineapple chunks earlier that morning, and half of it was still sitting on the counter, waiting to be put away. One of the kids asked, "Mama, may I have the rest of the pineapple?"

I answered, "Wait just a minute. I've gotta go change sister's diaper, and then I'll come back and help you with it."

You already know what happened, don't you? I came back into the kitchen after changing the diaper, and there was the pineapple, spilled all over the floor. The sticky juice had splattered everywhere—not just on the floor but up on the doors of the cabinets and under the refrigerator—then had been tromped through and tracked into the living room by another little one. It was one giant mess.

I drew in a breath. *This is* not *what I need right now,* I said to myself. I couldn't even get to the mop without walking through the pineapple juice.

Then another voice came into my head: *I'm giving you grace to do what's right. Are you going to have the right response?*

The words had to have come from God, and yet it almost seemed as if they were coming from the anxious child standing before me in the middle of the mess, his little face worried, his eyes as big as giant marbles.

We looked at each other for one long moment. Then I squatted down in front of him and said, in a soft, calm voice, "What did Mommy say?"

He swallowed hard as a tear rolled down his cheek. He repeated what I had told him—to wait and I would help him get some pineapple.

"That's right. That's what I said," I told him, trying to remain calm in that same, soft voice. "Now I want you to go to your room and wait for Mommy. I'm going to clean up this mess, and then I'll be there in a little bit."

Don't think my anger was under control just because I didn't yell at him. That wasn't it at all. The attitude of my heart at that moment was, *Okay, Lord (pant, pant, pant), I'm about to explode right now. This is absolutely more than I can handle on my own, but I know You're helping me. So I'm gonna do what You say; with Your help, I'm gonna stay calm and speak in that soft, low voice.*

I cleaned up the sticky mess; it took quite a while, but it gave me time to cool down and think about the lesson I had taught the children from the Wisdom Booklet—the proper response to our anger—and suddenly I felt a surge of God's grace filling me with peace and erasing all traces of bitterness and frustration.

I went to my son, waiting nervously in his room, and was able to lovingly explain to him, in a soft, gentle voice, why he needed to always obey me: not just because he might make a big mess if he disobeyed but also because I loved him and didn't want him pulling things down that could hurt him or spill and get into his eyes or cut him with sharp edges.

"There are things you don't understand right now that Mommy does understand," I told him. "Sometimes I don't have time to explain why I'm telling you to do something or not to do something, but you can trust that it's because I love you and not because I'm trying to spoil your fun or make you wait for something you really want. God is teaching you patience—while He's teaching me how to teach you."

This heart-to-heart talk with my little guy was the beginning of a

whole new level of child training for me; I was learning the value of a soft voice. Oftentimes as I spoke with my children that way while encouraging or correcting them, I was reminded of another Bible passage, a story from 1 Kings 19 that tells how, while Elijah was hiding in a cave on Mount Horeb, "the LORD passed by."

A great wind roared by the cave, "but the LORD was not in the wind." Nor was He in the earthquake that followed, or the fire that came next. But after all that, there came "a still small voice," the voice of God.

In the days surrounding Josie's birth, she and I were so sick and weak I couldn't quite imagine a day would come when we would pose for a photo like this.

That day happened many years ago, but even now, I still struggle with anger. Sometimes I feel it welling up inside of me, and my natural response is to lash out, say harsh words, and raise my voice, but then I'm reminded of the damage that kind of response causes: I can see in my children's faces that their spirits are crushed, and I feel so much guilt. It produces a damaged relationship, and I have to go back and ask them to forgive me.

Each time it happens, I think, *I don't want to have to do that again!* I realize God is training me to tame my tongue and to choose joy over exhaustion and weariness. I *choose* to smile and be joyful because my children are precious to me, and I can't think of a better way to spend my life than investing it in the lives of my children and my grandchild—and, I hope, more grandchildren and great-grandchildren to come. What I do now affects generations to come. As a reminder to me, a plaque hangs in my room that urges me to "Be a Joyful Mother of Children!"

ALFREDO SPAGHETTI

1 quart heavy whipping cream
1 stick (½ cup) butter
8 ounces (2 cups) Parmesan cheese
1 teaspoon salt
1 pound cooked spaghetti, drained

In large saucepan, warm whipping cream and butter until butter is melted. Remove from heat. Slowly blend in Parmesan cheese and salt with wire whisk until thoroughly blended. Cover, let stand 10 minutes, till thickened. Stir in cooked spaghetti. Makes 6 servings.

CONSISTENCY IS KEY

Another important goal is consistency. I am trying to train my children to obey the first time they're told, whether I'm asking a three-year-old to put her big sister's markers back where she found them or asking a five-year-old to sit quietly at the table for school or instructing all the youngest ones *never* to climb on the outside railing of the staircase in our living room.

Jim Bob and I aren't rigidly strict disciplinarians. We know children make mistakes and use poor judgment—and, sometimes, so do their parents. We are thankful God is patient and "longsuffering" with us. Through our own mistakes, we've learned the importance of consistently training our children according to biblical principles.

I mentioned this earlier in the book, but it's worth repeating here. If I ask a child to do something and he doesn't do it, or vice versa, or if I let a child get away with something she knows not to do, then a few minutes later there's going to be another little act of misbehavior, and a little later there will be another, bigger misbehavior. Before long there will be behavior that requires serious attention, often resulting in tears. That's not what either of us wants.

I've learned that I need to *immediately* attend to that first little incident. If it's really minor, I simply let the child know I've seen it and tell him or her to *stop*. Or if it's one of the little boys driving an "outside toy" inside the house, maybe I have the child sit at the kitchen counter for five minutes or have him or her stand quietly beside me while I'm doing dishes, cooking, or attending to something else, until I can tend to the child.

The children need to know that when Mama says something in her soft, quiet voice, she means it—and she means it the first time. I don't yell (anymore). In fact, sometimes my children say they know when I'm *really* serious because my voice gets even softer than usual! Each one must learn there are consequences for bad behavior and rewards for good behavior. All communication must be done with a gentle spirit, like a judge calmly determining the outcome of a case.

Love and consistency are the keys!

THE HEART OF HOMESCHOOLING

People often ask us why we've chosen to homeschool our children. Let me share with you the reasons. Early in our marriage, even before Josh was school age, Jim Bob and I committed to homeschooling him as well as any other children we might have.

The first reason was to fulfill the teaching of Deuteronomy 6:5–7:

> And thou shalt love the Lord thy God with all thine heart, and with all thine soul, and with all your might. And these words, which I command thee this day, shall be in thine heart: And thou shalt teach them diligently unto thy children, and shalt talk of them when thou sittest in thine house, and when thou walkest by the way, and when thou liest down, and when thou risest up.

We personally felt that homeschooling was the best way for us to accomplish the goal of training our children to love God with all their heart, soul, mind, and strength, when they get up, sit down, walk, and are going to bed as commanded in Deuteronomy.

The second reason we homeschool is that we want our children to be free to become who God wants them to become without negative peer pressure and without the influences that could lead to involvement in drugs, alcohol, and immorality.

Even though Jim Bob went to a Christian school from grades six through twelve and had a lot of godly teachers, as he looks back on his school years he sees that the kids had more social influence over their fellow students than the teachers did. In contrast, we want our children to be surrounded by positive peer pressure from godly Christian influences during their most formative years.

The third reason is that we don't want our children indoctrinated in atheism, socialism, evolution, and other worldly philosophies and behaviors eight hours a day, which is happening in many schools. We believe as parents that we are responsible for every influence we allow our children to be around. We are training our children with a Christ-centered education, and we use many resources, such as www.answersingenesis.com, which teaches not only evidence that God supernaturally created the earth but also how evolution is impossible.

The fourth reason we homeschool is that we want our children to become best friends with each other and be close as a family. Our opinion is, if you can learn to get along and resolve conflicts with your brothers and sisters day in and day out, you can learn to get along with anyone. It's a beautiful thing to see this truth lived out!

When we decided to homeschool, I loved it, but as our family grew, it sometimes seemed absolutely overwhelming. Jim Bob would be gone all day, sometimes from sunup to sundown, answering wrecker calls that came into our towing business. Even in those early years he thought he had a big family to support (little did he know!), and he felt the pressure weighing on him tremendously. Those days usually left me as the only parent available to teach, train, and correct all our little guys throughout the day.

While my intention was to teach our children, it seemed that sometimes, through our studies together, God was teaching me more than I was able to teach them. Responding appropriately to anger was just one of the lessons I was learning. I also saw how our children learn more from our responses and actions than from our words, and the

importance of being consistent in training and discipline was proven to me again and again. Then came the biggest lesson of all.

One afternoon when I'd finally managed to get all of the babies down for their naps and all the school-age children seated around the table, I opened up our curriculum and suddenly felt completely inadequate for the task at hand. It just seemed to be too much to do—almost impossible. How could I possibly teach my children all the things I wanted them to know: reading, writing, math, science, history, medicine, government, and everything else? I was starting to question why I had ever thought homeschooling was a good idea.

I can't do this, Lord. It's just too much, I mentally moaned.

His answer seemed to come as quickly as my next breath: *If you can do only one thing, Michelle, do the most important thing: get My Word into their hearts and minds in such a way that they hunger and thirst for it.*

I was reminded how Jesus had summarized God's Word for His followers. Basically, He told them the most important commandments were to love God and to love others as they loved themselves. If they made those two goals their priorities, everything else would fall into place, He said. "Seek ye first the kingdom of God and His righteousness and all these things shall be added unto you."

Not long after that moment, the idea I mentioned earlier about "salting the oats" came to mind. It's the idea of making God's Word so appealing and interesting—so salty—the kids hunger for it. We began focusing more on memorizing Scripture, working on it together to put motions with the words and embedding them in our hearts.

In addition to memorizing God's Word, we also study it as the owner's manual for our lives. We read it aloud to each other just for the pure enjoyment of hearing it, or we read it silently, absorbing it into our minds. I *know* our children are absorbing it because they will come back and quote it later or refer to it when they share a situation they're struggling with.

We try to surround our children and ourselves with God's Word, and we try to get it into our heads and our hearts through as many

of our senses as possible. One way we do this is to "write it upon the doorposts," using decorative lettering to copy Bible phrases, as well as encouraging quotes from Christian leaders, onto the walls of various rooms.

In addition to including Bible reading and memorization in our homeschool time, Jim Bob reads and explains Scripture passages to the children at night during Bible time. Some people ask if we skip over the Bible stories that include murder, adultery, stealing, or other sinful behavior. The answer is no. We use those stories as teachable examples of someone who did wrong and incurred God's consequences as a result. We prefer those stories to television and movie plots that sometimes feature someone doing wrong without any consequences, or even getting rewarded for committing the crime.

MEDITATE? IN *OUR* HOUSE?

At the Basic Life Principles Seminar, which we highly recommend, we heard Dr. Bill Gothard talking about the value of memorizing and meditating on Scripture. He said, "When Joshua faced the awesome giants of his day, he was given the command to meditate upon God's Word day and night, so that whatever he did would be successful" (see Joshua 1:7–9).

Remembering Dr. Gothard's words, I (Michelle) thought of an idea. I set a little CD player on my nightstand so we can listen to recordings of Alexander Scorby reading the entire King James Version of the Bible. He has a wonderfully strong but mellow voice. I set it to play continuously, with the volume barely above a whisper, and Jim Bob and I fall asleep hearing the inspiring words of the Bible.

That practice has been a great blessing to me, especially during stressful times or times of spiritual struggle. I feel like I'm being fed God's Word intravenously! Now I listen to similar recordings on my iPhone, or I turn on another CD player when I'm working in the kitchen or elsewhere in the house.

The Bible is the truth we base our lives upon, and we've taught our children to do likewise. We have only a short time with them before they're grown and living away from home, and we want to spend every possible moment filling their hearts with our love and their minds with God's Word.

The Bible says when God's Word goes out, it does not come back void (see Isaiah 55:11), and I've certainly seen the truth of that statement. I've learned that when I can't find the CD of a certain passage of Scripture, I should ask my children about it before I look further. More than likely, one of them has been listening to it through the day or as he or she falls asleep to it at night.

The Bible says, "The evening and the morning were the first day" (Genesis 1:5), which we understand as meaning that our day actually begins the evening before. Maybe that's why it seems that whatever I go to bed thinking about sets the course for the next day. Many nights, while it is quiet, I spend time alone with the Lord, pouring my heart out to Him, praying for my family and for others, and thinking about how His Word applies to every aspect of life.

This is one of the ways we meditate on Scripture in the busy, noisy Duggar family. It's interesting to see how, as we go through life and have to make important decisions, we filter our choices through those scriptures and Bible principles we've learned and studied. To me, that's what wisdom means: looking at everything in life from God's perspective.

USING THE INTERNET FOR GOOD

Speaking of wisdom, we agree with most of the world that the Internet is one of the greatest inventions in our lifetime, providing quick availability of knowledge about every subject imaginable. But the Internet also has the greatest potential to destroy souls with instant, unlimited access to all sorts of immorality. We tell our children, "Welding metal together is an incredible process. It is interesting to watch, but if you don't protect your eyes, you will go blind! Similarly, if men, young and

old, do not have internet protection and accountability, they will scar their eyes, which are the windows to the soul." For that reason, we have set up multiple safeguards on our Mac computers, creating parental controls that strictly limit Internet access.

I realize that the limits we set for our children may be different than those set by others, but so many have asked us about it that I want to share our thinking with you here.

During their free time, our kids can go to more than seventy-five prescreened websites for fun and educational information and activities. Some of their favorites are lifeatthepond.com and focusonthefamily .com. The sites they're able to visit don't include any search engines or websites that have full-web search engines as part of the site. We also double-check to verify that any embedded YouTube videos on those pre-approved sites don't also have a YouTube search engine.

If the kids need to go to the open Internet to research something, they need an accountability partner to sit alongside them as they go on the web, and before they can begin, Mom or one of the older girls must type in the Internet-protection password. They're the only ones who know it.

Last year we acquired a few iPhones. They are handy and fun to use; we can check the bank balance or the ten-day weather forecast in an instant. But because they are Internet enabled, they also need to be password protected. The ones used by Dad and the boys don't have Safari or any other application that leads to a search engine.

To keep an iPhone safe from open Internet access, you have to thoroughly examine every application you are considering, as well as anything it links to and from. Even with the Safari web browser turned off, sometimes an ad on an application will lead to the open Internet. As parents we must guard our family and ourselves from wasting time on computers and allowing access to sites that could destroy our souls.

Social networks like Facebook, MySpace, Twitter, and chat rooms are quickly connecting the world. If used in the right way, they can be powerful tools for sharing God's redemption plan and for offering per-

sonal testimony about how God is working in your life. But they can also be dangerous, allowing exposure to immoral messages and images and wasting a lot of time!

Grandma Duggar has told our kids for years, "Show me your friends, and I will show you your future." Open access to social-networking sites can expose us to "friendship" that can have a harmful effect on our hearts and minds.

Consider this: Christ did not command us to go out and make friends; He told us to make *disciples* (see Matthew 28:19). We tell our kids, If your goal is to win *friends*, you'll probably end up doing a lot of compromising to keep their friendship. If your goal is to love and *disciple* others, people who hang out with you will be challenged to follow God's vision for their life, and you will have true friendships where each encourages the other to live for God!

The Learning Channel maintains a Facebook page for our series, *19 Kids and Counting,* but at this point none of our children living at home has a Facebook, MySpace, or Twitter account, even though there have been many impersonators out there pretending to be one of us.

GIRL TALK

When our girls are turning twelve, or whenever it seems appropriate for them, I (Michelle) give them a little gift we call a "womanhood kit" that includes some personal feminine products, perfume and deodorant, a razor, and sanitary pads, as well as some girlie stuff: maybe some translucent powder, lip gloss, and pretty hair clips or barrettes.

Then we spend some special time together, usually beginning with lunch, where I can talk to my daughter about some of the changes that are or will be happening in her body. I explain how this is the beginning of a new and exciting season of life, and I share some of the things her big sisters and her mom know about—things like cramps and Midol, for example! I laugh, telling her about the "phenomenon" that seems to cause most of the older girls in the family to go through their men-

strual cycle at about the same time. It's just one of those things that happens when a bunch of women live and work together.

I'll talk to her about how she'll soon start having those funny feelings whenever she's around boys. And how God wants her to stay pure mentally and physically until she's married; then we'll probably shop for a purity ring. It's just a simple band, but she gets to pick exactly what she wants, whether it's embossed or smooth. It's to remind her of her priority to stay pure in heart, soul, and body.

We explain to our older children, both girls and boys, that they have different areas of weakness. We share the Bible's warning about how dangerous it is to make "provision for the flesh, to fulfill the lusts thereof" (Romans 13:14). For instance, I have told my girls that romance novels are to women what pornography is to men. They stir up your emotions with unreal fantasies. In contrast, God's Word tells us to think on things that are honest, pure, lovely, and of a good report (see Philippians 4:8).

For these reasons, we try not to have things around our home that would set up our children for failure in moral purity, whether it be magazines that contain sensual ads or newspaper inserts that portray immodesty.

A PRIORITY OF PURITY

President Teddy Roosevelt said, "To educate a child without teaching morality is to educate a menace to society." In today's world, the entertainment industry glamorizes intimate physical relationships with multiple others outside of marriage as being irresistible and acceptable. But the truth is, God designed the intimate love relationship for only one man with one woman within a lifelong marriage commitment. Anything other than that is asking for painful and serious consequences.

Jim Bob loves to teach our children by telling great stories or creating analogies that they can relate to. He has an incredible ability to

make a truth from God's Word come alive and become real in their hearts and minds.

To explain the importance of purity (saving yourself for the one God has made for you), he told the older children, "Imagine that your parents are going to surprise you and give you a brand-new bike for Christmas. Two weeks before Christmas, they buy your bike and hide it in the storage shed in the backyard. But then the boy next door sneaks into the shed and borrows your new bike; he stunt-rides it up and down the back alley.

"On Christmas morning your parents lead you out to the shed to reveal the special gift they bought for you, and as they open the door and say, 'Surprise!' they're just as surprised as you are. You're *all* shocked to see that the bike looks like it's been thrown off a cliff. The front fender is missing, and the front tire is warped so it rubs on the frame. It's dirty, the paint is all scratched and chipped, and the seat has a big rip in it. It looks worse than something you would have bought at a garage sale.

"I'm sure you would still be grateful for the bike, and you would have fun riding it, but it won't be in the condition your parents had hoped and dreamed it would be when you received it. You would miss out on a lot of the enjoyment they meant for you to have.

"In that same way, we don't want any boy (or girl) to come and steal your purity. It's vital to be patient and wait for the one God has for you and to not 'play around' in situations where you could be tempted to compromise your purity. What kind of gift do you want to be for your future spouse?"

Another story Jim Bob shares starts with a disgusting image: "What if we were at a meeting with about one hundred other people and the speaker asked that a large cup be passed around and that everyone spit in the cup? What if you happened to be all the way in the back—the last person on the last row—and when the cup finally came to you the speaker asked you to drink out of the cup? What would you do?"

All of our children say, "Yuck! That's nasty! Gross! That makes me sick just thinking about it!"

Then Dad explains to our older children, "That's what it's like if you have intimate physical relations with several partners. Physical relations outside marriage promote venereal disease, cervical cancer, and a host of other problems."

God can forgive any wrong choices a person is willing to confess and forsake, but there are still painful consequences to be endured. Our heavenly Father loves us, and His goal is not to take away our fun but to protect us from things that will hurt us.

MAN TO MAN

Physical purity is important to us and to our children. Jim Bob talks to our sons at about the age of eleven or twelve and discusses the facts of life to whatever degree he believes they can handle at that age (some mature faster than others).

He talks about how their bodies start to change, and he explains that the reason for their God-given attraction to girls is so that one day they will get married. He also emphasizes the importance of staying pure in mind and in body and how every man has temptations. He encourages them to come and talk to him, day or night, when they are struggling with anything, and he begins asking them on a regular basis

I (Jim Bob) work hard to maintain a strong, loving relationship with all ten of our sons so that they will feel free to tell me the concerns of their hearts.

how they are doing with their thought life and other purity issues that men face.

OVERCOMING TEMPTATIONS

We talk to our children frequently about their feelings, and we maintain an attitude of openness so they feel safe coming to us anytime about anything that's troubling them. That includes feelings and thoughts of a sensual nature, which are inevitable among adolescent and teenage children. We tell our kids, "The power of sin is in secrecy."

We say, if Satan can get you to *think* about doing things that are wrong, it's just a matter of time before he presents a situation that tempts you to *act* on your secret desires. At that point he has you right where he wants you.

You know better than to do what he tells you to do, we say. But sin can make you stupid. He tells you that doing this bad thing will bring you pleasure, and you're tempted to believe him. Sure, there may be temporary pleasure—until the consequences arrive. Then the guilt sets in as well. Once Satan has a stronghold in one area of your life, he tries to take over the rest of it too.

We've told our kids that most bank robbers don't just walk in and rob a bank on impulse. Maybe they can't pay their bills and they wonder where they're going to come up with the money. Instead of thinking about how they could work to earn what they need, they start dreaming about what they would do if they had all the money the bank has. They start coveting the bank's money, and then they start dreaming up ways they could steal it without getting caught. This mind-set could have started with something as simple as stealing a piece of candy when they were kids.

Maybe they think about robbing the bank for quite a while. Then, one day, they put their thoughts into action. They rob the bank, and they get caught and spend the rest of their lives in prison!

Where did they first go wrong? When they robbed the bank? No, the

wrongdoing started before that; it started when Satan put the lazy, covetous thought in their minds. We teach our kids to "[bring] into captivity every thought to the obedience of Christ," quoting 2 Corinthians 10:5. And we remind them of something Grandma Duggar has always said: "If a person will lie to you, he will steal also." Major misdeeds and wrongdoings often get their start in what may have seemed inconsequential at the time: a wayward thought, a covetous idea, or a little white lie.

COMMUNICATING OPENLY, WITH LOVE

We explain to our children the importance of maintaining a clear conscience with God and others. We teach them how that's possible, by sharing what Jesus taught His followers: that we should confess our sins so we aren't weighed down by guilt. God's Word says, "He that covereth his sins shall not prosper: but who so confesseth and forsaketh them shall have mercy" (Proverbs 28:13).

Following that guidance, we encourage our children to share with us their mistakes and temptations as well as their troubling thoughts and feelings. We tell them if they've done something wrong (or a whole bunch of things) they need to confess it to God to be free from the guilt that will otherwise make them miserable.

We pray together with the child, asking God to wipe the slate clean and thanking Him for the wonderful gift of forgiveness. Then they go to the person they have offended, if that kind of mistake is what's being confessed, and ask for forgiveness.

When they tell us the thought or temptation that's bothering them, or when they confess the hurtful or mean-spirited thing they may have said or done, we talk to them about how harmful temptations can lead them to behaviors that damage their relationship with God and with their family and friends. Talking to us about those feelings can be freeing; once their "secret" is shared, its grip on their life is released.

Whenever our kids share their hearts with us we know it's important to keep a calm look on our faces and not to overreact to whatever

they share with us. Otherwise the kids will think, *I can't tell Mom and Dad about this bad thought I've had; they'll think I'm a horrible person.*

Nothing could be further from the truth. I (Michelle) tell them there's nothing they can say, do, or think that will cause us to stop loving them.

I ask them, "Who do you think put that thought in your head?"

They acknowledge, "Satan did!"

Satan has used similar temptations throughout the centuries, planting doubt and lies in the minds of men and women as he's tried to lead them away from God's truth. I want our children to realize that *everyone* faces temptations from time to time—even Mama and Daddy. In fact, the Bible records many dramatic stories of failure as a result of temptation. From the strongest man who ever lived, Samson, to a man after God's own heart, David, biblical heroes through the ages were tempted by Satan's lies; many fell victim to those lies and failed as a result. God put their stories of failure in the Bible so we can see how the consequences played out when they listened to Satan. We pray that, by God's grace, we won't go that same route.

But the stories also tell us how God restored them to full relationship with Him when they confessed their sin and asked forgiveness. For example, when David, who committed adultery and even murder, came to repentance, God forgave him and eventually blessed him.

We teach our children these lessons so they're ready, not *if* temptations come but *when* they come. "You *will* be tempted to do wrong," I tell them. "So don't be surprised; be prepared!"

We also remind them that the Bible says they're not going to experience a temptation that hasn't already threatened someone else. In fact, I encourage them to memorize 1 Corinthians 10:13, which says, "There hath no temptation taken you but such as is common to man: but God is faithful, who will not suffer you to be tempted above that ye are able; but will with the temptation also make a way to escape, that ye may be able to bear it."

Their older siblings, and even their parents, have probably had the same thoughts or feelings they're having, I say. But by clinging to God's

Word and asking for His help, they will be able to withstand whatever temptation comes their way.

This kind of confession and discussion help keep our relationship with our children strong. But it's not just children who need to learn these kinds of communication skills. I (Michelle) tell our children, "When you learn how to share your mistakes and your temptations with your parents, who love you more than anything, you'll be laying the foundation of communication skills you'll use someday with your spouse. Then you can communicate openly and honestly with your mate just like Daddy and I do now.

"As husband and wife, we are each other's accountability partner. When Daddy is tempted, you can be sure he shares it with me. We talk about it and pray about it together. He does the same for me when I share a problem with him."

A friend of ours who has worked with juvenile delinquents tells young people, "You're going to be okay if you just keep talking, being open and honest. If you do that, you'll make it." Open, loving communication, we say, is one of the keys to strong, stable, loving relationships.

Note: Some children may not feel their parents are a safe place to share their hearts. If the child thinks that the parents will repeat what they have shared with others, they won't feel the freedom to open up.

As a parent, if you have failed in these areas you need to go back and ask forgiveness.

Our whole family helped out in the campaign rallies when Jim Bob ran for the US Senate in 2002.

17

• Jim Bob's Lifelong Hobby •

Husbands, love your wives,
even as Christ also loved the church, and gave himself for it.
—Ephesians 5:25

Michelle and I got married in 1984, three days after my nineteenth birthday and two months before her eighteenth. I was the happiest guy in the world, having a girl like Michelle accept my marriage proposal. But most people back then probably thought I didn't have a lot going for me.

I'd been an average student in high school. I worked in a grocery store, where advancement opportunities were limited. I was a good, hard worker, but on paper, my credentials looked pretty weak. Thank goodness Michelle was able to see that my potential lay not in my résumé, but in my heart.

She knew I loved God and loved her and that I had committed my life to following God with my whole heart. Since the first night I met Michelle on a church visitation, my prayer had been that God would allow her to be mine and that I could become her spiritual leader. When the first part of that prayer was answered, I committed myself to doing all I could, with God's help, to becoming the spiritual leader husband, and eventually the spiritual leader father, that God wanted me to be. My lifelong hobby is my family. In the following pages, I'll share some of the ways this hobby has developed as I've matured. Maybe what I've

learned will encourage other husbands and fathers to make their families their hobby, as well.

Praying About Financial Decisions

Although I wasn't a strong student during my youth, as an adult I've developed a passionate love for learning Bible principles. That change in me may have been triggered by a speaker I heard years ago who preached from James 1:5, which says, "If any of you lack wisdom, let him ask of God, that giveth to all men liberally, and upbraideth not; and it shall be given him."

As our family grew (baby Jinger was number six) we knew we needed a solid financial foundation to be able to live frugally and care for our children.

I prayed for wisdom and sought to become the man God wanted me to be. In the years since I heard that sermon I've attended many Christian conferences and seminars aimed at teaching men to become godly husbands, fathers, and Christian leaders. One of those seminars, Jim Sammons's Financial Freedom series, mentioned earlier, changed how we thought about and managed our family's finances (see the Resources section for more information).

Jim Sammons's goal was to be financially independent by age thirty. He borrowed money to play the stock market and did quite well—until several of the companies he'd invested in with borrowed money went broke. Instead of being financially independent at age thirty, he was completely upside down. At that point, he says now, God had him

right where He wanted him. He started studying God's Word and applied it to his everyday life. As he turned his heart toward God and started applying His principles, God blessed him. Eventually he ended up paying off all his debts and gaining the financial independence he'd hoped for. His success has continued to the point that now he has paid cash to build several shopping centers.

The most important thing the Sammons program taught us was to pray about decisions relating to our personal and business finances and to base our financial practices on a biblical model. In our first book we described several of the amazing miracles we've experienced as we've followed that ideal, and each passing month seems to bring more lessons and more opportunities as we continue to follow that biblical standard.

Sammons's teaching also includes many marriage and family principles as he shares his own transparent life testimony in a humorous way. Michelle's favorite chapter is titled "Husbands, Listen to the Cautions of Your Wife."

Jim Sammons says that one way of "making ends meet" is not a matter of increasing income as much as it is decreasing expenses by utilizing present resources more efficiently. He teaches how to find God's will and how to seek His direction. So many times we have prayed about a potential investment and made an offer, and the offer was rejected or sometimes countered with a higher price than we thought we should pay. When that happens, we accept it as God closing the door on that investment at that time.

Sometimes as we pray for God's guidance about a financial decision, we see His blessings unfolding in seemingly unrelated and totally unexpected ways. For example, weeks before our extended stay in Little Rock, Josh had told me about a great deal on a fifteen-passenger van for sale by a rental-car agency. When we went to look at it, the salesman mentioned that the company was looking for a new location to rent in Springdale. We ended up buying the van, and shortly after that, I found a property on Springdale's main highway that had been on the market

awhile. We were able to purchase it for a very good price, with a closing date a few weeks away in early December 2009. Right before that closing date, however, Michelle's health problems developed.

I called the company handling the closing and explained that I was in Little Rock and couldn't make it to the scheduled closing in Springdale because my wife and baby were in the hospital. They said they also had an office in Little Rock.

While I was in that Little Rock office, signing papers to complete the sale, I mentioned that we were looking for a house to rent. As we said in an earlier chapter, that comment in that place resulted in our renting the Cornish house.

Next I called the car-rental manager about the property we had just bought and asked if he would be interested in taking a look at it. Just now, as we are finishing this book, we signed a twenty-year lease with that company.

God is so good. When we let Him control our lives, He accomplishes far more than we could ever imagine.

Avoiding Debt, Embracing Frugality, Saving for Emergencies

The second principle we adopted after going through the Financial Freedom seminars was to eliminate debt in both our personal and business finances. For more than twenty years, we've followed the principle in Romans 13:8, which says, "Owe no man any thing." Not a day goes by that we're not thankful for that lesson, especially in today's challenging economy. We've seen too many families and businesses make presumptions about the future, go into debt—and lose everything.

We've observed that when people finance big purchases, they usually pay more than they should because they're concentrating on the monthly payment instead of the total cost. They don't realize that when finance charges are added, they're paying two to five times as much for the new item as they would have paid to buy the same or similar used

item that would have met their needs just as well. Too many times these debt-burdened buyers end up with a boatload of stuff they don't need or that they soon discard or set aside (sometimes having to get a rental unit to store it), but they're stuck with the payments long after the items are gone. That kind of financial pressure forces them to work longer hours and be away from their families more.

We completely understand that sometimes you want something *now*, and if you don't finance it, you have to wait, which might be uncomfortable. For instance, our house wasn't air conditioned when we moved into it. We saved our money and used window fans for about a year, until we could pay cash for a new system (and what a relief *that* was!). When three of our kids needed braces but we could afford to pay only for one, the others had to wait a little while until the budget could accommodate more orthodontia.

Saving money to buy something teaches patience and discourages impulsive purchases, so of course it's something we not only practice ourselves but also teach our children. The young ones receive money as gifts and occasionally receive monetary rewards for helping with household jobs. They save their money in a piggy bank or some other kind of container they can keep in their locker (every child has one—and a lock to go on it) or else their earnings are recorded in their account in the "family bank." When they've saved up enough to buy something, we take them shopping for it.

All our children know that the Duggar motto is "Buy used and save the difference," and they're becoming as frugal with their money as we are with ours. Some of them have gotten to the point where they really don't like to spend money! Jinger is gaining a reputation as a bargain-hunting champion. When Jinger and her older sisters go thrift shopping to buy clothing items for the family or to the store to buy some groceries, the girls usually come by my (Jim Bob's) office to say good-bye as they're heading out the door. Michelle is trying to break me of my habit of jokingly telling them, "Love you! Don't spend any money!" She says Jinger takes that message too seriously. She ends up

standing at the store thinking, *This is really a good bargain. But Daddy said not to spend any money . . .*

Many people asked us whether we have accepted government assistance to help cover medical expenses with Josie's crisis. The answer is no. We have never accepted government assistance of any kind, and I pray we never have to. It's a good safety net for those who need it, but we have insurance—and savings—that so far have kept us from needing additional help.

That's not to say the out-of-pocket medical bills haven't been costly. Michelle's emergency medical flight from Rogers to Little Rock, which

Jinger is one of our thriftiest thrift-store shoppers.

wasn't covered by insurance, cost ten thousand dollars.

Josie's December 10, 2009, birth meant we had to pay her and Michelle's insurance deductible for 2009 and then pay their 2010 deductibles a few weeks later. After that, almost all of their medical expenses were covered by insurance. We had been paying thousands of dollars a year for insurance premiums over the years. With a pretty healthy family and a twenty-five-hundred-dollar deductible, sometimes I wondered if the high monthly premiums were a wise investment. After all, we really hadn't had a major health-related expense. But all that thinking quickly evaporated when Michelle (and then Josie's) health crises erupted. Also, having had an insurance license at one time, I understood the importance of spreading the risk out over thousands of people. Everyone's premiums together easily cover the costs of the relatively few major claims that occur among the policyholders.

My Main Hobby: Being the Duggar Dad

Providing financially for my supersize family could be an all-consuming, high-pressure role for me, but as we have trusted God and followed His principles, we have seen Him supernaturally provide every step of the way and meet our needs. Together we pray about upcoming decisions, and we trust God to provide the opportunities and guidance we need.

Living debt-free, I'm able to focus more of my attention on my family. I don't play golf, don't own a fancy bass boat, and don't take off for weeklong hunting trips with buddies. My family is my hobby, and I spend every minute I can enjoying it.

Because we live debt-free, I (Jim Bob) am able to enjoy more fun activities with my family—like heading to the go-cart track with (from left) Jessa, Joseph, John-David, Jinger, and the rest of the kids old enough to "drive."

Because I run our commercial rental property business from home, I'm able to mingle real estate and family responsibilities throughout much of each day. When repairs are needed on any of our properties, some of my children go along with me to help or to learn. When Michelle and I are looking at property, it's quite common for us to take along a child or two—or sometimes a whole busload. When I'm on the phone at home talking business, there is usually lots of background noise. This is not an inconvenience for me; it's what I've chosen, and I feel incredibly blessed. I like nothing better than being surrounded by my family.

I try to have a learning spirit and glean from successful fathers and businessmen. I discovered some interesting ideas recently in nearby Bentonville, where Sam Walton started the Walmart business empire.

Sam was an amazing man. He built the world's largest retail company, and that company started and is still run out of that small Arkansas town. The original store, Walton's Five & Dime, has been turned into a visitors center where "Sam's Rules for Building a Business" are on display. Reading them, I saw how Sam's built up a successful business, but I also could see how his ideas could help me build up my family. For example, just as Sam's ideas inspired his "associates" (employees) to feel ownership as partners in the company, I could see how those same ideas could help inspire my children's love and devotion to God and to each other.

Sam's rules are reprinted in the Resources section of this book. Read them and see if they don't inspire you too. For instance, Rule 1 is "Commit to your business. Believe in it more than anybody else. . . . If you love your work, you'll be out there every day trying to do it the best you possibly can, and pretty soon everybody around will catch the passion from you—like a fever."[1] I hope it's obvious to my family that I'm totally committed to them and I like nothing better than spending time with them.

I especially like Sam's "Rule 3: Motivate," which says, in part, "Keep everybody guessing as to what your next trick is going to be. Don't become too predictable."

That's what I try to do with my family when I say, "Tomorrow we're going to do something really special"—and then refuse to say what special thing Michelle and I have planned for them. Sometimes I get on our home's intercom and call, "Everybody come to the kitchen right now. I've got something to show you," and then we might do something like the hillbilly waterslide in the front yard. Or I say, "Attention, all Duggars! Everybody on the shuttle bus! We're going to go do something really fun," and we head out for some playtime at our favorite park.

Of course I work out these little (and sometimes big) surprises ahead of time with Michelle, and she helps shape the family's schedule to accommodate things like field trips to a local ostrich farm or to a

historic or scenic place in our area, or, while we were in Little Rock, a trip to the zoo or a family expedition up Pinnacle Mountain. I try to fill our family with a "spirit of funness" and keep them guessing what the next fun thing will be.

Not all of the surprises are fun, however; sometimes they're challenging but rewarding. One evening in Little Rock I told our older girls (The older boys were back in Tontitown doing some home maintenance projects so they missed out on this adventure!) I had something special planned for the next day, and when they woke up I told them we were going to go donate blood! I reminded them that Josie had received more than a dozen blood transfusions, and this was one way we could give back in the same way that others had given to our family.

Now, I don't know anybody who *enjoys* being poked with needles. Our daughter Jill and I share an especially deep dread of that kind of thing, and—wouldn't you know?—I had to be stuck twice because

In thanksgiving for all the blood Josie was given during her hospitalization, the older girls and I donated blood while we were in Little Rock.

I moved while the phlebotomist was having trouble hitting the vein. But afterward, we wore our Band-Aids as proudly as our little guys do when they're showing off a boo-boo. And we all agreed that donating blood was a good thing to do.

Sam Walton's rules advise business leaders (and dads) to "communicate everything you possibly can," "appreciate everything your associates [and children] do," and "listen to everyone in your company [or family]." We look for ways to incorporate Sam's advice into the way we parent our children.

One thing Sam *didn't* listen to was the negative people who told him not to open a tenth, one hundredth, or one thousandth store, worrying

that he might end up with more than he could manage. Adamantly following his core principles, he eventually became a billionaire and at one time was the richest person in America.

In the same way, by taking on the responsibility for more children over the years, Michelle and I have incurred a lot of criticism, with people questioning how in the world we would be able to take care of and provide for all of those kids. Despite that criticism, we stuck to our core principles, and God has provided and met our needs every step of the way. We consider each one of our children priceless. With nineteen children who love the Lord, we feel like the richest people in the world!

CONTROLLING ANGER

In families of any size—in fact, in any relationship—anger, especially uncontrolled anger, never produces the best results. Too often an angry dad's response to an upsetting situation causes more damage than the event itself. Sure, kids make mistakes and do dumb things, innocently or deliberately. But disciplining and correcting the child while seething with rage can cause irreparable harm to the child's heart and spirit, and cause damage to the parent-child relationship that might take years to heal. The Bible says, "The wrath of man worketh not the righteousness of God" (James 1:20).

I tell people I never had an anger problem until I had children, and then, it seemed, I'd get mad at the kids about things that would never have upset me before I became a father. Again I gained great wisdom at a seminar, one that included descriptions of how destructive a father's (or anyone's) anger can be. One of the dangers about anger is that it feeds on itself; it can easily build to an unhealthy state and become destructive.

Adopting an idea learned at the conference, I asked my family to forgive me and I gave our children permission to help me identify if I am talking with sharp words or an angry spirit. I told them when they sense that I'm mad about something and my anger is building, they

have permission to touch my arm gently, whisper in my ear, and say, "Daddy, I think you're getting angry."

That sweet comment always snaps me back into "sensible mode." It's like dumping ice-cold water on a hot head. I realize what's happening, ask God to help me have the right response, and I regain control. This isn't to say our kids never do things that could make Michelle or me mad, but we try to follow the same guidance we teach our children, remembering that too often someone's response to a hard situation causes more damage than the event itself.

(A comment from Michelle: I would like to add that Jim Bob is really determined to control his anger, and this routine of the children reminding him about losing his temper is rarely needed.)

LISTENING TO EACH OTHER

Anger can also be a destructive force in a marriage, as well as in child-rearing; it's important not to let little things build into frustrations that can erupt in angry outbursts that can damage a couple's relationship.

When Michelle and I got married twenty-seven years ago, we were so in love we just overlooked each other's shortcomings. As time went on, however, it turned out that there were just a *few* little things about us that got on our spouse's nerves. We did our best to ignore them, knowing how important it is not to have a critical attitude. So those little things that bugged us stayed locked up inside our heads. Oh sure, we might make a suggestion about the spouse's behavior from time to time, but that spouse probably took it as just that: a suggestion.

For instance, when we got married, I had a fun way of taking off my socks and doing an athletic, basketball-shooting maneuver—well, it was fun for me, though not for Michelle. I would sit down on the bed, pull off a sock, wad it into a tight little wad, and then toss it over the back of our open bedroom door (the basketball "hoop"). I was actually pretty good at getting each sock over the door and into a pile back in the corner, which made it very convenient for Michelle. She could just

grab the pile of wadded-up socks and carry them to the laundry room. What a good husband I was!

Michelle liked the idea of having all my dirty clothes in a pile, but she *hated* the sweaty, stinky, wadded-up socks. Because they were wadded up so tightly, the sweaty socks didn't ever dry out while they were waiting to be laundered. They just got stinkier and stinkier, and then Michelle would have to pull and pull and *pull* to get them flattened out so they would get clean in the washer (and dry in the dryer).

She took it as long as she could—probably several months or even a year. (She is a *very* patient person.) Then she said something like, "Jim Bob, would you please not wad up your socks? It's good to put all your dirty clothes in a pile behind the door, but it's a lot of work to unwad your socks."

I said, "Okay!" And for a few days, I didn't wad up my socks. But over time I forgot, and the old habit took over again. Michelle didn't immediately comment, so the wadded-up-sock tossing continued. Then she might say, "Jim Bob, please don't wad up your socks," and I'd stop again for a couple of days and then start doing it again. Then Michelle came to me one day with a laundry basket of wadded-up socks. "Honey, this really bothers me. Would you *please* stop doing that?"

I finally got the message, and I stopped wadding up my socks.

Actually, it's hard for me to think of anything Michelle does that's annoying; she's one of the sweetest, most caring people ever. But, well, yes, there is *one* little thing. Because she's so caring and thoughtful, she sometimes sees things the rest of us miss. Instead of procrastinating, she tries to take care of those needs immediately whenever she runs across them—including when I call to her, "Hey, Michelle! Come here real quick!" She answers, "I'll be right there!" But on her way she wipes the baby's running nose, scrapes cereal off the counter and puts away the box so the kids don't spill it again, rinses her hands in the sink and then decides it needs scrubbing, and *then* she finally hurries up to me and says, "Here I am!"

I might say, "I wanted you to see something cute Jackson and Johannah were doing, but I'm sorry, you just missed it!"

Over the years, we've both tried to work on correcting our little annoying behaviors that tend to irritate each other. It's important to say that we wouldn't have known these behaviors were irritable if the spouse hadn't pointed them out. It's imperative to have good, clear communication and listening skills within a family, and we constantly work on improving them. I tell friends just a little more work, and Michelle will have me trained!

STILL LEARNING TO COMMUNICATE

Attending marriage seminars, conferences, and retreats together is a great way for married couples to enjoying a "date weekend" while also learning how to strengthen their marriage. A couple of our favorites are Whatever It Takes (for information, go to www.witministries.com) and A Weekend to Remember (www.familylifeministries.com).

Another conference that had a strong impact on our marriage was Chris and Anne Hogan's Noble Partners Marriage Conference (www.noblecall.org), which we attended about four years ago. The conference focuses on "courageous conversations" that help couples communicate with and understand each other. During the conference, couples are guided in identifying divisions that have crept into their relationship, whether they are newlyweds or have been married fifty years.

Even though we had been married twenty-three years at that point and had a good marriage, we learned new insights about how to ask each other questions to get to the heart of important issues.

During a courageous conversation, the husband is advised to ask his wife, "What is your most pressing issue?" The question seeks out what the wife wants to discuss about the need, concern, worry, fear, priority, or challenge in the marriage and the family, including its finances or its future.

She answers the question, describing what is, to her, the most pressing issue, and then it's important for the husband to rephrase what he heard her say to make sure he understood correctly. He can say, "What I think I heard you say was . . ."

When it's clear that the message has been understood, he continues, "How is this situation affecting you?" Then he listens carefully to his wife's answer, repeating and rephrasing what he has heard. The wife clarifies, if necessary.

When a woman feels she is being heard and truly listened to, she will begin to open up and share her heart—and true communication happens. In a courageous conversation, the husband's next question is, "What will the future be like if nothing changes?"

The wife's response helps him understand the consequences of doing nothing about this matter that is burdening her.

The next question gets to the real heart of the matter when, with a humble heart, the husband asks, "What do you see as my responsibility for this issue?"

This question creates an opportunity for the wife to open her heart to her husband and for the husband to gain genuine understanding of her true needs. It's crucial at this point that the husband doesn't make excuses for character flaws or imperfections but simply acknowledges what has been said.

If at this point he begins to explain, complain, or blame his wife in response to what she is saying, the conversation will fail. On the other hand, this can be a turning point in the conversation if the husband agrees to pray about and work on those areas that have been brought to his attention and the wife realizes that, while she may feel she is the victim, she also has responsibility for helping resolve the issue.

When this issue has been completely discussed, it's wise for the husband to ask, "In addition to this issue, is there something else?"

There may not be time to get to all the core issues in one sitting—in fact, husbands, you may need a pen and paper to write down a long list

during your first courageous-conversation exercise! The couple may then reverse the procedure, with the wife asking the questions.

The conclusion of the conversation is the time for the couple to pray together, asking God and each other for forgiveness. Remember that, as you work through the important issues in your marriage, you are not responsible for your spouse's past mistakes, his or her hurtful words and actions. It is imperative, however, that you humbly ask God and your spouse to forgive *you* for *your* offenses. Before God and your mate, you can make *your* part right. (The *Love Dare* book is an excellent resource for those in a marriage relationship in which only one spouse is trying to make it work.)

Once your marriage issues are discussed in this way, you can work on problems and set future goals. By sharing a mutually agreed upon vision for the future and working toward it, you and your spouse can restore enthusiasm and a sense of partnership in your marriage. Then, as you see improvements as a result of your courageous conversations, you'll no doubt be motivated to work through other issues at regular intervals and to continue communicating this way.

You can also resolve to dedicate yourselves and your family to God. Without Him, we humans are naturally self-centered.

UNDERSTANDING WHAT'S IMPORTANT

During one of the marriage seminars we attended, the leaders described how, in a typical couple's relationship, a stay-at-home wife will want to tell her husband all the challenges that happened while he was at work. Hearing the wife's description of her trying day, the typical husband assumes she is asking for advice on what she could have done differently to resolve the situations that arose.

What she's really wanting, in most cases, is just for the husband to be quiet, listen as she shares her heart, and understand all the obstacles and emotions she faced that day. Then she wants him to show her compassion, love, and care, acknowledging what she went through.

ONE OF OUR FAVORITE COOKBOOK RESOURCES

Kim Cahill's *No-Guesswork Cooking Cookbook: Recipes You Can Trust* is the cookbook we grab most often. When we need to cook for a crowd or just for our family (which is a crowd!), we trust this cookbook to give us all the information we need to pull off a meal with no worries. We love the fact that it guides you through making everything from scratch if you want to—or you can use one of the variations listed to make the cooking go much faster.

It has a built-in self-standing cover and special glossy pages to protect the recipes from the messiest little chefs and helpers. Available from www.iblp.org.

She *doesn't* want "how you could've solved all the problems" advice.

Another communication issue we've encountered over the years is that I sometimes don't pick up on something Michelle is trying to tell me. There have been many times when she has talked with me (Jim Bob) about a number of pressing things that need my attention. I would make a mental list as I listened, categorizing her thoughts and prioritizing what I thought was most important to her. That system meant some things (the ones I thought weren't priorities) were left undone—and Michelle was left feeling disappointed that I didn't catch on to what she meant and, as a result, I didn't follow through with what *she* felt was a priority.

We were about twenty-four years into our marriage when we finally came up with a way to avoid these headache situations. It's a super-simple concept, but it has made a big difference in our relationship. Are you ready? Here it is: when Michelle has something to say that's very important to her, she'll make sure she has my full attention and then she will say, *"Jim Bob, this is really important to me!"*

GIVE US GODLY HOMES

Years ago we heard a song titled "A Christian Home" at another marriage conference we attended. We adopted this song as our family song, and through the years we have enjoyed singing it as a prayer to the

Lord during Bible time or at church. It is sung to the tune of "Be Still My Soul." The song opens with "Oh, give us homes built firm upon the Savior . . . Where ev'ry child is taught His love and favor." You can find the complete lyrics to the song at http://lyrics.astraweb.com/display//177/hymns..unknown..a_christian_home.html.

18

• Do the Duggars Date? •

*Therefore shall a man leave his father and his mother, and shall cleave
unto his wife: and they shall be one flesh.*
—Genesis 2:24

We're often asked about our hopes for our children's future and
how they will find eligible mates. People want to know, do the
Duggars date?

The answer is yes—but only after marriage! In fact, Jim Bob and I
(Michelle) just enjoyed a date night earlier this week when we went out
to eat with another couple on a double date.

Before marriage? No, our children do not date—not as most people
would define dating: a boy and girl getting together with little or no
supervision, just going out for the temporary pleasure of enjoying each
other's company. We've chosen, as a family, not to play the dating game,
hoping to avoid a lot of the inherent pitfalls. (We highly recommend
Joshua Harris's book *I Kissed Dating Goodbye*.) We believe that dating
can lead to unstable emotional attachments, improper touching, and
building a relationship solely on physical attraction rather than emotional and spiritual connection. Having a dating relationship with person after person and breakup after breakup simulates what is happening
in so many marriages today. Too many couples get married with the idea
that if it doesn't work out, they'll break up and find someone else.

When men and women establish a close, intimate relationship with
someone of the opposite gender, they give away a piece of their heart.

Then, as they move through break-ups and new relationships, they give away more and more pieces until, when they finally find the person they decide to marry, they may have a broken heart and a load of guilt left over from wrong choices in the past.

This is a relatively new phase of parenting for us as our older children mature and enter this season of life. We are still learning, with Joshua being our only child to marry so far. Still at the beginning of this important decision-making stage, we're gaining experience about what the Bible says in regard to relationships and the healthiest way they should be established. There will be many things to learn as we walk through this season of our family's life!

We expect that finding a life partner will be a unique process for each one of our young adults, but

Josh and Anna's marriage in 2008 and Mackynzie's birth in 2009 opened a new chapter of parenting— and grandparenting—for us. We love it!

we've agreed on some basic ideas to prepare them for this stage. We are committed to guiding our young-adult children in waiting, evaluating, considering, pre-engagement, engagement, marriage, and *then* dating.

Waiting: Preparing Yourself

When the time is right—meaning, in God's timing—He will bring your intended spouse into your life. Until then you wait, preparing

yourself to become the person God wants you to be in every area of your life.

Waiting begins with the idea that as a marriage-age young person, you're not involved in self-focused dating relationships but are instead seeking God's leading. It teaches contentment as you rest confidently in your belief that God has given you everything you need for your happiness.

Waiting creates a special time as God becomes your best friend. This is also a time when you seek discernment and advice from parents and friends who also are seeking God in their lives. Waiting means denying your physical urges as you hold fast to your goal of receiving God's best in His timing, not yours. Remember, the best things in life are worth waiting for! Waiting helps you appreciate that custom-made person when God brings him or her into your life to be your marriage partner.

As our daughter Jill explained it to a friend, "Often, dating is going out with guys without thinking about marriage anytime soon. *Waiting* is preparing myself to be a godly wife—the kind of girl a godly guy is looking for. That's the girl I want to be!"

Evaluating: Upfront Examining of Character

As young people get to an age when they are noticing the opposite gender, not only are they waiting, but they quickly need to learn to start *evaluating*. Even in their early teen years they need to write out a list of character qualities they want in a future spouse. It's also good to write out a separate list of negative qualities they *don't* want.

The two lists will help teenagers and young adults look past outward appearances to see who someone really is before they get emotionally involved—because once an emotional attachment forms, love becomes blind, character deficiencies are excused, and an unrealistic optimism sets in. You start believing that once you're married your spouse will become that person you said you want him or her to be. Grandma Duggar states, "A lot of people mistakenly think they can alter them at the altar!"

We've talked with our young adults about what kind of person they

hope to marry. We've said there will be many "prospects" at times, but a large percentage of those candidates can be eliminated by evaluating them on their private "What I Desire in a Spouse" and "What I *Don't* Want in a Spouse" lists. By evaluating the potential spouses they encounter, they'll see that only a very few have a genuine godly focus.

One day Jana asked, "Mama, what is the most important quality a future spouse should have?"

I (Michelle) asked for time to pray about my answer, and then, later, I told her the most important thing I appreciate about her daddy is knowing my heart is secure with him. I know I can trust him to lovingly listen to whatever I need to tell him. I know Jim Bob loves God more than he loves himself, and he puts God first in his life. He shows that by expressing it in words but also in the way he lives. He shares his heart with me, including the most vulnerable things about himself; he's open and honest with me because he wants to keep his heart pure before God. That gives me a solid security that nothing else can provide; all the money in the world couldn't buy it.

A few months before Josie's birth in 2009, we renewed our wedding vows on our twenty-fifth anniversary with our eighteen children and daughter-in-law Anna as our attendants.

When we first got married, we were scraping by financially, but that didn't matter because we were deeply in love. I didn't think it was possible to be happier than I was then (little did I know!). Over the years our love has grown and matured. We have weathered many life storms together, and we're actually closer, happier, and more in love now than

we were back then. I told Jana, "I love and admire your daddy so much; I still want to spend the rest of my life with him! I pray that each one of you girls find someone like your dad."

Jana listened carefully. Then she and the other older girls talked about it and they decided to put together some basic evaluations for a spouse. Their individual lists vary a little; here's a composite sample of what our older girls desire to find in a young man.

1. He has to be a deeply committed Christian with a ministry mind-set.

2. He has to love Jesus as much as I do.

3. He has to have a servant's heart and a desire to win others to Christ.

4. He needs to be emotionally and spiritually steady.

5. He needs to have common sense and constantly seek God's wisdom.

6. He needs to treat his mom and sisters with respect.

7. He needs to be a diligent worker who is able to provide for his family (but all the girls agree that this doesn't mean they expect him to be wealthy).

8. He needs to be willing to humble himself and admit his mistakes and shortcomings. Then he has to be willing to ask forgiveness and gain a clear conscience from those he has offended.

9. Even though inward character is the most important, he has to be someone they are attracted to spiritually, emotionally, mentally, and physically.

10. He needs to have a learning spirit and be a man of good character like Dad.

Here is the girls' list of what they *don't* want in a future spouse.

1. A lack of godly focus or purpose in life.

2. Quick to anger.

3. Self-centered.

4. Overly focused on hobbies.

5. Lack of manners.

6. Lack of self-control.

7. Lazy.

8. Ongoing moral issues (without brokenness.)

9. Dishonest.

10. Involved in drugs, smoking, drinking, chewing tobacco—or hangs out with those who are involved in them.

Now, this doesn't mean that someone who has had struggles in these areas would never be considered; God forgives, and so do we. But by God's grace, he would need to work on these areas to be considered a possibility.

These are not comprehensive lists; no doubt, your children's requirements will be different. We offer our girls' lists here hoping they can spark a discussion in your family and perhaps help your older children start thinking about making their own.

Until the day comes when that young man or woman appears in their lives, our children are becoming the people God wants them to be. They are learning skills that will help them support their families and create love-filled, God-focused homes. First Corinthians 7:32 says, "He that is unmarried careth for the things that belong to the Lord, how he may please the Lord." The girls are hoping to become the kind of wise and virtuous wife and mother described in Proverbs 31. They

have gained great insights from Sarah Mally's book, *Before You Meet Prince Charming*, and they recommend it to every young lady.

Considering: Is This Person a Potential Spouse?

Our older sons have their own similar lists of what they're looking for in a life partner. But before one of them identifies a godly young lady who surpasses his rating checklist and might be considered as his potential spouse, he needs to make sure he also meets all the requirements on his checklist for himself. First he needs to have his own spiritual life on track with God. Second, he needs to have his life and finances in order so he can support a family. Third, if he's in the middle of training or college, he needs to consider whether this is the right time for marriage.

If all those conditions line up and after much prayer, if he believes this girl could be a potential spouse, we would encourage him to talk with the girl's dad to see if the girl would have any interest in getting to know him for the purpose of considering each other as a potential life partner. Yes, this can be kind of scary, but if it's meant to be, it will work out. If it's not God's will, it won't.

Working through the girl's father is less intimidating for the young lady than approaching the girl directly, and it gives her the freedom to express her true feelings to her father. He can then relate those feelings

We had such a good time at the Orr Family Farms in Oklahoma that we literally jumped for joy on the farm's giant jumping pillow.

to the young man. If the girl shows interest, the father and the young man can get to know each other.

Jim Bob recently shared with our older kids a wonderful example describing how a father had a heart-to-heart talk with a young man who was interested in his daughter.

This young man was a hard worker and had saved up all summer to restore an older classic car that he was driving. The dad asked about his car and about the time, energy, and money that had gone into fixing it up. The boy described how long and hard he'd worked to earn the money to buy the car and how many hours he'd spent restoring it.

The dad explained that he knew how it felt to invest his life savings and his energy into something. He told the boy he had poured his life into his daughter; she was priceless to him. All of her life he had protected and provided for her at all cost.

It is important that a dad or a godly father figure help discern a young man's character and level of spiritual maturity and evaluate his intentions.

Most of our daughters will probably wait for a guy to contact their dad; then there will be discussion and prayer about whether she is interested, or whether she wants to get to know the boy better to see if she might become interested. Potential life partners might be identified when a son or daughter spots a godly young person with good character and suggests that we include them in some family ministry or outreach activity so the two have an opportunity to interact while surrounded by our family. If the two eventually agree that they are each other's potential life partner, we probably would invite the whole family to fellowship with us so we can see the interworkings of their family dynamic. We believe you don't just marry the person; you marry into the family.

As potential life partners surface, these young adults will spend time getting to know each other in group settings to see what interests they have in common, how their personalities connect, and watching to see how each other reacts in various situations.

In our family, we're sure that lots of brothers and sisters will be weighing in and giving advice about what they think of each potential brother-in-law or sister-in-law. There is wisdom in many counselors. This "considering" time rolls along without any commitments, except the commitment to pray and seek God's will.

SLOPPY JOES

1 pound ground turkey
½ cup ketchup
½ cup barbecue sauce
½ envelope dry onion soup mix
2 teaspoons liquid smoke flavoring

Brown and season meat; drain. Add all other ingredients, heat through. Serve on buns; love it!

We have heard many unique, supernatural stories of how God has brought couples together, so we don't say the considering time has to happen a certain way. But we've also heard many tragic stories of couples who damaged their relationship right from the beginning by mishandling their time of getting to know each other. So we believe something like this suggestion should be considered.

The main focus is to guard the emotions of our young people so they don't prematurely give their hearts away—and then regret it later. Instead, they should be encouraged to keep their heart for the one God made for them.

Pre-Engagement: Getting to Know Each Other Better

The most important decision in your life, next to accepting Christ as your Savior, is the decision about whom you're going to marry. This decision determines your future. If you pick the right person, you can have a special relationship in which both of you give 110 percent and consistently build each other up. On the other hand, if you settle for less than God's best, it can be an "evil for evil" relationship in which there is constant back-and-forth arguing, fighting, and put-downs.

(If you are married and in that situation now, we recommend John Reiger's Intimacy in Marriage course, which helps in dealing with challenging relationships.)

So many times people don't want to give God this area of their lives because they think they can do a better job of picking out a spouse than He can.

When a couple has gone through all of the above steps, and they both believe, along with their family, that this is a possibility, then the young man would formally ask the girl's father's permission to get to know the girl and work toward possible engagement.

During this time the couple has more freedom to get to know each other in a deeper way, but always in the presence of others. It is an evaluation process. After close character and compatibility examination, a lot of couples realize this is *not* the one they are to marry.

We tell our kids, you're never going to find a perfect person because that young man or young woman doesn't exist. Still, you shouldn't settle for anything less than God's best.

Engagement

When the couple and their parents believe that this relationship is God's plan, the young man should again go to the girl's father and ask for the daughter's hand in marriage. During the engagement stage the couple probably endures more temptations than at any other time, because they are two young people in love, planning their future dreams together, and emotions and feelings are inevitably strong. That's why we recommend a short engagement and a lot of accountability!

Marriage—for Life

Marriage is not a test drive. At your wedding you're vowing before God that, for better or worse, richer or poorer, you will be together and love each other until death do you part.

How does a couple confirm that this marriage is God's will? When a man and woman who are individually dedicated to God and who love each other determine that they can do more together for the kingdom of God than they can do alone, *that* is the time to get married.

Marriage is one of the most amazing concepts God instituted, merging two people from diverse backgrounds into one being in mind, spirit, and body.

We pray that the single people who read this chapter will commit their love lives to God and then trust Him to bring into their path the spouse He intends for them. Trust is the key. "Trust in the LORD with all thine heart; and lean not unto thine own understanding. In all thy ways acknowledge Him, and He shall direct thy paths" (Proverbs 3:5–6).

JOSH AND ANNA

A few days after Josh met Anna at the concession stand of an ATI homeschool conference in 2006, he told Jim Bob that God had just revealed to him who he was supposed to marry. Jim Bob said, "Let's pray about it and see if God confirms it."

Meanwhile, Josh had also caught Anna's eye.

The Duggar girls and the Keller girls also met at the conference, and they quickly became good friends. After everyone went home, the girls started talking on the phone on Tuesday nights, usually on the speakerphone so everyone could join in. Sometimes Josh or one of the Keller boys would join the conversation too.

Early in January 2008, Anna's brother Daniel invited Josh to come to Florida to help with a week of seminars being presented by the Keller family's prison ministry. After Josh and Daniel worked on the seminar together, Josh talked to Mr. Keller about his feelings for Anna. Her dad had already asked her if there was anyone she thought might be the man God intended for her, and she had mentioned Josh. So Mr. Keller was ready that day when Josh approached him. He gave Josh permission to start talking to Anna on the phone to get to know her better.

Prayers and phone calls continued—and became more frequent. Josh and Anna talked to each other but always with their siblings lis-

tening on the speakerphone. Both became convinced that they were the ones God had intended for them, but it came as a shock to Anna, on her twentieth birthday, when Josh showed up with a diamond ring and proposed to her! He had asked permission of Anna's parents, of course, and after much prayer, all of us were absolutely certain this was God's will. An October wedding date was set.

Josh purchased a pink cell phone for Anna upon their engagement, and they were allowed to talk without siblings listening in during their many conversations from June until their wedding in October.

INTIMACY: ENJOYING YOUR PARTNER

Attention, parents: the contents of this section may be unsuitable for young children.

Jim Bob and I work hard to give our big family a solid foundation in faith, love, character, and joy. In addition, Jim Bob carries most of the responsibility for providing for our family financially. But here's something that may surprise you: our goals and responsibilities for our large family are secondary to our responsibilities to each other. Our relationship comes first!

Our children's safety and well-being are top priorities for us. But along with my (Michelle's) devotion to Christ, my relationship with Jim Bob is the underpinning of our family; it's the solid ground beneath that foundation we're building for our children. The Bible points out the disastrous difference between a house built on rock and a house built on shifting sand (see Matthew 7:24–27). We want our godly marriage to be that rock for our family, creating a foundation that points each one of them to a relationship with Jesus.

The thing that distinguishes marriage from all other relationships is the intimate spiritual, emotional, and physical connection between a husband and a wife. We've shared throughout this book many aspects of our spiritual and emotional life; now we want to address the physical aspects of a loving marriage as well. We believe too many of modern

culture's messages about this very special relationship are warped and twisted.

Physical intimacy is one of the delights of marriage. Right before Jim Bob and I were married, Dr. Ed Wheat, a well-known Christian author and also our family doctor at the time, counseled us and gave us copies of his incredible books and audio messages, which include insights about physical intimacy and pleasure in marriage. (We recommend that every married couple read his books *Love Life for Every Married Couple* and *Intended for Pleasure*.)

Dr. Wheat taught us from a medical and spiritual perspective how to maximize our special time together as a couple. We quickly found out how much fun it is for a married couple to learn together, discovering God's amazing design and enjoying the wonderful gift of pleasure He has given husbands and wives! Twenty-five years later, we passed along to Josh and Anna as a wedding gift the same books and materials Dr. Wheat had given us when we got married.

After Jim Bob and I were married, a Christian friend of mine, Gayla, gave me some more great marital advice. She had been married about eighteen months earlier, and she told me, "Michelle, when the honeymoon is over, and the newness wears off, here's something to remember: men are geared differently than women. They need the physical relationship more often than we women. Keep the perspective that you are the *only* one who can fulfill that special need in his life." Through the years those words would ring in my ears at the end of a long day when I was exhausted.

The marriage relationship is all about yielding to each other's needs. We belong to one another. I am his, and he is mine! With God's grace we can do for each other what we ought to do, even when we don't feel like it. Without His grace we are selfish and tend to foster an evil-for-evil response toward each other that will destroy our relationship. The reward that comes to both of us as we choose to be unselfish toward each other is that our love deepens and we keep the home fires burning.

Most of us women probably build intimacy more through loving

communication and spending quality time together than through being physically intimate. At the top of my intimacy list is how Jim Bob treats me, how he talks to me, and how he shows me that he cherishes me. *Cherishing* means seeing great value in someone, protecting her and praising her to others, and that's what Jim Bob does throughout the day. He shows his love for me by *telling* me he loves me, by calling me just to say hi whenever we're apart, or by showing respect by doing things like opening doors for me or planning a date night for us to go to my favorite restaurant.

Early in our marriage we learned more about understanding each other's needs, in part, through two Bible study booklets: *Seven Basic Needs of a Wife* and *Seven Basic Needs of a Husband* (see the Resources section for ordering information).

By far the most precious way Jim Bob demonstrates his love to me is by protecting and guarding our relationship as he willingly shares his heart with me. A man's natural tendency is to not share his real needs with his wife; he wants her to admire him as a success. But before honor must come humility. A husband wins his wife's love more by sharing his specific failures than by reporting his successes. We strive to be totally open and honest with each other by sharing our thoughts and struggles as well as our hopes and dreams.

It's vital that a husband and wife share everything in their hearts with each other. We experience great freedom when we both release before God and each other any thoughts, struggles, or temptations we are having. In our marriage, we both realize that freedom doesn't give us the right to do what we selfishly *want* but the power to do what we selflessly *ought*. Personally, I feel this freedom allows for the deepest intimacy a husband and wife can experience together. I'm so grateful to God for Jim Bob's honesty and humility. It gives me a deep love, admiration, and respect for him and a real sense of security in our marriage relationship. We realize how much we need each other.

The Bible instructs husbands and wives not to withhold physical intimacy with each other "except it be with consent for a time"

(1 Corinthians 7:5). We do agree to abstain from physical intimacy during certain times. As mentioned earlier, we choose to follow Old Testament guidelines of abstinence for forty days after the birth of a boy and eighty days after the birth of a girl. We also abstain for seven days after the start of my menstrual cycle.

We practice self-control during those times of abstinence, and for me it's a time of rest (except for struggling with menstrual cramps!). We find that the time of abstinence builds anticipation and excitement, and when we come back together, we enjoy renewed passion and an increased desire for each other. We personally believe it is wrong to touch oneself for sexual pleasure because God wants us to wait for each other and learn self-control. Only a husband and wife together should meet those needs for one another.

Our children grow up feeling secure and confident that nothing will shake the bond their parents are seeking with each other and with God. With a broad smile and a happy tone, Jim Bob tells the kids, "I love your mama, and I'm so grateful to God she married me!"

Josie, our miracle baby, on her first birthday.

Our children understand that Dad and Mama have dedicated their lives to loving and serving God and each other, and that is the foundation of our love for them. We let them see that love played out as we show appropriate affection to each other throughout the day with quick kisses and hugs or by holding hands as we sit and talk. For our intimate affection, however, we have a good, strong lock on our bedroom door!

Our love has deepened over the past twenty-seven years of marriage.
I love Michelle more now than ever!

• P.S. Answering the Big Question •

~

I have set before you life and death, blessing and cursing;
therefore choose life that both thou and thy seed may live.
—Deuteronomy 30:19

A couple of months after Josie was born, we started hearing the question "So, are you going to have more children?" The best way to answer that question is to reaffirm what we continue to believe.

For several years now, sharing our beliefs publicly has put us in a different light than most of our nation's culture. As we joyously celebrate the birth of each new child, we realize that there are people who condemn us for the choices we have made. In fact, *People* magazine in mid-February 2010 put our picture on the cover with a line asking, "How many kids are too many?"

We are glad to live in a land where everyone can express his or her opinion. We don't let the negative opinions bother us. Nor do we let them influence what we continue to believe, including what God says about children: they are a gift and a blessing and a reward from Him. It's probably impossible for anyone to fully understand the depth of His love for His children, but those who have endured the death of a child, experiencing the deepest grief and sorrow, might come a little closer in understanding. God knew that agony as He watched His only Son die on the cross—on our behalf. Imagining (or remembering) yourself in the midst of such a heart-wrenching loss gives you a much

clearer picture of how precious life is. The value of that one life is worth more than all the riches in the world. We are so thankful for each one of our children.

God's love truly does multiply! We are experiencing it as we enjoy the family He has given us.

We write these words not knowing what the future holds for us; but we know who holds the future, and we place our trust in Him. It might be that by the time you read these words, I will be pregnant again, if that's God's will for us. Or it may be that Michelle's child-bearing days are over due to menopause or simply because it's God's will. It's true that there are risks involved, perhaps greater risks than we've faced before. But the truth is, our hearts haven't changed. We are grateful to God for each child He has blessed us with, and our love for children has grown deeper with each passing day. We still desire to love children the way God loves them, and we consider children one of His greatest gifts.

So to answer the question "Are the Duggars going to have any more children?" we say, "If that is God's will for us, we would love to have more!"

We believe children are a gift from God, and with nineteen children,
a daughter-in-law, one granddaughter (and, as of this writing,
our first grandson on the way), we feel incredibly blessed!

• Resources •

For more resources we have found helpful, go to www.duggarfamily.com.

AUDIO AND VIDEO RESOURCES

Christian movies by Sherwood Pictures, the ministry of Sherwood Baptist Church that has also produced the popular Christian movies *Flywheel, Facing the Giants, Fireproof,* and *Courageous.* www.sherwoodpictures.com

Pastor S. M. Davis preaching videos. www.solvefamilyproblems.com

The principles taught by Jim Sammons in his Financial Freedom series have been life-changing for us. www.iblp.org/iblp/discipleship/financialfreedom.

Other websites we like as a source of audio and video resources:

www.titus2.com

www.unshackled.org

www.saicff.org

www.wallbuilders.com

BIBLE STUDIES

Seven Basic Needs of a Wife and *Seven Basic Needs of a Husband.* http://store.iblp.org/products

BOOKS

Randy Alcorn, *Does the Birth Control Pill Cause Abortions?* (Sandy, Ore.: Eternal Perspective Ministries, 2007). Available from www.epm.org/store/product/birth-control-pill-book/.

Kim Cahill, *No-Guesswork Cooking Cookbook: Recipes You Can Trust.*
Available from www.iblp.org.

Alex Kendrick and Stephen Kendrick, *The Love Dare* (Nashville: B&H
Books, 2008).

Sarah Mally, *Before You Meet Prince Charming* (Cedar Rapids, Iowa:
Tomorrow's Forefathers, 2006, 2009), 40–41.

Dr. Ed Wheat and Gloria Okes Perkins, *Love Life for Every Married
Couple* (Grand Rapids, Mich.: Zondervan, 1997).

Dr. Ed Wheat and Gaye Wheat, *Intended for Pleasure: Sex Technique and
Sexual Fulfillment in Christian Marriage* (Grand Rapids, Mich.: Revell, 1976).

Other websites where we find Christian books:
www.christianbook.com/
www.visionforum.com/

CHILDREN'S RESOURCES WEBSITES

www.jonathanpark.com/
www.majestymusic.com/
www.visionforum.com/news/enn//
www.whitsend.org/

CONFERENCES AND SEMINARS

A Weekend to Remember (www.familylifeministries.com)
ALERT Academy Homeschool conferences (www.alertacademy.com)
Basic Life Principles seminar (www.iblp.org)
Journey to the Heart http://iblp.org/iblp/discipleship/journeytotheheart/
Noble Partners Marriage Conference (www.noblecall.org/conferences/)
Whatever It Takes (www.witministries.com)

ENCOURAGEMENT RESOURCES

Free daily success e-mails: http://iblp.org/iblp/discipleship/dailysuccess/
Vision Forum Family Resources: http://www.visionforum.com/
Other websites where we find ideas for sharing encouragement:
www.bbnradio.org/
www.oneplace.com/
www.tdharmon.com/
www.livingwaters.com/
www.focusonthefamily.com/

Homeschool Resources

Accelerated Christian Education. www.aceministries.com.

The Advanced Training Institute, source of the Wisdom Booklets we use as well as other homeschool materials. http://ati.iblp.org/ati/.

Christ-centered homeschool materials that teach how God supernaturally created the earth and how evolution is impossible. www.answersingenesis.com.

CollegePlus! is a Christian-based distance-learning program that helps students earn their fully accredited bachelor's degree in a fraction of the time and cost of the traditional university system. www.collegeplus.org.

Home School Legal Defense Association is a nonprofit advocacy organization established to defend and advance the constitutional right of parents to direct the education of their children and to protect family freedoms. www.hslda.org.

Oak Brook College of Law, a Christian law school providing education and training in law and government policy in the context of a biblical and historical framework. www.obcl.edu.

Switched on Schoolhouse (SOS) software from Alpha Omega Publications. www.AOPhomeschooling.com.

Verity Institute, another Christian-based distance-learning program that offers dual high school and college enrollment in association with Thomas Edison State College, Indianapolis, Indiana. www.verityinstitute.org.

Internet Filter Service

American Family Online: http://www.myafo.net/

Ministry Opportunities

SOS Ministries International is a faith-based, not-for-profit ministry that desires to minister to the physical and spiritual needs of people throughout the world by feeding the hungry, clothing the poor, embracing the orphan, providing education and medical attention to the destitute, and giving hope to the hopeless through the Word of God. This is the group that organizes the mission trips to El Salvador in which we participate. www.sosminternational.com.

Other websites offering ministry-opportunity ideas and resources:
www.gospelink.org/
www.gfa.org/
www.reversalministry.com/
www.ican-online.org/

Modest Clothing Resources

We find modest clothing at these websites or retailers:
Swim Wear: www.wholesomewear.com
Skirts: Cato Fashions & Accessories: www.catofashions.com
Tops: Christopher & Banks affordable fashions: www.christopherand
banks.com

Sam Walton's Rules for Building a Business[1]

RULE 1: COMMIT to your business. Believe in it more than anybody else. I think I overcame every single one of my personal shortcomings by the sheer passion I brought to my work. I don't know if you're born with this kind of passion, or if you can learn it. But I do know you need it. If you love your work, you'll be out there every day trying to do it the best you possibly can, and pretty soon everybody around will catch the passion from you—like a fever.

RULE 2: SHARE your profits with all your associates, and treat them as partners. In turn, they will treat you as a partner, and together you will all perform beyond your wildest expectations. Remain a corporation and retain control if you like, but behave as a servant leader in a partnership. Encourage your associates to hold a stake in the company. Offer discounted stock, and grant them stock for their retirement. It's the single best thing we ever did.

RULE 3: MOTIVATE your partners. Money and ownership alone aren't enough. Constantly, day by day, think of new and more interesting ways to motivate and challenge your partners. Set high goals, encourage competition, and then keep score. Make bets with outrageous payoffs. If things get stale, cross-pollinate; have managers switch jobs with one another to stay challenged. Keep everybody guessing as to what your next trick is going to be. Don't become too predictable.

RULE 4: COMMUNICATE everything you possibly can to your partners. The more they know, the more they'll understand. The more they understand, the more they'll care. Once they care, there's no stopping them. If you don't trust your associates to know what's going on, they'll know you don't really consider them partners. Information is power, and the gain you get from empowering your associates more than offsets the risk of informing your competitors.

RULE 5: APPRECIATE everything your associates do for the business.

A paycheck and a stock option will buy one kind of loyalty. But all of us like to be told how much somebody appreciates what we do for them. We like to hear it often, and especially when we have done something we're really proud of. Nothing else can quite substitute for a few well-chosen, well-timed sincere words of praise. They're absolutely free—and worth a fortune.

RULE 6: CELEBRATE your successes. Find some humor in your failures. Don't take yourself so seriously. Loosen up, and everybody around you will loosen up. Have fun. Show enthusiasm—always. When all else fails, put on a costume and sing a silly song. Then make everybody else sing with you. Don't do a hula on Wall Street. It's been done. Think up your own stunt. All of this is more important, and more fun, than you think, and it really fools the competition. "Why should we take those cornballs at Walmart seriously?"

RULE 7: LISTEN to everyone in your company. And figure out ways to get them talking. The folks on the front lines—the ones who actually talk to the customer—are the only ones who really know what's going on out there. You'd better find out what they know. This really is what total quality is all about. To push responsibility down in your organization, and to force good ideas to bubble up within it, you *must* listen to what your associates are trying to tell you.

RULE 8: EXCEED your customers' expectations. If you do, they'll come back over and over. Give them what they want—and a little more. Let them know you appreciate them. Make good on all your mistakes, and don't make excuses—apologize. Stand behind everything you do. The two most important words I ever wrote were on that first Walmart sign: "Satisfaction Guaranteed." They're still up there, and they have made all the difference.

RULE 9: CONTROL your expenses better than your competition. This is where you can always find the competitive advantage. For twenty-five years running—long before Walmart was known as the nation's largest retailer—we ranked number one in our industry for the lowest ratio of expenses to sales. You can make a lot of different mistakes and still recover if you run an efficient operation. Or you can be brilliant and still go out of business if you're too inefficient.

RULE 10: SWIM upstream. Go the other way. Ignore the conventional wisdom. If everybody else is doing it one way, there's a good chance you can find your niche by going in exactly the opposite direction. But be prepared for a lot of folks to wave you down and tell you you're headed the wrong way. I guess in all my years, what I heard more often than anything was: a town of less than 50,000 population cannot support a discount store for very long.

CHARACTER QUALITIES[2]

Operational Definitions of Character Qualities

ATTENTIVENESS vs. Unconcern — Showing the worth of a person by giving undivided attention to his words and emotions — Hebrews 2:1	**SENSITIVITY** vs. Callousness — Exercising my senses so that I can perceive the true spirit and emotions of those around me — Romans 12:15	**JUSTICE** vs. Fairness — Personal responsibility to God's unchanging laws — Micah 6:8	**COMPASSION** vs. Indifference — Investing whatever is necessary to heal the hurts of others — I John 3:17	**GENTLENESS** vs. Harshness — Showing personal care and concern in meeting the needs of others — I Thessalonians 2:7	**DEFERENCE** vs. Rudeness — Limiting my freedom in order not to offend the tastes of those God has called me to serve — Romans 14:21	**MEEKNESS** vs. Anger — Yielding my personal rights and expectations to God — Psalm 62:5
ORDERLINESS vs. Disorganization — Preparing myself and my surroundings so that I will achieve the greatest efficiency — I Corinthians 14:40	**INITIATIVE** vs. Unresponsiveness — Recognizing and doing what needs to be done before I am asked to do it — Romans 12:21	**RESPONSIBILITY** vs. Unreliability — Knowing and doing what both God and others are expecting me to do — Romans 14:12	**HUMILITY** vs. Pride — Recognizing that God and others are actually responsible for the achievements in my life — James 4:6	**DECISIVENESS** vs. Double-mindedness — The ability to finalize difficult decisions based on the will and ways of God — James 1:5	**DETERMINATION** vs. Faint-heartedness — Purposing to Accomplish God's goals in God's timing regardless of the opposition — II Timothy 4:7-8	**LOYALTY** vs. Unfaithfulness — Using difficult times to demonstrate my commitment to God and to those whom He has called me to serve — John 15:13
RESOURCEFULNESS vs. Wastefulness — Wise use of that which others would normally overlook or discard — Luke 16:10	**THRIFTINESS** vs. Extravagance — Not letting myself or others spend that which is not necessary — Luke 16:11	**CONTENTMENT** vs. Covetousness — Realizing that God has provided everything that I need for my present happiness — I Timothy 6:8	**PUNCTUALITY** vs. Tardiness — Showing high esteem for other people and their time — Ecclesiastes 3:1	**TOLERANCE** vs. Prejudice — Acceptance of others as unique expressions of specific character qualities in varying degrees of maturity — Philippians 2:2	**CAUTIOUSNESS** vs. Rashness — Knowing how important right timing is in accomplishing right actions — Proverbs 19:2	**GRATEFULNESS** vs. Unthankfulness — Making known to God and others in what ways they have benefited my life — I Corinthians 4:7
WISDOM vs. Natural Inclinations — Seeing and responding to life situations from God's frame of reference — Proverbs 9:10	**DISCERNMENT** vs. Judgment — The God-given ability to understand why things happen — I Samuel 16:7	**FAITH** vs. Presumption — Visualizing what God intends to do in a given situation and acting in harmony with it — Hebrews 11:1	**DISCRETION** vs. Simple-mindedness — The ability to avoid words, actions, and attitudes which could result in undesirable consequences — Proverbs 22:3	**LOVE** vs. Selfishness — Giving to others basic needs without having as my motive personal reward — I Corinthians 13:3	**CREATIVITY** vs. Under-achievement — Approaching a need, a task, an idea from a new perspective — Romans 12:2	**ENTHUSIASM** vs. Apathy — Expressing with my spirit the joy of my soul — I Thessalonians 5:16,19
SELF-CONTROL vs. self-indulgence — Instant obedience to the initial promptings of God's Spirit — Galatians 5:24-25	**REVERENCE** vs. Disrespect — Awareness of how God is working through the people and events in my life to produce the character of Christ in me — Proverbs 23:17-18	**DILIGENCE** vs. Slothfulness — Visualizing each task as a special assignment from the Lord and using all my energies to accomplish it — Colossians 3:23	**THOROUGHNESS** vs. Incompleteness — Knowing what factors will diminish the effectiveness of my work or words if neglected — Proverbs 18:15	**DEPENDABILITY** vs. Inconsistency — Fulfilling what I consented to do even if it means unexpected sacrifice — Psalm 15:4	**SECURITY** vs. Anxiety — Structuring my life around that which is eternal and cannot be destroyed or taken away — John 6:27	**PATIENCE** vs. Restlessness — Accepting a difficult situation from God without giving Him a deadline to remove it — Romans 5:3-4
ALERTNESS vs. Unawareness — Being aware of that which is taking place around me so that I can have the right responses — Mark 14:38	**HOSPITALITY** vs. Loneliness — Cheerfully sharing food, shelter, and spiritual refreshment with those God brings into my life — Hebrews 13:2	**GENEROSITY** vs. Stinginess — Realizing that all I have belongs to God and using it for His purposes — II Corinthians 9:6	**JOYFULNESS** vs. Self-pity — The spontaneous enthusiasm of my spirit when my soul is in fellowship with the Lord — Psalm 16:11	**FLEXIBILITY** vs. Resistance — Not setting my affections on ideas or plans which could be changed by God or others — Colossians 3:2	**AVAILABILITY** vs. Self-centeredness — Making my own schedule and priorities secondary to wishes of those I am serving — Philippians 2:20-21	**ENDURANCE** vs. Giving-up — The inward strength to withstand stress to accomplish God's best — Galatians 6:9
TRUTHFULNESS vs. Deception — Earning future trust by accurately reporting past facts — Ephesians 4:25	**OBEDIENCE** vs. Wilfulness — Freedom to be creative under the protection of divinely appointed authority — II Corinthians 10:5	**SINCERITY** vs. Hypocrisy — Eagerness to do what is right with transparent motives — 1 Peter 1:22	**VIRTUE** vs. Impurity — The moral excellence and purity of spirit that radiate from my life as I obey God's word — II Peter 1:5	**BOLDNESS** vs. Fearfulness — Confidence that what I have to say or do is true and right and just in the sight of God — Acts 4:29	**FORGIVENESS** vs. Rejection — Clearing the record of those who have wronged me and allowing God to love them through me — Ephesians 4:32	**PERSUASIVENESS** vs. Contentiousness — Guiding vital truth around another's mental roadblocks — II Timothy 2:24

• Notes •

Chapter 7. Living Under the Microscope

1. For a more detailed analysis of how birth-control pills work, see Randy Alcorn, *Does the Birth Control Pill Cause Abortions?* (Sandy, Ore.: Eternal Perspective Ministries, 2007). Available as a PDF download from www.epm.org/store/product/birth-control-pill-book/.

Chapter 17. Jim Bob's Lifelong Hobby

1. Sam Walton, *Made in America* (New York: Bantam/Doubleday/Dell, 1993), p. 314.

Resources

1. This list of rules is given out at the Walton/Walmart Visitors Center in Bentonville, Arkansas, and is included in *Sam Walton: Made in America* (New York: Bantam, 1993), pp. 314–17.

2. http://ati.iblp.org/ati/family/curriculum/characterqualities.pdf?show=true.